**Bantam/Britannica Books**

**Unique, authoritative guides
to acquiring human knowledge**

What motivates people and nations? What
makes things work? What laws and history lie
behind the strivings and conflicts of
contemporary man?

One of mankind's greatest natural endowments
is the urge to learn. Bantam/Britannica books
were created to help make that goal a reality.
Distilled and edited from the vast Britannica
files, these compact introductory volumes offer
uniquely accessible summaries of human
knowledge. Oceanography, politics, natural
disasters, world events—just about everything
that the inquisitive person wants to know about
is fully explained and explored.

The Encyclopaedia Britannica staff for
BANTAM/BRITANNICA BOOKS

Editor          Frank Gibney
Executive Editor          Richard Pope

THE U.S. GOVERNMENT: HOW AND WHY IT WORKS

Subject Editor          Bruce L. Felknor
Editorial Assistant          Beverly Gay
Art Director          Cynthia Peterson
Editorial Production Manager          J. Thomas Beatty
Production Coordinator          Elizabeth A. Chastain
Index Supervisor          Frances E. Latham
Senior Indexer          Helen A. Peterson

Encyclopaedia Britannica, Inc.
Chairman of the Board          Robert P. Gwinn
President          Charles E. Swanson

BANTAM/BRITANNICA BOOKS

# The U.S. Government

**How and Why It Works**

**Prepared by
the Editors of
Encyclopaedia
Britannica**

51414

THE U.S. GOVERNMENT: HOW AND WHY IT WORKS
Bantam edition/November 1978

ISBN 0-553-12485-4

*Published simultaneously in the United States and Canada*

*Bantam Books are published by Bantam Books, Inc. Its trademark,
consisting of the words "Bantam Books" and the portrayal
of a bantam, is registered in the United States Patent Office
and in other countries. Marca Registrada.
Bantam Books, Inc.,
666 Fifth Avenue, New York, New York 10019.*

Printed in the United States of America

# Foreword:
# Knowledge for Today's World

One of mankind's greatest natural endowments is the urge to learn. Whether we call it knowledge-seeking, intellectual curiosity, or plain nosiness, most people feel a need to get behind the newspaper page or the TV newscast and seek out the background events: What motivates people and nations? What makes things work? How is science explained? What laws and history lie behind the strivings and conflicts of contemporary man? Yet the very richness of information that bombards us daily often makes it hard to acquire such knowledge, given with authority, about the forces and factors influencing our lives.

The editors at Britannica have spent a great deal of time, over the years, pondering this problem. Their ultimate answer, the 15th Edition of the *Encyclopaedia Britannica*, has been lauded not merely as a vast, comprehensive collection of information but also as a unique, informed summary of human knowledge in an orderly and innovative form. Besides this work, they have also thought to produce a series of compact introductory volumes providing essential information about a wide variety of peoples and problems, cultures, crafts, and disciplines. Hence the birth of these Bantam/Britannica books.

The Bantam/Britannica books, prepared under the guidance of the Britannica's Board of Editors, have been distilled and edited from the vast repository of information in the Britannica archives. The editors have also used the mine of material in the 14th Edition, a great work in its own right, which is no longer being published because much of its material did not fit the design imposed by the 15th. In addition to these sources, current Britannica files and reports—including those for annual yearbooks and for publications in other languages—were made available for this new series.

All of the Bantam/Britannica books are prepared by Britannica editors in our Chicago headquarters with the assistance of specialized subject editors for some volumes. The Bantam/Britannica books cover the widest possible range of topics. They are current and contemporary as well as cultural and historical. They are designed to provide *knowledge for today*—for students anxious to grasp the essentials of a subject, for concerned citizens who want to know more about how their world works, for the intellectually curious who like good reading in concise form. They are a stepping-stone to the thirty-volume *Encyclopaedia Britannica*, not a substitute for it. That is why references to the 15th Edition, also known as *Britannica 3* because of its three distinct parts, are included in the bibliographies. While additional research is always recommended, these books are complete unto themselves. Just about everything that the inquisitive person needs to catch up on a subject is contained within their pages. They make good companions, as well as good teachers. Read them.

The Editors,
*Encyclopaedia Britannica*

# Contents

51414

# *Introduction*: On Understanding American Government

Government has been defined in many different ways by a long list of philosophers and social scientists from Plato and Confucius to those of the present day. These definitions have frequently been cast in terms of the purpose of government. The most commonly acknowledged purpose, or end, has been either justice or the public good. Conflicting views have insisted that it has rarely achieved either ideal.

There has been a tendency since the nineteenth century to discard ends as a key to defining government and an inclination to concentrate on the process of government—how government works. This is known as the functional view, which might be defined as government by a large or small group of people who control the operations of and changes in an organization. The destructive results of nihilism (the philosophy of negation involving a rejection of traditional morality, authority, and order), however, have taught the perils of ignoring the ends of government.

## Classifying Governments

Since the days of Plato and Aristotle, governments have been classified in a great many different ways. Plato saw the several forms of political order (*politeia*) as corruptions of the ideal order that he delineated in the *Republic*. Aristotle built upon this foundation, while introducing some significant changes—not in terms of the ideal but rather in those of the standard, or model. He called this model *politeia* (polity), or political order as such. In Aristotle's terms there was, in government, good and bad rule of one (monarchy or tyranny), of a few (aristocracy or oligarchy), or of many (democracy or polity). His concept of the ideal political order corresponds to the idea of a constitutional democracy in the United States, whereas he used the word *democracy* by itself to denote the rule of a majority unrestrained by a written constitution. Without retaining their precise Aristotelian meaning, these terms have become a part of the general political vocabulary of modern man.

In the sixteenth and seventeenth centuries it was customary to divide governments into two types: monarchical (headed by a royal family) and republican (headed by one or more who is not a monarch). The word *republican* is used in the U.S. Constitution, which provides that each state shall have a "republican form of government." Perhaps the classification of most universal significance is that which is determined by the key aspect of the pattern of control: is power concentrated or divided? Stable power is based on organization and the control of organization.

Without common objectives, there can be neither organization nor power. To avoid a situation in which conflicting objectives predominate, power must be divided; different groups in the community may be entrusted with different tasks and charged with restraining other groups. Thus a valid basis for classifying governments may be found in the extent to which they are constitutionalized. Constraint and consent are the two intertwined bases of power and control. Most human organizations and their governments can be ranged between the unrealistic extremes of complete constraint and complete consent.

The modern use of the word *republic* derives from dual ideas: the absence of monarchy and the presence of some degree of common concern for the welfare of the state and for citizen participation in public affairs. The anti-monarchical view constituted a major element in the American Revolution, as did the twin ideas of consent of the governed and the rights of man.

In the United States *republic* has special connotations and is frequently used as historical justification for denying that the United States is truly a democracy in the original sense of the word. The bases for this contrast are (1) the ancient and purist use of *democracy* to denote small-scale, direct democracy; (2) the classical fear, which continued at least to the end of the eighteenth century, of such democracy as unstable and fickle; (3) the Ciceronian interpretation, which widely influenced the U.S. founding fathers, of the Roman republic as a mixed and balanced government; and (4) the revival by French political philosopher Montesquieu in the eighteenth century of the idea of democracy as direct and small scale and his insistence that democracy was impossible in a large state, which could be at best a representative republic. These ideas were studied and combined by a number of the founding fathers—especially by James Madison, who used *republic* as a technical designation for representative government as opposed to *direct democracy*. He insisted on the necessity for a system of checks and balances against the dangers of straight majoritarian decision in a legislature elected by majority on a single principle of representation. The insistence that *republic* is not synonymous with direct democracy or absolute majoritarian democracy, but rather with constitutional democracy, is valid in the specific U.S. context.

## The Role of the Constitution

Constitutionalism in its broadest connotation may be defined as a government that is limited by a constitution. Such a constitution may be constructed in a great variety of ways. It may be built around a monarchy, or it may be a republican scheme; it may set up a parliamentary executive or some other kind; it may or may not contain a bill of rights. Whatever the detailed arrangements, a constitution will always seek to make certain that no one man, or group of men, is in a position to exercise legitimate power without some effective restraint. Usually such restraint would require power to be relinquished, to be shared, or to be renewed periodically at the hands of the electorate. No matter how skillfully balanced, the ultimate sanction for the maintenance of any constitutionalism lies in the determination of the people to maintain it. This rule has in the last analysis decided the success or failure of every constitutional government.

There used to be much concern over whether a constitution was rigid or flexible. Scholars comparing the situation in the United States and Great Britain (as for instance British historian James Bryce) were fond of dwelling upon this theme. More realistic analysis has disclosed this difference to be rather elusive. *Rigid* and *flexible* are ill-defined words that hide rather than expose the real problems. The Third French Republic, for example, had a constitution that proved too easy as well as too difficult to change. It was a question not of general rigidity or flexibility but rather of the constitution itself being badly drawn. The U.S. Constitution is usually classed as rigid, yet, in the twentieth century, it could add and then discard a provision for prohibiting the sale of liquor.

## Evolution of Federalism

Much more central and significant to the study of government is the problem of federalism. Any constitution that guarantees independent jurisdiction to a number of component units of government can be characterized as a federal constitution. Leaving the insoluble problem of exactly who is sovereign (supreme) in a federal setup, we may say that federalism is a system of government under a constitution that divides political power between a central authority and a number of component territorial units. Even the most effectively centralized government will grant some measure of decentralized authority to local bodies. In terms of objectives, constitutional federalism seeks to balance general and common objectives with particular and conflicting objectives. The Swiss Constitution, for example, leaves all educational matters to the cantons (small political divisions) so that those cantons with a French- or Italian-speaking majority may differentiate themselves from the German-speaking majority in the country as a whole.

Federal patterns of government frequently owe their existence to a preceding federation, or league, of governments. It is, therefore, possible to analyze such governments practically in terms of the institutions that are characteristic of such federations. The United States is a good example. Three characteristic federal institutions are (1) a legislative assembly composed of representatives of the component units or states, as if they were equals or near-equals; (2) an executive in which, or in the selection of which, the component territorial units participate; and (3) a judicial body or bodies for the settlement of disputes between the states and the central government according to a charter or constitution.

In a nonparliamentary form of constitutional government the executive may be of the conciliar type (illustrated by the seven-person administrative council of Switzerland) or of the presidential type. In the United States the president, for all practical purposes, is elected by the people (actually, by a majority of voters in each state) and thereby becomes the leader of his political party. In all matters of general policy involving legislation or the spending of funds he must successfully manage his party in Congress or prove ineffective. Grave difficulties confront him if, through election, the Congress becomes dominated by the opposition party, which happened to Woodrow Wilson in 1918, to Herbert Hoover in 1930, to Harry S. Truman in 1946, and to Dwight D. Eisenhower and his Republican successors since 1954. The lack of party discipline or a broad executive appeal, however, sometimes makes it possible to exert effective leadership with the support of votes from the opposition party. This occurred for many years in the state of New York where Democratic governors had to work with Republican legislatures. The evolution of government in the United States presents a unique synthesis of a modern republic built on representative democracy, federalism, and constitutionalism.

## Development of the American System

In the American colonies before 1763, relations with Great Britain had hardly been harmonious; in fact, contests for power and position had become chronic. The colonists had striven steadily to achieve control of their local affairs and had actually reached that goal in Connecticut and Rhode Island before the end of the seventeenth century. In the other colonies they had encountered resistance by British (or British-appointed) governors, councillors, judges, and other officials. The colonists had endeavored to make the elected lower house of the assembly the dominant force in every colony. In these struggles the lower house had gradually seized the initiative with regard to money bills and then with regard to legislative questions in general. It had also invaded the area of executive authority. In all the colonies it was claimed that for domestic affairs the lower house was the counterpart of the English House of Commons; such was in fact the case, although in British theory the colonial legislatures were merely municipal bodies.

Upon the end of the Seven Years' War (1763), George III, king of England, and the British ministry (executive body) determined to seek the enlargement of the number of British troops garrisoned in North America. The decision was a momentous one. Parliament had accepted a recommendation from the ministry that seventy-five regiments be kept in service throughout the world, including seventeen to be stationed in North America, and that the colonists be required to pay their share of the cost.

Over the next decade myriad aggravations continued and increased. Finally, in 1772, the Boston town meeting created a committee of correspondence to communicate about such matters with the smaller towns and with other provinces. Thus an effective instrument for resistance was brought into existence. One by one the colonies formed similar committees. By early 1774 all the colonies but two, Pennsylvania and North Carolina, shared in the network.

The Massachusetts lower house took control of the province. Assuming the guise of a provincial congress, it became, in effect, a revolutionary government. Following that example Patriots (those who wished to assert independence of

British rule) everywhere began to turn the lower houses of their legislatures into revolutionary bodies. They organized committees of safety, dealt harshly with aggressive Loyalists (those who wanted to retain British rule), sent protests to London, and elected delegates to the First Continental Congress, which met at Philadelphia in the fall of 1774.

This Congress gave the Patriot cause greater breadth, depth, and force. Its fifty-six members, representing all of the colonies except Georgia, were lawyers, country gentlemen, and merchants—respectable and responsible men; and America followed them. They made it clear that Britain would not be permitted to subdue Massachusetts without interference from the other colonies. They demanded repeal of the oppressive Coercive Acts (by which Parliament sought to impose military rule over Massachusetts) and the Quebec Act (which attempted to shift control of the rich northwest lands to the province of Quebec). The Congress went so far, in fact, as to brand these acts—together with several other measures taken after 1764—as unconstitutional. The members called for a return to the "old days" of 1763—and more. They urged the British Crown to abandon its right to name the councillors in the royal colonies. In a forthright manner they questioned the authority of Parliament, though carefully refraining from petitioning it for redress. The Congress did, however, send an appeal to the Crown as well as a direct appeal to the British people asking for a redress of grievances. It also endorsed a declaration of rights, which accused the British government of violating colonial charter rights, their own rights as Englishmen, and man's natural rights.

The inclusion of the concept of natural rights was of great importance. Previously the colonists had chosen to rely principally upon their rights as British citizens, even though some of their leaders had invoked the idea of the rights of mankind. British law and custom, however, had not turned out to be such a safe stronghold of American liberties after all. The colonists were moving away from the narrower argument concerning the rights of Englishmen toward the more fundamental one of the natural rights of man.

Fifteen months after the beginning (April 1775) of actual hostilities, the Second Continental Congress (now including Georgia) met. On July 2, 1776, it "unanimously" (by the vote of twelve colonies with New York abstaining) resolved that "these United Colonies are, and of right ought to be Free and Independent States."

# I. The American System of Government

*"... the last, best hope of earth."*

—Abraham Lincoln

# 1.
# The Unique Constitution

The Constitution of the United States was written in Philadelphia during the summer of 1787 by a convention of fifty-five delegates. After ratification by the necessary number of states, it went into effect on March 4, 1789. Under that brief and well-drafted document—the oldest written constitution in operation in the world—the country prospered and remained united; the basic rights of people proved to be secure, in spite of all the profound changes that followed: economic, social, cultural, and political.

Many factors explain the continuing vitality of this eighteenth-century document. In contrast with some lengthy state constitutions that are loaded down with provisions designed to appease transient interests, it is a concise and well-written document of about seven thousand words, confined to the expression of basic, permanent principles in broad terms. The U.S. Constitution does no more than organize basic political institutions—describing the framework of government while leaving the details to legislative action. However, it limits the scope of government by guaranteeing individual liberties. Finally, the door is left open for adaptation and change through usage, interpretation, and workable methods of amendment.

Another reason for the Constitution's success is that it was rooted solidly in historical experience, containing little that was new or experimental. Its authors drew their ideas from English law and practice, from actual colonial experience, and from the state constitutions and the Articles of Confederation. In a real sense the Constitution was an outgrowth and indeed the climax in the ancient struggle for liberty as expressed through the great traditions of English common law. It was not imposed by a foreign power or dictated from above by a ruler, nor was it—as with many later constitutions—the product of military defeat. It was an act of free will, a triumph of apparent human reason in an age of European turmoil, a symbol of good government in an epoch of modern political upheaval. In a pluralistic country of separate states the document also served as a powerful center of loyalty for the diverse peoples who made up the population of the United States.

## The Declaration of Independence

One can say, as John Adams did, that this now famous Declaration of Independence contained nothing really novel in its political philosophy—which was derived from the writings of John Locke, Algernon Sidney, and other English theorists. It may also be asserted that the argument offered was not without flaws in history and logic. The Declaration substantially abandoned contention based on the rights of Englishmen and put forth instead the more fundamental doctrines of natural rights and of government under contract. Claiming that Parliament never truly possessed sovereignty over the colonies and that the Crown could rightfully exercise it only under contract, it contended that George III, with the support of a "pretended" legislature, had persistently violated the agreement between himself as governor and the colonists as the governed.

Few now claim that government arose among men (as Locke and Thomas Jefferson did), and the contract theory has lost vogue among political scientists. Many of the Declaration's assertions were in fact partisan and not uniformly defensible. The defects in the document, however, by no means support the conclusion that it is unsound. On the contrary, it was in essence morally just and politically valid. Even if the right of revolution cannot be established on historical grounds, it nevertheless rests solidly upon ethical ones. The right of the colonists to government ultimately of their own choice is hardly deniable, and close scrutiny of the behavior of the British government and of the colonists after 1763 reveals persuasively that the grievances of the Americans were neither trifling nor transient.

The Congress raised a noble standard to which the future country could rally in the War of Independence and afterward. Some of the phrases contained in the Declaration have continued to exert profound influence during the course of U.S. history, especially the proclamation: "We hold these truths to be self-evident, that all men are created equal, that they are endowed by their Creator with certain unalienable Rights, that among these are Life, Liberty, and the pursuit of Happiness." While the meanings of these phrases, together with conclusions drawn from them, have been endlessly debated, the Declaration has served to justify the extension of political and social democracy within the country. Appeals to it as "higher law" superior even to the federal Constitution were frequent in the middle third of the nineteenth century and still continue. Abraham Lincoln emphatically declared that his political philosophy was based upon it.

Plans of colonial federation had been proposed several times before the period of the American Revolution. The movement that finally led to independence forced some degree of unity, and the Continental Congress became the outward symbol of unified political action. What political direction the revolutionary movement received came through the continuance of that organization (without any formal written instrument of union), which proved highly inefficient. It was replaced by the Articles of Confederation in 1781.

## The Fledgling Union

The Articles established a loose union, with little in the way of a national government and with no power in that government to raise revenue or to enforce its laws directly upon individual citizens throughout the country. The government had the authority to ask the states to act but not to compel action by either the state or its citizens. It had power to make treaties but no power to enforce state observance of such treaties. Each state had power to impose restrictions upon trade with other states, and a state with the geographical advantages of New York was in a position to impose and did impose burdensome restrictions upon the commerce of the neighboring states of New Jersey and Connecticut.

The fledgling union could not function effectively under such a system. These conditions led to the assembling of the Constitutional Convention in 1787 and to the framing and adoption of the Constitution of the United States, under which the present government was instituted two years later. The Constitution was framed with specific reference to the difficulties presenting themselves before its adoption. A governmental organization was established independent of those in the states and with power to enforce its laws directly upon citizens within those states. Critical powers were conferred, the most important of which allowed the central government to control interstate and foreign commerce, to levy taxes, to raise federal revenue independently of the states, and to direct foreign relations.

The new government was thereby constituted with real authority. The history of the federal system since 1789 is to a large extent a history of the expanded authority and importance of the national government under this Constitution.

## Division of Authority

The framers of the Constitution accepted it as an unchallengeable maxim that the only way to avoid governmental tyranny was to separate the legislative, executive, and judicial powers and functions. This the Constitution does in the so-called distributive clauses—declaring that all legislative powers are vested in the Congress; all executive powers in the presidential office; and all judiciary powers in the courts. The separation of powers is not only a political theory about the proper organization of government but also a doctrine of constitutional law.

A fundamental feature of the U.S. constitutional system is the division of political authority between two levels of government—national and state. The Constitution as originally enacted attempted to deal with problems that were national in scope while leaving the states free to handle matters of purely local concern.

What is the authority granted to the national government? Express legislative powers, couched in most cases in broad language, are conferred on Congress in a series of eighteen paragraphs in Article I, section 8, of the Constitution. In even more general terms, powers are conferred on the executive and judicial departments of the United States. Certain powers are of such a character that they must be exercised exclusively by the national government—such as levying federal taxes, borrowing money on the credit of the United States, constituting federal tribunals inferior to the Supreme Court, and establishing a uniform rule of naturalization. Others are made exclusively national by specific prohibitions upon the states. The federal power to coin money is supplemented by forbidding the states to do the same. The federal war powers are made exclusive by prohibitions upon the states. The federal treaty-making power is strengthened by forbidding state treaties altogether and by prohibiting state agreements or compacts without the consent of Congress. Other powers are of such a nature that they may be exercised by either of two governments but not by both. The grant of such a power to the central government makes it exclusive.

Of necessity, some of the powers granted to Congress are not exclusive. In such matters states may exercise authority similar to that of the national government in the same field. Congress has exercised only in small part its power to fix the standard of weights and measures, and there is valid legislation in all the states on this subject. The Constitution itself expressly provides for concurrent authority over the militia. Under a general grant of power to regulate interstate commerce, Congress has full power, but the states may legislate in regard to local needs and circumstances unless Congress otherwise directs.

All powers of the national government must be found within the terms of the Constitution. It has no others. This by no means implies, however, that all powers must be expressly granted by that document. In fact the Constitution grants a number of important powers in broad terms to Congress and to the other departments of the national government.

Although the national government is limited to its enumerated powers, several important facts about these powers must be noted. (1) The national Constitution, and statutes and treaties adopted pursuant to it, constitute, in the language of Article VI, "the supreme Law of the Land; . . . any Thing in the Constitution or Laws of any State to the contrary notwithstanding." This means that any state law, otherwise valid, must yield if contrary to a valid federal law, since the latter is the supreme law of the land. (2) To supplement the enumerated powers expressed in broad terms, the "elastic" clause (Art. I, Sec. 8) states that Congress shall have the authority "To make all Laws which shall be necessary and proper for carrying into Execution" the various powers vested in the national government by the Constitution.

Under the Constitution, the states as such are guaranteed their territorial integrity and are expressly recognized as units in the organization of the national government. They are treated as units in the election of president and vice-president and of members of the national legislature. They also have a decisive share in the process of amending the federal Constitution. Most important, the Tenth Amendment to the Constitution specifically reserves to the states or the people all "residual rights" not granted to the United States or prohibited to the states by the Constitution.

## The National Legislature

Irrespective of population, the states are equally represented by two members each in the United States Senate, and in proportion to their population in the House of Representatives. By the terms of the Constitution no state may without its consent be deprived of its "equal suffrage in the Senate."

U.S. senators are elected for six-year terms, arranged so that one-third of the members are elected every two years.

Representation in the national House of Representatives is based upon population. Under the Constitution, each ten years, after the decennial federal census, the Congress determines how many members will constitute the House of Representatives. This number is then divided into the total population of the states. In this manner a ratio of representation is obtained, although each state, no matter how small its population, is entitled to at least one representative.

Members of the House of Representatives are elected for two years, and the whole membership changes at the same time. Each state is required to be divided into districts equal to the number of members it has in the House of Representatives; but if the number of representatives apportioned to a state is increased, and the state legislature makes no reapportionment of districts within the state, then all representatives are elected by the state at large. Each member of the House is required to be a resident of the state from which he is chosen.

The Constitution also provides that the House of Representatives "shall have the sole Power of Impeachment" (Art. I, Sec. 2, cl. 5); however, "The Senate shall have the sole Power to try all Impeachments" (Art.I, Sec. 3, cl. 6). In other words, the lower house must bring the indictment but the upper house must serve as the jury.

## The Presidential System and Judicial Powers

Under the Constitution the federal government has adopted the presidential system of executive leadership as distinguished from cabinet or ministerial systems of the United Kingdom and many other countries. Under the presidential system there is an independent executive elected for a fixed term and holding office during that term irrespective of whether he is or is not in political harmony with the legislature. Members of the legislative bodies are elected at fixed times and for fixed terms, and no power is vested in the executive to dissolve them or to force elections at any other time. The principle of separation of powers as applied in the United States precludes any member of the executive department from having a seat in a legislative body. Under this system the president has genuine executive authority. In addition, use of the executive veto gives the president great power to influence or control legislation.

The Constitution expressly authorizes the president to make certain appointments to office; with the country's growth, the national administration and the number of such appointments have naturally grown as well. The more important appointments are subject to confirmation ". . . by and with the advice and consent of the Senate." In cases of malfeasance, the Constitution provides for removal of the president and any of the civil officers by the process of impeachment.

A judicial body for the settlement of disputes between central and local authorities is found in all federal systems. In the United States the Supreme Court is charged with this duty. The Constitution also provides for "such inferior courts as the Congress may from time to time ordain and establish." The judges of these courts are appointed by the president of the United States and hold their offices during good behavior. They are removable only by the cumbersome machinery of impeachment. Article III, which provides for a federal judiciary, also defines treason—the only crime so specified in the Constitution.

## The Role of State Governments

Under the federal system, the states are units within the country, not governments independent of the nation. The limitations imposed upon the states by Article I, Section 10, of the Constitution clearly indicate the purpose of establishing a single national system. States are forbidden, without the consent of Congress, to "keep Troops, or Ships of War in time of Peace, enter into any Agreement or Compact with another State, or with a foreign Power, or engage in War, unless actively invaded, or in such imminent Danger as will not admit of delay." They are forbidden to enter into treaties, alliances, or confederations. These types of limitations upon the states show a definite intention to deprive the states of any independent existence as national governments in themselves. This intention is supported by the language making the "Constitution, and the Laws of the United States which shall be made in Pursuance thereof; and all Treaties made, or which shall be made, under the Authority of the United States" to be the supreme law of the land.

Yet the powers retained by the state governments are broad and comprehensive. Subject only to the condition that the form of government be republican, the states organize their own central and local governments and provide revenues for the support of these governments. The state courts administer the great body of law affecting the rights of individuals and the suppression of crime. Education is under the direct control of the states and of the local governments created by them. The same condition applies to the construction and maintenance of highways and to the great mass of governmental details with which the citizen comes into daily contact.

The role of the states in federal government is recognized in a variety of ways. In the selection of the president, voting by the states in the electoral college is a partial recognition of the states as special entities. Thus the president is not elected by a majority of the whole people but by a combination of state majorities. State power is also reinforced by "senatorial courtesy," an unwritten custom that requires the president to accept recommendations for certain federal officers functioning within any state by the senior senator of that state.

### Law of the Land

Article VI, which declares the entire Constitution and laws and treaties under it to be the supreme law of the land, goes on to stipulate that "the judges in every State shall be bound thereby." It also specifies that all state and federal legislators and executive and judicial officers "shall be bound by oath or affirmation, to support this Constitution; but no religious test shall ever be required as a qualification to any office or public trust under the United States." Another section of the article validates public debts contracted under the Articles of Confederation. The final, brief Article VII provides for ratification.

Article I, creating the Congress of the United States and setting forth its powers, contains half of the entire Constitution. Section 8 sets the framework for all federal legislation, its eighteen sections outlining the awesome authority of the national Congress. The remarkably comprehensive, yet concise, Constitution creating this government is the oldest such document still in force in the world, and it has been admired and studied since the time of its adoption.

# 2.
# The Evolving Constitution

Historians have often declared that two great questions were posed in the American revolutionary era: how should power be distributed between Britain and America, and how should power be divided among the Americans? There has been some inclination to believe that the answer to the second question was such that one should think in terms of two revolutions: the external revolution, referring to the separation of America from Britain; and the internal revolution—the sum of political, social, and economic changes that took place within America itself.

During and after the War of Independence the Patriots had to create a new governmental system. With few exceptions they were republicans after 1776, partly from necessity, mostly from conviction. There was only one person who could be put forward as a candidate for chief executive—George Washington, and he wished to be neither king nor dictator.

The Patriots, so hostile to King George III of England, had transferred their dislike to the institution of monarchy. The majority of them feared concentration of power, whether in the hands of one man or of several. They were federalists rather than nationalists and insisted upon making every colony into a state. While they were generally in favor of a central government, many of them believed that its authority should be severely restricted: monarchy did not go well with a federal system.

Agreeing that they must have republican institutions, the Patriots had to decide what sort of republican system they wanted. From 1774 to 1776 British officials were driven from the colonies, which then reappeared as states. During the same period the Continental Congress developed into a national government, continuing to function as such until 1781, when the Articles of Confederation (the first national constitution) were adopted. The Congress was a revolutionary assembly until that year, and its powers were severely limited even after the Articles were approved by the states. The authority of the central government was largely confined to military, foreign, territorial, and Indian affairs, and it was dependent upon the states for the bulk of its funds. There

51414

was, therefore, more reform undertaken in the states than at the national level.

## Conflicting Ideologies

Struggling in state elections, conventions, and legislatures to shape the country-to-be, the Patriots divided roughly into three groups—conservatives, liberals, and radicals. In the main, the conservatives wished as little change as possible, aside from separation from Britain. They were planters, merchants, lawyers, and clergymen of established churches, supported by other folk fearful of too great change. The conservatives had substantially been partners in power with Britain before 1775, and they wished to inherit the authority formerly wielded by Britain.

The liberals wished neither to preserve the status quo nor to carry out domestic revolution quickly. Less numerous than any other group, the liberals were lawyers, planters, newspaper publishers, and politicians who sought to combine the maintenance of order and financial stability with a zeal for reform and justice. They were devoted to personal rights and—commonly deistic or agnostic—they were enemies of established churches. With the help of radicals and sometimes the conservatives, they carried through many reforms.

The radicals desired political and social leveling; they might also be called democrats in the twentieth-century use of the word. In general, the radicals were mechanics, farmers, and debtors—men who had something to gain from economic, social, and political reform. They believed not only that human beings (except, perhaps, women and those of African descent) were equal but also that American institutions should be remolded accordingly. A few idealists among educated men sympathized with the radical cause and gave it leadership. Less articulate than the other groups, the radicals achieved their successes chiefly in alliance with the liberals.

There were gradations within the three divisions, of course, and men did not invariably, clearly, or continuously belong to any of them. It should also be observed that the conservatives were not opposed to every sort of change and that the radicals had great respect for property rights. Conservatives, for example, could and did call for the abolition of both the African slave trade and slavery itself.

In the contest for control of the new government, the conservatives were at a disadvantage. The Loyalists, who were in the main natural allies to the conservatives, were discredited and excluded from office. Moreover, the liberals and radicals could and did demand substantive reforms in compensation for their sacrifice in the war. The conservatives were also weakened by the fact that they had committed themselves to the concept of the rights of mankind in the struggle with Britain. Construing those rights broadly when denouncing British "tyranny," they could not now quickly reduce their scope after the crisis had passed. They were strong enough, however, to prevent a domestic revolution; the liberals triumphed at the time—the radicals would have their way later.

Clashes among the Patriots became evident when they undertook to draft written constitutions for the states. The radicals wanted the suffrage to be widely extended, even to all white males; the conservatives preferred to restrict it to men of property; the liberals wished to offer the vote to all responsible and capable citizens. The radicals favored a unicameral (one-house) legislature; the conservatives, a bicameral (two-house) body with the upper chamber representing those who owned property; the liberals, bicameral, but with the upper house not dominated by men of large property. Most Patriots feared strong governors, but the conservatives were somewhat more favorable to a single strong head than were the other groups. The conservatives wanted independent and appointed judges who would be free from popular caprice; radicals and liberals preferred judges elected for short terms, to help establish the superiority of the legislature over the judiciary. The conservatives favored indirect choice of members of the upper house by state legislatures; the other groups opposed it. The conservatives supported long terms of office; the others, short. The conservatives and the liberals advocated a sound money policy; the radicals liked cheap paper money and legal tender provisions as means of lightening debt.

## From Colonies to States

The results of the contests over these issues varied from state to state and from time to time within a state. In most of the states there was compromise. Nevertheless, the transformation of the colonies into states brought with it great political change and the opening of the door to political democracy. Although state constitution-makers paid solemn lip service to the principle of separation of powers, the legislative branch was usually made more powerful than the executive and judicial branches, which were to a degree at its mercy. A two-house legislature was generally adopted, partly in keeping with the pattern set in colonial days. The senate (as the upper house came to be called) was not made an unassailable stronghold of privilege, however. A governor was commonly given little authority. It is apparent that the Patriots transferred their dislike of British-appointed governors to their own under the new regime. Property and taxpaying qualifications for voting were continued or revised, and thus the franchise was gradually expanded. In sum, the new states established a political order that was soundly republican, though not wholly democratic.

Also of great import for the future were the changes made by the revolutionary generation with respect to constitutional rights and processes. By common consent a written constitution was put into effect in every state. Moreover, whether placed in a constitution or separately enacted, a bill of rights protecting individual liberties became part of the fundamental law of every state. The chances of future constitutional alteration in accordance with the popular will were thereby increased. The power of the popular will was also enhanced by provisions for constitutional conventions and referenda. The first state constitutions were often made in haste amid pressure of other business by revolutionary bodies, but this procedure aroused public displeasure. Everywhere a demand arose for constitutions formed by conventions specially chosen for the purpose. It was also insisted that their work be submitted to the voters for ratification. These devices were securing acceptance before the end of the War of Independence, and they soon became embedded in American political tradition. Government by written compact (which could, however, be altered) became standard throughout the states.

## "National" vs. "Federal" Governments

When the colonists declared their independence they agreed that the new union of states must have a common government, but they disagreed then—as they continued to disagree for generations—about the kind of government it should be and, above all, about the amount of authority it should have. One group of leaders in 1776 wanted a strong central government with the power to regulate trade, control finance, dispose of western lands, curb state legislative majorities, and intervene within the states to maintain order. They wanted what came to be called a "national" government, but at that time such leaders were in a minority. They were opposed by most of the men who had been the aggressive revolutionary leaders—men who had denied the authority of Parliament over the colonies and who had insisted that each colonial legislature was supreme within its own domain. Equally important in their political thought was their distrust of powerful government and of people in political office. They believed that when human beings gained political power they inevitably tried to gain even more power and that in so doing they often corrupted government and subverted the liberties of the people. Therefore, when the revolutionary leaders wrote the state constitutions, they limited the power of officeholders and protected the people from government by bills of rights.

## The Articles of Confederation—Federalism in Practice

When persons who held such beliefs took up the formation of a constitution for the United States they rejected a document proposed by the "nationalists." The Articles of Confederation, finally adopted by the Continental Congress in 1777 and sent to the states for ratification (secured in 1781), provided for a strictly "federal" government that had no authority over the states or their citizens. The Articles declared specifically that "each state retains its sovereignty, freedom, and independence" and all powers and rights not "expressly delegated to the United States, in Congress assembled." Delegates to the Congress were elected annually by the state legislatures and were subject to recall at any time. Distrust of power seekers was expressed in the provision that no man could be a member of Congress for more than three years in any six. Congress was denied the power of taxation—a logical reflection of the long fight against the taxing power of the British Parliament. Nor did Congress have the power to regulate trade, although it was given the exclusive right to make treaties.

Opposition to granting the taxing power to Congress was so overwhelming that it was not even debated, but lesser issues, which continued to be problems in later constitutional history, were debated fully. One was the question of representation. The states with large populations insisted that they should have more votes in Congress than the small states. The latter, plus those leaders fearful of a powerful central government, insisted on the equality of the states and established the rule that each should have one vote. A second issue was the apportionment of common expenses. The northern states, assuming their lands to be of high value, argued that population was the best index of wealth and ability to pay. The southern states, with poorer land and large populations, established the principle that expenses should be apportioned according to the value of improved lands. The most important conflict concerned western lands. Five states had definite western boundaries, and they insisted that Congress should have control. The other states, some with claims extending to the Pacific Ocean, inserted a provision in the Articles prohibiting Congress from interfering with the lands of the states. Maryland refused to ratify the document because it was a "landless" state; this position was backed by speculators with interests in the region claimed by Virginia. Finally, Virginia ceded the Old Northwest to the United States, thereby requiring Congress to nullify speculators' claims. As a result, Maryland was forced to ratify on March 1, 1781.

For all the evident distrust of centralized power embodied in the Articles of Confederation, the document both limited the independence of the states and granted significant authority to Congress. Indeed, it contained many of the important provisions later incorporated in the Constitution of 1787. The citizens of each state were guaranteed the privileges of the citizens of any state to which they moved. Provision was made for the extradition of criminals fleeing from one state to another. A court of arbitration, under the supervision of Congress, was provided for the settlement of disputes among the states. The freedom of the states was limited by the powers granted to the federal legislature. Congress had the sole power of making peace and war and appointments of military (except regimental officers) in the service of the United States. It had sole control of diplomatic negotiations. It could borrow money, issue paper money, and fix the value of currency coined by it and the states. It had the sole authority to fix weights and measures, establish and manage a post office, and manage affairs with the Indians not a part of any state. Despite the lack of coercive authority over the states and their citizens, then, the Articles of Confederation obviously set a pattern for many important provisions of the Constitution that followed.

The "federal period" (1781–89) during which the Articles of Confederation served as America's constitution was a time of political and social stress. The American federation was little more than a league of sovereign states. The Continental Congress under the Articles was ignored abroad, on the verge of bankruptcy at home, and generally unable to solve the complex social and economic problems of the period. Yet many of these problems, such as demobilization and a postwar depression, were not the fault of weak government. Moreover, the government under the Articles—despite its inherent weaknesses—could point to a number of genuine achievements. By providing the American people with experience in using a written constitution, the Articles paved the way for greater unification. A rudimentary executive branch evolved from the offices of secretary for foreign affairs and superintendent of finance. These two offices, created during the military and financial crisis of 1781, eventually became the Department of State and the Treasury Department. The War Department, established by Congress in 1785, was carried over intact into the federal government under the Constitution. The Confederation government managed to settle state claims to western lands and to establish territorial government for the Northwest Territory. In fact, the Northwest Ordinance of 1787 set precedents of immeasurable significance for all future settlement and government of the country's western territories.

## Defects and Disillusionment

Despite these accomplishments, the government of the Confederation faced a variety of economic and social problems that undermined its support and furnished ammunition to those who desired a stronger central government. The problems of military demobilization were complicated by governmental insolvency and the depreciation of paper money. Indeed, experience with governmental incompetence during the war had convinced most army officers of the need for a strong central government.

Among the misfortunes of the Confederation government was the fact that it coincided with an economic depression—a typical postwar depression that began with an orgy of consumption at the end of the war and a big increase in imports from Europe. By the spring of 1784 the country was in a severe commercial depression characterized by a scarcity of money and glutted markets. This situation was somewhat mitigated, however, by the expansion of trade, no longer limited to the British Empire. The economy was fundamentally sound and the depression relatively brief; prices were rising by early 1787, but in the meantime the depression created a number of important political issues that escalated the demand for a stronger central government.

During the Revolution the Continental Congress and most of the states had issued certificates of debt (short-term negotiable promissory notes) that circulated as money. The effort to redeem these certificates at the end of the war drastically reduced the amount of money in circulation and aggravated the depression. Debtors, unable to obtain the cash necessary to pay what they owed, demanded that the states print more paper money; soon the subject became the hottest political issue of the Confederation period. By 1786 seven states had adopted paper money. Where merchants were willing to accept this paper money, it worked well and circulated at its face value. Elsewhere, it depreciated in varying degrees. In Rhode Island the Providence merchants refused to accept it and closed their shops to avoid being paid in worthless money, causing commercial chaos. Unfortunately, the successful use of paper money in several states was generally overlooked amid the uproar over Rhode Island. Thoroughly alarmed, merchants and creditors joined the rising chorus of demand for a strong central government that could prohibit the states from emitting bills of credit, which were paper bills based on a state's credit and circulated as currency. (The present Constitution does indeed prohibit this practice in Article I, Section 10.)

## Calls for Reform

The inadequacy of the Articles of Confederation was evident to many even before they were ratified. Even those who generally favored the Articles agreed that some revision was necessary. The inability of Congress to levy taxes, its dependence on the states for voluntary contributions, and the lack of any power over interstate commerce were the most glaring defects. Alteration of the Articles was difficult because amendments required the unanimous consent of all thirteen states. As early as 1781 Congress asked the states for power to levy customs duties in order to pay off the revolutionary debts. All except Rhode Island agreed, and five years later—when that state finally ratified the proposal—New York withdrew its consent. Attempts to obtain the power to regulate interstate and foreign commerce were similarly frustrated by the fear of southern states that northern merchants would dominate their trade. In desperation Congress in 1786 appointed a committee to review the weaknesses of the Articles and suggest remedies. Although the committee approved a comprehensive series of recommendations designed to increase the powers of Congress, and even to create a federal judiciary, it was too late. Nationalists by then were completely disillusioned with the Articles; they were looking for ways of summoning a convention to set up a new framework.

The leader of this movement was James Madison of Virginia. A progressive who guided the Statute for Religious Freedom through the Virginia Assembly in 1786, Madison was also a believer in strong, stable government. He had a powerful ally in George Washington, who in 1784 had reaffirmed his long-established interest in improving communication with the West. In so doing, he took a leading part in promoting plans for improving navigation of the Potomac and Chesapeake waterways. In March 1785 the two men arranged a conference of Maryland and Virginia legislators at Mount Vernon (but in which Washington did not participate). The meeting helped to smooth the way for a joint Virginia-Maryland project, but the cooperation of Pennsylvania was seen to be needed because western routes also involved that state. This factor inspired Madison and Washington to use the regional meeting as a springboard to broader discussions; Madison arranged to have an invitation to the Annapolis Conference (1786) extended not only to Pennsylvania but to all the states so that problems of commerce in general could be discussed on a national scale.

The need for such a meeting had become increasingly evident because of problems confronting foreign and domestic commerce. Since recognition of U.S. independence in 1783 Britain had scorned the idea of a commercial treaty with the new country (which some of the British referred to as the "disunited states") by suggesting that not one treaty but thirteen would be needed. The Barbary pirates were thwarting the efforts of U.S. citizens to trade with the Mediterranean area. Moreover, the new country's "perpetual ally," France, was too involved in its own mercantilist (trade) policy to have room for commercial "friendship." These foreign factors, as well as the problems connected with interstate commerce, caused the belief to spread that the only solution lay in changing the Articles of Confederation.

## The Annapolis Conference

In spite of the apparent need for concerted action, only Virginia, New Jersey, Delaware, New York, and Pennsylvania were represented at the Annapolis Conference (September 11–14). No delegates were named from Maryland (nominally the host state of the convention), Connecticut, Georgia, or South Carolina. Although delegates were chosen from New Hampshire, Massachusetts, Rhode Island, and North Carolina, they did not attend. Of the twelve men who went to Annapolis, Alexander Hamilton and James Madison in particular hoped to widen the agenda to include more than commercial matters and to use the convention as a sounding board for broad revision of the Articles of Confederation. The delegates realized, however, that with only five of the thirteen states represented they could neither deal with national commercial problems nor recommend changes in the Articles. They therefore drew up an address to the states citing the authority given to the New Jersey delegation as a useful example and urging that another meeting of commissioners from all the states be called to examine the defects in the system of government and to design a plan to correct them. In agreeing to this address the delegates stretched their authority to the utmost, but in so doing they in effect issued the call that resulted in the Constitutional Convention. Deliberately vague so as to alarm no one, the resolution was endorsed by the Continental Congress under prodding from Madison. Twelve states responded (all except Rhode Island), and on May 25, 1787, a total of fifty-five delegates began to assemble in Philadelphia.

## The Constitutional Convention

Thomas Jefferson, who was U.S. minister to France at the time, referred to the Philadelphia convention as an "assembly of demigods," and it certainly was a distinguished collection of statesmen. The Virginia delegation alone included, besides Washington and Madison, Gov. Edmund Randolph, George Mason (who had written the Virginia Declaration of Rights), and the brilliant lawyer George Wythe. Pennsylvania sent Benjamin Franklin and Robert Morris, while South Carolina sent John Rutledge and Charles C. Pinckney, both prominent in the Revolutionary conventions. Alexander Hamilton of New York, William Paterson of New Jersey, and Rufus King of Massachusetts all contributed clearheaded, positive views to the deliberations. Oliver Ellsworth of Connecticut, thoughtful and sober, helped to solve several difficult problems. Gouverneur Morris of Pennsylvania was especially responsible for the clear language in which the Constitution was cast.

The convention quickly decided to make a new constitution rather than try to amend the Articles of Confederation. Its basic elements were contained in the Virginia (large state) Plan, prepared before the opening of the convention by the Virginia delegation; it was drafted largely by Madison and proposed by Edmund Randolph. This called for the creation of a powerful central government, including a bicameral congress with the representation of each state based on its population or wealth. Agreement was quickly reached (May 30) that ample power must be vested in the central regime, and also (June 12) that the Constitution when finished should be presented for ratification to specially elected conventions in the several states rather than to their legislatures. Later it was stipulated that the Constitution should be put into motion when nine such conventions had voted approval. It was thereby arranged that the Constitution should have as its basis the sovereign will of the people.

## Conflict and Compromise

The bases for representation in Congress proposed in the Virginia Plan, however, encountered serious opposition. From the time of the first Continental Congress each colony-state had possessed (as in the convention itself) one vote; the use of a ratio of numbers or wealth would obviously destroy that system and would give the larger states—especially Massachusetts, Pennsylvania, and Virginia—a heavier representation. Bitter protests came from delegates of the small states, who were influenced not only by state pride but also—and especially—by fear that members of the Congress from the large states would combine their votes to dominate the others. Massachusetts, Pennsylvania, and Virginia—with support from Connecticut, the Carolinas, and Georgia—urged the principle of proportional representation for both houses of the congress-to-be. The rest clung to their belief that the votes of the large states would be cast in bloc—although Madison correctly predicted that voting would be in accordance with sectional, economic, and social beliefs rather than with size.

Insisting upon equal representation, therefore, the small states rallied behind the New Jersey (small state) Plan, offered by William Paterson of that state on June 15. This scheme proposed a unicameral legislature in which all states had an equal vote and would have materially increased the powers of the Congress beyond those granted in the Articles of Confederation. Provision was also included for an executive and a judiciary. The debate lasted until mid-July and was the most serious conflict in the convention. It became evident that constitutional reform would fail unless meaningful concession was made to the small states. On June 11 Roger Sherman of Connecticut proposed a compromise in which representation would be proportional in one house of the Congress and equal in the other. To conciliate the large states, power to introduce money bills would be given only to the first house, subsequently named the House of Representatives. The Connecticut Compromise, made effective by votes taken on July 16 and 23, assured both sides that their interests would be protected, and the convention moved relatively quickly to approve the other features of the Virginia Plan. Before the end of July the emerging document was sent to a Committee on Detail.

Other difficulties did arise because of conflicting sectional interests, chiefly those of the North and the South. Northern delegates desired representation in the House of Representatives to be in proportion to wealth or free population. Those from Maryland southward insisted that Negro slaves be taken into account either as persons or as property. On the other hand, northern spokesmen wished to count slaves in the apportionment of direct taxes, but southerners were reluctant to do so. After a bitter wrangle a compromise permitted states to count each slave as three-fifths of a person for purposes of both taxation and representation.

Other delicate problems between North and South arose from divergent opinions regarding export duties, regulation of the oceanic slave trade, and navigation acts. The southern delegates desired prohibition of export duties and laws that might give northern merchants a monopoly of southern maritime trade. Men from the deep South also desired a bar against action by Congress to destroy the slave trade. New Englanders sought to secure as much of the southern seaborne traffic as could be gotten for Yankee merchants; and along with delegates from the upper South they desired to abolish the oceanic commerce in slaves. The Connecticut delegation helped materially in arranging a sectional bargain on these controversial issues that, in addition to the earlier compromise on the slave count, came to be called the "Great Compromise." These agreements prohibited any interference with the importation of slaves until 1808, granted Congress the power to regulate foreign trade but required ratification of all treaties by a two-thirds vote of the Senate, and forbade Congress to levy export taxes.

The convention also harmonized its views on various other political matters. It enumerated the powers of the central government; provided for a single executive chosen by a complicated system in which the voters, the states, and the Congress were all to play parts; laid down an outline for a federal judiciary; and adopted a system of checks and balances designed to prevent domination of the federal government by the president, the Congress, or the judiciary. The delegates did not provide specifically for judicial review of legislation, but they apparently expected it to take place. They declared the Constitution to be "the supreme Law of the land." They also failed to insert a full federal bill of rights, partly at least because they thought one unnecessary.

In September the entire document was referred to a Committee on Style. At last, on Sept. 17, 1787, it was signed (by all except sixteen delegates—including George Mason and Edmund Randolph of Virginia and Elbridge Gerry of Massachusetts).

## Debate Over Ratification

In its last dying gasp the Continental Congress recommended the Constitution to the people, and a prolonged debate ensued. Supporters of the Constitution, seizing the initiative, began calling themselves Federalists, a term which emphasized the "federal" character of the Union and the rights retained by the states. Opponents were thus forced to call themselves Anti-Federalists. Ratification procedure was outlined in the Constitution—state legislatures were bypassed in favor of specially elected conventions, and the assent of only nine states was required to put the Constitution into effect. Delaware (the first to ratify), New Jersey, and Connecticut experienced little difficulty in approving the Constitution; all were small states that could not hope to survive without a continental union. In Pennsylvania the Federalists moved with almost unseemly haste to summon a convention and approve the Constitution in December 1787—before the opposition could organize. Georgia, thinly populated and badly exposed to Indian attack, followed suit in January. Massachusetts, whose convention was almost evenly divided, was the first to experience serious opposition. There the Federalists obtained approval by a variety of devices, including a hint to vain but influential John Hancock that he might be the first president. In the spring of 1788 Maryland and South Carolina ratified the Constitution by substantial majorities; both states were dominated by wealthy merchants and planters who desired a strong, orderly government. With the approval of New Hampshire in June, the Constitution went into effect—but it could do little without the assent of New York and Virginia. In both states a majority of the people opposed the new plan of government.

## The Federalist Papers

To persuade the voters of New York, a series of eighty-five essays—published in newspapers in 1787 and 1788—urged the virtues of the Constitution. They were written by Alexander Hamilton, James Madison, and John Jay. Distinguished for their cool logic and insight into problems of government, these works became a classic statement of American governmental theory. The authorship of some of these Federalist papers is a matter of dispute among historians, but it is clear that Hamilton wrote the majority of the papers. Taken together (as they were later published), they presented a masterful exposition of the new federal system and of the major departments in the central government. They also argued that the existing government under the Articles of Confederation was defective and that the proposed Constitution would remedy its defects without endangering the liberties of the people.

As a general treatise on republican government, *The Federalist* is distinguished for its comprehensive analysis of the means by which the ideals of justice, the general welfare, and the rights of individuals could be realized. The authors assumed that the primary political motive of human beings was self-interest and that people—whether acting individually or collectively—were selfish and only imperfectly rational. The establishment of republican government would not of itself provide protection against such characteristics. The representatives of the people might betray their trust; one part of the people might oppress another; both the representatives and the people themselves might give way to passion or caprice. The possibility of good government, therefore, lay in the devising of political institutions that would compensate for human deficiencies in both reason and virtue in the ordinary conduct of politics. This was the predominant theme in late eighteenth-century political thought in the United States and accounts in part for the elaborate system of checks and balances written into the Constitution.

Of particular note is the tenth essay. In it Madison rejected the commonly held belief that republican government was possible only for small states. He argued that stability, liberty, and justice were more likely to be achieved within a wide area with a large and heterogeneous population. Though frequently interpreted as an attack on majority rule, the essay is in reality a defense of social, economic, and cultural pluralism and of a composite majority formed by compromise and conciliation. Decision by such a majority, rather than by a monistic one representing but a single interest, would be more likely to be in accord with the proper ends of government. This distinction between a "proper" and an "improper" majority typifies the fundamental philosophy of the *Federalist*: republican practices (including that of majority rule) were not "good" in themselves but only insofar as they constituted the best means for the pursuit of justice and the preservation of liberty.

The reasoned arguments of Hamilton, Madison, and Jay—plus the fear of being left out of the Union—ultimately converted enough delegates to approve the Constitution. In North Carolina an initial convention rejected the document, but in 1789 a second convention approved it after the federal government had already been established. Rhode Island, which had not even bothered to summon a ratifying convention, finally joined the Union in 1790 under the threat of being treated as a foreign country. Elections were held in the fall of 1788, the first Congress assembled in New York City in the spring of 1789, and on April 30 George Washington was inaugurated as the country's first president.

## "An Almost Perfect Document"

There has been much dispute among scholars concerning the achievement, intentions, and motivations of the men who made the Constitution and secured its adoption. In the latter part of the nineteenth century and the early years of the twentieth both popular and scholarly opinion held that the Constitution was an almost perfect document made by wise and altruistic men. It was generally believed that its adoption rescued the United States from political and economic anarchy during the years following the Revolutionary War. In 1913, however, historian Charles A. Beard in *An Economic*

*Interpretation of the Constitution of the United States* stimulated more sophisticated analysis. Beard contended that the making and ratification of the document were the work of men who were merchants, lawyers, manufacturers, and capitalists—men who were dominated primarily by interests in personal property, especially national certificates of indebtedness. He also offered data tending to indicate that the Constitution was opposed by a majority of the American people—that its adoption was "undemocratic." Other writers in his wake claimed that the adoption was the equivalent of the counterrevolutionary reaction following the French Revolution.

It should be observed that the process of adoption was as "democratic" as any employed in the ratification of state constitutions at the time; furthermore, the provisions of the document were approximately as "democratic" as those of the average contemporary state constitution. It is impossible to prove, therefore, any remarkable conservative reaction in 1787–88. Moreover, scholars have properly pointed out that the possession or nonpossession of certificates of indebtedness could not of itself have determined attitudes toward the Constitution. Indeed, as historians Robert E. Brown and Forrest McDonald have since asserted in critiques of Beard's work, conclusive evidence is lacking that economic status in general dictated either allegiance or opposition to the Constitution. In the debates over the influence exerted by the economic situations of persons and classes, arguments in behalf of the Constitution as a supportive agent for the general good have received insufficient attention. Yet it is clear enough that it offered promise of economic benefits to the country as a whole and of solid improvements in the management of foreign affairs, national defense, and Indian matters. It offered the promise of a dignified and respectable central government in which the new country could and did take pride. It was a document that quickly became admired and respected around the world.

# 3.
# The Flexible Constitution

The procedure for amending the U.S. Constitution is outlined in Article V. Amendments may be proposed by two-thirds vote of both houses of Congress or by a convention called by Congress on the application of the legislatures of two-thirds of the states. Although such conventions are suggested from time to time, none has yet been convoked, since all amendments have been initiated by Congress. The amendment must then be ratified either by three-fourths of the state legislatures or by conventions in as many states. Congress decides which of the two methods of ratification shall be used. Only the Twenty-first Amendment (1933), repealing the Eighteenth (Prohibition) Amendment, called for the convention method of ratification by the states.

By the mid-1970s only twenty-six amendments had been added to the Constitution since 1789. Since the first ten amendments (the Bill of Rights) were submitted and ratified (1791) at the same time, however, and were numbered separately only for purposes of electoral convenience, it could hardly be said that the Constitution had in fact been amended twenty-six times. It would be more accurate to say that it was amended on only seventeen occasions. Furthermore, the Eleventh Amendment, forbidding suits against states in federal courts, and the Twelfth, correcting an error in the original operation of the electoral college, were purely technical in character, and the Twenty-first Amendment merely canceled out the Eighteenth. The most far-reaching—the Thirteenth, Fourteenth, and Fifteenth amendments, imposing important new restraints upon the states—were adopted as a direct consequence of the Northern military victory and occupation of the South at the close of the U.S. Civil War (1861–65).

If a state legislature ratifies a proposed amendment, the Supreme Court has ruled, it may not reconsider its vote later and vote against it; but if the legislature votes against the proposed amendment, it is free to reconsider and vote in favor of it (*Coleman* v. *Miller*, 1939). One reason given for this dual approach is that the Constitution speaks only of ratification; perhaps a better reason is that the court believes that such questions are political and therefore within the control of Congress. If Congress wishes to accept a ratification or chooses to ignore a legislature's change of mind, the Court believes there is nothing that it can with propriety do about it. In the cases of the Eighteenth, Twentieth, Twenty-first, and Twenty-second amendments, and the proposed Twenty-seventh, Congress stipulated that each must be ratified within seven years. While Article V is silent on the subject of a time limit for ratifying, the Supreme Court has ruled that this limiting power is a fair inference from the language of the article, since submission and ratification are successive stages (*Dillon* v. *Gloss*, 1921).

## The Bill of Rights

In the state conventions called (starting in 1787) to ratify the Constitution, nearly every state had proposed changes. Most of the criticism centered on the lack of a bill of rights. One of the champions of a bill of rights for the federal Constitution was Thomas Jefferson. In 1787 he had written to James Madison from Paris that "a bill of rights is what the people are entitled to against every government on earth."

The Bill of Rights derives from Magna Carta (the English Bill of Rights) as well as from the colonial struggle against king and parliament accompanied by a gradually broadening concept of equality among the American people. Virginia's 1776 Declaration of Rights, drafted chiefly by George Mason, was an example of a notable state bill of rights.

The Constitution in its main body protects a number of rights. It forbids suspension of the writ of habeas corpus except in cases of rebellion or invasion (I, 9); prohibits state or federal bills of attainder and ex post facto laws (I, 9, 10); requires that all crimes against the United States be tried by jury in the state where committed (III, 2); limits the definition, trial, and punishment of treason (III, 3); prohibits titles of nobility (I, 9) and religious tests for officeholding (VI); guarantees a republican form of government in every state (IV, 4); and assures each citizen the privileges and immunities of the citizens of the several states (IV, 2). Yet wide popular dissatisfaction with these limited guarantees was expressed at the state conventions.

James Madison, who had promised at the Virginia convention to correct this deficiency, took upon himself the task of combining the 210 amendments suggested by the various ratifying conventions. The Congress adopted twelve items of Madison's proposed bill of rights and sent them to the states for ratification. The Senate refused Madison on a thirteenth, which would have protected religious liberty, freedom of the press, and the right to trial by jury from violation by the states. Ten of the twelve were ratified quickly and went into effect in 1791. The two that failed of ratification would have prohibited enlargement of the House of Representatives and would have forbidden Congress to raise its pay before an intervening election.

## Basic Freedoms

The First Amendment provided that "Congress shall make no law respecting an establishment of religion, or prohibiting the free exercise thereof; or abridging the freedom of speech, or of the press; or the right of the people peaceably to assemble, and to petition the Government for a redress of grievances." As to religion, persecution had been a factor in driving colonists to the New World in the first place; moreover, "respecting an establishment of religion," the leaders of established churches (particularly in New England) wanted protection from congressional interference. Where no church was established churchmen feared that establishment of one church might exclude others; in addition, the Baptists, growing in number, held to separation of church and state as a principle of their creed. The two freedoms of speech and press had been important issues between Americans and the Crown since early colonial times. In 1690 the first American newspaper, published by Benjamin Harris, had been suppressed in its initial issue in Cambridge, Mass. The acquittal of journalist Peter Zenger in New York in 1735 reflected a later commitment to a free press. The right to petition the government for redress of grievances is closely associated historically with freedom of assembly. The political theory of the American revolutionary era emphasized strongly that the colonists were entitled to all the historic guarantees of English liberty, among them freedom of petition. (Thomas Jefferson in the Declaration of Independence significantly listed the flouting of "petitions for redress" as a major grievance against the king.)

Hostility to standing armies found expression in the Second and Third amendments in a guarantee of the people's right to bear arms and in limitation of the quartering of soldiers in private houses. Amendments four through eight relate to the judicial processes of prosecution, trial, and punishment. The Fourth secures the people against unreasonable searches and seizures affecting persons, houses, papers, and effects, and provides that no warrants shall be issued except upon probable cause, supported by oath or affirmation, and particularly describing the place to be searched and the person or things to be seized. The fifth requires grand jury indictment in prosecutions for major crimes and prohibits double jeopardy for a single offense. It provides that no person shall be compelled to testify against himself and forbids the taking of life, liberty, or property without due process of law, or the taking of private property for public use without just compensation. The Sixth, in criminal cases, guarantees the defendant the right to a speedy and public trial by an impartial jury, to be informed of the nature of the accusation against him, to be confronted with witnesses against him, to have compulsory process for obtaining witnesses in his favor, and to have assistance of defense counsel. The Seventh preserves the right of trial by jury in civil suits and makes jury findings incontestable, and the Eighth forbids excessive bail or fines and cruel or unusual punishment.

The Ninth and Tenth amendments underscore the general rights of the people. The Ninth protects unenumerated residual rights of the people, and the Tenth reserves powers not delegated to the United States to the states or the people.

Of them all, the First and Fifth amendments are the most far-reaching, and their impact on the development of an American system of government and of an American national character has been profound. It is the Fifth that makes the Constitution's first reference to "due process of law"—an idea whose first concrete expression in Anglo-American law appears in the 39th article of Magna Carta (1215) in the royal promise that "No free man shall be seized or imprisoned or outlawed, or in any way destroyed; . . . excepting by the legal judgment of his peers, or by the laws of the land." In subsequent English statutes and in elucidating commentaries of Magna Carta, the references to "legal judgment of his peers" and "laws of the land" are treated as substantially synonymous with "due process of law."

## Amendments Eleven and Twelve

Only two amendments intervened between the ratification of the Bill of Rights in 1791 and the Civil War. The Eleventh, adopted in 1795, forbids suits against states in federal courts. The Twelfth corrected a constitutional error that came to light in the presidential election of 1800. In this case, the winning political slate was the Republican one of Thomas Jefferson and Aaron Burr, which won seventy-five electors. Since each of them cast one vote for Jefferson and one for Burr (as the Constitution provided), the two Republican candidates ended in a tie. Although Burr was clearly intended to be vice-president, he refused to withdraw from the presidential contest, and the election was thrown into the House of Representatives, where the Federalists possessed a "lame duck" (defeated officeholders still in office until the inauguration of their successors) majority. Against the advice of Hamilton, who regarded Burr as a "modern Catiline" (insurrectionist), the Federalists supported Burr and deadlocked the House for thirty-six ballots. At the end of February 1801 the crisis ended when a few moderate Federalists cast blank ballots, enabling the Republicans to elect Jefferson. The flaw in the Constitution that made this situation possible was remedied by the Twelfth Amendment, adopted in 1804, providing that the offices of president and vice-president be voted on separately in the electoral college.

## Civil War Amendments

The Thirteenth, Fourteenth, and Fifteenth amendments were the immediate outcome of the Civil War. The Thirteenth Amendment (1865) abolished slavery, while the Fifteenth (1870) forbade denial of the right to vote "on account of race, color, or previous condition of servitude." The Fourteenth (1868) was regarded for a while by the courts as limiting itself to the protection of the freed slaves. The Fourteenth Amendment provides that all persons born or naturalized in the United States are citizens of the United States and of the states wherein they reside (this meant that blacks were thereafter to be citizens without regard to their previous condition of servitude); it also provides that "No State shall make or enforce any law which shall abridge the privileges or immunities of citizens of the United States; nor shall any State deprive any person of life, liberty, or property without due process of law, nor deny to any person within its jurisdiction the equal protection of the laws."

While these Civil War amendments do not expressly make applicable to the states all of the guarantees of the first ten amendments, the Supreme Court later established that the terms *liberty* and *due process of law*, as used in the Fourteenth Amendment, make available against state action certain fundamental rights guaranteed to accused persons in the original Bill of Rights. The basic rights referred to are "implicit in the concept of ordered liberty," for, if they were sacrificed, "neither liberty nor justice would exist" (Justice Benjamin Cardozo, *Palko* v. *Conn*, 1937).

Thus many of the protections of the people against the federal government found in the First, Fourth, Fifth, Sixth, and Eighth amendments have been extended to protect them against similar encroachments by the state as well. In this way judicial construction of the Fourteenth Amendment accomplished what Madison would have accomplished with his thirteenth proposed element for the Bill of Rights—a proposal that the Senate did not allow to be presented to the people.

## Taxation, Electoral Reform, and Prohibition

An income tax had been imposed by the U.S. Congress in 1862 to meet Civil War expenditures. Unpopular and widely evaded, it expired a decade later. Reimposed in 1894, it was held to be unconstitutional by the Supreme Court on the grounds that certain portions of it were direct taxes and therefore were invalid because the tax was not apportioned according to population as required by the Constitution. An immediate attempt was made to sanction income taxation by constitutional amendment; this culminated in the Sixteenth Amendment, effective in 1913, which empowered Congress "to lay and collect taxes on income." In that same year the Seventeenth Amendment was ratified, modifying Article I of the Constitution and providing that U.S. senators be elected by popular vote instead of by state legislators.

Prohibition of intoxicating liquors had been a goal of assorted reformers in America since the mid-nineteenth century. Its progress among the states was irregular but by the end of World War I half of the U.S. population lived in "dry" states. During the war a temporary wartime Prohibition Act was passed to save grain for use as food. In 1917 the Hobson resolution for submission of the Prohibition Amendment to the states received the necessary two-thirds vote in Congress; the Eighteenth Amendment was ratified on Jan. 16, 1919, and went into effect a year later.

The opponents of Prohibition began to organize from the moment the law came into effect. By 1929 the demand for some change was considerable. In February 1933 the Senate and House adopted a joint resolution proposing the Twenty-first Amendment to the Constitution repealing the Eighteenth. It was ratified in 1933.

## Voting Rights and Technical Reforms

Another reform effort, based on the idea of political equality rather than morality, brought about the Nineteenth Amendment after years of struggle by the women's suffrage movement. Wyoming gave women full political rights from the beginning of its statehood. Similar rights were won in New York in 1917, the movement's greatest victory yet. Women by 1918 had acquired equal suffrage with men in fifteen states — the only instance in the world where the voters themselves gave the franchise to women. Congress sent the amendment to the states, and it was ratified before the 1920 election.

Later extensions of voting rights were appended to the constitution in the 1960s. The Twenty-third Amendment, adopted in 1961, gave residents of Washington, D.C., the right to vote for president by providing the District with three electoral votes like any of the smallest states. The Twenty-fourth Amendment abolished payment of the poll tax (a fixed fee at the polling place) as a requirement for voting in federal elections. Fueled by the civil rights movements of the 1960s, it was adopted in 1964. The franchise was extended to eighteen-year-olds by the Twenty-sixth Amendment in 1971.

The remaining three amendments that were adopted during the country's first two centuries affected the presidency and the Congress. "Lame duck" sessions of Congress, meeting after the election of a new Congress and president in November but before the presidential inauguration the following March, were abolished by the Twentieth Amendment, ratified in 1933. It provided that thereafter the Congress elected in November should begin its session the third day of the following January, and that the president should be inaugurated January 20 instead of March 4.

The Twenty-second Amendment was set in motion by the disquiet of conservatives over Pres. Franklin D. Roosevelt's flouting of the tradition that U.S. chief executives would not seek a third term. It forbids election to a third term and debars a vice-president who has succeeded to the presidency for a period of longer than two years from being elected president more than once. It was ratified in 1951.

Presidential succession was the subject of the Twenty-fifth Amendment, adopted in 1967. It provides for the president to fill by appointment a vacant vice-presidency, and for temporary succession to office in case of a president's disability. Had it been in force in 1919, Vice-President Thomas R. Marshall might have been acting president during President Woodrow Wilson's long illness. Half a century later, when scandals forced the resignation of Vice-President Spiro Agnew and then President Richard M. Nixon, the Twenty-fifth Amendment provided an orderly basis for the appointments of two vice-presidents, Gerald R. Ford and Nelson Rockefeller.

Various amendments have been proposed but failed of ratification, and many more have been suggested but never adopted by Congress for submission to the states. A number of these ideas have been adopted by various states. Several of them were embodied in another approach to constitutional government at the time of the Civil War: the constitution of the Confederate States of America, the seceded South.

This Constitution throughout its framework was a modified copy of the Constitution of the United States, for the Southerners had insisted time and again that they had no quarrel with that document. Their objection was to the way the North was interpreting it. But there were important additions and clarifications that made it one of the most interesting documents in U.S. history.

The president was to serve for a term of six years and be ineligible for reelection; the president might veto separate items in appropriation bills; with the consent of Congress, cabinet members might have seats on the floor of either house; a budget system was adopted, and Congress was not authorized to increase items in a budget except by a two-thirds majority; after the first two years the Post Office Department was required to be self-sustaining; the foreign slave trade was prohibited; and no law could relate to more than one subject. By way of clarification, Congress was forbidden to foster any industry by a protective tariff, appropriate money for internal improvements, or limit the right to take slaves into a territory. Although there was a provision for a Supreme Court, the Confederate Congress never set one up, fearful of the power it might assume.

When the United States celebrated its bicentennial, the Constitution had been in effect 187 years. In that time it had been amended, in the main, sparingly and with sobriety and restraint. It had not, despite temptations and occasional attempts, been festooned with ceremonial proclamations and legislation in the guise of amendments. Yet the amending process, cumbersome by design, had worked well enough to put to rest any fears about its rigidity.

# 4.
# Tripartite Government: The Separation of Powers

To the framers of the U.S. Constitution, it was axiomatic that there was only one sure way to forestall tyranny by the government they were creating. That was to divide its powers and to place in three separate departments the essential functions of the legislative, the executive, and the judicial.

This view reveals that the founding fathers were obliged once again to the views of seventeenth-century English philosopher John Locke. In his *Two Treatises of Government* (1690) Locke had written a refutation of absolutist theories of government: "Freedom of men under government is to have a standing rule to live by . . . a liberty to follow my own will in all things where that rule prescribes not, not to be subject to the inconstant, uncertain, unknown arbitrary will of another man."

To secure this freedom, Locke favored a mixed constitution: the legislative should be an elected body, whereas the executive would usually be a single person, the monarch in Locke's day. He thus argues for a separation of legislative and executive powers. The people are *ultimately* sovereign, though it is not always clear in Locke's theory where the *immediate* sovereignty lies.

The French philospher Montesquieu, writing little more than a generation later, carried the separation idea further. His treatise *L'Esprit des lois,* a major contribution to political theory, abandoned the classical classification of governments as monarchy, aristocracy, and democracy. Montesquieu assigned to each form of government an animating *principle:* the republic, based on virtue; the monarchy, based on honor; and despotism, based on fear.

The most famous chapter of this work was written as early as 1734, and on publication in 1748 it became perhaps the most important piece of political writing of the eighteenth century. It was admired and held authoritative in England, inspired much of the Declaration of the Rights of Man of the French Revolution, and influenced the major part of the Constitution of the United States. Here he developed the theory of the separation of powers. Dividing political authority into the legislative, executive, and judicial powers, he asserted that in the state most effectively promoting liberty these three powers must be distributed among different individuals or bodies acting independently.

In England almost the only strict application of the doctrine of the separation of powers was the tradition that the executive should never interfere with the judiciary in the exercise of judicial functions. On the other hand it was regarded as right and proper that the judiciary could interfere with the executive whenever a minister or a department was shown to have acted illegally. In this way the concept of the rule of law came gradually to be identified with the idea that judges, in ordinary legal proceedings in ordinary courts, could pronounce upon the lawfulness of the activities of the executive.

## The American Version

In the United States the same conception of judicial restraint upon the executive prevailed, but the other aspects of the doctrine of the separation of powers were acknowledged as the idea was embodied in the federal Constitution and the state constitutions. A *complete* separation of powers was not considered feasible by the framers, so they modified the doctrine by adding the notion of "checks and balances," whereby each of the three branches of government would be checked and balanced by the others. This actually strengthened the power of the courts to review the actions of the executive.

In the light of subsequent constitutional experience, it became clear that the triple separation of powers was only one means of solving a broader constitutional problem: how to insure the restraint of governmental power by dividing it without carrying such division to an extreme incompatible with effective government. Federalism, the division of power between coexisting territorial jurisdictions, was another means of achieving this purpose. When seen as part of this broader design, the classic functional division of power loses some of its rigidity and dogmatic purity. The combination of separation of powers with the geographical divisions of federalism has characterized the U.S. Constitution.

## Lessons of History

The concept of the separation of powers has been sharply attacked, in the name of both democracy and efficiency, by fascists and communists who have radically rejected the idea of dividing governmental power and have insisted upon the need of concentrating it in the hands of ruling party groups dedicated to the revolutionary transformation of society. In the late eighteenth century, English political philospher Jeremy Bentham and other critics started to object to the inhibiting effect of the separation of powers, insisting that the system does not actually operate, that it cannot be made to work. Experience with the totalitarian dictatorships of the interwar and post-World War II era, however, forced reconsideration. One conclusion was clear: constitutional democracy *presupposed* a balanced system of divided powers, for only within such a system could the citizen hope to enjoy a measure of independence and freedom through a guarantee of civil liberties.

# II. Federal Government: The Three Branches

*"I know no safe depository of the ultimate powers of the society but the people themselves; and if we think them not enlightened enough to exercise their control with a wholesome discretion, the remedy is not to take it from them, but to inform their discretion."*

—Thomas Jefferson

# 5.
# The President

The framers of the federal Constitution provided for the office of president in one succinct sentence: "The executive power shall be vested in a President of the United States of America" (Art. II, Sec. 1). The very brevity of this provision has afforded ample opportunity for the evolution of the presidency into the extraordinary office it has become.

The framers found their model for the office in that of the state governor. They lifted several provisions for the office of governor directly from state constitutions and put them into Article II. Just as the constitution of every state made the governor commander in chief of its military forces, for example, so the president was made commander in chief of the armed forces of the country.

The Constitution requires that the president be a natural-born citizen of the United States and be at least thirty-five years old. A president must have been a resident of the United States for fourteen years at the time of inauguration, though such residence need not have been continous. The Constitution also provides that the president shall receive a compensation for his service that shall be neither increased nor decreased during his term. Congress periodically fixes the presidential salary plus expense and travel allowances as well as pension provisions.

The president is elected for a four-year term, but the Constitution originally placed no limit on the number of terms a president might serve. Alexander Hamilton, in *The Federalist,* argued for unlimited reeligibility. George Washington opposed placing any limit on the number of terms a president might serve and, though retiring at the end of his second term, he had no intention of setting a precedent. Thomas Jefferson was the first president (1801–09) who favored setting a precedent for only two terms, and during the next 130 years the two-term limit was assumed to be permanently established by an inflexible custom—notwithstanding Grant's unfulfilled wish for a third nomination in 1876.

During World War II the Democratic National Convention nominated Pres. Franklin D. Roosevelt for a third term, apparently on the assumption that a change of administration would not be prudent in the midst of a world crisis that might suddenly involve the United States in war. Roosevelt was elected for a third term in 1940 and for a fourth term in 1944, thereby shattering the two-term precedent.

As part of the postwar reaction against strong executive leadership, the Twenty-second Amendment to the Constitution was adopted in 1951 to limit the president to two terms. "No person shall be elected to the office of the President more than twice, and no person who has held the office . . . , or acted as President, for more than two years of a term . . . shall be elected to the office . . . more than once." Pres. Harry S. Truman was exempted. On assuming office the President takes the oath of office prescribed by the Constitution: "I do solemnly swear (or affirm) that I will faithfully execute the Office of President of the United States, and will to the best of my Ability, preserve, protect and defend the Constitution of the United States." Since Washington's day every newly elected president has delivered an inaugural address describing the basic policies he plans to follow.

## Presidential Powers

The Constitution makes the president the country's chief executive with this succinct injunction: ". . . he shall take Care that the Laws be faithfully executed" (Art. II, Sec. 3). Article I, Section 7, gives the president a strong veto power. All bills passed by both houses of Congress must be submitted to the president. To veto a bill he declines to sign it and instead returns it to the house of origin with his objections. If each house then votes by a two-thirds majority to pass it over the veto, the bill becomes law without presidential approval. If the president fails to return a bill within ten days, excluding Sundays, it becomes law without his signature. If, however, Congress adjourns before the ten days have elapsed, the president may kill the bill simply by failing to act upon it. This is the pocket veto, and it is absolute.

The proclamation is a historic form of executive action in England and the United States. Presidential proclamations and executive orders are the chief ways in which a president may initiate action. While some proclamations of a president are merely informative or advisory, others are exercises of essentially legislative authority delegated by statute or inferred from powers vested in the president by the Constitution. Two of the most famous are Washington's Proclamation of Neutrality (April 22, 1793), and Lincoln's Proclamation of Emancipation (Jan. 1, 1863).

# Presidents of the United States

| | Name | Served | Party |
|---|---|---|---|
| 1. | George Washington | 1789–1797 | Federalist |
| 2. | John Adams | 1797–1801 | Federalist |
| 3. | Thomas Jefferson | 1801–1809 | Democratic-Republican |
| 4. | James Madison | 1809–1817 | Democratic-Republican |
| 5. | James Monroe | 1817–1825 | Democratic-Republican |
| 6. | John Quincy Adams | 1825–1829 | Democratic-Republican |
| 7. | Andrew Jackson | 1829–1837 | Democratic |
| 8. | Martin Van Buren | 1837–1841 | Democratic |
| 9. | William H. Harrison | 1841 | Whig |
| 10. | John Tyler | 1841–1845 | Whig |
| 11. | James K. Polk | 1845–1849 | Democratic |
| 12. | Zachary Taylor | 1849–1850 | Whig |
| 13. | Millard Fillmore | 1850–1853 | Whig |
| 14. | Franklin Pierce | 1853–1857 | Democratic |
| 15. | James Buchanan | 1857–1861 | Democratic |
| 16. | Abraham Lincoln | 1861–1865 | Republican |
| 17. | Andrew Johnson | 1865–1869 | Democratic |
| 18. | Ulysses S. Grant | 1869–1877 | Republican |
| 19. | Rutherford B. Hayes | 1877–1881 | Republican |
| 20. | James A. Garfield | 1881 | Republican |
| 21. | Chester A. Arthur | 1881–1885 | Republican |
| 22. | Grover Cleveland | 1885–1889 | Democratic |
| 23. | Benjamin Harrison | 1889–1893 | Republican |
| 24. | Grover Cleveland | 1893–1897 | Democratic |
| 25. | William McKinley | 1897–1901 | Republican |
| 26. | Theodore Roosevelt | 1901–1909 | Republican |
| 27. | William H. Taft | 1909–1913 | Republican |
| 28. | Woodrow Wilson | 1913–1921 | Democratic |
| 29. | Warren G. Harding | 1921–1923 | Republican |
| 30. | Calvin Coolidge | 1923–1929 | Republican |
| 31. | Herbert Hoover | 1929–1933 | Republican |
| 32. | Franklin D. Roosevelt | 1933–1945 | Democratic |
| 33. | Harry S. Truman | 1945–1953 | Democratic |
| 34. | Dwight D. Eisenhower | 1953–1961 | Republican |
| 35. | John F. Kennedy | 1961–1963 | Democratic |
| 36. | Lyndon B. Johnson | 1963–1969 | Democratic |
| 37. | Richard M. Nixon | 1969–1974 | Republican |
| 38. | Gerald R. Ford | 1974–1977 | Republican |
| 39. | Jimmy Carter | 1977– | Democratic |

The executive order is never merely ceremonial. It is the principal mode of administrative action on the part of a president of the United States. It came into use before 1850, but the numbering system that was inaugurated about 1895 goes back only to the administration of President Lincoln.

The Constitution gives the president the power to nominate and, by and with the advice and consent of the Senate, to appoint all major executive officers. He may appoint inferior executive officers independently. He may "fill up all Vacancies that may happen during the Recess of the Senate, by granting Commissions which shall expire at the End of their next Session" (Art. II, Sec. 2). Customarily the Senate confirms the president's nominations of Cabinet appointees without question. The Constitution is silent as to the president's power to remove appointees without the consent of the Senate. The First Congress (1789–91) assumed without legislative action that he could not be held responsible for enforcing the laws unless he had unrestricted power to remove subordinates in whom he had no confidence.

This was the issue that the Radical Republicans forced in the Andrew Johnson administration, legislating a denial of the president's right to remove appointees, and leading directly to the impeachment effort when he refused to abide by the restriction. Although the position of the First Congress and Andrew Johnson was ultimately upheld, this was not until 1926, when the Supreme Court ruled in *Myers* v. *United States* (272 U.S. 52).

Under the Constitution, the president is commander in chief in time of peace as well as in time of war. He has at all times unlimited authority to direct movements of land, sea, and air forces. This unlimited discretion enables a president to direct movements of the armed forces that may provoke hostilities with a foreign nation and leaves Congress no alternative but to declare that a state of war exists. President James Polk in 1846, for example, ordered U.S. troops into disputed border territory where a clash with Mexican troops initiated the Mexican War.

President Lincoln gave the commander-in-chief power an extraordinarily broad interpretation during the U.S. Civil War. He suspended the privilege of the writ of habeas corpus, increased the personnel of the army and navy, acquired vessels for the navy, proclaimed emancipation of the slaves, and initiated his own plan of reconstruction of the states whose citizens had been in rebellion—all powers generally assumed to belong to Congress. Lincoln asked Congress to authorize some of his acts retroactively, and it did so.

Although the Constitution empowers Congress "To provide for calling forth the Militia [of the states] to execute the Laws of the Union, suppress Insurrections and repel Invasions" (Art. I, Sec. 8), the president may in the meantime have also used the federal armed forces for these purposes. There was no federal army when Congress enacted the legislation in 1794 that enabled President Washington to assemble 15,000 state militiamen and suppress the revolt in western Pennsylvania against collection of the federal excise tax on whiskey stills. In 1861 President Lincoln interpreted the secession movement in the very phrases of the statutes of Washington's administration when he called upon the governors of the states for 75,000 militiamen to suppress combinations obstructing the enforcement of federal laws in states that had passed ordinances of secession. In 1957 President Eisenhower, utilizing the power Congress had authorized, mobilized the militia of Arkansas under his power as commander in chief, thereby taking it out of the control of Gov. Orval Faubus, who had been defying a federal court order. President Eisenhower then utilized federal armed forces to prevent further interference with the court order which directed limited desegregation in a school at Little Rock, Ark.

The Constitution invests the president with "Power, by and with the Advice and Consent of the Senate. To make Treaties, provided two thirds of the Senators concur" (Art. II, Sec. 2, cl. 2). Usage has established the practice that the president, either directly or through his agents, negotiates treaties and submits them to the Senate for action. In addition to treaties, the president frequently negotiates with foreign governments executive agreements, which have all the effect of treaties although they are not referred to the Senate.

"The President is the sole organ of the nation in its external relations and its sole representative with foreign nations," declared John Marshall as a member of the House of Representatives in 1799. The Constitution provides that the president, "by and with the Advice and Consent of the Senate, shall appoint Ambassadors, other public Ministers and Consuls" (Art. II, Sec. 2), who become, in effect, the president's personal diplomatic representatives abroad. Only the president can "receive Ambassadors and other public Ministers," and only the president can dismiss foreign diplomatic representatives.

The Constitution provides that the president "shall have Power to grant Reprieves and Pardons for Offenses against the United States, except in cases of Impeachment" (Art. II, Sec. 2). A "reprieve" suspends the penalties of the law while a "pardon" remits the penalties. The president may not grant a pardon before the commission of an offense but may do so at any time after its commission. Since impeachment and conviction of officers of the United States is an exclusive function of Congress, the president is forbidden the power of pardon in such convictions. In like manner Congress may not interfere with the president's power of pardon.

The president's influence in the national government rests upon the powers granted him by the Constitution and by federal statute, upon political factors not found in constitutions or statutes, and upon the personality of the president and his capacity for political leadership. The influence of the presidency varies with the man who occupies the office and with the circumstances that surround him.

With Washington's willing acquiescence, his secretary of the treasury, Alexander Hamilton, assumed bold leadership of the executive departments. He drafted and promoted passage through Congress of the administration's measures known ever since as the Hamiltonian program. Hamilton's competent and aggressive leadership, however, no less than the nature of the legislation he sponsored, aroused a determined opposition. Rallying around Thomas Jefferson, this opposition (the Anti-Federalists) formed the first Republican Party, succeeded in electing Jefferson president in 1800, and brought about a striking change in the very nature of the presidency. The center of gravity in the government passed from the executive to the legislature, where it remained until the administrations of Andrew Jackson (1829–37).

Jackson was the very model of a strong president, and his rejection of South Carolina's nullification theory and his veto of the renewed charter of the Bank of the United States effectively shifted the center of gravity in the government back to the executive branch, where it had been in Washington's administration. The presidency had taken another sharp turn.

Even more than Jackson, Lincoln used the unexplored power of commander in chief and thereby to reshape the presidency into an instrument of extraordinary power for resolving emergencies—all with a confident touch and incomparable ingenuity.

The high prestige Lincoln's hand had given the presidency went into a generation-long decline after his death. Pres. Theodore Roosevelt (1901–09) used his executive power to meet rising public demands for reform. He reinvigorated the long-ignored Sherman Anti-Trust Act and demanded government regulation of industry, becoming the first U.S. president to envision the federal government as an umpire upholding the public interest in conflicts involving big business, big labor, and the consumer. Roosevelt strengthened the Interstate Commerce Commission, interposed federal authority in a major labor dispute, set in motion a national conservation policy to preserve public lands and forests, broke a deadlock in negotiations over the Panama Canal, and brought Russia and Japan together in peace negotiations after the Russo-Japanese War of 1904. In the course of all this he greatly expanded the powers of the president, thus in a most appropriate fashion introducing the office to the looming complexities of the twentieth century.

Pres. Woodrow Wilson (1913–21) demonstrated the possibilities of presidential leadership in legislation. Utilizing the long neglected provision of the Constitution that the president "shall from time to time give to the Congress Information of the State of the Union, and recommend to their consideration such Measures as he shall judge necessary" (Art. II, Sec. 3), he got an unprecedented program of important measures—regulating business—enacted by Congress in his first term. Wilson added a dramatic touch by resuming the delivery of presidential messages in person, for the first time since the administration of John Adams 112 years earlier.

## The New Deal

Pres. Franklin D. Roosevelt (1933–45) introduced new features into the pattern of presidential leadership in legislation. The "fireside chat," an informal talk broadcast by radio to the nation generated public pressure on Congress in support of the president's program. It became an established device, greatly augmented by the advent of television. President Roosevelt also initiated the practice of accompanying a proposal for legislation with an already prepared bill. He also used patronage shrewdly.

The massive recovery and reform legislation and executive action of Roosevelt's New Deal unalterably changed the role of president and dramatically expanded the scope and power of the executive branch of government.

Lyndon B. Johnson was a master legislative strategist when he succeeded (Nov. 22, 1963) the assassinated John F. Kennedy. Johnson shrewdly exploited the national grief and guilt as well as his own skills in working his way with legislators. He enjoyed prodigious success. The Congress in the next few months denied him little he asked in Kennedy's name and his own. After his election in November 1964 he concentrated most of his energies on his "Great Society" program. He got from the Congress a mass of welfare legislation larger than any in U.S. history. It was an extraordinary period. Most observers feel that there was brought about in that period a volume of social change greater than that which in other times and places had come to pass only through revolution.

Johnson, however, ran afoul of public sentiment that opposed increasingly massive U.S. intervention in the Vietnam War. Not in this century had there been so angry an outcry against any president's foreign policy. Johnson became the personification of evil in the political arena. By the end of 1967 it became apparent that he would be unlikely to win renomination. Johnson had significantly increased the power of the presidency on the domestic front, but his Vietnam misadventure resulted in a heavy blow to the prestige of the office, the executive branch, and government itself. The result was a perceptible diminution of a vital aspect of presidential power, the power to rally and focus public support for U.S. foreign policy and, ultimately, any U.S. policy.

## Andrew Johnson

Other presidents, one of whom was Andrew Johnson, of course have involuntarily diminished the power or stature of the office. Johnson's presidency foundered on the enormous problems of reconstructing the South. He adopted Lincoln's view that the establishment of Reconstruction policy was an executive prerogative and accepted the main features of Lincoln's policy, infuriating the Radical Republicans who dominated Congress. The times demanded a president who was tolerant, broad of view, and politically adept. By temperament and experience Johnson lacked these qualities, and the breach between him and the Republican Congress widened. As president, Johnson had been placed in an almost impossible situation, for he had no large personal following; he was president by accident and was the titular head of a party whose policies and leaders he distrusted. Standing almost alone, he faced the complexities of Reconstruction that had taxed even Lincoln's greater capacities, and that led eventually to his impeachment, which failed of conviction. But Johnson's protracted wrangle with Congress and contradictions of his policies by members of his own administration brought the prestige and power of the presidency into a near-eclipse by comparison with the Lincoln administration.

## The Cabinet

In the United States the president's Cabinet is altogether different from the British cabinet. It is composed of the heads of different executive departments, but the members do not have seats in Congress and their tenure does not depend on favorable votes on administration measures. The existence of the Cabinet and its operation are matters of custom rather than law because the Cabinet as a collective body has no legal existence or power. The Constitution does not mention a cabinet, but it does assume, in incidental references, that Congress will establish executive departments. One of these references says that the president may require written opinions from executive department heads— all that remains of an attempt by some members of the Constitutional Convention to provide for a specific presidential advisory council. The word *cabinet* was first used publicly by James Madison in 1793.

George Washington inaugurated the practice of consulting regularly with his department heads as a group. In 1789 he wrote that the first three executive departments had been instituted because of "the impossibility that one man should be able to perform all the great business of the state." Quite naturally he turned to subordinates in the executive branch for help, the more so since the Senate, anxious to preserve its legislative independence, was reluctant to act as an intimate advisory council. From the outset Washington sought advice—in informal conversation and writing—from the three department secretaries and the attorney general. In 1791–92 he began to consult occasionally with this group of four on important and confidential matters.

Washington's habit of calling regular and frequent Cabinet meetings began a tradition that has been followed by every succeeding president. But it is important to remember that the Cabinet exists solely to help the president carry out his functions as the country's chief executive. He is virtually free to use it or not as he wishes. The president may consult with Cabinet members before making a particular decision but the responsibility for making that decision is nevertheless completely his. If he does not choose to consult with Cabinet members there is little they can do about it. A story is told about a disagreement in Abraham Lincoln's Cabinet that found the president's viewpoint opposed by all the members of the group. Lincoln called for a vote and announced the results—"One aye, seven nays: the ayes have it."

Some presidents have relied on their Cabinets a great deal, and others have done so relatively little. The great variety in usage is accounted for by differences in the kinds of problems under consideration and, most importantly, by the differences in ability, temperament, and working habits of individual presidents. Attendance at meetings has been restricted to department heads of Cabinet rank.

Many different factors enter into the president's selection of his Cabinet. Ordinarily all members are of the same political party as he. Some may be personal friends unknown to the public; others may be political leaders of national reputation. Normally the group contains representatives from different sections of the country. The desires of pressure groups may influence the selection of certain members.

While nominations to the president's "official family" must be confirmed by the Senate, confirmation is normally given promptly and without objection. (Only a few have ever been rejected.) Cabinet appointment is for the duration of the administration; however, the president may dismiss any member at pleasure, without approval of the Senate. Dismissals are rare, but individual resignations have been fairly common. Department heads may also be removed by impeachment, but such action is extremely rare. In 1876 impeachment proceedings were brought against Secretary of War William W. Belknap, but he was not convicted.

Under the Presidential Succession Act of 1886, the Cabinet was given a special role in the event that both the president and vice-president died, resigned, were removed, or were unable to serve. The members of the Cabinet were next in line of succession, beginning with the senior member, the secretary of state. The Presidential Succession Act of 1947 modified this procedure to place the Speaker of the House of Representatives and the president pro tempore of the Senate ahead of the Cabinet members. In 1967 the Twenty-fifth Amendment provided for presidential appointment of a vice-president before the 1947 order was ever used.

## Ceremonial Duties

Early in his first term Washington, who by education and natural inclination was minutely careful of the proprieties of life, established the rules of a virtual republican court. In both New York and Philadelphia he rented the best houses procurable, refusing to accept the hospitality of others because he believed that the head of the country should be no man's guest. He returned no calls and shook no hands, acknowledging salutations by a formal bow. He drove in a coach drawn by four or six smart horses and with outriders and lackeys in rich livery. He attended receptions dressed in a black velvet suit with gold buckles, with yellow gloves, powdered hair, a cocked hat with an ostrich plume in one hand, and a sword in a white leather scabbard. After being overwhelmed by callers he announced that except for a weekly levee (reception) open to all, persons desiring to see him must make previous engagements. On Friday afternoons Mrs. Washington held more informal receptions, at which the president appeared and chatted gravely with both ladies and gentlemen. Though the presidents of the Continental Congress had made their hospitality partly public, Washington, who entertained widely and invited members of Congress in rotation, insisted that his hospitality be entirely private. He served good wines, and the menus were elaborate, but some visitors complained that the atmosphere was too "solemn." Indeed, his simple ceremony offended many of the more radical Anti-Federalists, who did not share his sense of its fitness and accused the president of conducting himself as a king.

The first president did establish two important and enduring democratic traditions, however. Eschewing a pompous title with overtones of aristocracy, Washington asked to be addressed in his official capacity simply as "Mr. President." This proved to be a superb choice, intuitively selected, and in keeping with the spirit of democracy in the fledgling republic. He also made the distinct gesture of deferring to the legislative branch of government by going before the assembled Congress to make his first State of the Union address— he did not ask the Congress to come before him.

With the passage of time the president has become increasingly burdened with ceremonial duties. The elaborate ritual of his inauguration, suggestive of a royal coronation, is but the first of such activities. He awards medals to military heroes, buys the first poppy at the annual Veterans of Foreign Wars sale, greets delegations of firemen, Boy Scouts, Elks, Eagles, Daughters of the American Revolution, and other organizations, issues the Thanksgiving Proclamation, lays a wreath on the Tomb of the Unknowns, lights the White House Christmas tree, and receives visiting monarchs. Nor can it be doubted that these acts of the chief of state strengthen the powers of the chief executive. More than once the electorate has chosen as president a symbol rather than one who, by an appropriate apprenticeship in public administration, has been prepared for the presidency.

## Politics

The office of president is an eminently political one. Theodore Roosevelt's characterization of the presidency as "a bully pulpit" is famous. And indeed the White House has been recognized as a forum for moral suasion by every occupant. Not all have used it effectively, but all have tried.

Those presidents whose command of rhetoric has been substantial have fared better than others, and some of them perhaps—notably Lincoln—worked long and hard at it. His best ideas and finest phrases did not occur in impromptu speeches. Rather, long-remembered sayings were written out ahead of time and rewritten with meticulous revisions. Some resulted from a gradual growth of thought and phrase through many years. One of his recurring themes—his central theme—was the promise and the problem of self-government. As early as 1838, he spoke of "the capacity of a people to govern themselves." Again and again he returned to this idea, and steadily improved his phrasing. In his first message to Congress after the fall of Fort Sumter, he declared that the issue between North and South involved more than the future of the United States. "It presents to the whole family of man the question whether a constitutional republic, or democracy—a government of the people by the same people —can or cannot maintain its territorial integrity against its own domestic foes." And finally at Gettysburg he made the culminating, the supreme statement, concluding: "that from these honored dead we take increased devotion to that cause for which they gave the last full measure of devotion—that we here highly resolve that these dead shall not have died in vain—that this nation, under God, shall have a new birth of freedom—and that government of the people, by the people, for the people, shall not perish from the earth."

In the realm of political maneuvering and negotiating, presidents have used variations on the carrot-and-stick approach, the carrot usually being the awarding of an appointment of some sort to a constituent of a friendly legislator. The name of Jackson is usually linked with the origins of the spoils system (political patronage appointments) but the practice of removing unsympathetic officeholders and replacing them with supporters of a president's own views actually began in 1801 with Jefferson. Moreover, Jackson did not carry out the practice either uniformly or to excess. Even in the era of civil service for the vast majority of federal positions there remain enough appointive openings to supply much incentive. Indeed sometimes, as in the Ford administration and the beginnings of Jimmy Carter's (1977), large numbers of policymaking positions go long-unfilled or manned by temporary occupants.

Presidents who are not themselves skilled at the niceties of "politicking" have often relied on defter assistants, a practice begun with Washington and Hamilton.

The shadowy figure of "Colonel House," Edward M. House, loomed large in the first election campaign (1912) of the self-righteous Woodrow Wilson. A veteran and adroit political adviser to a succession of Texas governors, House quickly won Wilson's confidence and affection. He refused any Cabinet position for himself but came to be regarded as Wilson's "silent partner" in all administrative and political matters. After the outbreak of the European war in July 1914 he was recognized as Wilson's chief agent for foreign relations.

U.S. participation in the war brought a vast enlargement of House's role. He cooperated intimately with the Allied war missions and headed the U.S. mission to an Inter-Allied conference in London and Paris. The president turned to House for advice in drafting his war aims speeches—especially the one containing the fourteen points. In the autumn of 1917 Wilson entrusted House to organize an American program for the peace conference.

When the Germans requested peace negotiations in October 1918, Wilson chose House as his representative in the Inter-Allied conferences where the reply to the German appeal was formulated. House persuaded the Allied chiefs of state to accept Wilson's fourteen points as the basis of the ultimate peace settlement. He became one of the five U.S. commissioners to the peace conference and sat with the president on the commission that drafted the covenant of the

League of Nations. His influence was pervasive, and his share in the settlement of critical issues important, but his ties to the president were gradually loosening. The very gift at compromise that made him valuable to Wilson drove them apart as the president—even after he came to see compromise unavoidable—found that process extremely distasteful.

Other presidents have used alter egos in various ways. Franklin Roosevelt's Harry Hopkins carried enormous authority in his respective spheres of activity. Richard Nixon's, H. R. Haldeman and John D. Ehrlichman, exercised tremendous power and influence for years, and are notorious now for organizing and conducting the cover-up of White House complicity in the Watergate scandals.

Appropriately, however, the ultimate responsibility for the conduct of the presidency resides in the man elected to that high position. "The buck stops here," read a plaque on Harry Truman's desk. Its blunt accuracy fairly reflects that president, whose courage and candor place him among the men who have enhanced the honor and stature of the office of president of the United States. Among the presidents remembered less favorably is Andrew Johnson's successor, Civil War general Ulysses S. Grant, who came to office in 1869 at age forty-six, the youngest man elected president up to that time and the most inexperienced in politics. The scandals of his two administrations, all revolving around unwise appointments and dishonest associates, dismayed and sickened Grant and still further lowered the repute and the power of the presidency.

### Scandal and Succession

The prestige that Pres. Theodore Roosevelt had restored to the office was reduced by the scandals of the Warren Harding administration (1921–23). Except for the president, corruption reached into the highest levels of government.

The administration of Richard M. Nixon (1969–74) brought certain distinctions to the presidency before it was brought down by scandal of a different sort. He had moved boldly to relax tensions with the Soviet Union and end hostility with the People's Republic of China. But the Watergate scandal and its cover-up tarnished Nixon's enhancement of the presidency in foreign affairs and ultimately drove him from office (August 1974) in the deepest crisis of confidence in the history of the presidency. Following so closely on the heels of Lyndon Johnson's debacle in Vietnam, the successive blows of the Watergate revelations wrought terrible damage to the fabric of U.S. political life. The most beneficial aspect of the twenty-nine-month interregnum of Gerald R. Ford that followed was that the conspicuous decency of the man and his intentions restored as much tentative respect for government as it did.

It was the threat of impeachment that drove Nixon from office. The president in pursuit of his duties is not subject to judicial process despite the silence of the Constitution on the matter. This immunity is derived by judicial interpretation from the implied separation of powers of the Constitution, which signifies that the judiciary may not interfere with the executive. However, the president, along with other civil officers of the United States, may be impeached and, if convicted, removed from office. The House of Representatives initiates impeachment proceedings against the president by passing resolutions consisting of articles of impeachment charging him with "Treason, Bribery, or other high Crimes and Misdemeanors." "Managers" appointed by the House of Representatives prosecute the accused president on trial before the Senate sitting as a court, with the chief justice presiding when the president is on trial. The president is not present in person but is defended by his legal counsel. Conviction requires a two-thirds vote of the senators. The only penalty the Senate can impose is removal from office.

Critics of the impeachment process have feared on one hand that it was so cumbersome that it would never be used and on the other that it was so easy to initiate that it might be used by a heavy partisan majority in Congress to punish an executive for belonging to the wrong party. In experience neither fear has been justified. The process is cumbersome, but by the 1970s it had been seriously undertaken only twice at the presidential level (though much more frequently at lower levels). Although Congress had substantial and important grievances against Andrew Johnson, there were of course important partisan elements in the impeachment of a Democratic president by a Republican House of Representatives. Yet a Republican Senate refused to convict him, though narrowly. There also were some partisan elements in the move toward impeachment of the Republican Nixon by a Democratic House, yet most Republican members agreed with the majority that impeachment was warranted as the facts of the Watergate scandal and cover-up emerged.

The vice-president is elected with the president and for the same term. The Constitution provides for vice-presidential succession to the presidency when that office is vacant. It also originally provided that: "In Case of the . . . Inability [of the president] . . . [his] Powers and Duties . . . shall devolve on the Vice President . . . ." No authority to determine inability was named, however. To provide for the eventuality of both offices becoming vacant, Congress in 1947 determined that the succession goes first to the Speaker of the House of Representatives, next to the president pro tempore of the Senate, and then to Cabinet members in the order in which their departments were created. In 1967 the Twenty-fifth Amendment provided that the vice-president succeeds to the presidency if the president declares his inability to the president pro tempore of the Senate and the Speaker of the House or if the vice-president and a majority of the Cabinet declares the inability. Presidential notice of "no inability" goes to the same congressional officers and is thereupon effective, unless contested by the vice-president and a majority of the Cabinet or by a body designated by Congress; then a two-thirds majority of both houses can overrule the president. If the vice-presidency is vacant the president appoints a vice-president subject to confirmation by a simple majority of both houses. If both offices become vacant simultaneously, the act of 1947 applies.

Both Johnson and Ford had been vice-presidents who succeeded to the presidency. The conditions governing that succession, including custom and precedent as well as Constitution and statute, have by no means always been clear.

When William Henry Harrison died on April 4, 1841, one month after his inauguration, John Tyler succeeded to the presidency. The opposition proposed to recognize him as acting president only, but Tyler successfully claimed all rights and privileges of the office, including the title President of the United States. To the offices of president and vice-president Tyler contributed a valuable precedent, namely, that when a vice-president succeeds to the office of chief executive he becomes *president* and not *acting president.*

Forty years later, Pres. James A. Garfield was shot by a disappointed office seeker. For eighty days Garfield lay near death, performing only one official act, the signature of an extradition paper. His long disability raised for the first time the problem of succession of a living president. The daily bulletins of the physicians made it abundantly clear that the president was unable to perform the duties of his office. Before the end of July the problem was being discussed in letters to the press, and later it was analyzed in magazine articles by leading constitutional lawyers.

It was generally agreed that, in such a case, the vice-president was empowered by the Constitution to assume the powers and duties of the office of president. Would he then serve merely as acting president until Garfield recovered, or would he receive the office itself and thus displace his predecessor? Because of a certain ambiguity in the pertinent provision (Art. II, Sec. 1, cl. 6) of the Constitution, and in view of the precedent established in 1841 by Tyler when he, the vice-president, took the oath of office as president after Harrison's death, opinion was divided.

Congress was not in session, but the seven members of the Cabinet agreed that the vice-president should assume the powers and duties of the president. But on the question that had already troubled the constitutional lawyers the cabinet was also divided, three holding to the view that the vice-president would merely become acting president and four, including the attorney general, that Chester Arthur would become president of the United States. In view of this possibility, all seven agreed that no action should be taken by them without first consulting Garfield. Since in the opinion of the doctors this was clearly impossible at the time without endangering their patient's life, no further action was taken either by the Cabinet or by the vice-president before the President died on Sept. 19, 1881.

The lengthy illness of Woodrow Wilson after World War I peace negotiations did not raise succession questions as openly or insistently as had the public assassination and lingering decline of Garfield. Wilson was forced to give up a cross-country tour attempting to rally support for the League of Nations, and return to Washington, D.C., in a state of complete collapse. On October 2 he suffered a thrombosis that impaired the control of the brain over the left side of his body. The physical prostration of the president left him isolated from men and affairs. Entirely apart from the confusion that was thus occasioned in the conduct of public business, it shattered hopes of a speedy ratification of the Versailles Treaty. No one else was capable of leading the fight for ratification or possessed enough authority to arrange a compromise. On November 13 the Senate approved reservations to the treaty that the President denounced.

Efforts to arrange a compromise during the succeeding weeks proved fruitless. With something of his physical health regained, with his mind nervously active, but with his grasp of affairs unrealistic, the president drafted a far-fetched plan for submitting the issue to popular vote at a special election. Recognizing the practical difficulties of such a plan, he insisted that the only way out was to "give the next election in the coming November the form of a great and solemn referendum."

Despite some improvement in the spring and summer of 1920, Wilson's physical condition never amounted to a genuine recovery, and he was dead within three years. His second wife, Edith Bolling Galt Wilson, protected the ailing leader from every possible political anxiety during his illness, which extended, with occasional remissions, from September 1919 to March 1921 when he left office. In the process of sheltering him she contributed greatly to the isolation that put political realism beyond his reach. She also assumed much of the responsibility belonging to the office of president. Had the Twenty-fifth Amendment been in force in 1919, Vice-President Thomas R. Marshall might well have seen service as the country's first acting president.

Consideration of presidential succession necessarily incorporates consideration of death or disability by attempted assassination. Four U.S. presidents have been murdered: Lincoln, Garfield, McKinley, and Kennedy. Attempts have been made to assassinate three others: Franklin Roosevelt, Truman, and Ford (twice). One former president, Theodore Roosevelt, was shot at, and one presidential aspirant, Robert Kennedy, was killed.

## Secret Service

Immediately after McKinley's murder (1901), agents of the Secret Service, a crack investigative agency of the Treasury Department, were assigned to guard Pres. Theodore Roosevelt. In 1913 Secret Service protection was extended to the person of the president-elect and in 1917 to the members of the immediate family of the president.

Authority to guard the vice-president at his request was given the Secret Service by act of Congress in 1951. It was later extended to the vice-president, the president- and vice-president-elect, and the families of former presidents.

# 6.
# The Federal Bureaucracy: The Executive

The U.S. government carries on its various functions other than those of a legislative or judicial character through a variety of departments, boards, commissions, government corporations, and other agencies. Although they are often thought of as in the executive branch, they are by no means all under the president's control.

Some are actually agencies of the legislative branch—for instance, the Library of Congress, with its legislative reference service that offers a pool of experts available to the committees and the individual members of Congress; the U.S. Government Printing Office, headed by the public printer; and the federal government's audit agency, the General Accounting Office under the comptroller general, who serves for the exceptionally long term of fifteen years.

A somewhat larger number of agencies are neither in the legislative branch nor under the president's orders but are controlled or directed by individuals appointed by the president with the advice and consent of the Senate. These agencies, often spoken of as independent regulatory commissions and boards, are usually created by statute as bipartisan establishments and deliberately placed outside the reach of the president's legal power of command. Most of the principal agencies of the federal government having quasi-legislative and -judicial functions are of this type, such as the Interstate Commerce Commission, the Federal Trade Commission, the Federal Power Commission, the Securities and Exchange Commission, and the National Labor Relations Board.

Within the executive branch, thus narrowly defined, there are further distinctions between agencies. One group is formed by the government corporations, for example, the Tennessee Valley Authority and the Export-Import Bank of the United States. Another category is represented by the considerable number of agencies that are comparable in many respects to departments but lack this title. These agencies include the Veterans Administration, the National Science Foundation, the General Services Administration, and the U.S. Postal Service. Many are headed by a single administrator like the departments; others are directed by plural bodies, like the independent regulatory commissions and boards. Again, like the departments, most of these executive agencies perform functions that in some way directly affect the public or parts of it. A few executive agencies, however, have the task of attending to needs of management that exist throughout the executive branch—for instance, the Civil Service Commission for recruitment, classification, and other aspects of personnel administration, and the General Services Administration for office space, procurement of supplies, and disposition of records.

## Executive Departments

The most important category of federal agencies is formed by the so-called executive departments, relatively few in number but collectively the backbone of the executive branch. The twelve executive departments of the federal government, in order of their official rank, are these: State followed by Treasury, both since 1789; Defense, established in 1949, with its three military departments, Army (created as War Department in 1789), Navy (1798), and Air Force (1947); Justice (1870), with antecedents reaching back much further; Interior (1849); Agriculture (1862); Commerce (1903); Labor (1913, previously joined with Commerce); Health, Education, and Welfare (1953), as an elevation of the former Federal Security Agency; Housing and Urban Development (1965); Transportation (1966); and Energy (1977).

The Executive Office of the President, a staff organization created in 1939 to assist the chief executive in the general direction and coordination of the departments as well as of other agencies of the executive branch, is not itself a department. It is a presidential establishment for purposes of program planning, analysis of problems and issues, review and formulation of proposals, and administrative control. The Executive Office of the President has included, among others, in recent years the White House Office, the Office of Management and Budget, the Council of Economic Advisers, the National Security Council, the Central Intelligence Agency, the Domestic Council, the Office of Economic Opportunity, the National Aeronautics and Space Council, and an Office of Emergency Preparedness.

On the president's level, the concerns with particular functions that emerge from the departments and other agencies of the executive branch are met by the counterpressure of a government-wide orientation. Such broader orientation is typical of the presidency, as the foremost organ for the expression of national points of view under the Constitution. Between the Executive Office of the President, as a staff organization looking at matters across the board, and the departments of the executive branch, each absorbed in its own functions, there develops a creative tension. The outcome, ideally, is a constructive interchange, with a broadening effect upon decisions. Realistically, however, it is also possible that the result, in the individual case, is determined by political compromise.

Departmental strength is a product of many factors, one of which is size. By quantitative measurements, the departments, like the other agencies of the executive branch, show striking variations. The largest, by a wide margin, is the Department of Defense. One measure of the growth of the departmental system is the increase in civilian and military personnel in the executive branch. The grand total rose steadily from less than 1,000 civilian employees and 1,300 military personnel during Washington's administration to more than 2.5 million and about 3 million, respectively, in the second half of the twentieth century.

Like the heads of almost all executive agencies, department heads are appointed by the president with the advice and consent of the Senate. Only department heads bear the distinctive title of secretary—as, for instance, secretary of labor. The title is not common to all, however. The top officer of the Department of Justice has the designation of attorney general, dating back to the beginnings of the republic.

Department heads have neither the right nor the duty of participation in the affairs of Congress, as is normally the case under parliamentary government. On the other hand, the principle of Senate approval of the president's choices for his official team carries with it certain limitations to be observed in the exercise of his appointive power. For one thing, men with a passion for unpopular causes, a reputation for unorthodox opinions, or a lofty disdain for politicians do not make good material for presidential nominations, whatever their wisdom and integrity. There is also the matter of geographic balance in picking candidates, besides other factors of political strategy that no president can ignore. But affiliation with the opposite party is not necessarily a bar, for on occasion a bipartisan appearance is politically desirable.

As far as their relationship with Congress is concerned, department heads confine their role essentially to supplying information and advice, often as pleaders, mostly in testimony before congressional committees. In such testimony, as in other public statements, the members of the president's team are supposed to reflect his policies. But the interest they have in advancing their departmental programs may induce them to be more responsive to the legislative committee dealing with the department's affairs or to organized groups that regard themselves as the department's clientele than to the goals sought by the president. To be sure, in a formal sense, expressed by the Constitution, department heads are the subordinates of the president; he can fire them at will. Yet a disciplinary action so extreme is practical only on very rare occasions, when in the nature of all circumstances its application would not inflict serious damage upon the prestige of the president's administration. As a matter of fact department heads are able to move rather freely in a no-man's-land of political convenience, checked only by such factors as their loyalty to the president and their fear of the price of a full-scale conflict with him.

Only department heads and the U.S. representative to the United Nations are automatically members of the Cabinet. The president, however, is free to request the regular attendance of other officials, such as the director of the Office of Management and Budget. The practical importance of the Cabinet and its efficiency in performance are roughly proportionate to the president's own intentions and working methods. For lack of a necessary constitutional function the Cabinet operates as a meeting of presidential advisers, but the president does not withdraw behind the Cabinet. There is thus no collective responsibility of the Cabinet for the government's program, in the sense of British political doctrine. When it comes to getting the president's approval for a particular matter, a department head settles the business directly with the president or his staff assistant rather than propose it for the Cabinet agenda. It is then left for the president to make sure that the subject has the benefit of scrutiny by additional eyes before he commits himself.

Assurance that such scrutiny is provided as a normal procedure is perhaps most evident in the field of proposed legislation. Under arrangements made initially in 1921, the Bureau of the Budget (renamed the Office of Management and Budget in 1970) became the presidential clearinghouse for legislative proposals advanced by executive agencies. The test question in this matter is whether or not the individual proposal is in accord with the president's program. In furnishing clearance, the Office of Management and Budget not only is guided by decisions made by the president but also seeks the advice of all other agencies having an interest in the particular matter, thus helping to establish a common position within the executive branch. In addition, when agencies are asked by congressional committees to convey their views on pending bills, the same clearance procedure is applied. If an agency insists, it may send its views to the Congress when it differs from the views of other agencies or from the Office of Management and Budget, but this is rare. In such an event, the agency must add the finding of the budget office concerning the relationship of the bill to the president's program. The same kind of consultation throughout the executive branch is obtained by the budget office before a proposed executive order is passed on to the president for his consideration and signature.

## Departmental Organization

In basic internal organization, the departments show considerable similarity. The top nucleus is generally known as the secretary's office. Upon it converge the demands for decisions that rise constantly in the normal course of business from the next lower level—the great functional groupings made up of bureaus, offices, or divisions. These, in turn, are subdivided successively as need requires, down to the smallest working unit. One can imagine the departments as a mighty cluster of central agencies. In actual fact, however, the headquarters organization of the departments at the nation's capital in Washington, D.C., is usually only the smallest part. More than nine-tenths of all federal employees are stationed in the field, mostly throughout the United States.

Departmental direction is, therefore, in great part a matter of communication, as in all far-flung and large-scale organizations. No department can be much more than the reflection of its sense of purpose. Such sense of purpose and broader objectives may remain distant and rather blurred images for the rank and file, preoccupied with what is close at hand. This tendency toward personal isolation, never completely overcome by even the most resourceful kind of coordination, may make the department as a unified whole a rather distant goal for all but those occupied with general management. The individual employee's allegiance may be limited, therefore, to the particular unit or sector in which he works, especially when the department is a multipurpose one or is the outgrowth of many changes.

Withdrawal into the small-scale world of the individual working group—a world to be kept secure, agreeable, neat, and unmolested by bigger things outside—is a familiar trait of bureaucratic behavior. It is a trait that should not be condemned rashly because, paradoxically, it also has a certain therapeutic value. It is an antidote to the growth of a bureaucracy so unified in an independent concept of mission as to rise above control by elective policymakers. The vast physical expansion of the executive branch of the federal government in the twentieth century has often been lamented. It has been seen as a forerunner to what is predicted by some as the coming tyranny of the managers. But the habits of bureaucracy as they manifest themselves in the departmental operations of the federal government are all on the other side. In the United States bureaucracy, in public administration, is a force created by division; it is not a single body with its own sense of direction.

Lack of unity in the permanent officialdom is thus a natural condition, promoted by the absence of a recognized higher career service reaching up right below the department head and his political aides, like the British administrative class. On the other hand, the respect accorded the administrative class in England demonstrates that a higher career service, under the pervasive influence of its own ethics, can be a strong restraint upon the zest for power among its members. So indoctrinated, the civil service is able to guard itself against both excessive solidarity and bureaucratic self-aggrandizement. U.S. civil servants, under a weaker service spirit and larger departmental entities, are more inclined to put priority on that part of the departmental program for which they have individual responsibility.

Single-handed, of course, a department secretary would accomplish little without multiplying himself, so to speak, by leaving part of the job to lieutenants in whom he can put his full political as well as personal confidence. These are the undersecretary and the assistant secretaries, occasionally also a deputy secretary, as in the Defense Department. Like the secretary himself, they are among the political officers who are appointed by the president with the advice and consent of the Senate. In contrast with past practice, these selections are rarely mere patronage appointments. The reason is the increased public pressure upon the president—in the day of the service state—to make a satisfactory record in the conduct of his administration, as a matter of good politics.

Yet presidents face considerable difficulty in persuading well-qualified citizens to undertake this kind of public service and to stay in the post after having accepted. Businessmen in particular, but also labor leaders and members of the professions, often require vigorous prompting to make themselves available for an indefinite tour of duty in Washington, D.C. This is not merely a matter of personal and family finances but also the reflection of a political environment notorious for its frustrations and its lack of charity in public criticism. Recruitment of top-caliber men and women for high political positions has emerged as one of the unsolved problems of U.S. government.

In each department the number of presidentially appointed top officials is small, although the impetus they give the department is noticeable. To extend themselves sufficiently far, they need special assistants such as policy advisers, contact men, or confidential assistants. The great bulk of the departmental personnel, however, consists of permanent employees having regular civil-service status.

Although civil servants legally can be shifted around to suit the preference of an incoming departmental high command, no department is easily stripped of its established ways. Actual performance, by and large, though showing variations within departments and from department to department, compares fully with the standards of private business.

In their day-by-day administration, almost all departments have come to place considerable reliance on groups of management specialists. Most of these are engaged in program planning, review of operations, budgeting, organization and methods work, personnel administration, accounting, and the like. In several departments, in 1950, all or most of these specialized elements of departmental management were combined under the new office of administrative assistant secretary, intended to be filled by career men.

## Reorganization

Year upon year, new administrative activities are authorized by Congress, and established ones either change or disappear because of changing circumstances and policies. In their cumulative effects, these changes make it necessary to reexamine the organizational structure of the executive branch at frequent intervals. Executive departments, however, are massive structures reinforced by precedent and tradition and cannot easily be changed. They are singularly unresponsive to the preachings of people stirred by a sense of organizational efficiency. Moreover, all the organized interests, economic and social, that have a stake in the departmental setup view with deep suspicion any marked departure from similar arrangements. Each interest is fearful of coming out the loser.

Real gains may be attained, however, by some patient, piecemeal improving. That has been done rather persistently. The usual procedure, applied on all levels of government in the United States, is to set up a formal inquiry into existing conditions, in the hope of bringing forth concrete recommendations with a fair chance of adoption.

These corrective bodies, pursuing a broadly evolutionary approach, have done useful work. One made history by breaking ground for the concept of the Executive Office of the President. Implicit in this concept was the idea that executive responsibility should be matched with sufficient authority and clearly centered in the top man, but its exercise should be bolstered by a balanced grouping of staff units bringing coordinating skill as well as specialized judgment to bear upon decisions. Another element in the working doctrine of executive reorganization was the demand that activities be fitted into patterns, each dominated by a basic governmental purpose. This criterion of departmentalization sounds simple but is much less so in practical application. Still another point of doctrine is the general rule that both the number of departments and the total number of agencies of the executive branch ought to be held to a minimum; that, ideally, the lesser agencies ought to be brought into some clearly defined relationship with one or another department, since the president's span of control is naturally limited; and that new public functions, especially while still experimental or when undertaken for the duration of an emergency, might best be constituted as—possibly temporary—agencies rather than as new departments.

With the president constitutionally the coequal partner of Congress in the performance of the tasks that have fallen to the federal government, it might be thought that he can do as he pleases in reorganizing the executive branch. But as a practical matter, it appears accepted that the president requires congressional authorization to reorganize the executive branch. Securing adequate authority for him is doubly important because evidence shows, as could perhaps be expected, that Congress, left to itself, is not a particularly good architect of executive structure.

Until the spring of 1977, Congress persistently refused to grant the president authority to carry out reorganization. Previously, it passed a succession of short-term reorganization acts—that of 1949 prolonged repeatedly by new legislation. Each laid down the same basic procedure, first adopted in 1939. The president had to present a specific reorganization plan to Congress. If Congress did not vote disapproval within sixty days, the plan would take effect.

Notwithstanding the insistence of Congress to steadily intensify its control of the "stop" button, this procedure on the whole worked quite well. Instances of congressional disapproval were infrequent—among them a rejected 1967 proposal to merge the departments of Commerce and Labor into a single department of business. Successful reorganization plans established the framework for the Executive Office of the President—one of the most important events in the modern administrative history of the federal government; strengthened the authority of top management on the departmental level; created the Department of Health, Education, and Welfare (1953), the Department of Housing and Urban Development (1965), the Department of Transportation (1966), and the Department of Energy (1977). The U.S. Information Agency was established in 1953 and the Equal Employment Opportunity Commission in 1965. Most reorganization plans, however, reallocated activities among existing agencies rather than creating new ones. The Environmental Protection Agency, for example, which was established in 1970, clustered all controls of water, air, solid wastes, pesticides, radiation, and noise hazards. It incorporated the Federal Water Quality Administration from the Interior Department; took on seven units still in the Department of Health, Education, and Welfare at the time, including the National Air Pollution Control Administration and Public Health Service functions relating to radiological health, solid waste, and pesticides; and incorporated the former Federal Radiation council and some functions of the Atomic Energy Commission.

Reorganization proposed by a presidential commission and accepted by Congress in 1970 stripped the former Post Office Department of cabinet status and created an independent

U.S. Postal Service. Although the former department had managed the largest business in the world, its basic management decisions affecting rates, employee wages, investment in facilities, and even numerous operational guidelines were made by Congress. In addition, postmasters were presidential appointees with life tenure, further reducing the management flexibility of the department's top staff.

From its earliest days the U.S. postal system continued to experience significant growth in mail volume without significant change in methods or mechanization. As a result of the deficits and dissatisfactions this promoted, considerable interest had been building to change postal procedures and organization significantly. The ultimate recommendation in this area was made in June 1968, when a presidential commission appointed to study the postal service recommended that the department be removed from Cabinet status and transformed into an independent government corporation (similar to the Tennessee Valley Authority) to be administered by a presidentially appointed board. This was fully implemented by the passage of the Postal Reorganization Act, signed by the president in August 1970, which created the U.S. Postal Service, effective in July 1971.

## Departmental Functions

The machinery for the conduct of the principal functions of the executive branch per se is as follows:

*1. Foreign Affairs.* The central figure in U.S. foreign policy is the president; he holds the final authority and personally makes the most critical decisions concerning foreign affairs. The organization charged with the conduct of the country's international affairs is the Department of State. Its head, the secretary of state, is the president's traditional principal adviser in the formation of foreign policy and his principal agent for its coordination and implementation.

The exact role played by the secretary of state is shaped by the philosophies and personalities of the president and the secretary. The secretary of state, however, will normally assist the president on international problems by presenting to him all elements of the problem, alternative courses of action, and essential differences of opinions, and by giving his own views and recommendations. In a more formal vein the secretary of state is a statutory member of the National Security Council, a body created in 1947 within the Executive Office of the President to assist the president in the clarification and resolution of the complex issues of national security. In 1947 the Policy Planning Council was created within the State Department to provide the secretary with the reflective analysis and creative proposals to suggest the future course of the country's diplomacy.

To implement foreign-policy decisions and conduct normal diplomatic relations with governments abroad the Department of State is organized into a Washington headquarters and about three hundred embassies, legations, consular posts, and special missions located in more than a hundred countries throughout the world. The U.S. ambassador to a foreign nation is the personal representative of the president and has full responsibility for the implementation of American foreign policy in the country of his assignment by all U.S. government personnel in that country. To handle the steady flow of up to two thousand or more daily messages exchanged with these foreign posts, the Washington offices of the department are organized into five regional bureaus, each one headed by an assistant secretary. These five regional bureaus represent Africa, Latin America, East Asia and the Pacific, Europe, and the Near East and South Asia. A separate bureau is organized to provide guidance and support for U.S. participation in international organizations such as the United Nations, and international conferences, numbering about six hundred annually. Other offices provide the secretary with expert advice on foreign economic matters, with scientific and technological aspects relating to U.S. foreign policy, and with research and analysis on foreign intelligence.

The U.S. Foreign Service recruits professional career foreign service officers and provides training progressively throughout their careers. These career personnel operate under the direction of presidential appointees at the levels of secretary, undersecretary, and assistant secretary. The Bureau of Security and Consular Affairs holds responsibility for the issuance of passports and visas as well as for the protection and welfare of American citizens abroad. Other bureaus within the department deal with public affairs, congressional relations, and educational and cultural-exchange programs.

The secretary's authority to "direct, coordinate, and supervise the interdepartmental activities of the U.S. government overseas" (except for military activities) is derived from a presidential statement of March 4, 1966. This responsibility is discharged primarily through the undersecretary and the regional assistant secretaries of state. The head of each regional bureau acts as the executive chairman of the Interdepartmental Regional Group. This group consists of designated regional representatives from the Department of Defense, the Agency for International Development (AID), the Central Intelligence Agency (CIA), the Organization of the Joint Chiefs of Staff, the U.S. Information Agency (USIA), and the White House or National Security Council staff. Regional matters requiring more attention are brought before the Senior Interdepartmental Group under the chairmanship of the undersecretary of state and composed of the directors of AID, USIA, and CIA plus the chairman of the Joint Chiefs of Staff, the deputy secretary of defense, and the president's assistant for national security affairs.

Two important additions to the traditional means of carrying on U.S. foreign relations have come into being since World War II. A program of foreign aid to Europe, first proposed by Secretary of State George Marshall in 1948, has evolved organizationally into a separate agency within the State Department. The Agency for International Development is responsible for administering nonmilitary assistance to selected countries throughout the world. This assistance is divided into categories of loans, grants, investment surveys, and development-research activities.

The second innovation, the Peace Corps, was proposed by President Kennedy in 1961. As an agency within the State Department the Peace Corps arranges for the placement abroad of volunteer men and women of the United States in developing nations of the world. These volunteers help fill the developing nations' critical needs for skilled manpower and seek to promote a better understanding between the American people and the peoples served.

**2. Finance: Revenue and Debt.** In the United States, as in Great Britain, the Treasury has been a vital factor in the development and the operations of the entire national administrative system. In the United States most managerial and many operational responsibilities originally developed in the Treasury Department. But as the government matured, managerial responsibilities gravitated toward the presidency, the biggest shift being effected in 1939 by the transfer of the Bureau of the Budget from the Treasury to the Executive Office of the President. Operational responsibilities have been transferred to other departments.

The Treasury maintains two primary responsibilities. First, the secretary of the treasury serves as fiscal adviser to the president, along with the Council of Economic Advisers and the Office of Management and Budget. Second, the department administers most revenue (mainly tax) collections, the manufacture of coin and currency, and many law-enforcement activities.

The responsibility for federal fiscal policy involves the Treasury in three major areas. First, it is the secretary of the treasury and his experts who present to Congress, for the president, the tax proposals of the executive branch, and who in turn serve Congress as principal sources of technical information. The proposals of the executive branch in these as in all other matters are simply presidential recommendations. Congress is constitutionally free to modify or ignore the recommendations and to initiate its own legislation.

A second area revolves around the Treasury responsibility to finance federal deficits and to oversee, with other agencies, the country's monetary, financial, and economic affairs. The department must minimize the cost of debt financing while supporting a money market capable of meeting public and private credit demands, of stimulating national economic growth, and of maintaining international monetary stability. Although policies of the Federal Reserve System may directly affect rates of interest on Treasury financing, the Treasury has no legal authority over that system. Nor has the Treasury direct control over many governmental lending programs, such as those providing building loans or agricultural credit. These and other activities beyond Treasury's control make Treasury's relationship with other agencies of crucial consequence to the economy. Treasury's regularized review of fiscal and economic affairs with the Office of Management and Budget and the Council of Economic Advisers has become known as the "Troika." It is called the "Quadriad" when it includes the Federal Reserve System, which is considered the backbone of the country's private banking business and chief guardian of sound money conditions.

The third area of policy guidance deals with the balance of payments and other aspects of international monetary and financial affairs. The Treasury's Office of the Assistant Secretary for International Affairs collects and analyzes current information about the economic positions and policies of other nations having a bearing upon United States financial and monetary programs. The Treasury negotiates, with foreign governments, international monetary arrangements and other aspects of international finance. The secretary serves as chairman of the National Advisory Council on international Monetary and Financial Policies, in effect a Cabinet committee for purposes of coordinating U.S. participation in international financial and lending institutions.

In the Treasury Department the fiscal and the administrative assistant secretaries represent the growth of the career civil service to the highest level. The fiscal assistant secretary is in charge of the Fiscal Service, including supervision of the Bureau of Accounts, the Bureau of the Public Debt, and the Office of the Treasurer of the United States, which is essentially the banking facility for the federal government. The assistant secretary for administration supervises the department's work in general management matters.

The main divisions of work in the Treasury demonstrate how broad its operating functions remain. Its chief components in addition to the Fiscal Service are the Bureau of the Mint, the Bureau of Engraving and Printing, the U.S. Savings Bonds Division, the Office of the Comptroller of the Currency (who supervises the so-called national banks), the Internal Revenue Service (which collects all federal taxes and has an extensive field service of its own), the Bureau of Customs (also with a field organization), and the U.S. Secret Service (responsible for physical protection of the president and certain other political leaders and for suppression of counterfeiting and forgery of federal and foreign currencies and financial obligations).

**3. Defense.** The mission of the Department of Defense is to provide, through its military strength, a solid foundation for the national policy of the United States. The forerunner of the Department of Defense, the National Military Establishment, was created by the National Security Act of 1947 and evolved from the experiences of World War II. While combat and service components of the Departments of the Army and the Navy fought together in various theaters of operation under unified direction of overseas commanders, the individual military departments reported separately to the president. The conflicting and competitive policies of these departments prevented a truly effective, coordinated, and unified military effort. To overcome this organizational deficiency the National Military Establishment was created, and the Cabinet post of secretary of defense was established to provide overall policy and direction of the military departments without destroying their individual identities. Concurrently the Air Force was created as a third military department on a coequal basis with the departments of the Army and the Navy.

The original National Security Act of 1947 provided the secretary of defense with limited authority and staff to exercise control. Subsequent amendments to the basic act in 1949, 1953, and 1958, however, greatly strengthened the authority and ability of the secretary to direct defense policy. In the 1949 amendment the Department of Defense as we know it today was established. In 1978 the Department of Defense was organized under the secretary of defense (a civilian), the deputy secretary of defense, a special assistant to the secretary and the deputy secretary, the Armed Forces Policy Council, two under secretaries of defense (for policy and for research and engineering), seven assistant secretaries (communications, command, control, and intelligence; comptroller; health affairs; internal security affairs, manpower, reserve affairs, and logistics; program analysis and evaluation; public affairs), and a general counsel.

The civilian secretaries of the military departments (Army, Navy, and Air Force) are responsible for the administration of their particular departments, and are responsible for training, equipping, and providing combat-ready forces to the respective commands. The combat forces of the Army, Navy, Air Force, and Marine Corps are under unified and specified combat commands, organized on either a functional or a geographic basis. A unified command contains combat forces from more than one service, such as the Pacific Command, which is comprised of all Army, Navy, Air Force, and Marine Corps units in the Pacific area. A specified command is composed of units from a single service; for example, only Air Force units are contained in the Strategic Air Command (SAC). SAC is the only specified command in the Department of Defense. The commanders of the unified and specified commands are responsible to the president and the secretary of defense. By secretarial delegation the Joint Chiefs of Staff exercise operational direction over the unified and specified commands.

The Joint Chiefs of Staff are the principal military advisers to the president, the National Security Council, and the secretary of defense. Ths Joint Chiefs of Staff consist of the chairman, who is the country's highest-ranking military officer; the chief of staff, U.S. Army; the chief of naval operations; the chief of staff, U.S. Air Force; and the commandant of the Marine Corps on matters concerning the Marine

Corps. The chiefs are appointed by the president to four-year terms. The Joint Chiefs of Staff are supported by the Joint Staff, which is limited by law to not more than four hundred officers. This staff, organized along conventional military staff lines, performs such functions as developing strategic concepts and war plans, reviewing the operating plans of the unified and specified commands, and establishing unified doctrine for operations. The Joint Staff also provides the Joint Chiefs of Staff with planning factors and requirements for the development of plans relating to the overall force structure. An assignment to the Joint Staff provides military officers a unique opportunity to work on coordinated plans and to develop an understanding of the integrated effort required under today's concept of joint operations.

Within the Department of Defense there are five defense agencies. These agencies were established to provide integrated and unified effort in support activities that generally cut across service lines. The defense agencies have consolidated functions that were previously fractionalized among the military services. The Defense Atomic Support Agency, Defense Intelligence Agency, and Defense Communications Agency report to the secretary of defense through the Joint Chiefs of Staff. The Defense Supply Agency and Defense Contract Audit Agency report directly to the secretary of defense.

As a top-level management tool, the Armed Forces Policy Council was established to advise the secretary of defense on broad policy matters. The council brings together the top civilian and military leaders so that all aspects of a problem can be exposed and alternative solutions explored. The secretary of defense is the chairman of the council; other members include the deputy secretary of defense, the secretaries of the military departments, the Joint Chiefs of Staff, and the director of Defense Research and Engineering.

Since the prime mission of the Defense Department is to provide military support for U.S. national policy, including foreign policy, close coordination with the Department of State is essential. The primary method of achieving this coordination is through the Senior Interdepartmental Group and the Interdepartmental Regional Groups.

The need for the military to consider implications of political, economic, and scientific factors in the development of military plans, supplies, and advice requires senior military officers to have a broad education in these disciplines. To this end, the military departments have established an extensive continuing-education system for their officers. Included in this educational system are joint-service schools such as the National War College, Armed Forces Staff College, and Industrial College of the Armed Forces, as well as individual service schools such as the Naval War College, Air University, and Army War College. These schools are conducted on a highly professional, graduate-school level to train future military leaders as broadly educated officers who understand the importance of political, economic, and scientific factors on military planning. The Department of the Army, through its Corps of Engineers, also performs important civil functions in improving rivers, harbors, and waterways for navigation, in constructing flood-control and similar projects in various parts of the country, and in administering the laws governing navigable waters.

*4. Justice.* In the U.S. system of separated powers, justice is determined primarily in the courts of law. The principal mission of the Department of Justice is to represent the federal government before those courts. Other major functions include advising the president and other executive agencies on legal matters; administering the Federal Bureau of Prisons, the Immigration and Naturalization Service, and the Community Relations Service; investigating violations of federal law; and coordinating federal law enforcement and federal assistance to state and local law enforcement.

The head of the department is the attorney general of the United States. Historically one of the earliest Cabinet positions, and—until the twentieth century—traditionally less political than most Cabinet offices, the attorney general has evolved into a combination of prosecutor, counselor, and administrator. He is assisted in these responsibilities by the deputy attorney general, who also coordinates the nearly one hundred U.S. attorneys' offices, located in each federal judicial district, and undertakes preliminary screening of recommendations of candidates for federal judgeships, whose nomination by the president must also be confirmed by the Senate. The third principal official in the department is the solicitor general, who, subject to rarely exercised review by the attorney general, determines which cases involving the federal government will be appealed and briefs and argues all cases in which the federal government appears before the U.S. Supreme Court.

Although routine litigation is handled by the U.S. attorneys in the field, specialized areas are handled centrally by the six litigating divisions. Of these, two divisions have broad policy authority to shape enforcement programs in specific areas. The Antitrust Division is responsible for enforcing the broad mandates of the Sherman and Clayton antitrust acts to maintain a competitive economy. By selecting cases to be litigated, and marshaling arguments and evidence in those cases, this division, through the courts, has significantly influenced national economic policy. A second major enforcement program is the responsibility of the Civil Rights Division. Formed to administer the Civil Rights Act of 1957, this division now also enforces the wide-ranging acts of subsequent years prohibiting discrimination in public facilities, public accommodations, voting, employment, education, and housing. The Criminal Division concentrates on such matters as organized crime, criminal fraud, political and election violations, and espionage and subversive activities. The Tax Division also processes all civil federal tax matters before all federal courts other than the Tax Court of the United States. The remaining litigating divisions are the Civil Division, representing the United States in all otherwise unassigned civil matters (including most claims in the Court of Claims), and the Land and Natural Resources Division, which supervises condemnation of property on behalf of federal agencies, litigation involving federally owned land, and administration of Indian claims. The Office of Legal Counsel, though not a litigating division, provides legal advice to the attorney general and to other agencies of the government.

A number of agencies within the department are responsible for investigation of federal criminal offenses. The Federal Bureau of Investigation (known widely as the FBI) is the largest single federal investigating agency in the United States. Operating parallel to but substantially independently from the rest of the department, this bureau maintains special-agent's offices in most major cities, as well as extensive laboratory and staff facilities in the capital. A major addition to the department was the Law Enforcement Assistance Administration, responsible for the administration of funds for state and local improvement under the Omnibus Crime Control and Safe Streets Act of 1968. The federal Bureau of Prisons operates all federal penal facilities, and also provides technical assistance to state penitentiary systems.

Within the department, but operating substantially independently, is the Immigration and Naturalization Service, which controls the entry of aliens into the country and supervises them during their presence in the United States. The Community Relations Service, with field offices in major cities, serves to maintain workable relations and communications between potentially hostile elements in various communities.

**5. Resources.** In this field the most important role is played by the Department of the Interior. The activities of the department center upon the management, conservation, and development of the natural resources of the United States. It also promotes the welfare of the inhabitants of the island possessions of the United States and of the Trust Territory of the Pacific Islands, in addition to exercising guardianship over U.S. Indians and promoting the interests of the natives of Alaska. The principal division of work on the department's top level is in terms of fish and wildlife, mineral resources, public-land management, and water and power development.

The Interior Department is divided into these main elements: the Bureau of Indian Affairs, trustee of the lands belonging to the Indians and source of public services to them, as long as they are not yet absorbed into American life; the Bureau of Land Management, responsible also for the granting of grazing permits on the public range; the Bureau of Mines, which has as its tasks the conservation of mineral resources, the conduct of research in mining and utilization of mineral substances, and the promotion of safety in the mineral industries; the Bureau of Reclamation, in many respects a rival of the Army Corps of Engineers as the builder of public works to bring water to the lands of the west, including development of power; the Fish and Wildlife Service; the Bureau of Outdoor Recreation; the Geological Survey, a research bureau engaged in compiling and publishing information about the nation's mineral, water, and other resources; and the National Park Service, with nearly three hundred national parks, historic sites, and recreation areas.

**6. Agriculture.** The foremost mission of the U.S. Department of Agriculture (USDA) is to promote the general interests of those who produce from the soil — *agriculture* being a collective term that includes enterprises organized as private corporations, owners of family farms, homesteaders, tenants, and sharecroppers. The mission of the department is not limited to farmers but is also directed to assisting rural communities, conserving and improving land, water, and timber, improving household management for families generally, and eliminating malnutrition.

Each USDA agency has its own primary functions. The Agricultural Stabilization and Conservation Service carries out price-support and production-adjustment programs. The Commodity Credit Corporation finances these programs. The Federal Crop Insurance Corporation insures crop-production costs against loss from weather, insects, and diseases. The Farmer Cooperative Service helps farmers help themselves through joint action. The Foreign Agricultural Service expands exports through market-development activities. The Farmers Home Administration extends credit to enable farmers to buy or improve their farms and finances farm and rural housing, recreational facilities, small rural business enterprises, and community water and sewer systems. The Rural Electrification Administration was created to bring electric and telephone service to rural people. (The Farm Credit Administration is an independent agency not under the control of the USDA.)

The Soil Conservation Service provides technical and financial help to individuals and communities in conserving and improving land and water resources. The Forest Service manages the country's 155 national forests and 19 national grasslands. The Agricultural Research Service and the Cooperative State Research Service which work closely with state agricultural experiment stations and forestry institutions, carry out research on the production, marketing, and utilization of agricultural products as well as research on nutrition and the control and eradication of plant and animal diseases and pests. The Economic Research Service and the Statistical Reporting Service provide economic and statistical information on crops and livestock, prices and income, conservation and rural development, foreign agriculture, and other data. The Extension Service, the education arm of the department, helps farmers, rural residents, and the general public apply research and technology to farm, home, and community improvement and operates programs of youth development. The Agricultural Marketing Service grades and inspects agricultural commodities, provides marketing services, and promotes fair play in agricultural markets. The Food and Nutrition Service administers the food stamp program and other programs of food assistance to children and the needy.

**7. Commerce.** The responsibilities of the federal government in the field of commerce, broadly defined, are widely scattered. The Commerce Department is essentially a service agency with almost no regulatory duties except export-import controls and strategic-materials stockpile management. Its Bureau of Economic Analysis performs long-range as well as short-run analyses of the national economy, which are made available in the form of the monthly *Survey of Current Business*. Other domestic services are provided by the Bureau of Domestic Commerce and the Economic Development Administration. The Bureau of International Commerce publishes *Commerce America*, and other internationally-oriented bureaus deal with East-West trade and resources and trade assistance.

The department performs a number of basic national services. These are represented by the Bureau of the Census, as one of the federal government's major fact-finding and statistical agencies; the National Bureau of Standards, conducting for the government fundamental research and related technical activities in physics, mathematics, chemistry, and engineering; the Patent Office; and the Maritime Administration, concerned with aid to shipping. In 1970 the National Oceanic and Atmospheric Administration (NOAA) was created to conduct research on the atmosphere and marine resources. The functions of the Bureau of Commercial Fisheries, formerly in the Interior Department, were transferred to NOAA, which also oversees the tasks formerly under the Environmental Science Services Administration, the parent body of the Coast and Geodetic Survey and the National Weather Service. Of considerable importance to the national economy are independent agencies, such as the Federal Home Loan Bank Board, the Federal Deposit Insurance Corporation, and the Small Business Administration, which provides financial and other assistance to small business.

**8. Labor.** The fundamental mandate of the Department of Labor is to foster the welfare of U.S. wage earners, improve their working conditions, and advance their opportunities for profitable and rewarding employment. The department's organizational structure takes into consideration new emphasis on the disadvantaged and the more traditional focus on the workingman. Primary responsibility for the training of the disadvantaged lies in the Employment and Training Administration, which also administers the U.S. Employment Service and oversees state employment services; the Unemployment Insurance Service, which reviews state unemployment-insurance operations; the Bureau of Apprenticeship and Training, which formulates standards for the training of skilled workers in industry; and the Job Corps and other programs for the training of disadvantaged youth.

A variety of services for wage earners are provided by the Wage and Labor Standards Administration, and safe working conditions are prescribed by the Occupational Safety and Health Administration. Employees' Compensation is charged with the administration of the accident-compensation program for federal employees and certain types of private employment subject to federal legislation. The Women's Bureau serves as a focal point for efforts to make more effective use of abilities and potentials for women in all aspects of society. The Wage and Hour and Public Contracts Division assures minimum rates of pay, in general, and protection of youthful workers against exploitation, in particular, and supervises the observation in government contracts of fair employment.

Concern with labor-management relations is centered in the Labor-Management Services Administration. The Office of Labor-Management and Welfare-Pension Reports requires the public disclosure of the financial affairs of labor organizations and regulates some of their internal procedures, particularly with respect to the election of union officers. The Office of Veterans Reemployment Rights helps veterans returning from military service obtain reemployment and related benefits with their former employers. The Office of Labor-Management Relations Services participates in particular dispute-problem situations.

Other bureaus include the Bureau of Labor Statistics, the main repository within the federal government of information about employment, manpower, productivity, earnings, hours and wages, industrial relations, accidents, price trends, and costs, as well as standards of living. This information is made public in special bulletins and in the *Monthly Labor Review.*

Essential additional functions are carried out by such separate agencies as the National Labor Relations Board, concerned with protecting collective bargaining and eliminating unfair labor practices; the Federal Mediation and Conciliation Service; and the National Mediation Board, applicable to railway labor.

*9. Health, Education, and Welfare.* The Department of Health, Education, and Welfare was established in 1953 as an elevation of the Federal Security Agency. Its total budget is the largest of all domestic departments. The department administers about 250 different programs, the oldest of which is the Public Health Service hospitals established in 1798. There are seven operating agencies in the department. The National Institutes of Health, the Health Services and Mental Health Administration (which includes the National Institute of Mental Health), the Food and Drug Administration, and the Environmental Health Service are the four operating units of the Public Health Service. Legislation in the 1960s greatly expanded the health activities of the department.

The Office of Education was for many years limited primarily to providing statistical information and technical advice along with some small programs of federal aid for limited categories of education. The enactment in the mid-1960s of federal legislation providing for major programs of federal aid to education changed the basic character of the office to an operating agency with extensive administrative functions and substantial funds for schools, colleges, and universities. The Social Security Administration, originally the Social Security Board, administers the social security program (old-age, survivors, and disability insurance) and the Medicare program. The social security program is the largest single insurance system in the world. The Social and Rehabilitation Service, established in 1967, includes the Community Services Administration, the Rehabilitation Services Administration, the Administration on Aging, the Assistance Payments Administration (which handles federal funds to the states for welfare), and the Medical Services Administration (which administers federal funds for Medicaid). The Office of Child Development reports to the office of the secretary of HEW.

Financial aid is provided through the department to the American Printing House for the Blind, Louisville, Ky.; Gallaudet College for deaf students, Washington, D.C.; Howard University, Washington, D.C., founded in 1867 to provide higher education for Negroes; and St. Elizabeths Hospital, Washington, D.C., a government institution for the mentally ill.

**10. Housing and Urban Development.** In 1965, upon the recommendation of President Johnson, Congress authorized the establishment of a new Cabinet Department of Housing and Urban Development. Robert C. Weaver was appointed the first head of the department and thus became the first

Negro to sit in a president's Cabinet. The nucleus of the department was the Housing and Home Finance Agency, which Weaver had headed since 1961. It was a large, diffuse organization that had developed over the years and included such agencies as the Federal Housing Administration, Urban Renewal Administration, and Public Housing Administration. Assistant secretaries administer the department's programs in research and technology, housing production and mortgage credit, metropolitan planning and development, renewal and housing management, model cities, and equal opportunity.

**11. Transportation.** The Department of Transportation was established in 1966 with appointment of its first secretary, Alan Boyd, formerly undersecretary of commerce. A consolidation of thirty-one previously existing agencies and bureaus, the department was concerned with problems ranging from rush-hour traffic to supersonic air travel, and including auto safety. Among the organizations included in the new department were such independent agencies as the Federal Aviation Agency and the St. Lawrence Seaway Development Corporation, and the following from other departments: the Bureau of Public Roads and the Great Lakes Pilotage Administration (Commerce); the Coast Guard (Treasury); and the Alaska Railroad (Interior).

**12. Energy.** In 1977 Congress approved President Carter's proposal of a Department of Energy, to coordinate and administer the energy functions of the federal government in the research, development, and demonstration of energy technology and the marketing of federally produced electric power. The department's mandate embraces energy conservation, the nuclear weapons program, regulation of energy production and use, and pricing and allocation. The Department of Energy absorbed the functions of the former Energy Research and Development Administration, the Federal Energy Administration, the Federal Power Commission, and four regional federal power administrations that generated and sold power. The secretary of energy heads the organization, which includes a deputy secretary, an under secretary, an executive secretariat composed of members of the Federal Energy Regulatory Commission, directors of administration and of procurement and contracts management, and a controller. Eight assistant secretaries are responsible for intergovernmental and institutional relations, international affairs, policy and evaluation, conservation and solar applications, environment, resource applications, energy technology, and defense programs. Two administrators are charged with economic regulation and energy information, and there are a director of the office of energy research, an inspector general, and a general counsel.

## Agencies

Some government agencies wax and wane in importance as presidents choose to use them. An example is the National Security Council, created in 1947 to advise the president on national security matters that require the coordination of domestic, foreign, and military policies. Its members are the president, vice-president, secretary of state, and secretary of defense. The need for a national policy-coordinating group more formal in character than the presidential Cabinet was not recognized in the United States until the eve of World War II, when a standing liaison committee consisting of the undersecretary of state, the chief of naval operations, and the army chief of staff was created. With the onset of war, however, policy coordination was provided personally by the president.

Following World War II, congressional investigation focused attention on the lack of coordination that had been a factor in the Pearl Harbor disaster, and there was general pressure for reorganization of defense agencies. The suggestion for a National Security Council (NSC) originated in studies by a staff of experts appointed by James V. Forrestal, then secretary of the navy. The NSC was established by law in 1947, with a staff of its own. After President Eisenhower took office in 1953 the NSC was given new importance and its staff was strengthened by the formation of a planning board. An operations coordinating board was also established.

With the accession of Kennedy as president in 1961, the old structure disappeared. The NSC was, at first, scarcely used at all. It did not meet until after the abortive Cuban invasion of April 1961 but thereafter met more frequently. Johnson used it more regularly, and Nixon gave the NSC even greater prominence, which continued under Ford and Carter.

One of the agency's responsibilities is for control of the Central Intelligence Agency (CIA), which was established in 1947 to advise the NSC on security matters; to coordinate all departments and agencies in relation to foreign intelligence; to correlate, evaluate, and distribute intelligence information to the appropriate agencies; to deal with certain matters common to all intelligence agencies; and to perform such other intelligence functions as the NSC might direct.

Though an independent agency, the Civil Service Commission is discussed here because of its role in staffing the executive department, as well as most other arms of the federal government. It is headed by three commissioners, not more than two of whom may belong to the same political party, appointed for six-year terms by the president with the advice and consent of the Senate. The commission has its central office in Washington, D.C., ten regional offices in principal cities, and sixty-five boards of examiners nationwide. The commission is responsible for policy and instructions to guide federal departments, recruiting and examining, setting position classification standards, personnel investigations, retirement programs, life and health insurance, training, inspection of agency personnel programs, and executive assignments.

Over the years emphasis in the work of the commission has gradually shifted from fighting the spoils system to the development of progressive personnel practices and the maintenance of a true career employment system. In addition to the increasing coverage of the merit system both by legislation and executive order, principal advances after 1883 were the classification of positions by duties and a systematic pay plan (1923); a retirement act (1920); and an extension of the merit system by law to state programs financed in part with federal grants-in-aid. A salary reform act (1962) and subsequent additions called for gradual pay increases for white-collar employees directed toward achieving comparability with pay for work of the same level of difficulty in the private sector. An executive inventory system was begun in 1967.

Not controlled by the Civil Service Act are such agencies or groups as the Foreign Service, the Commissioned Corps of the U.S. Public Health Service, the Tennessee Valley Authority, the Federal Bureau of Investigation, and the Department of Medicine and Surgery of the Veterans Administration. These units have separate merit systems of their own, tailored to their particular needs; nevertheless, they may be covered by the same salary, training, life insurance, health insurance, retirement, and other laws that apply to the regular civil service.

# 7.
# The Federal Bureaucracy: Regulatory and Independent Agencies

Federal regulation of business proceeds under Article I, Section 8 of the Constitution. The most important clause is that referred to as the interstate commerce clause, the clause that gives Congress power "to regulate Commerce . . . among the several states." After decades of court decisions the clause has been broadly interpreted, particularly since the late 1930s, and it seems that the clause is unlikely to impose significant limits on federal regulatory powers in the future. As the Supreme Court put it in a 1946 case, federal power to regulate interstate commerce "is as broad as the economic needs of the nation."

## Regulatory Agencies

The need for administrative regulation first became apparent in the United States in the railroad industry, and it was out of the attempts to deal with the railroad problem that the first modern U.S. administrative agency, the **Interstate Commerce Commission** (ICC), was developed. Established by the Interstate Commerce Act of 1887 and with its powers expanded by the Hepburn Act of 1906 and subsequent statutes, the ICC is composed of eleven members, appointed by the president and confirmed by the Senate, who serve for staggered terms of seven years. The commissioners may be removed only for cause, and have been able, in practice, to function free from direct presidential control. This has led some to characterize them as a "headless fourth branch" of the government.

The ICC is the classic example of a quasi-judicial regulatory agency. As such, it applies the broadly stated legislative policies to concrete cases by a procedure patterned upon that of the courts. The commission fixes reasonable rates for commerce between states and ensures that they are observed. It grants licenses to those seeking to engage in interstate transportation. It exercises the power of injunction (a legal writ of restraint) over discriminatory practices. The commission also performs important nonjudicial functions. It promulgates safety and other regulations. It controls railroad financing and planning. It gives specific form and content to the congressional policies expressed in the Interstate Commerce Act (as amended). Its position has been compared to that of a superboard of directors of the railroad industry. It also has extensive authority over motor carriers.

The assertion of governmental control in other economic fields led to the creation of many other regulatory agencies modeled upon the ICC. The first among these was the *Federal Trade Commission* (FTC), which was created in 1914 to prevent unfair methods of competition in interstate commerce. The law did not define "unfair methods of competition," leaving the door open for interpretation. Congress gave the FTC two distinct powers. First, the commission could investigate corporations and other business concerns and report its findings to Congress, the president, or the public at large. Second, the commission could issue a complaint against any offending business that was practicing unfair competition. It required the offender to reply, and testimony was taken under oath on the issue involved. The statute required the commission either to dismiss the complaint if the testimony was insufficient to establish unfair competition, or, if a case was made out, to issue an order to cease and desist from the offending method. Many of the complaints issued have been based upon charges made by one business competitor against another.

The FTC is composed of five members appointed for seven-year terms by the president, with the advice and consent of the Senate. Not more than three members may belong to the same political party. One commissioner is named by the president to be chairman of the commission and to be responsible for its administration.

Simultaneously with the passage of the Federal Trade Commission Act, Congress passed the Clayton Antitrust Act. Under it the FTC was entrusted with the prevention of unlawful price discriminations, tying contracts, stock acquisitions in competing corporations, and interlocking directorates. These anti-monopoly measures were strengthened to outlaw unfair or deceptive acts or practices in commerce as well as unfair methods of competition, thus granting the purchasing or consuming public the same protection that a merchant or manufacturer already enjoyed against the unfair methods of a dishonest competitor. Congress also provided definite and substantial civil penalties for violation of the commission's orders to cease and desist after they became final, although at first there had been no penalty for violation of the commission's orders unless they had been affirmed by a U.S. circuit court of appeals.

In response to the demand for greater consumer protection, Congress specifically prohibited the dissemination of false advertisements of food, drugs, cosmetics, and therapeutic devices. Where the use of such commodities might be injurious to health (or where falsely advertised with fraudulent intent), criminal penalties are imposed. The FTC was also authorized to bring suit in U.S. district courts.

The commission devised a procedure of trade practice conferences whereby an industry could participate in considering fair trade practice rules for its own regulation. Trade practice rules proposed by the commission following such conferences were then adopted after public hearings and had the force of law.

In 1934 Congress merged the seven-year-old Federal Radio Commission into a new *Federal Communications Commission* of seven members. The new agency's broadcast bureau regulated radio and later television operations; a common carrier bureau had similar power, transferred from the Interstate Commerce Commission, over interstate telephone and telegraph services. The commission assigns transmission frequencies and issues and renews licenses to radio and television stations and radio operators. It also exercises authority over all U.S. cable television operations.

The Securities Exchange Act of 1934 created the *Securities and Exchange Commission* (SEC) to administer federal securities regulation. All securities exchanges must be registered with the SEC, and before shares are traded on the exchanges registration statements must be filed with the exchanges and the SEC. The act governs such practices as short-selling, floor trading, concerted buying and selling for the purpose of artificially manipulating prices, hypothecation (pledging) of customers' accounts, and short-swing (within six months) "insider" trading in shares of a corporation by its officers, directors, and large shareholders. Brokers and dealers must register with the SEC, and supervision of their activities is carried out by the National Association of Securities Dealers, a private body that must be registered with the SEC and through which disciplinary action of its members is taken in accordance with SEC findings.

The 1934 act also gives the SEC broad rule-making powers, which it has exercised (1) to penalize fraud as broadly defined in the statute and rules; (2) to regulate sales made by mail or in interstate commerce; (3) to require that periodic reports be made to shareholders and filed with the SEC by corporations listed on exchanges; and (4) to supervise the solicitation of proxies of securities listed on exchanges. Under its antifraud rules SEC also undertakes to curb the activities of "boiler room operators," a term applied to organizations of securities salesmen using high-pressure sales tactics by telephone. The jurisdiction of SEC over proxy solicitation, reporting, and "insider" trading as to listed companies was greatly expanded by later amendments to include all corporations having assets of more than $1 million and five hundred or more shareholders.

The most important New Deal labor legislation was the National Labor Relations Act (NLRA) of 1935, usually called the Wagner Act. Its basic provision, Section 7, guaranteed employees the "right to self organization, . . . to bargain collectively through representatives of their own choosing, and to engage in concerted activities for the purpose of collective bargaining or other mutual aid or protection." Section 8 set forth and prohibited unfair labor practices by employers. The NLRA did not define unfair labor practices of unions and, indeed, contained no sanction against them at all. Later legislation—the Taft-Hartley Act of 1947 and the Landrum-Griffith Act of 1959—imposed restrictions on unions.

The NLRA made a three-member (later a five-member) *National Labor Relations Board* (NLRB) responsible for the prosecution and adjudication of all charges of unfair labor practices. The NLRB also determined which union was authorized to represent the employees in a specific labor unit and could hold elections among the workers to that end. The union selected by a majority of the employees voting was then recognized as the exclusive bargaining agent for the entire unit. The 1947 and 1959 laws broadened the regulatory responsibility of the NLRB accordingly.

Federal competence to enact air legislation was questioned as late as 1918 but eventually was justified on the basis of the familiar interstate commerce clause. When legislation was enacted concerning rules of flight, navigation lights, and licensing of aircraft personnel, it was held valid for purely intrastate operations on the ground that any departure from national standards would present hazards to interstate air navigation.

The Air Commerce Act of 1926 authorized the secretary

of commerce to make safety regulations, grant licenses and registrations, and to install and operate such facilities necessary to safe navigation as airway lights and radio stations. Those rule-making powers were transferred by the Civil Aeronautics Act of 1938 to a *Civil Aeronautics Board* (CAB), with a view to promote development of safe, efficient air services at reasonable charges under regulated competition. The Federal Aviation Act of 1958 continued the CAB and created a Federal Aviation Agency (now the Federal Aviation Administration) to control use of the navigable airspace and develop and operate air navigation facilities and air traffic control. In 1966 the agency was included in the Department of Transportation. The CAB regulates rates and routes on domestic operations. International routes are established in bilateral agreements negotiated by the State Department and approved by the president.

## Independent Agencies

To accomplish governmental business outside the realm of regulation, a variety of organizational approaches have been devised. One of these is the government corporation, a corporate body wholly or partly owned by the government and utilized primarily for business-type functions or services. First widely employed during World War I to provide the operating and financial flexibility required by certain emergency programs involving construction and operation of merchant vessels, trading in commodities, and other activities, the government corporation later became a common form of organization for public enterprises in nearly all countries and at all levels of government. The incorporated agency became the instrument for carrying out major parts of the national economic recovery program in the 1930s.

As defined by President Roosevelt when he recommended establishment of the *Tennessee Valley Authority* (TVA) in 1933, the government corporation's purpose is to provide an agency "clothed with the power of government but possessed of the flexibility and initiative of private enterprise." The TVA is a U.S. government agency created to control floods, improve navigation, and produce electrical power along the Tennessee River and its tributaries. During World War I the government determined to erect a couple of munitions plants at Muscle Shoals on the Tennessee River, plus a hydroelectric dam and a supplemental steam electric plant to power them. None of these undertakings had been finished by the end of the war, when it was decided to suspend construction work (though Wilson Dam was later completed). A half-dozen serious proposals to liquidate the government's $100 million investment at Muscle Shoals failed. Two bills providing for government development of the properties were approved by Congress, but vetoed. In 1933, with the United States in the grip of the Great Depression, President Roosevelt urged development of Muscle Shoals to put idle men to work and stimulate the economy of the region. Congress responded and established the Tennessee Valley Authority as a regional agency of the U.S. government. In legal form the authority was a public corporation; though it was a governmental agency it had many of the attributes of a private corporation. It was governed by a board of three directors appointed by the president by and with the advice and consent of the Senate.

The *Reconstruction Finance Corporation* (RFC), created by Congress in January 1932, played a major role in recovery from the depression. In moderating the epidemic of bankruptcies in the 1930s, the RFC helped lay the groundwork for economic recovery. Its purpose was to operate as an independent agency not subject to political influences. Applications for business loans would be considered on merit rather than political consideration; it was assumed that such loans would be made only when private financing was not available and when public interest would be served. Later, the RFC came to be used as a means of disbursing huge sums of money for other government agencies without the delays of getting appropriation bills through Congress. After years of criticism, it was abolished in 1957, its remaining functions transferred to the Housing and Home Finance Agency, the General Services Administration, the Small Business Administration, and the Treasury Department.

The *Export-Import Bank of the United States* is also a corporation. The bank's purpose is to assist in financing exports of U.S. goods and services. The bank was originally created to finance trade with the Soviet Union, whose government had just been recognized by the United States in 1933. It never did so, however, largely because of the breakdown of Soviet debt negotiations. A second Export-Import Bank was set up to finance trade with Cuba, and in 1935 the two banks were merged. In 1945 the bank was made an independent agency; a board of directors consisting of a president, vice-president, and three other directors is appointed by the president with the advice and consent of the Senate.

The economic crisis of 1933 occasioned establishment of the **Federal Deposit Insurance Corporation** (FDIC), to insure deposits in all member banks of the Federal Reserve System and qualified nonmembers. From 1921 to 1929 more than 5,400 banks closed. During the next four years the depression caused the failure of 8,812 more, with losses to depositors of more than $5 billion. Congress rejected many proposals to place deposit insurance on a national basis until the disastrous collapse of the banking system in 1932 made it imperative to take action to protect depositors. Thus the federal insurance program was launched with authority to insure deposits in eligible banks up to a maximum of $2,500 for each depositor (raised to $40,000 by 1974), and to regulate certain banking practices. Costs were to be met out of regular premium payments by insured banks. All members of the Federal Reserve System were required to insure their deposits, while nonmember banks—about half the U.S. total —were permitted to do so if they met FDIC standards. Similar insurance for savings and loan association depositors was provided in 1934 by the creation of the Federal Savings and Loan Insurance Corporation.

In 1933 the **Home Owners Loan Corporation** (HOLC) was established as another antidepression measure. It purchased from financial institutions about one million home-mortgage loans of borrowers who were having difficulty in meeting required repayments. The loans were recast into long-term loans (up to fifteen years) to be amortized through monthly payments over the life of the loan. Although the HOLC eventually had to acquire some of the properties securing the loans, by 1951 it was able to liquidate its $3.5 billion total investment without loss.

One of the more recent government corporations is COMSAT, the **Communications Satellite Corporation**, organized under the provisions of the U.S. Communications Satellite Act of 1962. COMSAT was created to be the U.S. participant in and manager of the International Telecommunications Satellite Consortium (Intelsat), a partnership of countries formed in 1964 to establish a global commercial communications satellite system. Intelsat owns the satellites and the ground control equipment as contrasted to the earth station communication terminals that are owned in the United States by COMSAT.

Other kinds of agencies, boards, and systems bear a variety of designations. They arose in profusion during the New Deal. One of these antidepression measures that was to have a lasting effect was the creation of the **Federal Housing Administration** (FHA) in 1934. Designed to restore lender confidence in mortgage loans and to broaden effective housing demand through liberal loan terms, thus stimulating construction employment, the National Housing Act provided for FHA mortgage insurance. The borrower pays a mortgage insurance premium, equal to 1/2 of 1 percent of the outstanding loan balance, and the lender is insured by FHA against loss of principal and interest, and partly against loss in foreclosure costs. Insurance claims are paid in long-term FHA debentures, guaranteed by the U.S. Treasury, thereby enabling the FHA to utilize its reserve to pay interest on debentures. Under this plan, acquired properties can be held off the market in order to avoid a glut that could depress existing home values and cause a decline in building.

FHA project-housing mortgage insurance was also made available to stimulate multifamily rental housing construction. An additional FHA program of insuring home improvement loans stimulated employment in the home-repair and modernization industry. The Housing Act of 1961 created a special below-market-interest-rate program under FHA for financing housing to serve lower-middle-income families. Successive legislative enactments continued and liberalized the basic mortgage insurance program of the FHA. In 1961 it was expanded to cover insurance of mortgages for condominium ownership, and in 1965 it was made available to cover the financing of assembling and improving land for new residential developments.

One of the most pervasive and important of U.S. governmental entities is the **Federal Reserve System,** the central banking authority of the United States. It acts as a fiscal agent for the government, is custodian of the reserve accounts of commercial banks, makes loans to commercial banks, and is authorized to issue the federal reserve notes that constitute the paper currency of the country. Before the establishment of the Federal Reserve System and after the liquidation of the second Bank of the United States in 1836, there was no central banking institution in the United States. The National Bank Act of 1863 and its consequences tended to concentrate the reserves of the country's commercial banks in a small number of large banks located in a few financial centers, notably New York City. Unusual demands for currency or credit periodically produced great financial stringency in the important financial centers, with consequent deflationary results. There was no system for changing the quantity of currency so that it would be responsive to the changing needs of the business community or to the continued growth of the country's economy.

The financial panic of 1907 led to studies that brought about passage of the Federal Reserve Act late in 1913. The Federal Reserve System consists of (1) a board of governors; (2) twelve federal reserve banks; (3) a federal open market committee; (4) a federal advisory council; (5) a consumer advisory council; and (6) the member banks. The board of governors (known until 1935 as the federal reserve board) consists of seven members appointed by the president and confirmed by the Senate. The chairman of the board is appointed by the president from the membership of the board for a period of four years. "The Fed" as it is called, is theoretically independent of the executive branch. The appointment of the members of the board of governors for terms of fourteen years—so arranged that one vacancy normally will occur every two years—is designed to provide a substantial degree of independence.

The country is divided into twelve federal reserve districts, each with a federal reserve bank—a corporation established pursuant to the Federal Reserve Act to serve the public interest and privately owned by the member banks. Each federal reserve bank is governed by a board of directors of nine members. Three may be bankers. Three must be actively engaged within the district in commerce, agriculture, or industry and not officers, directors, or employees of any bank. Three are appointed by the board of governors of the Federal Reserve System and must not be officers, directors, employees, or stockholders of any bank.

The twelve-member Federal Open Market Committee consists of the seven members of the board of governors and five members elected by the federal reserve banks. The committee determines federal reserve policy toward the purchase and sale of securities on the open market, a most powerful instrument of control over the money supply. The Federal Advisory Council consists of twelve members, one from each of the federal reserve districts. The Consumer Advisory Council was created in 1975 to advise the Board on relevant consumer matters and consumer protection laws.

Member banks are all national banks plus those state banks that meet the requirements and desire to participate.

Some agencies have been established to serve or advance particular constituencies. One such is the **Veterans Administration,** begun in 1930 to protect the interests of nearly thirty million U.S. veterans of military service. It operates a medical system that incorporated 171 hospitals in 1976 and administers educational, housing, and other benefits.

The **Small Business Administration** (SBA) was established in 1953 to extend loans to small firms that were unable to obtain credit from commercial banks. The SBA also assisted qualified small firms to obtain credit from commercial banks and to win government contracts; it also promoted research on small business problems.

The **Atomic Energy Commission** (AEC) was created in 1946 to put a civilian agency in control of the development and production of nuclear weapons for defense as well as in charge of the research and development of peaceful uses of nuclear energy in medicine, biology, agriculture, industry, and so on. In 1975 the commission was abolished and its functions relocated. The Nuclear Regulatory Commission oversees the safety of such devices as nuclear reactors in generating electric power and of other applications of nuclear technology. The research and development functions of the AEC were absorbed into the new Department of Energy.

The **National Aeronautics and Space Administration** (NASA) is another agency oriented to science and technology. It was set up in 1958 to bring into one body the responsibility for planning, coordinating, and conducting the U.S. program of space exploration. NASA's charter also provides for cooperation with other countries in space activities.

The government foundation is another type of agency worth noting. The **National Science Foundation** was established in 1950 to advance fundamental scientific research. Although tax-supported, it has an independent governing board and makes grants for research projects, fellowships, and related programs. Government took a similar role in advancing culture with the creation in 1965 of the **National Foundation on the Arts and the Humanities.**

For more than a century the government had been operating an establishment that merged scientific and cultural advancement in the unique **Smithsonian Institution.** It was founded in 1846 when Congress accepted a bequest of more than half a million dollars from an English scientist, James

Smithson. Smithson had willed that his estate should go "to the United States of America, to found at Washington, under the name of the Smithsonian Institution, an establishment for the increase and diffusion of knowledge among men."

The institution now embraces the National Air and Space Museum, the National Museum of History and Technology, the National Museum of Natural History, the Smithsonian Astrophysical Observatory, the John F. Kennedy Center for the Performing Arts, and many art galleries, collections, and activities.

Independent agencies are created by Congress from time to time as dictated by changing needs and dangers. U.S. efforts toward arms control were concentrated in 1961 in an *Arms Control and Disarmament Agency.* In 1974 Congress created a *Federal Election Commission* to oversee a new election law, administer campaign subsidies, and issue guidelines for campaign practices. The initial legislation provided for a commission appointed partly by the president and partly by Congress. The Supreme Court later ruled that all commissioners must be appointed by the president (with the consent of the Senate), since the agency's duties were executive rather than legislative, and in 1976 the commission was restructured to comply.

## The Merit System

The American tradition has been not only anti-aristocratic but often anti-intellectual. During the administrations of the first six presidents there was a tendency to retain in office the sons of the propertied and educated families of the Eastern seaboard. A drastic change occurred under President Jackson. Rotation in appointive as well as in elective office (except for the federal judiciary) became identified with the upsurge of democracy in the young republic. Jackson asserted that official duties could be made "so plain and simple that men of intelligence may readily qualify themselves for their performance." This view resulted not only from the admission of the new states as the Western frontier advanced beyond the seaboard but from the rise of political parties that related government jobs to services to the party in power. The increasingly sordid spectacle of a poorly paid and poorly chosen public service, changing with every incoming administration, and replaced by other patronage appointees of no greater competence and of less experience in their tasks, ensued for most of the nineteenth century. These jobholders tended to be loyal to the political boss who nominated them rather than to the department that paid them.

Two parallel forces finally prevailed to bring about the gradual emergence of the contemporary U.S. merit system for government employment. One was the persistent campaign of civil service reformers such as Carl Schurz to counteract the wave of corruption and scandals that took place after the Civil War, but a less known and equally potent force was the early entry of the government into scientific and technological fields and the growth of technical education through the land-grant colleges. The professional groups in these fields insisted on the appointment of administrators of qualification and merit. Not until the assassination of President Garfield by a disappointed office seeker, however, was the competitive civil service system finally authorized.

Every president since that time has extended the merit system. It is estimated that today more than ninety-nine percent of the nearly 2.9 million civilians in the federal service are in the merit system and continue in their posts when a new administration takes office in Washington. This fact often frustrates new presidents seeking to bend federal agencies in their own direction.

In the 1920s even members of the top ranks of the administrative services were known as "clerks." Since then at the federal level the earlier anti-intellectual tradition has virtually disappeared in the face of the complex demands of modern administration and of the great increase in the number of college graduates in government service.

The prestige and dignity of holding a government post in the career services of the federal government have advanced with the advent of merit principles. Salaries, pensions, and fringe benefits have been greatly improved. Training plans have been introduced, and there is a greater amount of lateral mobility as well as promotion from within, thus making the public service more attractive as a career for able people. There are still many improvements, however, to be made in perfecting the career services.

## Problems of Bureaucracy

Bureaucracy that suffers from organizational illness, as many authorities have pointed out, is not confined to governmental agencies and can be found in all kinds of large organizational units. In a democracy, however, there is a continuing need to prevent the worst bureaucratic tendencies found in government because of its power over private rights and lack of the corrective possibilities of the marketplace.

The two illnesses to which large organizations are prone are the polar tendencies of aggressiveness and recessiveness. The aggressive type is preoccupied with the extension of its jurisdiction, size, and power. The recessive type, on the other hand, suffers from a kind of inferiority complex; it shrinks from innovation, hesitates to assert itself, and tends to avoid responsibility and to shift it to others. A given agency may fluctuate between these two opposing tendencies, but as a rule it will lean toward one or the other. When an agency becomes too aggressive or recessive, an aspect of bureaucracy is at work. The respective influences of the permanent career staff and of the temporary policy staff are out of balance. The cure consists in restoring a balance between these conflicting forces of continuity and flexibility.

One of the phenomena observed in large organizations is the elevation of status over function as an objective. Officials in such organizations tend to give greater weight to the importance of their rights and prerogatives than to their duties. While a growing spirit of professionalism has often greatly enhanced the competence of public services, an excessive preoccupation with questions of status and rights of officials, as in the case of the medieval guilds, becomes a brake on flexibility and innovation.

The questions most frequently raised about civil service systems in which the incumbents enjoy tenure rights relate to their responsiveness vis-à-vis new policies as reflected in the election of a new administration, to their open-mindedness in regard to new methods and innovation, and to their industry and productivity. Many studies indicate that the widely held stereotype that all civil servants resist change, cannot innovate, and are lazy and unproductive is exaggerated. Agencies differ in their behavior just as people do, and there is much evidence that these traits are by no means universal and are to be found in large private organizations.

In the federal government the chiefs of the large operating agencies or bureaus are predominantly career men and women and can exercise considerable power in their alliances with congressional committees and supporting interest groups, often in defiance of the policies of the cabinet-level department head. Partly as a check on this tendency, the U.S. practice is to interpose political assistant secretaries between bureau heads and department heads.

After World War II, an old problem of bureaucracy reasserted itself in an acute new form: governmental secrecy. The cold war, which has kept world powers in a continual state of military preparedness with huge and increasing military budgets, and an accelerating rate of technological progress in weapons such as missiles and the atomic bomb, have brought great areas of governmental information into the secret or "classified" category. Civil servants continue to be examined not only for competence and integrity but for "loyalty and security," and have frequently been discharged or rejected on slender evidence. There is a large temptation in such times for officials to extend justifiable governmental secrecy to unrelated matters, and this may be used to cover up errors and to lessen the accountability of public servants.

The problem will continue to persist in the thermonuclear age. In spite of U.S. legislation requiring public disclosure, there may be no satisfactory solution until effective international control is established over the ultimate weapons and a more peaceful international atmosphere prevails.

In democratic societies the public mind still tends to accept the simple virtues as criteria of organizational health. Such characteristics as integrity, impartiality, responsiveness, progressiveness, efficiency, and courtesy are all signs of organizational health and freedom from the excesses of bureaucracy. Bureaucracy is ailing when an agency lacks these elements to any marked degree. Graft and corruption, favoritism, waste, backwardness, insensitivity to public needs, and idleness are all evidences of organizational disease. Elementary as these symptoms sound, they are not easy to overcome in a large, complex organization.

The democratic process is the best protection against bureaucratic disease. The right to question and to criticize is the most potent anti-bureaucratic hygiene, but new methods of internal evaluation and improvement in the many techniques used by public administration are increasingly being adopted by government agencies themselves. Applied psychology has contributed better methods of personnel administration and of appraising, stimulating, and rewarding good work and productivity. The social sciences have contributed useful techniques in the art of supervision and in regard to group behavior. Administrative research and in-service training have been fostered. The concepts of modern economics such as measures of "input" and "output" are beginning to be applied to innovations in program and performance budgeting. Government has been a pioneer in the adoption of the digital computer, and many agencies, performing great masses of transactions, have upgraded the efficiency of their services to the public, eliminating red tape and excessive paperwork. From time to time the press stimulates such improvement by publicizing outcries against suffocation by bureaucratic paperwork. The statistical sciences, aided by the computer, have improved the quality and quantity of factual data available as a basis for decision making on public policies and have made possible the use of operations research. Great progress has been made in the archival disciplines, which preserve and index documents of permanent value and dispose of unnecessary papers. Government accounting and auditing systems have been perfected. Many agencies are taking pains to humanize their services to the citizen and to issue forms and instructions in clearer and more understandable terms, reducing if not eliminating "gobbledygook" or bureaucratese. Advances have been made in improving the organizational structure of departments. In the acceleration of programs of scientific research and technical development, the government has used the device of letting out major projects under contract to private industry and universities. In fact a healthy bureau is one in which improvements such as these are continuously pursued.

Of even greater importance is the fact that many governments are introducing new methods aimed at preventing and remedying abuses that arise from the arbitrary use of administrative authority. A significant innovation in this field is the Scandinavian creation of the post of ombudsman, an official who is authorized to receive and deal with citizen grievances against departments and agencies; a number of countries are beginning to emulate this example. There is a growing practice of consultation by officials with citizen and employee groups.

In the United States widespread emulation of the Scandinavian practice is unlikely because in the end the citizen's representatives in Congress are his agents against the encroachments of bureaucratic excess. The war against the sicknesses of bureaucracy in the modern world, with its growing structures of complex organizations, is an incessant one, and eternal vigilance is the price not only of liberty but of the rendering of impartial and effective public service that free men demand of their governments in the modern democratic service state.

# 8.
# The Congress

The historical roots of the United States Congress are found in the parliamentary assemblies of the Middle Ages. Since that period there have developed in Western society the concepts of representation based on widespread elections for public office and an expanded legislative function that includes general control of the national government. Political ideas that were current in the eighteenth century, however, shaped the formal structure of Congress, the legal powers embodied in a written constitution, and the relationship between Congress and the president.

The basic theory under which Congress operates is that all official governmental action must have a legal base. This means that Congress must have a continuing watchdog relationship with the rest of the government and with society as a whole, to see to it that the existing law is adequate, and to create new law where necessary. Congress has become a great political regulator for adjusting conflict throughout the society as well as an agency for controlling government departments through law, personnel standards, appropriations, and criticism.

The U.S. Constitution of 1789 created a Congress with two houses having specific but restricted legal authority, and separated structurally from both the executive department and the judicial system. The two chambers have similar functions to perform, and they have adopted similar procedures for doing so. There are, however, certain differences.

The business of Congress has increased manyfold since the eighteenth century, but Congress has proved remarkably resilient in adapting itself to these demands. The policies adopted by the legislature over the years inevitably reflect the history of the United States and are in turn reflected in public law. Thus the political controversies that have embroiled Congress and the legislative solutions it has brought forth are an intrinsic part of the country's evolution. The study of Congress, like that of the government as a whole, cannot be divorced from the telling of U.S. history.

## House of Representatives
The House of Representatives has grown considerably since

the first Congress of 1789, which had 65 members. It reached the figure of 435 in 1912. On admission of Alaska and Hawaii as states, two additional representatives were automatically provided for under the Constitution, but at the next apportionment the membership returned to 435, the total authorized by statute. In addition there are a resident commissioner from the Commonwealth of Puerto Rico and a congressional delegate from Washington, D.C., who may join in debate but have no vote.

Membership of the House is reapportioned among the states every ten years, following the decennial census as required by the Constitution. The procedure for allocation is prescribed in the Apportionment Act of 1929 as amended. After receiving their quota of seats the states determine the size and boundaries of the congressional districts. The national law does not require a state to create single-member districts nor does it specify standards of compactness, uniformity, or contiguity that must be followed. In 1964, however, the U.S. Supreme Court ruled that congressional districts within each state must be substantially equal in population.

The biennial elections for the House of Representatives are held in the various states on the Tuesday following the first Monday in November, usually between candidates of the Democratic and Republican parties. Although national laws regulating elections are found in the corrupt practices legislation and the Federal Election Campaign Act of 1974, for the most part the elections are regulated by the states.

Increasingly in contemporary America a party may win the presidency but fail to win control of one or both houses of Congress. A president's party may also lose control of Congress in a midterm election. Such disparities in relative electoral strength may subsequently affect the relationship between the president and Congress.

Disputed election contests are referred to a court or to a House committee, but the final decision on eligibility rests with the House of Representatives, since the Constitution states that "Each House shall be the Judge of the Elections, Returns and Qualifications of its own Members. . . ." The constitutional provisions for eligibility as a Congressman specify a minimum age of twenty-five, U.S. citizenship for seven years, and habitation in the state from which elected. Residence in a congressional district is not a constitutional requirement for eligibility, but candidates normally reside in the district from which they are elected. The constitutional proviso that "no Person holding any Office under the United States, shall be a Member of either House . . ." has the effect of preventing members of Congress from heading governmental departments. This is one of the chief differences between parliamentary and congressional forms of government. If a member of the U.S. Congress accepts an offer to be, say, secretary of an executive department, he must resign his legislative seat.

Once elected, a member has certain constitutional privileges to protect him from interference in carrying out his duties. He is privileged from arrest (in all cases except treason, felony, and breach of the peace) during attendance at the sessions of Congress or in going to and returning from them. He cannot be questioned in a court of law "for any Speech or Debate" in either house, and he has certain privileges in the forms of travel allowance, administrative and secretarial assistance, the use of the mailing frank (free postage for official business), and office space. Beginning in 1977 the annual salary was set at $57,500 plus substantial travel and expense allowances and such added benefits as insurance and retirement programs.

In its internal organization the House of Representatives retains certain ancient parliamentary offices, including those of the Speaker of the House, the Clerk of the House, the Sergeant at Arms, and the doorkeeper. The historically ambivalent position of the Speaker of the House is revealed in the several functions the Speaker is required to perform, for he serves at once as servant of the House by presiding over its deliberations (in the performance of which he should be impartial) and as leader of his own party in Congress. In presiding over the House, the Speaker has the assistance of a skilled parliamentarian who is a permanent employee. The Clerk of the House has general charge of the records, but his jurisdiction does not extend to the staffs of committees or of members' offices. There is no central recruiting agency for the employees of Congress. Although some appointments are made purely on political grounds, there has been an increase in the professional competence of the entire staff since the enactment of the Legislative Reorganization Act of 1946.

Political parties developed within legislatures as a method for controlling the proceedings and mobilizing the necessary majorities to pass laws. In establishing the authority and the structure of a partisan organization the main problem is to provide sufficient control over the general lawmaking process so that the legislature will be able to act affirmatively, and at the same time permit members a reasonable measure of freedom of conscience and judgment in debate and voting.

That freedom is consistent with the heterogeneous nature of U.S. political parties and with the legal equality of elected representatives. The party structure is now quite diffuse, since earlier attempts to centralize control in the Speaker of the House or in the Rules Committee or in a caucus (a closed meeting) have been found unsatisfactory. The recognized party leaders, in addition to the speaker, are the majority and minority floor leaders and the party whips. The chairmen of committees also have considerable partisan influence. Indeed, party discipline waxes and wanes with the parliamentary skill and political dexterity and determination of such leadership figures as Speaker, Majority (or Minority) Leader, and committee chairmen. Moreover, in the contemporary Congress specific patterns of power, not infrequently crossing party lines, develop for the consideration and resolution of major policy issues.

A key unit of the party is the conference or caucus, where the main function is to develop a skeleton party organization that will be responsible for carrying on the day-to-day functions of the House. Party leaders are selected; committees are organized. In general, the parties attempt to secure representation at all the points in the political process where significant decisions are made. They provide the initiative in selecting the agenda, in developing the debate, and in mobilizing support for particular decisions, although they do not exercise exclusive authority in these areas. Control by each party over its own membership is not strong, and considerable latitude of action is granted individual members.

The committee system within Congress is an important adjunct to the work of the House of Representatives. The committees play a significant part in selecting and preparing bills for further consideration by the parent chamber, and their choice of bills may be influenced by the advice of the Bureau of Management and Budget, concerned governmental departments, or the attitude of the president. It is customary, but not mandatory, for committees to hold hearings on legislation at which interested parties are invited to give testimony. The committees also play a significant role in the control that Congress exercises over the governmental agencies; departmental heads and other responsible officials frequently called before committees to explain policy.

The committees have considerable autonomy and are not required to report back to the House all bills referred to them. However, a committee may be discharged from considering a bill further; this process requires a petition carrying the signatures of a simple majority of the members of the House. Legislation reported by a committee is placed on a calendar to await its turn, but if it is of sufficient importance it will be taken from the calendar and brought to the floor by means of a special rule reported by the Rules Committee. The function of this latter committee is to control both the flow of legislation considered by the House and the amount of time consumed in debate. On the floor of the House, committee members take the leadership in developing the debate on legislation previously considered in the committee.

In the late 1970s there were twenty-two House committees, which for the most part were organized around major policy areas. With the exception of some of the political leaders, all members are assigned to committees and are expected to participate fully. Each committee has a limited membership, and members normally belong to only one major committee. In view of the fact that membership on some committees is more desirable than on others, individuals do not necessarily get the assignment of their choice when they first enter the House of Representatives.

Members advance on their committee rosters through seniority, and traditionally the chairmanship has gone without question to that member of the majority party who has served longest on the committee. Since 1975 committee chairmanships have been subject to approval by vote in the party caucus. In modern times the committees have maintained professional staffs, many of whose members have a high degree of competence in their fields of activity. These staffs assist the committee in acquiring information and developing legislation, often aided by assistance from the Congressional Research Service of the Library of Congress.

### Senate

The organization of the Senate is in many ways similar to that of the House of Representatives, although its procedures are somewhat simpler. There is a less elaborate structure of political control, and, with its smaller membership, the Senate is able to take action on many items by unanimous consent agreements.

With the admission of Alaska and Hawaii as states in 1959,

there were one hundred members of the Senate, two from each state. The Seventeenth Amendment to the Constitution (adopted 1913) provides for the popular election of senators, whereas the Constitution initially specified that senators were to be elected by state legislatures. In most states the governor may fill vacancies by temporary appointment until the next regular congressional election, when any unexpired portion of the original term is filled at the polls.

The basic constitutional qualifications require a Senator to have been a citizen of the United States for nine years, to be an inhabitant of the state for which chosen, and to be at least thirty years old. The full term of office is six years, and one-third of the Senate membership is elected every two years. The popular election of senators on a statewide basis is an expensive proposition, particularly when added to the cost of conducting a primary campaign. Normally, the Senate appoints a special committee to investigate and supervise the conduct of elections, and complaints of unfair tactics or violation of law may be referred to this committee. The compensation of senators is the same as that of representatives, but appropriations for clerical assistance are somewhat larger.

The Senate is served by a staff that carries on functions similar to those of the staff of the House of Representatives. In particular, the Secretary of the Senate has custody of records and exercises general supervision of other employees, and the Sergeant at Arms has responsibility for security measures. The presiding officer is the vice-president of the United States, who is assisted by the president pro tempore of the Senate, an honorific, elected office (Art. I, Sec. 3). Each committee has its own staff, as does each senator.

Although partisanship and party organization are significant factors in senatorial behavior, the party structure of the Senate cannot readily be described by reference to an organizational chart. There are several political units, including for each party a conference, a policy committee, a steering committee, and a committee on committees. The position taken by influential senators, however, may be more significant than the action (if any) taken by a formal party structure. Each party elects a leader, generally a senator of considerable influence in his own right, who is in general charge of coordinating Senate activities, making arrangements with his opposite number for the consideration of legislation and defending party interests on the floor. This somewhat loose party organization is responsible for organizing the Senate, including the important function of naming members to committees. Each party also selects a committee to give assistance in senatorial campaigns, such as fund raising. Party members in Congress cooperate with the national political organization while retaining a degree of independence and freedom of action.

The Senate in the late 1970s had nineteen standing committees, which play a significant role in preparing legislation for consideration by the whole body. These committees also exercise control over certain government departments, to which in many cases they have delegated quasi-legislative powers. Chairmen are normally appointed under the seniority rule, with senators advancing in rank according to their length of service on the committee. Because of the strategic nature of their position the chairmen of important committees often exert considerable influence over public policy.

## House and Senate

There are several aspects of the business of Congress that the Senate and House share in common and that require common action. One item of common concern is the date for convening and for adjourning Congress. Congress begins its annual session in January (since the Twentieth Amendment), although the president may also convene either house on extraordinary occasions. The two houses customarily agree on a date for adjournment, although the president has authority (which he has never used) to adjourn Congress in the event agreement cannot be reached.

Another item of common concern is a joint session, which may occur when the president or other dignitary addresses both houses or when the electoral votes for president and vice-president are to be counted. A third item relates to certain subjects of mutual concern. To meet this common need, committees having membership drawn from both houses may be created, examples being the joint-conference committees (for adjusting disputes between different versions of legislation), the joint atomic energy committee, and the joint committee on printing.

The common interests of the houses of Congress also are served by several agencies that are in a very particular sense responsible to Congress or to its joint committees. These agencies include the Government Printing Office, the General Accounting Office, the Botanic Garden, and the Library of Congress. The independent commissions have an indeterminate status in the governmental structure; they are charged with carrying out the law of Congress, but they are not directly responsible to the president.

The House and Senate have similar functions to perform and have developed similar techniques and procedures for performing them. In considering legislation, the committees take up proposed bills, selecting for special attention those for which there is some political support and perhaps holding hearings on them. The public hearing, with testimony given by government officials and representatives of interested groups, has become an accepted adjunct of the congressional process. Many of the hearings before committees are published by the Government Printing Office.

The House and Senate follow slightly different procedures in reaching agreement on the legislation to be considered, but the process normally includes negotiation between both the committees concerned and the leaders of the parties. Debate is controlled more strictly in the House than in the Senate; a specific amount of time (several hours) is allotted in the House for considering the more important legislation, the time being controlled by committee leaders and reallocated to members who wish to participate in the debate. In considering legislation, the House may normally propose amendments, and on the demand of one-fifth of those present the vote is taken. The result of such a roll-call vote makes the position recorded by each representative a matter of public record. (The Senate has a similar provision.) A detailed account of the debate in Congress is recorded daily in the *Congressional Record*. Congress also publishes the *Congressional Daily Digest* and the *Congressional Directory*, and each house publishes its own *Journal*, which contains a concise record of the proceedings.

Senate debate is considerably freer than that in the House and less subject to rules and restrictions. In general, the practice is for the Senate to debate a measure until everyone has expressed his view, although occasionally it will be required that all debate be terminated at a specified time. The unanimous consent agreement is one of the factors that enables the Senate to complete action on minor business in a limited amount of time, leaving more time available for subjects of greater importance. The freedom of debate in the Senate may be abused by a filibuster, a device by which one or more members talk on interminably in hopes that the item will never be voted on. The rules provide for a method of terminating debate by the application of cloture, however, which in the late 1970s required the support of three-fifths of the members present and voting.

For an act of Congress to be valid, both the House and Senate must approve an identical document. Differences may be adjusted if one chamber or the other gives way, but often a joint conference committee is appointed to negotiate an adjustment of differences.

## The Legislative Process

In its annual sessions Congress has developed a routine for considering the various items of business that regularly arise. At the beginning of a session the president delivers his State of the Union Address required by the Constitution (Art. II, Sec. 3), in which he describes in broad terms the legislative program he would like Congress to consider. In February the president submits his annual budget message and the report on the economy prepared by the president's Council of Economic Advisers. The president also submits nominations and treaties for which the Constitution requires him to seek the advice and consent of the Senate. Inasmuch as the committees require a period of time for preparing legislation before it is considered on the floor, the legislative output of Congress may be rather small in the early weeks of a session; on the contrary, the legislative calendars tend to be crowded in the closing weeks of a session. Legislation not enacted at the end of a session retains its status in the following session of the same two-year Congress but dies at the end of it.

Meetings of the House and the Senate are customarily open to the public (a card from a member's office is ordinarily required); secret sessions are rare, although the need for occasional secrecy was clearly foreseen in the Constitution (Art. I, Sec. 5). The press gallery provides accommodations for representatives of various communications media. Regular sessions of Congress are not broadcast over either radio or television, but exceptions are made for addresses to joint sessions and for important open committee meetings. The increasing importance of the electronic media, especially television, steadily increases pressure on Congress to permit general broadcast coverage.

For some purposes, as we have seen, the president may be considered a functioning part of the legislative process. Congress also interacts continually with the various governmental agencies, either in making new policy or in determining the effectiveness of existing policy. If the electoral college fails to produce a majority of electoral votes for any one person, the Seventeenth Amendment provides that the House may select a president (each state delegation having one vote), and the Senate may select a vice-president. The power of Congress to provide for succession of the president and vice-president was modified by the Twentieth and Twenty-fifth amendments.

The Constitution requires the president (in Art. II, Sec. 3) to keep Congress informed of the need for new legislation, and the various departments and agencies are required to send Congress periodic reports of their activities. The president also submits treaties and certain types of nominations (in accord with Art. II, Sec. 2, of the Constitution) to the Senate for its advice and consent.

One of the most important legislative functions of the president, however, is that of signing or vetoing proposed legislation, as Article I, Section 7, of the Constitution mandates. The president's veto may be overridden by a two-thirds vote of each chamber. Nevertheless, the influence of the president's potential power of veto weighs importantly on Congress: it is easier to adopt legislation by a simple majority of those present and voting than it is to override by a two-thirds majority of the total membership of *both* houses. Therefore, a president's threat to veto may give him some influence in determining what legislation Congress will consider initially and what amendments will be acceptable. In addition to these legal and constitutional powers, the president has additional influence as leader of his party; he is in a position to mold party policy and to mobilize support for it both in Congress and among the electorate. Moreover, the president's power to command the attention of the news media (and thus the public) is usually greater than that of any member of Congress and often greater than that of the Congress as a whole.

The Supreme Court has no direct relations with Congress and does not give advisory opinions on the constitutionality of legislation. Decisions on such constitutionality by this and other federal courts, however, prescribe the constitutional perimeters within which Congress may act.

The representatives of special interest groups are not part of the formal structure of Congress, but they play a significant role in testifying before congressional hearings and in mobilizing opinion on select issues. The Legislative Reorganization Act of 1946 requires the registration of lobbyists who attempt to influence the passage of legislation.

## Congressional Authority

The basic assumption underlying official governmental action is that all acts of authority must have a legal base. In actual fact, many of the activities of Congress are not directly concerned with enacting law, but the ability of Congress to enact law is often the sanction that makes its other actions effective. The general theory under which Congress operates is that legal authority is "delegated" to the president or departments or agencies, and that the latter, in turn, are legally responsible for their actions. In some areas of delegated legislation, such as in proposals for governmental reorganization, Congress must indicate approval of specific plans before they go into effect. Congress may also retain the right to terminate legislation by joint action of both houses. The annual output of congressional legislation is found in the *United States Statutes at Large*; these laws are in turn codified in the *United States Code*. Rules and regulations (the terminology varies widely) based on legislation are found in the *Federal Register*, and this material is in turn codified in the *Code of Federal Regulations*.

Congress exercises general legal control over the employment of government personnel, the basic policy being contained in the Classification Act of 1923, as amended. Political control may also be exercised mainly through the Senate's power to advise and consent to nominations. This control, in the broadest sense, enables the Senate to set standards of policy and competence for appointments to high public office. It also may act as a check on the personnel policies of the service departments. When a senior senator of the same party as the president, however, recommends a high federal appointment in his state, it is virtually certain to be made; and senatorial courtesy has evolved to rule out approval of any nominee found "personally obnoxious" to a senator.

The Senate's authority over personnel may enable individual senators to exercise considerable influence on the selection of federal officers whose jurisdiction lies wholly within a state. Neither the Senate nor the House, however, has any direct constitutional power to nominate or otherwise select executive or judicial personnel. Nor does Congress customarily remove officials, although sustained criticism of personnel may lead to their removal by the president.

Congress may have recourse, however, to the seldom-used power of impeachment. In such proceedings the impeachment is made by the House of Representatives and the case is tried before the Senate, with a vote of two-thirds of the senators present required for conviction. The last impeachment trial was held in the Senate in 1936; in all, by the late 1970s there had been only four impeachment convictions.

The power to levy and collect taxes and to appropriate funds gives Congress considerable power in fiscal matters. The basic law outlining the broad procedures to be followed by the government in spending money and raising revenue is found in the Budget and Accounting Act of 1921, as modified by the Congressional Budget Act of 1974. The president has the initial responsibility for determining the proposed level of appropriations—a function performed with the assistance of the Bureau of Management and Budget—and submits to the Congress in February his estimates for the coming fiscal year. The budget committees of both House and Senate, with the assistance of the congressional budget office, analyze the president's requests and consider them in the light of their general responsibility to oversee expenditures and revenues as a whole. The budget committees also study and advise Congress of the effect on budget outlays of both existing and proposed legislation.

The House and Senate appropriations committees hold hearings on bills appropriating funds for the various divisions of the government, taking advantage of the opportunity to review past policy of the departments and agencies. Additional fiscal control is exercised by the General Accounting Office, a congressional agency which audits governmental spending and settles accounts, reports of its action being submitted to appropriate congressional committees.

The president's budget message includes references to anticipated revenue and, possibly, recommendations for changing the tax laws. However, Congress considers revenue measures independently; they are not an integral part of the process for appropriating monies. In either case, the House of Representatives assumes the initiative. Bills for raising revenue must originate in the House of Representatives, according to the Constitution (Art. I, Sec. 7), and by custom appropriation bills originate there also. Proposals for changes in the tax structure are made by the Treasury Department and are considered by the Ways and Means Committee in the House and by the Finance Committee in the Senate. The revenue committees are assisted in their work, such as estimating tax yield or the effect of tax change, by the professional staff of the joint committee on internal revenue taxation, in addition to their own staffs.

The critical function of Congress has developed from its concern with the effectiveness of existing legislation and the necessity for new legislation. The expression of criticism takes several forms, ranging from debate to special inquiry.

The most formal type of interrogation occurs when a committee or subcommittee conducts a special investigation, the object of the inquiry being set forth in a resolution passed by the parent body. In preparation for such an investigation, the general procedure is to grant a committee special authority to investigate a particular subject, special power being authorized to compel the attendance of witnesses and the production of certain printed materials. The exercise of this authority has, in turn, led to considerable adjudication in which the courts have been asked to determine the extent of Congress's power to investigate. The broad powers of Congress in this field have been upheld by the courts, although some cases have emphasized the importance of meticulous procedures. In the case of *McGrain* v. *Daugherty*, 1926, the Supreme Court said that "the power of inquiry—with process to enforce it—is an essential and appropriate auxiliary to the legislative function." This general principle has not been changed in subsequent judicial rulings.

One of the most contentious phases of investigations is, and has been, the refusal of witnesses to testify. In its early history, Congress itself punished stubborn witnesses, but subsequently it empowered the federal courts to try cases of contempt. The most effective claim for refusing to testify has been the protection offered by the Fifth Amendment to the U.S. Constitution, which provides, among other things, that "no person . . . shall be compelled in any criminal case to be a witness against himself." However, special legislation also provides that, under certain judicial conditions, committees may compel testimony by guaranteeing that the witness will be immune from prosecution arising from his testimony. In the important case of *Watkins* v. *United States*, 1957, however, the court held that the First Amendment protects a witness from identifying former Communist associates. Congress, the court said, has no "general power to expose where the predominant result can only be an invasion of the private rights of individuals."

# 9.
# Evolution of the Legislative Branch

The word *representation* in its broadest sense has roots that link it with the world of beliefs called magic. The modern governmental meaning of *representation*—a system enabling a large number of people to participate in the shaping of legislation and governmental policy—was not attached to the word until parliaments began to develop in the sixteenth century. Yet a certain magical element remained despite the continuous effort to rationalize the relationship called representation. French-Swiss political theorist Jean-Jacques Rousseau denied that representation of the will of the people was possible. It is generally agreed that representation of the electorate in modern elected assemblies poses real problems, because the views of both the representative and those represented are likely to change as time goes on.

In large modern countries the people cannot, of course, assemble in the marketplace as they did in democratic Athens or, at certain stages, in Rome. Only about thirty thousand citizens were eligible to participate in the assembly of ancient Athens, although actual attendance never ran that high. If the people of larger societies are to participate in government, they must select a few from their own number to represent them. Over a long period the methods for such elections have evolved; direct general elections have come to be accepted as the most "rational."

## Concepts of Representation

There has always been controversy between those who would have the representatives of the people act as delegates carrying out instructions and those who would have them be free agents acting in accordance with their best ability and understanding. Edmund Burke, British statesman and political philosopher, stated the latter alternative in his celebrated speech (1774) to the electors at Bristol: "Parliament is not a *congress* of ambassadors from different and hostile interests, which interests each must maintain, as an agent and advocate, against other agents and advocates; but parliament is a *deliberative* assembly of *one* nation, with *one* interest, that of the whole; where not local purposes, not local prejudices ought to guide, but the general good. . . ."

Yet Burke's idealistic conception accords neither with the reality of popular politics nor with the democratic ideal that the will of the people should prevail. The issue as to whose will is to prevail cannot be sidestepped by asserting with Burke that Parliament represents *one* nation, with *one* interest. This is true only in the abstract. The conflict of *various* interests and their possible relation to a more comprehensive public interest is the real issue.

Historically speaking, representative assemblies were developed in Europe in the late Middle Ages as an important part of the medieval constitutional order. Though great variations existed, the three estates (classes) were usually composed of nobility, clergy, and the city merchants (burgesses). In the English Parliament the higher nobility was joined with the higher clergy into one house of "Lords spiritual and temporal," while the lower group of squires (small landowners) and the burgesses came together as the Commons. This English system of two estates proved more viable than the continental system of three. The representatives of the lower estate were originally convened by the Crown in order to secure additional financial support for the realm. Quite naturally, they proceeded to present complaints and petitions in an effort to strike a bargain—in favor of their own class. They represented their class as agents of local powers and acted under instructions or mandates from these powers. Once an agreement was reached, however, the king and the two houses of Parliament acted together as "the king in Parliament" and were taken to represent the will of the whole realm. This background shows clearly that it is not justifiable to draw Burke's sharp distinction between agents with definite instructions and representatives speaking for one nation. An elected body is both: a deliberative assembly from *one* nation with *one* interest, that of the whole, *and* a congress of ambassadors from different and often hostile interests. This dualism in political representation cannot be escaped. Many political philosophers have tried to do it, but with unsatisfactory results. The Fascists and Communists have, by their insistence upon a monistic view, been forced into seeking some kind of religious or inspirational sanction, deifying (worshiping) the state, the proletariat (the common people or the folk), and their respective leaders. The duality of representing both the whole and one or another of its parts lies deeply embedded in all representative schemes.

Why did the concept of representation appear so late in the

history of mankind? Essentially, the answer must be that it was not needed before modern times. The great empires of Asia had been animated by religious beliefs in which the individual human being counted for little and his personal preferences for even less. In the ancient times of Greece and Rome, the small number of citizens making up the city-states made personal participation (also called direct democracy) possible. Aristotle deemed this participation so vital that he opposed altogether any political framework larger than the average city-state. Such personal participation became impossible whenever the city-state expanded beyond the local unit. Later the Romans undertook to incorporate the citizenry of each city of their Latin federation within the larger Roman citizenry by using various fictions, but the system broke down when republican Rome expanded far beyond its borders and the Romans adopted the Asiatic technique of deifying an emperor. The Roman Constitution contained elements of genuine representation, but they were crippled by the ascendancy of an unrepresentative Senate. By contrast, the spirit of corporate solidarity in the medieval towns, shires, monasteries, and cathedrals was sufficiently developed to make the group willing to participate in the larger community through group representatives. Unless such solidarity provides a common base of ideas, true representation cannot take place.

Except in small communities, constitutional government is impossible without a system of representation. A constitution restrains power by defining the functions of various power holders. Undivided power is unrestrained power. From a historical standpoint, the need for responsibility in government is the central objective in all the various systems of representation—even of supernatural schemes, such as that by which a king is supposed to represent God on Earth.

Ever since the sixteenth century, legislation has been considered the most important phase of governmental action. Legislation involves the making of rules binding upon the whole community. Such general rules, it was felt, should bear the closest possible relation to the community's general beliefs. A specific act of government may be justified in terms of a specific emergency, but no general rule can be considered valid without the assent of those to whom it applies. Since the citizenry is too large, representation therefore becomes essential. "No taxation without representation" is a vivid expression of this general view.

Deliberative processes are well suited to the relatively slow procedures of representative bodies. Nevertheless, the procedure of a well-organized representative assembly is arranged hopefully to result in action, namely the adoption of a law. Passage of such legislation requires workable compromise and careful adjustment of conflicting viewpoints. Through argument and discussion the area of agreement is determined in the representative legislature. It symbolizes the consent of the governed, which legislation presupposes.

With the rise of nation-states, legislative functions of government became increasingly differentiated from the executive and judicial, and the articulation of the "national will" occurred more and more through representative assemblies. As seats in England's Parliament became more valuable as a source of power, they became literally subject to auction and contest between the landed aristocracy and the new merchant and industrial classes. When it became apparent that governing power depended upon the successful organization of numbers of votes, the distribution of seats—hence of voting shares in national sovereignty—came under systematic examination among political philosophers and leaders. Principles of legislative apportionment were frequently stated methodically and mathematically.

## Apportionment

More vigorously debated was the problem of how legislative seats could be distributed to reflect the national will most accurately. The growth of democracy, the extension of the suffrage, and the rise of political parties have added to the complexity of the problem of delineating constituencies.

The pervasive issue of how to divide the electorate appropriately for election purposes is of great importance. As long as there are shifts of population, periodic readjustments of the boundaries of electoral districts are necessary to avoid gross injustices such as rotten boroughs (an election district with a small population but equal voting strength with other districts of comparable geographic size). In the United States and elsewhere this issue is a familiar one; recurrent political fights occur over reapportionment. Even with skillful handling, there are bound to be lags. Under adverse conditions, reapportionment becomes a "football" of party politics. Since a party needs only a small majority of votes in order to gain a legislative seat, it is tempting for the party in power to redraw the political map—that is, the boundaries of districts, wards, and other subdivisions—so as to distribute its voting power most effectively for election purposes. The resulting shapes of electoral subdivisions are often fantastic and not even always contiguous. A newspaper cartoonist once visualized the shape of a salamander in the outline of such a district constructed under Massachusetts governor Elbridge Gerry in 1812, and ever since the practice has been known as gerrymandering. It is easy to construct cases that illustrate how the same electorate may give a majority to the opposing party as a result of adroitly redrawn electoral boundaries.

In the United States each state is entitled to two seats in the Senate and to a number of seats in the House of Representatives according to the ratio of its population to that of the country. Every state is, however, entitled to at least one House member, regardless of population. The original constitutional apportionment set a ratio of one representative for each 30,000 inhabitants, counting all "free persons" but only three-fifths of "all other persons," notably slaves. By 1910 this ratio had become one representative for each 200,000 or more inhabitants. A 1929 act froze the total number of house seats at 435, to be reapportioned on a semiautomatic basis according to one of several mathematical formulas subject to congressional choice. In 1941 the formula known as the method of equal proportions was established.

The Constitution provides for the apportionment of representatives among states and for a census enumeration (Art. I, Sec. 3) to ensure equitable apportionment. The Constitution is silent, however, as to whether representatives shall be elected by districts or by the state at large. By 1842 there were twenty-two states electing representatives by districts and only six states electing at large. Thereafter the practice of electing by districts became general, except of course for states having only one representative.

## Continental Congresses

Like many other aspects of the Congress created in the Constitution of 1789, the apportionment provisions grew out of experience with the Continental Congress, the body of delegates that spoke and acted for the people of the colony-states of America collectively during the years 1774–89. As the delegates convened for the First Continental Congress they needed a chairman, and the historic choice of the terms *president* and *congress* was made at that time. Peyton Randolph of Virginia was chosen president of the Congress.

The manner of voting was an early subject of debate, with Patrick Henry urging that the delegation from each colony be given weight according to population. Spokesmen for the smaller colonies, however, insisted that each colony have one vote, and meeting their wishes was the price of unity.

The First Continental Congress rejected a plan to reconcile British authority and colonial freedom, adopting instead a declaration of personal rights, including those of life, liberty, property, assembly, and trial by jury. The declaration also denounced taxation without representation and the maintenance of the British army in the colonies without consent.

In addition, the First Continental Congress sent a petition to the king (though not to Parliament) and an address to the British people, demanding that Great Britain redress grievances accumulated since 1763 and that a return be made to the relationship (as the colonists conceived it) that had existed between the mother country and the colonies in that year. The Congress called for the formation of an association of the colonies to bring economic pressure upon the mother country. On adjourning, the delegates issued a call for a second congress to consider further steps in the light of the behavior of the British government during the interim.

Before the Second Continental Congress assembled in 1775, hostilities began at Lexington and Concord. The second assembly then voted to "adopt" the New England military forces that had converged upon Boston after the battles of Lexington and Concord and appointed George Washington commander in chief of the American Army. Assuming general direction of the colonial war effort, it acted as the provisional government of the colony-states, issuing and borrowing money, and setting up a postal service and a navy.

On July 2, 1776, the Congress "unanimously" resolved, with New York abstaining, that "these United Colonies are, and of right ought to be, free and independent states." Two days later it solemnly approved the Declaration of Independence to explain its decisive step.

The Congress continued to direct the American war effort. It also prepared the Articles of Confederation, which, after being sanctioned by all the states, became the first Constitution of the United States in March 1781. The Continental Congress functioned under the Articles until 1789, when it was replaced by the Congress created under the new Constitution.

Although debate in the constitutional convention of 1787 revealed widespread apprehension about possible excesses by a national executive—what has been feared recurrently in later American experience as an "imperial" presidency—the founding fathers also were desirous of avoiding domination of the national government by its legislature. The headlessness of the United States outside the Continental Congress demonstrated some of the problems of congressional government. The Congress with its shortcomings had been a laboratory in which were demonstrated the inadequacies of the Articles of Confederation that it had promulgated (under the pressures of war) to solve the problems of the legislature's own inadequacies.

## Parliamentary Positions

Naturally, many evidences remain in the present Congress, created by the 1787 convention, that demonstrate its lineal descent from the British Parliament. The presiding officer of the House of Commons is the speaker. The United States Constitution provides (Art. I, Sec. 2) that "the House of Representatives shall chuse their Speaker and other Officers. . . ." In accordance with the tradition in colonial assemblies, the speakers in the House of Representatives have been both parliamentary experts and political personalities.

From the beginning the speakership has generally been held by men with previous participation in state legislatures. Experience in the House of Representatives is normally required as well, but three members have been elected to the speakership during their first term in the House: F.A.C. Muhlenberg of Pennsylvania, the first Speaker, Henry Clay of Kentucky, and William Pennington of New Jersey. With the exception of these three, every Speaker has had prior service in Congress, ranging from one to sixteen terms.

Many famous men have served as Speaker of the House— James K. Polk, Schuyler Colfax, James G. Blaine, Thomas B. Reed, Joseph G. Cannon, Champ Clark, Frederick H. Gillett, Nicholas Longworth, and Sam Rayburn. Rayburn set a record for the longest service—nine terms, including two half-terms. Rayburn was Speaker even longer than Clay, who served six terms, five of them consecutive. More than one-third of the Speakers have come from the South, where Democratic influence has predominated since the Civil War.

In 1910 the House rebelled against the autocratic behavior of Speaker Cannon, and in March of that year a coalition of

Democrats and insurgent Republicans succeeded in drastically reducing his powers. They removed him from the Rules Committee, deprived him of the power to appoint standing committees, and restricted his right to recognize virtually at his whim members seeking to rise in debate.

The Presidential Succession Act of 1947 ranked the Speaker of the House first in line of succession in case of the death or disability of both president and vice-president. Relations between speakers and presidents have fluctuated between rivalry and harmony through the years. During periods of congressional supremacy the chair has challenged the authority of the White House; at other times popular presidents have dominated Congress. Despite the reduction in his powers, the Speaker continues to be at once the presiding officer and titular leader of his party in the House.

One of the most important committees of the Congress is the House Committee on Ways and Means. It takes both name and function straight from Parliament. In Great Britain the Committee on Ways and Means consists of the entire House of Commons, meeting under somewhat different rules from those prevailing for the Commons itself. This practice originated formally in 1707 but had actually developed on an informal basis earlier, when the Speaker of the Commons was a designee of the Crown. Parliament wished to increase its independence of the Crown and its privacy in acting on revenue measures by meeting under the chairmanship of one of its own members. At first the term "committee of the whole house" was used. By the middle of the seventeenth century the practice had developed of using two different designations when Commons met as a committee— Supply and Ways and Means. The Committee of Supply votes money for particular expenditures; the Committee on Ways and Means levies taxes.

In the United States the Ways and Means Committee, consisting of thirty-seven members of the House of Representatives, handles all measures in the House relating to the raising of revenues—including taxes, tariffs, and social security levies—and establishing debt policy. This was one of the earliest committees established in the House, first as a select or special committee, 1795, and then as a permanent or standing committee, 1802.

Like its British forebear, the committee originally handled both appropriations and revenue measures, but this placed too heavy a work load on the committee and concentrated too much power in its hands. To remedy this situation, control of expenditure measures was transferred to an Appropriations Committee, although not until 1865. Since the Constitution provides that all revenue legislation must originate in the House of Representatives, the Ways and Means Committee has occupied a somewhat more strategic position than its Senate counterpart, the Finance Committee. Gradually, however, the Senate adopted the practice of making drastic changes in tax measures after approval by the House, and the position of the two houses is now more nearly equal in practice. The Ways and Means Committee, however, makes more detailed examination of tax questions than does the Senate committee. Five members from Ways and Means and five from Senate Finance constitute the Joint Committee on Internal Revenue Taxation, serving both as a continuing means of liaison and as the conference committee by which House-Senate differences on tax bills are adjusted.

## Organization and Procedure

Prior to the adoption of the Twentieth Amendment in 1933, the president, vice-president, senators, and representatives assumed office on March 4 following their election, and the Congress met annually on the first Monday of December. Under this plan new members of the Senate and House, elected in November of an even-numbered year, did not take office until March 4; and, unless the president called a special session of Congress, the newly elected members did not actually begin to function until the regular session in the succeeding December, more than a year after their election. It was possible for the session (meeting from [say] December 3 of the election year until the next March 4) to be controlled by members who had failed of reelection. In order to avoid control of a session of Congress by such defeated members, who were termed "lame ducks," the Twentieth Amendment was adopted. This amendment provides that the terms of the president and vice-president begin on January 20 following their election; the terms of senators and representatives begin on January 3 following their elections; and Congress assembles each year on the same date. The president may on occasions convene the two houses in special session.

The organization and procedure of the two houses of Congress are to a large extent determined by the size and traditions of the two houses. The rules of the Senate permit great freedom of debate; those of the House of Representatives restrict debate and expedite business. In the House, amendments to a bill must be germane to its purpose; the Senate permits extraneous legislation to be tacked on as a "rider" to a bill likely to be adopted. Under the Senate rules obstructive tactics may be and often are resorted to, though such tactics relate in fact to relatively few measures. The House of Representatives, with its larger membership, would in fact be helpless with complete freedom of debate, yet both houses accomplish a large amount of legislative business.

While the House of Representatives elects its own Speaker or presiding officer, the vice-president of the United States is automatically the presiding officer of the Senate. The work of both houses developed largely by chance, and committees in each house, created for once important tasks, usually remained in existence long after their usefulness had ceased. The Senate in 1921 and the House of Representatives in 1927, however, reorganized their committees and materially reduced their number. But further additions began immediately, and multiplicity of committees, with conflicts of their jurisdiction in each house, led to confusion and interfered with joint action by committees of the two houses. With legislation enacted in 1946, fifteen standing committees replaced thirty-two in the Senate, and nineteen replaced forty-eight in the House. The act also specifically defined the authority of each committee and encouraged cooperation between the two houses. Under this system, however, subcommittees tended to proliferate.

For many years before 1911 the real leadership in the House of Representatives was vested largely in the Speaker, who personally made all appointments to standing committees. After 1911 the Speaker was relegated more distinctly to the position of presiding officer, and committees were elected by the House itself on the basis of selections first made by the party organizations. Although the majority and minority floor leaders have considerable influence over the progress of legislation through Congress, they share their power with the chairmen of the principal committees.

## Conflicts in Leadership

From time to time when congressional leadership has been strong and presidential leadership weak or inept, Congress has asserted firm control over the direction of the country. The first conspicuous, sustained example of this phenomenon was the period of congressional government beginning at the end (1865) of the Civil War. Its roots went back to December 1861 when Congress convened, dominated by Radical Republicans who were in open rebellion against President Lincoln's hesitancy to pursue the war for further ends than the reestablishment of the Union. To them it was senseless to fight the South without destroying its most potent resource, the slave labor system. Abolition alone assured Republican Radicals that the whole structure of Southern society would be torn apart and the political power of Southern Democrats destroyed. To the Radicals only the absolute subjugation of the South could achieve the objects of the war. They established a congressional Committee on the Conduct of the War that pursued officers into the field and held inquiries into all military disasters. It challenged both the administration's military policies and its choice of commanders. Under its charges many leading Democratic officers were removed, disciplined, and disgraced.

In April 1862 Congress, without the president's approval, proclaimed the abolition of slavery in the District of Columbia and two months later in the territories—all before Lincoln decided on his Emancipation Proclamation. In Congress the Radicals in his own party abused him unmercifully and even the most moderate Republicans refused to defend him. Only his consummate political skills kept the president from being overwhelmed. He barely managed to retain his secretary of state in the face of continued congressional demands for his removal. By shrewd political generalship, Lincoln managed to win renomination. Even with the solidly Democratic South out of the Union, however, he won by only fifty-two percent of the popular vote against the Democrat George B. McClellan, who had repudiated his own party's anti-war platform.

Thus Lincoln's own position was weak against a hostile Congress; consequently when he died less than six weeks after his second inauguration the prospects confronting his vice-president, Andrew Johnson, were bleak indeed. The end of the war was at hand, and the stage was set for a sustained Radical Republican fight for congressional domination of the reconstruction process.

Johnson acted decisively after a special session of the Senate recessed, but when the full Congress assembled in December 1865 it regarded the course of presidential reconstruction in the South with deep suspicion. Since the Thirteenth Amendment had been ratified in January of that year, the South, if restored according to presidential policy, would gain additional representatives for the freed Negroes. Under the leadership of the Radicals, Congress refused to receive the representatives of certain states even though they had met the president's requirements. A joint committee of fifteen (six senators and nine representatives) took the whole subject of Reconstruction under advisement. When President Johnson vetoed a bill giving the Freedmen's Bureau increased power, Congress retaliated by passing a concurrent resolution (March 2, 1866) against admitting any reconstructed state until Congress alone declared it entitled to recognition. Thereby Congress claimed the sole right to direct future federal policy toward the South.

This schism between the President and the Republican leaders in Congress became complete when on April 9 Congress passed the civil rights bill over Johnson's veto. This act declared freedmen to be citizens of the United States with the same civil rights as white persons and entitled to the protection of the federal government. Then, to place these provisions beyond the danger of overthrow by courts or congressional majorities in the future, Congress in June 1866 submitted to the states a proposed fourteenth amendment to the Constitution. This amendment gave a constitutional guarantee of citizenship and equal civil rights to freedmen. On matters of voting it gave each state the option either of granting the suffrage to the Negro or of suffering a proportionate reduction in the number of its representatives in Congress. For further protection of black rights Congress passed, over the president's veto, an act continuing the Freedmen's Bureau for two more years.

Having broken with the Republican leadership, President Johnson was forced increasingly to rely on Democratic support. The so-called National Union Convention, which met in Philadelphia in midsummer 1866 in an effort to abate sectionalism and endorse the president's policies, included a large number of war Democrats, moderate Southerners, some Republicans, and a few Whigs, especially from the border states. The convention declared that the Southern states had a right to representation in Congress. The Radicals, meeting in their own convention, declared for congressional policy. (Note that these were not nominating conventions; it was the middle of the presidential term.) During the congressional election campaign the president journeyed to Chicago, speaking at various cities along the route and abusing his opponents in intemperate language. The Reconstruction Act of March 2, 1867, provided that the Southern states should be placed under military government while the social and political program of Congress was being carried out. Passed over the president's veto, the act declared that no legal government or adequate protection for life or property existed in any seceding state except Tennessee. It divided the South into five military districts, placing each under an Army general who was responsible for the preservation of law and order. Existing civil governments were declared provisional and subject to the paramount authority of the United States to abolish, modify, control, or supersede them. Through military control Congress hoped to force the adoption of the Fourteenth Amendment as well as the acceptance of Negro suffrage in the state constitutions of the South. When conventions, chosen under black suffrage and excluding Confederate leaders, framed state constitutions that embodied all federal requirements, those constitutions could then be submitted to Congress for approval.

To prevent President Johnson from securing control of the military arm of government, Congress, also on March 2, 1867, passed the Tenure of Office Act. Designed to protect Secretary of War Edwin Stanton, who was secretly reporting Johnson's plans to the Radicals, this act forbade the president to remove civil officers without the consent of the Senate. Another act required Johnson to issue military orders only through General of the Army U. S. Grant. Powerful Republican leaders in Congress, awaiting their opportunity to rid themselves of Johnson permanently by impeachment, acted when the president finally did remove Stanton, thus defying the Tenure of Office Act. The impeachment trial, held in the spring of 1868, ended in Johnson's acquittal by a narrow margin—only one vote short of conviction.

There was more to the Radical Republican struggle with Johnson, but the foregoing is sufficient to demonstrate what determined leadership in a politically strong Congress can do to usurp presidential prerogatives and initiatives from a politically weak president whose leadership capabilities do not meet the demands of the era. The dominance won by Congress in the Reconstruction struggle lasted in some measure for most of the rest of the century. It was challenged by President Grover Cleveland (1880s), but otherwise not seriously tested until the time of Theodore Roosevelt (1901–1909). The remarkable age of scandals highlighted by the

Crédit Mobilier affair was in part a result of the high-handed, freewheeling attitude of an easily dominant Congress. It is interesting to note that President James Garfield, as he was shot (1881), was actively seeking to wrest back some of the chief executive's power long defaulted to the Congress.

Some years later President Wilson encountered congressional intransigence—fueled, to be sure, by his own stubbornness—that effectively destroyed his dream and crowning achievement, the League of Nations, when the Senate rejected U.S. membership in the League. Several political strains came together to defeat the League. One was that in the 1918 elections Wilson had lost Democratic majorities in both houses of Congress. This Republican dominance of the legislature continued unabated until the depression (1930), introducing, for one thing, a wave of isolationism that prevailed in Congress and the country until the eve of the Second World War (1939).

After the end of the war and the death of Franklin D. Roosevelt (1945), the 80th Congress was elected (1946) only to be dominated once again by conservative Republicans. Roosevelt's vice-president, Harry Truman, was in the White House. Congress ignored Truman's "Fair Deal" legislative program and asserted instead its own priorities. It curtailed spending, for instance, taking, as the chairman of the House Appropriations Committee put it, a "meat axe to government frills." It also enacted, over President Truman's veto, a new basic labor law removing some restrictions on management but imposing several new ones on labor unions.

Truman fought back in the campaign of 1948 and, to the surprise of nearly everyone, won election in his own right. He had campaigned hard against the recalcitrant 80th "do-nothing" Congress; with Truman were elected enough Democratic senators and representatives finally to give his party workable majorities in both chambers.

At the beginning of the 1970s mounting popular opposition to U.S. involvement in the Vietnam War was reflected in congressional opposition to presidential power to commit U.S. troops on foreign soil. This coincided with the paralysis of the Nixon administration by the Watergate scandals and introduced a new period of congressional assertiveness that lasted through the brief presidency of Gerald Ford. One enduring effect of this period was the enlargement of congressional participation in the federal budget-making process through the creation of powerful budget committees.

In the eight years of Republican presidents Nixon and Ford, Congress was totally controlled by Democrats. For administration proposals to succeed, it was necessary to augment Republican minorities with ad hoc clusters of Democrats willing to deviate from party discipline on certain issues. The tactic, of course, is nearly as old as the two-party system, for in practice there have been periods many decades long when Congress was overwhelmingly controlled by one party or the other, whatever the affiliation of the president.

## Procedural Change and Self Regulation

Such periods of control are a factor in the weight of tradition in the operation of the Congress. Procedural change occurs slowly. The example of the filibuster is a case in point. The name was originally given to buccaneers and is probably derived from the Dutch *vry buiter*, "freebooter"; it was revived in the United States to designate adventurers who, after the end (1847) of the war between Mexico and the United States, organized expeditions within the United States to take part in West Indian and Central American revolutions. Its modern use denotes one who engages in private warfare against any state.

With the passage of time the term has taken on another meaning applicable to legislative bodies and especially to the U.S. Senate. It refers to the practice of delay and interminable debate whereby a determined minority seeks to prevent the majority from expressing its will in legislation. The intent is to wear out the majority so that, either from fatigue or under the pressure of other business, it will give up and either lay aside the pending measure or alter it significantly to induce the minority to abandon the filibuster.

In most deliberative bodies, attempts at filibustering can be prevented by the parliamentary action of "moving the previous question." This motion, like those to adjourn or to "lay on the table," is not debatable. If this motion carries, then the vote on the pending business must be taken immediately. The U.S. Senate had such a "previous question" rule from 1789 to 1806, and it had been widely used in the British Parliament in the seventeenth and eighteenth centuries. From 1789 to 1828 the presiding officer of the Senate also had, in practice, the unappealable power to stop superfluous motions and tedious speeches, and evidence seems to indicate that this power was indeed used by vice-presidents John Adams, Thomas Jefferson, and Aaron Burr.

In 1825 John Randolph of Virginia was elected to the Senate and proceeded to make irrelevant and tedious speeches that Vice-President John C. Calhoun refused to rule out of order. Three years later the Senate not only specifically provided that the presiding officer had such powers but also made his rulings appealable to the Senate itself. Apparently the purpose was to strengthen rather than weaken Senate discipline by adding the weight of the majority to questions of parliamentary order. A rule of relevancy was also available.

In 1872 Vice-President Schuyler Colfax ruled that "under the practice of the Senate the presiding officer could not restrain a Senator in remarks which the Senator considers pertinent to the pending issue." With this ruling, the heyday of the filibuster had arrived. During the so-called Progressive era, from 1907 to 1917, the filibuster was used a number of times on ideological grounds, notably by Sen. Robert M. La Follette, Sr., against several bills, including Wilson's armed merchant ship bill of March 1917.

This filibuster by the so-called willful eleven senators during the closing days of the 64th Congress, as relations with Germany reached a crisis, led to the adoption of cloture (closing of debate) provisions as the new Congress convened. Under pressure from Sen. Thomas J. Walsh of Montana, Rule XXII was amended so that a petition of sixteen senators to close debate on "any pending measure" should (after two days' delay) be brought before the Senate for a vote and could be passed by the affirmative votes of two-thirds of those present and voting. If this motion carried, then each senator would be entitled to speak for not more than one hour on all motions, and dilatory motions or amendments were to be ruled out of order.

In the entire history of this version of Rule XXII (1917–49), the closing of debate was successfully invoked on discussion of the Treaty of Versailles in 1919, the World Court in 1926, and on two other occasions. Despite frequent attempts, cloture was never affirmatively voted for the so-called civil rights bills of the 1930s and 1940s (federal bills against lynching and use of the poll tax as a prerequisite to voting) nor on bills relating to fair employment practices.

In 1949 a determined effort was made to modify Rule XXII so that the invocation of cloture would not be so difficult. The move backfired and resulted in making the process even more difficult by requiring the votes of two-thirds of all members of the Senate. Ten years later, however, the old rule was restored. Because of the difficulty of obtaining a two-thirds vote, cloture has seldom been invoked in the Senate. Efforts have occasionally been made to stop filibusters conducted by southern senators who opposed civil rights bills, but no such effort succeeded until 1964, when cloture was invoked to permit a vote to be taken on the bill that became the Civil Rights Act of that year.

The Constitution provides (Art. I, Sec. 5) that each house may "punish" its members for disorderly behavior, that it may expel a member with the concurrence of a two-thirds vote, and that it shall be itself the judge of the "qualifications of its own members." From time to time, the actions of certain members have resulted in a congressional rebuke. Following a period in which Sen. Joseph R. McCarthy of Wisconsin made but failed to prove widespread and extravagant charges of Communist infiltration into government, the Senate, by a vote of 67–22 on Dec. 2, 1954, "condemned" the senator for acting "contrary to senatorial ethics," obstructing its "constitutional processes," and impairing its dignity. A controversy arose over whether the senator had actually been censured by this resolution.

A decade later in March 1967, the House of Representatives voted to exclude for misuse of public funds New York Rep. Adam Clayton Powell, who prior to his reelection in 1966 had been chairman of the House Committee on Education and Labor. Powell was subsequently reelected, however, by his constituency and took his seat in January 1969.

Another case of censure arose in the Senate on April 27, 1967, when the Select Committee on Standards and Conduct recommended that Connecticut Sen. Thomas J. Dodd be censured "for his conduct, which is contrary to accepted morals, derogates from the public trust expected of a Senator and tends to bring the Senate into dishonor and disrepute." Dodd was accused of using political funds for personal expenses and of thirteen instances of double-billing for travel.

House and Senate adoption of relatively stringent ethics codes in the mid-1970s—partly in response to general reaction to the Watergate affair—offered another illustration of the fact that Congress does conform, even if slowly, to the popular will in its organization and procedures as well as in enacting legislation. Its evolution, like its performance, is affected by time, events, and men. Codes of ethics, however, are unlikely to daunt those seekers or wielders of influence who are determined to evade them.

# 10.
# The Federal Judiciary

The structure of court organization in the United States reflects the division of functions characteristic of the federal form of government. Each state has its own independent, comprehensive system of courts, capable of adjudicating almost every conceivable controversy, and ordinarily subject to no higher judicial authority. At the same time there exists a system of national courts established to perform distinctively national functions. To a considerable extent the state and national (or federal) courts exercise concurrent jurisdiction, but in certain cases the federal courts have exclusive jurisdiction, and in matters of national law they exercise the supreme judicial power.

## Structure

Two short sections of the U.S. Constitution provide for the establishment of a federal system of courts and define the federal judicial power. The judicial power is vested "in one supreme Court, and in such inferior Courts as the Congress may from time to time ordain and establish." The judges are appointed by the president, with the advice and consent of the Senate. They hold office "during good Behaviour"—that is, they can be removed only by impeachment—and their compensation cannot be diminished during their continuance in office.

The federal judicial power extends to nine classes of cases: (1) all cases, in law or equity, arising under the Constitution, the laws of the United States, and treaties made under their authority; (2) all cases affecting ambassadors, other public ministers, and consuls; (3) all cases of admiralty and maritime jurisdiction; (4) controversies to which the United States is a party; (5) controveries between two or more states; (6) controversies between a state and citizens of another state; (7) controversies between citizens of different states; (8) controversies between citizens of the same state claiming land under grants of different states; and (9) controversies between a state, or the citizens thereof, and foreign states, citizens, or subjects. The power granted with respect to the 6th and 9th classes of cases was narrowed in 1798 by the Eleventh Amendment, which withdrew from the federal courts jurisdiction over suits against a state by citizens of another state or by foreign states and their subjects.

The Supreme Court has original jurisdiction over all cases affecting ambassadors, other public ministers, and consuls, and over cases in which a state is a party. In the other enumerated cases, its jurisdiction is appellate (relating to appeals) and is subject to congressional regulation. In addition to the courts thus provided for, Congress has power to establish courts with plenary (complete) jurisdiction for the District of Columbia and other federal territories.

Implementation of the judicial article of the Constitution was a major task of the first Congress in 1789. After providing for a Supreme Court, Congress made the historic decision to establish a system of inferior courts instead of relying entirely on the state courts, in the first instance, to decide cases within the federal judicial power.

The plan for inferior courts has undergone changes from time to time, notably in 1891, when circuit courts of appeals were established, and in 1911, when the old circuit courts, which shared original jurisdiction with the district courts, were abolished. Under the organization in existence in the late 1970s, the court of first instance was the district court, the country being divided into ninety-four districts. The districts are grouped into eleven judicial circuits, in each of which is a court of appeals with jurisdiction to review decisions of district courts within its territory. The membership of the courts of appeals varies from three to nine judges. The Supreme Court opens its term in the District of Columbia on the first Monday in October of each year, exercising the original jurisdiction invested in it by the Constitution; a limited jurisdiction to review directly the decisions of district courts; a largely discretionary jurisdiction to review decisions of the courts of appeals; and a limited jurisdiction, also largely discretionary, to review decisions of state courts. Since 1925 the Supreme Court has been able to limit its appellate work to cases that are important to the national interest or to the administration and development of the law. Congress has also established certain specialized courts, such as the court of claims, the customs court, the court of customs and patent appeals, and the tax court.

Contrary to popular supposition, the Supreme Court is not the court of last resort on all questions of law. It is only when some provision of the federal Constitution, or an act of Congress, or a treaty is involved, or some right under federal law is asserted, that the Supreme Court has power to review decisions of state courts. Even this limited power of review, though it was established in the first Judiciary Act (1789), was repeatedly challenged by the states during the nineteenth century, despite the Supreme Court's definitive decision upholding its constitutionality in *Martin* v. *Hunter's Lessee*, 1816. In the great majority of cases, which involve only questions of common law or local statute, no appeal lies to the U.S. Supreme Court.

In the same year the eleven courts of appeals dispose of almost 3,000 cases, consisting primarily of appeals from district courts but including also appeals from certain administrative agencies and a few original proceedings. The district courts dispose of more than 110,000 cases. The largest single category consists of prosecutions for violation of federal criminal laws (about 37,000); the second largest (32,000) consists of bankruptcy cases (bankruptcy being one of the subjects concerning which the federal Congress exercises legislative power). In about 20,000 cases the United States or a federal officer is a party. In the remaining category of private civil litigation (21,000 cases), about sixty percent are controversies between citizens of different states, about thirty percent arise under federal law, and about ten percent are in admiralty.

## Early Years

A primary weakness of the United States under the Articles of Confederation was the inability of the government to enforce its laws through a national judiciary. In the Philadelphia convention opponents of strong central government argued that a federal judiciary would merely duplicate the functions of state courts. To avoid conflict the convention agreed to a vaguely worded compromise providing for "one supreme Court, and such inferior Courts as the Congress may from time to time ordain and establish."

Oliver Ellsworth of Connecticut was the acknowledged Federalist leader of the U.S. Senate in the first Congress. He was chairman of the committee to establish the federal court system and the chief author of the Federal Judiciary Act of 1789, the principal basis of the court structure. The Ellsworth Judiciary Act was a clear victory for the nationalists. It created the office of chief justice, to which Washington appointed the New York attorney John Jay, and it authorized five associate justices. Below the Supreme Court in the federal judicial hierarchy were three circuit courts and thirteen district courts. To ensure the supremacy of federal courts the act provided for appeals from state to federal courts in cases involving the Constitution, treaties, or federal laws.

When the chief justiceship became vacant in 1796, Washington appointed Ellsworth to that office, but his service on the high court was cut short in 1800 by ill health. That was the same year as Jefferson's election to the presidency, which he interpreted "as real a revolution in the principles of our government as that of 1776 was in its form." Jefferson was overstating the case, for most Republicans were just as "aristocratic" as the Federalists. Both parties represented the rich, the wise, and the wellborn; both were led by gentlemen trained in the art of government.

Actually, the spectacular feature of the "revolution of 1800" was an attack on the federal judiciary. Republican suspicion of the national judiciary was reinforced by the partisan behavior of Federalist judges during the Sedition Act trials. In January 1801 during the waning days of their power, the Federalists succeeded in expanding the number of circuit and district courts, and President John Adams filled the newly created judicial offices with staunch Federalists. Another last-minute appointment was a new chief justice, John Marshall, whose nationalism would dominate the Supreme Court for the next thirty-six years.

Fearful lest their entire legislative program be undermined by Federalists in the judiciary, the Republicans upon taking office immediately repealed the Judiciary Act of 1801. They then attempted to remove from office a justice of the Supreme Court, Samuel Chase, an arch-Federalist who had conducted several of the sedition trials in 1799. Impeached by the House of Representatives, Chase was tried before the Senate in the spring of 1805. Though probably guilty of judicial misconduct, Chase was held not guilty of a "high crime or misdemeanor," the requirement for removal set forth in the Constitution. His acquittal by the Senate in March 1805 ended the Republican assault on the judiciary.

The Constitution, in Article III, gives the Supreme Court a status independent of the will of Congress. Since the Constitution is silent on such matters as the size of the court and the scope of its appellate jurisdiction in the judicial hierarchy, however, the Supreme Court itself is subject in important respects to congressional action.

The first Judiciary Act provided for a chief justice and five associate justices. In 1807 the membership was increased by law to seven, in 1837 to nine, and in 1863 to ten. In 1866, as part of the effort by Congress to curb the appointing power of President Johnson, a statute reduced the membership to seven as vacancies should occur, and in fact the court declined to eight members. But in 1869 an increase to nine was provided, at which size the court has remained. Tenure is during good behavior, subject to expulsion by conviction on impeachment as provided in Article II, Section 4, of the Constitution. Only one justice of the Court has ever been impeached—Samuel Chase—but he was acquitted in 1805. By an act of 1937, a member of the Court who has served for ten years or more may retire with full compensation upon reaching the age of seventy.

Appointments to the Supreme Court, as to the lower federal courts, are made by the president with the advice and consent of the Senate. Eleven nominations have been rejected by the Senate, the latest being in 1969 and 1970. All appointees have been lawyers, but there has been no other pattern of selection. It can be said that geographic distribution has been a factor as well as the political outlook of the nominees: not so much their partisan affiliation as an outlook on problems of statecraft congenial to the chief executive and the Senate.

The judicial opinions of a number of justices have surprised and disappointed the presidents who appointed them. A somewhat different case was that of Abe Fortas, appointed to the Court in 1965 by Pres. Lyndon Johnson. After publicity about his outside financial activities, Fortas resigned in 1969 under pressure, the first justice in the Court to do so.

Two chief justices, Edward D. White and Harlan F. Stone, were advanced to that office while associate justices. Charles Evans Hughes (chief justice 1930–41) served as associate justice before resigning in 1916 to run for president. The longest tenure, thirty-four years and eight months, was that of Stephen J. Field (1863–97).

## Judicial Review

The power of the U.S. courts to rule on the constitutionality of legislation and to refuse to enforce legislation that in their judgment violates the Constitution has come to be known as judicial review. Few courts in the world have this extraordinary power. A statute passed by Parliament may indeed violate the constitution of the realm, for example, a gross statutory invasion of free speech, but no English court has the right to refuse to enforce it on constitutional grounds. Parliament is sovereign; but in the United States the Constitution, as construed by the courts as the embodiment of the will of the whole people, is sovereign.

With the following statement by John Marshall, chief justice of the United States, in *Marbury* v. *Madison* in 1803, the constitutional practice of judicial review is generally considered to have begun:

> *It is a proposition too plain to be contested that the Constitution controls any legislative act repugnant to it or that the legislature may alter the Constitution by an ordinary act. Between these alternatives there is no middle ground. The Constitution is either a superior, paramount law, unchangeable by ordinary means, or it is on a level with ordinary legislative acts and, like other acts, is alterable when the legislature shall please to alter it. . . . So if a law be in opposition to the Constitution, if both the law and the Constitution apply to a particular case, so that the court must either decide that case conformably to the law, disregarding the Constitution, or conformably to the Constitution, disregarding the law, the court must determine which of these conflicting rules governs the case. This is of the very essence of judicial duty.*

Compelling as Chief Justice Marshall's logic now appears, there was in fact no express warrant for it in the actual text of the Constitution. The successful assertion of the power of judicial review in *Marbury* v. *Madison* rested ultimately on the Supreme Court's own ruling, plus the absence of effective political challenge to it by the Jeffersonians. In fact, as Charles Evans Hughes noted in his Columbia University lectures, contemporary criticism of *Marbury* v. *Madison* was directed mainly at those portions of the opinion where the Court, by way of obiter dictum (an incidental opinion that is not binding), declared that the justices of the peace had a right to receive their commissions. Chief Justice Marshall's expression of views on this point was particularly resented by President Jefferson. As to those parts of the chief justice's opinion that dealt with the function of the Court in passing upon the validity of legislation, there was in fact some historical precedent for Marshall's action in the control exercised by the privy council, the highest tribunal of the old British colonial empire, in relation to the American colonies before 1776.

At the beginning of the nineteenth century, whether the Constitution had created a federation or a country was not a question on which agreement could have been reached. It fell to John Marshall, and to the Supreme Court under and beginning with Marshall, to set forth the main structural lines of the judicial aspect of government.

## Landmark Cases

In *McCulloch* v. *Maryland*, 1819, upholding the second Bank of the United States, the Court gave a liberal interpretation to the necessary and proper clause of the Constitution and thus equipped Congress with supplementary powers of great potentiality. A counterpart was the decision in *Gibbons* v. *Ogden*, 1824, holding that a state could not confer a monopoly of interstate steamboat traffic, thus establishing the Court as a guardian of the free national market against local commercial self-interest.

The Court of Chief Justice Roger B. Taney, although on the whole more sympathetic to the concerns of the states, by no means reversed the current. *Bank of Augusta* v. *Earle*, 1839, established the capacity of a corporation chartered in one state to do business in another; and the *Charles River Bridge Co.* v. *Warren Bridge Co.* case, 1837, while sustaining the power of a state to charter a company in competition with one operating under a prior grant from the state, served to stimulate the development of new forms of interstate transportation. The *Genesee Chief* (1851) extended federal admiralty jurisdiction to inland navigable lakes and rivers, rejecting the English rule that such jurisdiction was confined to tidewaters. Pointing out the divergence between the English and American topography, Taney's opinion is at once a declaration of independence and an avowal that constitutional interpretation should conform to the facts of life.

Unhappily, Taney's reputation was derived too largely from the *Scott* v. *Sanford* (Dred Scott) case (1857). This decision, holding that Congress lacked power to prohibit slavery in the territories, foreclosed one avenue of compromise between North and South and helped to precipitate the Civil War. The war itself produced the *Ex parte Milligan* case (1866), a notable landmark in the field of civil liberties, declaring that trial of civilians by military commission is unlawful outside the theater of military operations while the civil courts are still capable of functioning.

The post-Civil War amendments to the Constitution were construed in the *Slaughterhouse* cases (1873) and the *Civil Rights* cases (1883) not to have worked a radical transformation in the basic structure of U.S. federalism. The first of these decisions ruled that the privileges and immunities of citizens of the United States, safeguarded by the Fourteenth Amendment, must be narrowly interpreted to include only those privileges peculiar to national citizenship and not such asserted rights as the opportunity to engage in common occupations. The second decision established the position that the amendments provide a federal guarantee against racial discrimination by state but not by private action.

The due-process clause of the Fourteenth Amendment was used in the late nineteenth and early twentieth centuries to strike down economic legislation that did not commend itself to the social philosophy of a majority of the justices serving at that time. Perhaps the high-water mark was reached in *Lochner* v. *New York*, 1905, invalidating a law that limited the workday of bakers to ten hours; in time the case became less notable for the decision than for the stinging dissent of Justice Holmes. Later this dissenting position was definitely established as the law of the land in *Nebbia* v. *New York*, 1934, a decision that gave broad scope to economic legislation affecting prices, wages, and the hours of labor by renouncing the view that there is a closed category of businesses so affected with a public interest that for them alone is such regulation constitutionally permissible.

The New Deal program of Pres. Franklin D. Roosevelt at first foundered on restrictive constitutional decisions of the Court. But the tide turned with the *National Labor Relations Board* v. *Jones and Laughlin Steel Corp.* case (1937), upholding federal authority over collective bargaining in industries in which work stoppages would affect interstate commerce. The opinion of Chief Justice Hughes was able to draw support from an earlier opinion of his in the *Shreveport* case (1914), where federal authority over intrastate railroad rates was sustained on a showing of their effect upon competitive interstate traffic. Congressional power over industry and agriculture has been validated to an extent ample for legislative purposes. Restraints in the interest of the states have become a matter of congressional discretion rather than constitutional compulsion.

The decision in *Brown* v. *Board of Education,* 1954, holding that separate but equal facilities for Negroes in public schools do not meet the constitutional standard of equal protection of the laws, created the greatest problem of compliance faced by the Court since the Marshall period. But the Court as an arbitral institution meanwhile won firm acceptance if not always similar public understanding. Despite changes in membership after Earl Warren was succeeded as chief justice by Warren E. Burger, the Court held firm to the principle of desegregation by ruling unanimously in *Swann* v. *Charlotte-Mecklenburg Board of Education,* 1971, that busing of pupils could be ordered by a court in order to overcome racial imbalance that was a legacy of segregation by law.

In *Baker* v. *Carr,* 1962, and succeeding cases, the Court invalidated, under the equal-protection clause, grossly disproportionate state legislative districts, over the dissent of Justice Felix Frankfurter, who warned that the Court was entering a "political thicket." The political process was safeguarded in a different way when the Court held in *N.Y. Times Co.* v. *Sullivan,* 1964, that the guarantee of freedom of the press protected a newspaper from liability for defamation of a public official provided the falsehood was not published knowingly or recklessly.

In another series of cases the Court applied various provisions of the federal Bill of Rights to state criminal trials, under the due-process guarantee of the Fourteenth Amendment. The application of freedom of the press to broadcasting was clarified in *Red Lion Broadcasting Co., Inc.* v. *FCC,* 1969, upholding the "equal time" and "fairness" doctrines of the Federal Communications Commission; those requirements, the Court declared, did not materially burden the station proprietors and had the merit of providing listeners with a broader spectrum of opinion, thus enhancing rather than diminishing the essential values of the First Amendment. *Mapp* v. *Ohio,* 1961, required the exclusion of evidence obtained through an unconstitutional search and seizure; *Miranda* v. *Arizona,* 1966, required the exclusion of confessions secured from a person under arrest without giving him an opportunity to consult counsel or offering to provide counsel if he is indigent.

The death penalty was held invalid as "cruel and unusual" punishment, at least as applied in a non-uniform and unpredictable way (*Furman* v. *Georgia,* 1972. A 1976 decision, however, clarified the Court's position. In *Gregg* v. *Georgia,* a 7–2 majority ruled that the death penalty was not necessarily cruel and unusual and that it is not necessarily imposed in an arbitrary and capricious way where the decision-making process involved in its imposition is carefully controlled by clear and objective standards aimed at even-handed treatment. A related decision, *Woodson* v. *North Carolina*, held mandatory death sentences unconstitutional. These lines of cases indicate how the Court exercised the power of judicial review with increasing intensity to assure more responsive and responsible government.

While the Supreme Court possesses the ultimate power of declaring federal and state legislation invalid on constitutional grounds, it has exercised this power with great restraint. Fewer than ninety federal statutes had by the late 1970s been so declared, though the number of state statutes held invalid was much larger. The Court will exercise this power only if necessary to decide cases and controversies and will not, as a few state courts will, give mere advice to Congress or to the executive in the form of advisory opinions. Judicial review, therefore, always grows out of concrete litigation where the rights of adversary parties are actually involved. Furthermore, the Supreme Court imposes a number of its own restraints upon the exercise of judicial review. It always begins with the assumption that the legislative body did not intend to violate the Constitution when it adopted the challenged statute. Therefore the burden of proof rests upon the party who questions the validity of the statute.

If the Court can possibly decide the case without ruling on the constitutionality of the statute, it prefers to do so; it comes to constitutional questions last, not first, and seeks to dispose of cases on minimal grounds. If a statute is susceptible of any reasonable interpretation that will save it, the Court will adopt that interpretation. In cases of reasonable doubt, the constitutionality of legislation will be upheld. The Court will not hold a statute invalid on such vague grounds as that it violates natural justice, or the spirit of the Constitution, or the principles of republicanism.

The Court takes a strict view of the question of who is eligible to raise constitutional questions to litigation; to be able to sue in court, a party must have a direct and substantial interest at stake. It has been held that a mere citizen and lawyer has insufficient interest to question in court the qualifications of a particular justice for his office (*Ex parte Levitt*, 1937). A mere taxpayer as such does not have sufficient interest in the U.S. treasury to attack in court the validity of a federal appropriation act (*Frothingham* v. *Mellon*, 1923). This rule, which bars federal taxpayer suits, closed the door to a possible flood of litigation that would have been most embarrasing to the government. Further, a statute may be assailed only by one who relies upon an alleged invasion of his own constitutional rights; one does not have standing to sue in behalf of others.

Finally, the thrust of judicial review is limited by the doctrine of the political, nonjusticiable question. In other words certain questions arising under the Constitution are regarded by the Court as being political in character and therefore outside the scope of judicial action. The Constitution declares in Article IV, for example, that "The United States shall guarantee to every State in this Union a Republican Form of Government." It was early decided (*Luther* v. *Borden*, 1849), however, that whether a particular state government is republican in form is for the political branches of the government (Congress and the president) to decide, not the courts. Similarly, the president's duty to see to the faithful execution of the laws is political and therefore not subject to judicial process (*Mississippi* v. *Johnson*, 1867).

Many military questions, such as the necessity for calling out the militia, plus foreign policy questions, such as whether the government has recognized a particular foreign government or international boundary or treaty, are considered political in character and therefore nonjusticiable. Some of the most unfortunate decisions of the Court have been marked by a disregard of the Court's own canons.

Writing in 1928, Charles Evans Hughes characterized three ill-starred decisions as self-inflicted wounds: the Dred Scott case, the first legal tender cases, and the income-tax cases. Each of these was in time uprooted: the first by the Civil War, the second by an overruling decision, the third by the Sixteenth Amendment to the Constitution. Each was a needlessly precipitate decision: the first because it could have been resolved on a nonconstitutional ground of state law; the second because one member of the Court, holding a decisive vote, was on the verge of retirement for disability; the third because the interests of the complainants—corporate stockholders—did not require the relief that the Court granted. It is noteworthy that judges who have been deeply sensitive to the demands on constitutional law made by a changing social order—Justice Louis D. Brandeis most conspicuously—have also been most insistent on the Court's observance of its professed canons of self-limitation.

## Symbolic Role

It has been argued with some force that the functions vested in the Supreme Court are tolerable only in a country that is basically agreed on its fundamental premises. It has been further argued that judicial review on the U.S. model would be impossible where there are deep philosophic cleavages, and that the U.S. practice is a corollary of the pragmatic American spirit. It can be said, however, that the relationship is one of interaction. The practice of judicial review, by a reflexive effect, serves to soften the edges of ideological weapons and to promote accommodations on a working basis. The Court operates in the context of specific facts; it does not so much choose between absolutes as it endeavors to reach a mediating solution; and it holds itself open for reconsideration of doctrine at a later time in the light of changed circumstances and fuller experience.

By virtue of the reasoned elaboration of its opinions in addition to the tradition of dissent, judicial review serves continually to clarify, refine, and test the large philosophic ideals that are written into the Constitution. Ideals are thus translated into working principles for a federal union under a rule of law. Beyond its specific contributions, this symbolic and pragmatic function may be regarded as the most significant contribution of the Supreme Court to the life of the country.

Judicial review of state legislation takes place with regard to such tangible factors as transportation and communication, and such political factors as national parties and presidential leadership. The chief technical instrument employed by the Court in this aspect of its work has been the constitutional commerce clause (Art. I, Sec. 8), which confers power on Congress to regulate commerce among the states. This clause has been applied from the time of Marshall to nullify state laws of taxation or regulation that discriminate against or unduly burden interstate commerce. The national market has thereby been maintained against the grosser demands of local commercial protectionism. The process has been one of accommodation, requiring in each case an appraisal of the state law in the light of local need compared with the inroad on the larger market. Marshall's Court tended to stress the national imperative, Taney's the concerns of local welfare. At no time in its history, however, has it been possible for the Court to avoid making close judgments on a pragmatic basis.

The assertion of national interest that spelled the doom of many state laws has served ultimately to vindicate national power when Congress has legislated. Beginning with the Interstate Commerce Act of 1887 and the Sherman Anti-Trust Act of 1890, Congress increasingly took over the regulation of sectors of the economy that previously were regulated ineffectively or not at all because of judicial restraints and practical inhibitions on the states.

A series of decisions, of which the child labor case in 1918 was the most conspicuous, threatened for a time to create a no-man's-land in which neither the federal nor state governments would have constitutional power to legislate effectively. The federal government was thus denied power because the objective of the law was employment practices, and the state governments were denied power because the interstate importation of articles of commerce is immune from state prohibition. Not until the overruling of the child labor case in 1941 was the federal power over commerce placed on a firm basis. Subsequently the Court sustained far-reaching applications of the commerce power by Congress, of which perhaps the most striking was the setting of maximum acreage quotas for the production of wheat, including wheat that is consumed on the farm itself.

As the commerce clause has been the chief doctrinal source of national power over the economy, the due-process and equal-protection clauses have been the principal sources of protection of persons and corporations against arbitrary or repressive acts of government. The guarantee of life, liberty, and property against deprivation without due process of law, enforceable against the states by virtue of the post-Civil War Fourteenth Amendment, has been interpreted by the Court to protect against the substance of certain legislation as well as against arbitrary procedures. Accordingly, during the first third of the twentieth century the Court invalidated important social and economic measures, including state laws setting minimum wages and maximum prices. Liberty of contract was construed in light of a laissez-faire philosophy shared by a dominant majority within the Court. Against this paralyzing judicial treatment of experimental legislation, Justices Holmes and Brandeis voiced a current of powerful dissents. Beginning in about 1940 the doctrine embodied in these dissents became the law of the land, and thereafter no significant economic legislation was found repugnant to the constitutional guarantees.

The field of civil liberties has had a markedly different history. Not until the 1920s was it established that the rights safeguarded against federal incursion by the First Amendment—freedom of speech, press, assembly, and religious exercise—are safeguarded also against action by the states, as part of the liberty guaranteed by the Fourteenth Amendment. As the Court has become more tolerant of economic controls, it has taken a more stringent view of laws that curtail the First-Amendment liberties and the procedural guarantees of the Bill of Rights. Insofar as these changing standards of judicial review have been rationalized, the justification is that the special concern of the Court is with process and structure; that political liberties are at the base of representative self-government; and that if normally the people must look to political processes for the correction of harsh or unwise legislation, the Court for that very reason must remain vigilant to strike down measures that repress the political process itself.

The guarantee of equal protection of the laws in the Fourteenth Amendment has had a development similar to the evolution of due process of law. Originally designed for the benefit of the emancipated blacks, soon utilized as a shield against social legislation, it came to serve as a barrier to racially discriminatory laws.

In a steady series of cases the Court invalidated a variety of restrictions directed at blacks: exclusion from voting in party primary elections, racial zoning, enforcement of restrictive covenants in real-estate deeds, exclusion from state-maintained unversities, and forced segregation in public schools and on public conveyances.

Race is not the only status that has been safeguarded under the equal-protection clause against invidious legislative classification. The expanded guarantee of equal protection has been extended to aliens, illegitimates, the indigent, and women. How far such protection should be the function of the judiciary, and how far it should depend on legislative action under the power of Congress to enforce the Fourteenth Amendment, is a basic question that will increasingly engage the attention of the Court as new ideals of equality are pressed for recognition.

It is hardly surprising that a tribunal exercising authority of such gravity, delicacy, and finality has frequently found itself the object of popular or partisan attack. Given the generality of the great constitutional provisions and the task of applying that document to an evolving social, economic, and political order, the Court cannot escape the responsibility of rendering judgments that provoke dissatisfaction in some quarters and for some time.

A number of the strongest presidents have been pitted at one time or another against the Court, among them Jefferson, Jackson, Lincoln, and both Roosevelts. Nevertheless, in the United States the Constitution was regarded from an early date as law of a superior order and of a more permanent character than legislative acts. Under the first state constitutions legislatures were the dominant organs of government. They abused their wide powers and helped develop a feeling that legislative authority should in some measure be curbed. Gradually the courts took on the role of declaring statutes invalid when they conflicted with constitutional provisions. Apparently the framers of the U.S. Constitution were of the opinion that it would be a function of the federal courts to preserve the powers of state and country under the Constitution. Except for a few provisions that are regarded as committed to the political organs of government, it may therefore be said that placing language in a written constitution makes such language judicially enforceable as against the legislative bodies. Whereas Parliament is the supreme lawmaker under the English system of government, in the United States the written Constitution as finally construed by the courts is supreme, restricting the powers of president and Congress and protecting the civil and political rights of the citizens.

## Jurisdiction and Procedure

For all the importance of judicial review, most of the Supreme Court's business comes to it in its appellate jurisdiction. Depending on the nature of the decision in the state or lower federal court, the route to the Supreme Court is by appeal or *certiorari*, which means "to be informed" in Latin. It is a procedure by which a higher court may call up the records of a lower court for examination. The higher court may, therefore, review questions of law or correct errors in the proceedings of lower courts and, in general, offer protection against excesses by the lower courts.

An appeal to the Supreme Court invokes its obligatory jurisdiction. A petition for *certiorari* calls on its discretionary jurisdiction. The development of this two-pronged authority reflects a response by Congress to a long struggle by the Court to cope with the volume of cases annually docketed. In 1891 a measure of relief was afforded by the Circuit Court of Appeals Act, setting up intermediate courts (of which there are eleven, in ten circuits and the District of Columbia) having final authority over appeals from federal district courts except in case of exceptional public importance. The same act put a belated end to the circuit-riding duties of Supreme Court justices.

The Judiciary Act of 1925 carried the reforms further. Initiated by the Court itself, under the sponsorship of Chief Justice William Howard Taft, the act greatly limited obligatory jurisdiction and gave the Court itself a large measure of control over its own business by classifying most types of cases under the heading of review by *certiorari*; such cases can be disposed of without full briefs or oral argument, where they do not qualify by their importance for an exercise of the Court's discretionary power of review. Members vote on each petition for *certiorari*, as in other actions. The affirmative vote of four justices suffices for the granting of *certiorari*, since at that stage the question is simply the appropriateness of the case for review. The number of cases that are filed annually in the Court exceeds four thousand. Of this total, about nine-tenths are disposed of summarily, mainly by the denial of petitions for *certiorari*.

The cases not thus disposed of are set down for oral argument after the filing of briefs. The time allowed for oral argument is limited, ordinarily to one-half hour for each side. At a conference of justices following a week of oral arguments, the cases heard are decided, and the responsibility for writing each opinion of the Court is assigned to a particular justice by the chief justice (or by the senior associate justice if the chief justice is in the minority in a case). The practice of writing dissenting opinions has been followed since the time of the Marshall Court; the first resolute dissenter was Marshall's colleague William Johnson.

Although the justices of the Supreme Court are authorized to sit in lower federal courts, ever since the elimination of their circuit function, it has been an extraordinary event for a justice to do so. This holds true at least until he retires from the Court, when he may be assigned, at his own request, to service in the lower federal courts. In addition, a justice may occasionally be called upon to act individually, in chambers, on a specific motion. Otherwise, he will perform his functions as a member of the Court.

The second tier of the federal judiciary is made up of the U.S. courts of appeals for the eleven circuits, each circuit consisting of a definite geographic area. The officers of these courts are referred to as judges rather than justices, the latter title now being reserved, in the federal system, to members of the Supreme Court. Usually the judges within each circuit sit in panels of three, but occasionally, because of the importance of the case, the entire membership of the court of appeals for a circuit will sit together. Basically, the work of the courts of appeals is to review judgments entered by the lower federal courts and, as prescribed by statute, to review decisions of administrative agencies. Like the Supreme Court, each circuit court has a clerk and, in addition, each judge has the services of a bailiff, a law clerk, and a secretary.

The trial court level is made up of about a hundred district courts, a district being a smaller geographical area within a circuit. Although the number of judges within each district varies widely, each of them usually sits individually and presides over trials or other initial aspects of the litigation process. There is a clerk and a marshal for each district court. The marshal, in addition to his other duties, is in charge of service of process (summons) and generally has the powers of a sheriff. The personal staff of each district judge ordinarily, but not necessarily, will include a law clerk, a secretary, and a bailiff. Although most of the business of the district courts is the original trial of the cases allocated to the federal courts by congressional legislation, they also function, to a limited extent, as bodies for the review of decisions of certain administrative agencies.

In this latter capacity, and in other extraordinary circumstances, the court will be made up of a circuit judge and two district court judges, sitting without a jury. When these special three-judge panels are convened, review of their decisions is directly by the Supreme Court rather than by the appropriate circuit court.

The district courts have the service of additional judicial officials. Commissioners for the district courts act as committing magistrates in criminal cases and are authorized to issue search warrants and arrest warrants. Referees in bankruptcy cases in each district act as judicial officers, subject to review by the district court judges. The trial courts may also make use of referees, masters, assessors, and others, who will hear evidence for the purpose of reporting to the court or to determine its admissibility in evidence or on depositions.

Outside the regular hierarchy of the federal courts are courts charged with the disposition of cases involving specialized subject matter. The specialized function of each court is indicated by its title. These include the court of claims, which entertains suits against the United States and which is also empowered to review judgments of the district courts in certain cases where the suit is against the United States; the court of customs and patent appeals; the customs court; and the tax court.

The right of trial by jury was guaranteed in Article III of the Constitution—but only in criminal cases. Indeed this point was repeatedly stressed by opponents of the Constitution while ratification was pending in 1787–89. The jury was a popular institution in the colonies and was widely used in both civil and criminal cases throughout the American colonial period. It was revered for its service in impeding the enforcement by colonial authorities of unpopular British laws.

Before the Constitutional Convention was held, most of the state constitutions already safeguarded the jury trial in civil as well as criminal cases. In the state conventions to ratify the Constitution, the absence of a civil jury trial guarantee was considered infinitely more objectionable than the document's failure to mention freedom of speech or press; in fact, it was principally reverence for civil jury trial that led to the popular demand for inclusion of a comprehensive Bill of Rights. The Seventh Amendment accordingly guaranteed jury trial in all common-law cases where the amount involved exceeds twenty dollars, and the Sixth Amendment reaffirmed the right of jury trial in criminal cases.

The jury system has been the subject of both enthusiastic praise and vigorous criticism. Critics propose a variety of reforms designed to improve the caliber of jury personnel and to increase the trial judge's control over the jury, by means such as the use of special-verdict procedures and the restoration of the judge's power to comment on the evidence.

The future of the jury system is not easy to predict. It has not survived on those parts of the European continent that experimented with it during the nineteenth century, and in England it is currently in decline, being virtually nonexistent in civil cases. It is still widely used, however, in both civil and criminal litigation in the United States.

# III. Checks and Balances

"The condition upon which God hath given liberty to man is eternal vigilance; which condition if he break, servitude is at once the consequence of his crime and the punishment of his guilt."

—John Philpot Curran

# 11.
# Separation at Work: Tensions and Conflicts of Tripartite Government

Tensions and conflicts between branches of the U.S. government should surprise no one, since the very concept of the separation of powers was instituted to create balance. The doctrine of judicial review must inevitably result in conflict between the legislative and the judicial branches whenever the doctrine is applied. In addition the probability of conflict between the administration and Congress is great whenever strong leadership resides in both places. The likelihood of tensions between the executive and the judiciary, however, is perhaps less self-evident, even though some of the resulting confrontations have made conspicuous history.

## Early Developments

The genius of the government that the Constitution of 1787 created, of course, is that the interbranch tensions are creative tensions and that the conflicts offer some prospect of resolution. This is nothing like the structured anarchy that prevailed under the Articles of Confederation. George Washington viewed the chaotic political condition of the United States after 1783 with frank pessimism, declaring in May 1786 that "something must be done, or the fabric must fall, for it is certainly tottering."

Washington presided over the convention called in 1787 to "render the Constitution of the Federal Government adequate to the exigencies of the Union." He wrote of his hope "that the convention may adopt no temporizing expedients, but probe the defects of the Constitution to the bottom, and provide a radical cure." The weight of his character did more than any other single force to bring the convention to an agreement and obtain ratification of the instrument afterward. "It or dis-union is before us to chuse from," he wrote in a letter published in a Boston newspaper.

When all that had been done and he had been elected and reelected president of the new country, Washington engaged with customary caution, methodical precision, and sober judgment in helping make the new government work. Every president's "honeymoon" with Congress and the public ends eventually, and Washington's was over by 1795. At that time occurred one of the earliest instances of conflict between the executive and legislative branches of government.

The treaty of commerce that Chief Justice John Jay had negotiated with Britain, which Washington signed on June 25, 1795, provoked a bitter discussion, and the House of Representatives called upon the president for the instructions and correspondence relating to the treaty. The president, who had already clashed with the Senate on foreign affairs, refused to deliver these papers, and firmly maintained his position even in the face of an acrimonious debate.

Other examples of interbranch tension followed, notably Pres. Andrew Jackson's battles with Congress over the Bank of the United States. The Bank figured in pulling and hauling between president and Congress for more than a decade. Henry Clay, who had championed a rechartered Bank in the Senate, was defeated for president by Jackson over that very issue in 1832. The Kentucky senator continued to challenge Jackson throughout his second term. He pushed through the Senate resolutions (expunged in 1837) censoring the president for removing government deposits from the Bank of the United States. He managed to prevent the confirmation of Martin Van Buren as Jackson's minister to England.

Because of his identification with the Bank issue, Clay was passed over for the Whig presidential nomination in 1840 in favor of William Henry Harrison, who won the election and died after thirty days in office. His vice-president, John Tyler, was a former Democrat and now a Whig ally of Clay, though he was a states' rights champion while Clay was a nationalist.

Tyler, so recent a convert to the Whig banner, was hardly a plausible national leader for that party. Clay moved boldly to fill the leadership vacuum and hoped to control the policies of the administration. In a special session of Congress, Clay proposed four major measures—one of them the establishment of a national bank. The contest was now joined between the nationalist senator and the states' rights president. Tyler signed two of the acts and vetoed two, including the National Banking Act. Clay declared that he would "drive the president before him" on the issue, and the Senate presented the president with a second bank bill providing for a fiscal "corporation." Tyler vetoed it, and his entire Cabinet resigned in protest (though Secretary of State Daniel Webster completed certain treaty negotiations first).

## Abraham Lincoln

Years later the Civil War occasioned serious conflicts between Pres. Abraham Lincoln and Congress—conflicts which grew even sharper as the end of the war and the start of Reconstruction approached. In the waning years of battle, Lincoln's policy for the defeated South was not clear in all its details, though he continued to believe that the main object should be to restore the "seceded states, so-called," to their "proper practical relation" with the Union as soon as possible. He possessed no fixed and uniform program for the region as a whole. As he said in the last public speech of his life (April 11, 1865), "so great peculiarities" pertained to each of the states, and "such important and sudden changes" occurred from time to time, and "so new and unprecedented" was the whole problem that "no exclusive and inflexible plan" could "safely be prescribed."

With respect to states like Louisiana and Tennessee, he continued to urge acceptance of new governments set up under his "ten percent plan" during the war. (This plan provided for the reestablishment of a state government whenever ten percent of the voting population of 1860 had taken the prescribed oath of allegiance.) With respect to states like Virginia and North Carolina, he seemed willing to use the old rebel governments temporarily as a means of transition from war to peace. He was on record as opposing the appointment of "strangers" (carpetbaggers) to govern the South. He hoped that Southerners themselves, in forming new state governments, would find some way by which whites and blacks "could gradually live themselves out of their old relations to each other, and both come out better prepared for the new." He suggested a program of education for freedmen and that the vote be given immediately to some blacks—"as, for instance, the very intelligent, and especially those who have fought gallantly in our ranks."

Lincoln, however, and the extremists of his own party stood even farther apart in early 1865 than they had a year before. Some of the Radicals were beginning to demand a period of military occupation for the South, the confiscation of planter estates and their division among the freedmen, and the transfer of political power from the planters to their former slaves. In April 1865 Lincoln began to modify his own stand in some respects and thus to narrow the gap between himself and the Radicals. He recalled the permission he had given for the assembling of the rebel legislature of Virginia, and he approved in principle—or at least did not disapprove —Secretary of War Edwin M. Stanton's scheme for the military occupation of southern states. After the Cabinet meeting of April 14, Atty. Gen. James Speed inferred that Lincoln was moving toward the Radical position. "He never seemed so near our view," Speed believed. What Lincoln's Reconstruction policy would actually have been had he lived to complete his second term can only be guessed, for he was shot that very night. What is clear is that he spent the last year of his life deeply engaged in the interdepartmental conflicts and tensions that were inevitable given a strong president, strong leadership in Congress, and important national issues.

## Andrew Johnson

Vice-Pres. Andrew Johnson inherited all Lincoln's problems and more. His differences with Congress have been examined previously. In essence they were the same as Lincoln's— variations in personal style apart. Both believed that Reconstruction policies should be set forth not by Congress but by the president; Congress believed the reverse.

First under Lincoln and later under Johnson, presidential programs of remarkable leniency were inaugurated. Lincoln's "ten percent plan" had been put into effect during the war in areas occupied by federal forces. Under a presidential proclamation of December 1863, the plan was used in Louisiana, Tennessee, Virginia, and Arkansas. It had slowly evolved from Lincoln's experiences with the border states and with military governments set up in occupied areas and from his own changing concept of the country. It was, in substance, an invitation to the Southern people to reorder their political structure and to take up their places again in the nation.

Based upon the assumption that reconstruction of a state government was exclusively an executive function and solely a political affair, the plan precipitated a bitter struggle between the President and the Radical wing of his own party in Congress. Once the Radicals had grasped the fact that Lincoln's program did not include social and economic rebuilding of the South, they began to challenge his control and direction of the machinery of Reconstruction. Their own more stringent program was embodied in the Wade-Davis Bill passed in July 1864. Lincoln, hoping to "reanimate the states" under presidential supervision before Congress reconvened, killed the Wade-Davis Bill by means of a pocket veto (an executive's indirect veto by allowing a bill to remain unsigned until after a legislature's adjournment).

When Lincoln was assassinated in April 1865, Johnson, a Southern Unionist who had been elected vice-president on the Lincoln ticket in 1864, continued Lincoln's moderate program with only minor modifications. He of course alienated the Radicals just as Lincoln had, and when Congress reconvened in December 1865, the Radicals were again prepared to challenge presidential control of Reconstruction. On the first day of the new session the struggle was begun when Congress refused to seat as newly elected members "Confederate Brigadiers" from southern states, and created the Joint Committee on Reconstruction.

The climax of this struggle between the executive and legislative branches of government was reached in the election of 1866, when both sides attempted to win popular support for their programs. Johnson's own intemperate outbursts against the opposition, coupled with such reactionary developments within the South as the rejection of the Fourteenth Amendment (except by Tennessee, which was readmitted in 1866), race riots in Memphis and New Orleans, and passage of repugnant "Black Codes" (restricting the freedom of blacks) by Johnson-supported state governments, seriously weakened the president's position and helped the Radicals win a smashing victory in the election. With what appeared to be a mandate from the voters in states that participated in the election, the Radicals in Congress abruptly took over control of the Reconstruction process from the executive.

Congressional control of the Reconstruction experiment was assured by passage (March 1867) of Reconstruction Acts that were specifically designed to undo the work of Lincoln and Johnson. As a result of these acts, the ten remaining Southern states were divided into five military districts, each commanded by a major general of the U.S. Army. These officers were to supervise the reconstruction of the states in their respective districts until such time as a new constitution could be drawn up in each state and approved by Congress. With the Southern states thus firmly in hand, the Radicals further strengthened their legislative influence by impeaching President Johnson (who escaped conviction by the margin of one vote in the Senate).

The impeachment trial was presided over with conspicuous dignity and fairness by Lincoln's designee as chief justice, Salmon P. Chase. Chase's chief defect as a statesman was an insatiable desire to become president. His willingness in 1864 to head an anti-Lincoln movement, even while serving as secretary of the treasury in Lincoln's Cabinet, verged on disloyalty and led to such "mutual embarrassment" that Lincoln accepted his resignation in June 1864. Nevertheless, several months later Lincoln, despite misgivings created by Chase's presidential ambitions, appointed him chief justice, a position that Chase held until his death in 1873.

The court in Chase's tenure came squarely to grips with unconstitutional legislation stemming from the rampant Radical Republicans controlling Congress. In *Mississippi* v. *Johnson*, 1867, and *Georgia* v. *Stanton*, 1867, Chase led the court in refusing to enjoin the president or a member of his Cabinet from enforcing the Reconstruction Acts. In the important case of *Texas* v. *White*, 1869, Chase declared secession a nullity and the federal union indissoluble. Courageous stands against the military trial of civilians (*Ex parte Milligan*, 1866) and against test oaths designed to penalize former Confederates (*Cummings* v. *Missouri*, 1867, *Ex parte Garland*, 1867) upheld traditional freedoms against excesses of Congress and military occupation forces.

The intransigence of Congress did not subside with the end of Johnson's administration. Pres. Ulysses S. Grant negotiated a treaty of annexation with Santo Domingo, which he believed offered a valuable naval base, opportunities for investment, and a possible solution to race problems. Although he forced Atty. Gen. E. R. Hoar out of his Cabinet for opposing annexation and managed to get his opponent, Sen. Charles Sumner, deposed as chairman of the Foreign Relations Committee, Grant was unable to get the treaty through.

## Grover Cleveland

Grover Cleveland in his two separate terms was embroiled in several significant conflicts with Congress. Cleveland was the first Democratic president since James Buchanan a quarter of a century earlier. Because of the brevity of his career in national politics before becoming president, Cleveland had only a limited acquaintance with leaders of his own party. He accepted literally the constitutional principle of the separation of powers and opened his first annual message to Congress (December 1885) with an affirmation of his devotion to "the partitions of power between our respective departments." This appeared to be a disavowal of presidential leadership, but it quickly became apparent that Cleveland intended to defend vigorously the prerogatives that he believed belonged to the chief executive.

During his first term (1885–89) Cleveland was confronted with a divided Congress—a Republican Senate and a Democratic House. This added to the complexities of administration, especially in the matter of appointments. Cleveland was a firm believer in a civil service based on merit rather than partisan considerations, but as the first Democratic president in a quarter of a century he was under great pressure to remove Republicans in appointive offices and to replace them with Democrats. He followed a line of compromise. In his first two years he removed the incumbents from about two-thirds of the offices subject to his control, but he scrutinized the qualifications of Democrats recommended for appointment and in a number of instances refused to abide by the recommendations of his party leaders. He thus offended both his fellow Democrats and the reformers who wished no partisan removals. Although his handling of patronage alienated some powerful Democrats, he scored a personal triumph when he persuaded Congress to repeal the obsolete Tenure of Office Act of 1867, which Republican senators had threatened to revive in order to embarrass him.

Cleveland was a conservative on all matters relating to money, and he was inflexibly opposed to wasteful expenditure of public funds. This caused him to investigate as many as possible of the hundreds of private bills passed by Congress to compensate private individuals, usually Union veterans, for claims against the federal government. In more than two hundred cases he judged these claims to be ill founded and vetoed the bills. He was the first president to use the veto power extensively to block the enactment of this type of private bill. The flurry of private pension bills had been stimulated, in part, by the growing surplus in the Treasury. In every year from 1879 to 1890 there was an excess of revenue over expenditures, a circumstance that encouraged suggestions that public funds be appropriated for a variety of purposes. The surplus also focused attention upon the tariff, which was an important source of this excess revenue. In 1883 Congress had reviewed the tariff and made numerous changes in the rates, increasing the tariff on some items and reducing it on others, without materially decreasing the revenue received.

Cleveland believed that the surplus presented a real problem. It hoarded in the Treasury money that could have been in circulation, and it encouraged reckless spending by the government. Like many other Democrats, he disliked the high protective tariff. After waiting in vain for two years for Congress to meet this issue boldly, Cleveland adopted the extraordinary tactic of devoting his entire annual message in 1887 to a discussion of this question and an appeal to lower the tariff. The House then passed a tariff bill generally conforming to Cleveland's views, but it was rejected by the Senate, and the tariff became a leading issue in the presidential campaign of 1888.

Cleveland was narrowly defeated in 1888, despite a minuscule popular plurality. In 1892 he was nominated for the third time and ousted Benjamin Harrison in a three-way race in which the third-party Populist candidate won a million of the nearly twelve million votes cast. Cleveland's second administration proved to be a stormy one. Shortly after his inauguration a financial panic struck the country, leaving in its wake one of the most serious depressions ever suffered by the United States. The public, uncritical, its temper on edge, blamed Cleveland and the Democrats for the disaster. To compound his difficulties, the President found his party in Congress drifting away from his leadership.

His first major fight involved the repeal of the Sherman Silver Purchase Act of 1890. The government had kept $346 million worth of "greenbacks" (inherited from Civil War days) in circulation and had issued, under the terms of Silver Purchase Acts, nearly $600 million in silver coin and certificates. The Treasury had accumulated over the years a gold reserve of more than $100 million to protect its currency, but in April 1893 drains on the Treasury reduced the reserve below the $100 million mark. The president, alarmed at the threat of inflation, called the Congress into a special session to repeal the Sherman Act. The House promptly passed the repealing act but the Senate refused.

The new Congress had Democratic majorities in both houses, and if it had a mandate to do anything, it was to repeal the McKinley tariff. It had no mandate whatever on the silver issue, and more than half of its Democratic members came from constituencies that favored an increase in the coinage of silver. Cleveland faced a herculean task in forcing repeal through Congress, but by the use of every power at his command he gained his objective. The Sherman Silver Purchase Act was repealed at the end of October by a bill that made no compensating provision for the coinage of silver. Cleveland had won a notable personal triumph, but in the process his party was hopelessly split and in large sections of the country he had become the most unpopular president of his generation.

The extent to which Cleveland had lost control of his party became apparent when Congress turned from silver to the tariff. The House passed a bill that would have revised tariff rates downward in accordance with the president's views. In the Senate, however, the bill was so altered that it bore little resemblence to the original measure, and on some items it imposed higher duties than the McKinley Act. It was finally passed in August 1894. Unwilling to veto the measue and risk losing badly needed revenues, the President signified his dissatisfaction with its high rates by allowing it to become a law without his signature.

## Theodore Roosevelt

When McKinley's lingering death put Theodore Roosevelt into the White House (1901), his first public announcement indicated there was to be no change from McKinley's policies. It soon became apparent, however, that the new president would not follow the same course as his predecessor. Roosevelt was worried about western demands for further control of trusts, for the regulation of railroads, and for a reduction in the tariff. He was aware that the price of inactivity might be a catastrophe for the Republicans in 1904 and defeat for himself, but he was also acutely aware that both the Senate and the House were tightly controlled by conservative Republicans who were bitterly opposed to western demands for reform. His answer to this situation was to ask for relatively little in the way of controversial legislation and to use his executive power to the full in appeasing the rising discontent.

Accordingly, Roosevelt's legislative harvest was slim. He was a past master in the art of using patronage and the influence of the White House to gain his ends, but he was also adept at compromise and was always willing to take half a loaf rather than none. His legislative achievements, therefore, never fully measured up to his promises and were apt to disappoint the most zealous of reformers. Nevertheless, in the two years he secured passage of the Pure Food and Drug Act and a bill giving the Interstate Commerce Commission effective regulatory power over railroads. To obtain the passage of both acts through a reluctant Congress, Roosevelt used his presidential power without stint. He also pushed his powers to the limit in creating public parks and national forests from federal lands. His actions in protecting coal and mineral lands and water power sites from falling into private hands, and in supporting the zealous efforts of James R. Garfield, his secretary of the Interior, and Gifford Pinchot, the chief forester, to serve the public interests angered many members of Congress.

The most effective check on Roosevelt's power came with the financial panic of 1907. As several great financial houses closed their doors, Roosevelt's conservative enemies blamed the president's continued trust-busting, his regulatory measures, and in particular his oral indictments of big business as the primary reason for the financial distress. From the autumn of 1907 Roosevelt's relations with Congress became increasingly stormy. While the presidential messages in 1907 and 1908 contained even more demands for reform, little was accomplished except for routine measures.

## Woodrow Wilson

Although Woodrow Wilson's political experience was limited to a term as governor of New Jersey, his performance in that role indicated great promise. From the first moment of his administration, beginning in 1913, Wilson made it evident that he was determined to be a strong chief executive and the real legislative leader of his party. As a professor of politics he had admired the British parliamentary system in which the prime minister was the most powerful figure in the legislative process. Wilson could not sit in Congress as the prime minister sat in Parliament, but he did the next best thing by appearing before Congress in person to read his message— the first president to do so since John Adams. He did not hesitate to use the patronage power in bargaining with members of Congress.

Like Theodore Roosevelt, he was not reluctant to appeal to the people over the heads of the lawmakers. Extremely skillful in his use of language, he couched his public speeches in a strain of idealism that had an enormous appeal for the masses. Out of power for sixteen years and disciplined by defeat, the Democrats were willing to accept, for a time at least, direction from the White House. This happy combination resulted in the passage of one of the most comprehensive legislative programs in the country's political history, including the first general reduction in tariff schedules in thirty years, and a provision for a graduated income tax made possible by the adoption of the Sixteenth Amendment.

The second important legislative triumph was the passage of the Federal Reserve Bank Act, destined to become the base of the national financial structure. The establishment of the Federal Trade Commission in 1914 provided for the use of federal powers to assure competitive conditions in trade. The Clayton Anti-Trust Act met the demands of labor by prohibiting injunctions in labor disputes unless necessary to prevent irreparable damage and by proclaiming that strikes and boycotts were not violations of federal law. The achievement of such far-flung legislation in these four fields of taxation, banking, trade, and labor practices went far toward creating a new social and economic atmosphere. But Wilson's brilliance as legislative leader and strong president were casualties of World War I and the peace treaty ending it, plus Wilson's own abhorrence of compromise, in addition to his poor health toward the end of his regime.

On July 10, 1919, President Wilson submitted to the Republican-dominated Senate the Treaty of Versailles, which included a Covenant providing for a League of Nations. Three weeks later, the Foreign Relations Committee began unprecedented open hearings on the pact, eventually advising acceptance subject to fourteen reservations. Despite prolonged debate centering on four key changes, the Senate on November 19 rejected the treaty both with and without reservations. Efforts to compromise with the White House proved futile, and on March 19, 1920, another vote on the treaty with reservations missed the required two-thirds majority by a margin of seven votes.

In large measure political factors explain this turn of events. The Republican Party's leadership did not want to hand Wilson an impressive achievement on the eve of a presidential election. Furthermore, even internationally oriented Republicans did not approve of the Covenant in its existing form, preferring to rely on moral suasion rather than on force to maintain peace. Party considerations demanded that these moderates be united with Republican irreconcilables utterly opposed to the League concept. Thus the Senate weighted down the pact with conditions unpalatable to Wilson.

Meanwhile, other factors weakened Wilson's effort to appeal to the country at large. He had alienated the vital support of political independents by harsh suppression of wartime dissent and by agreeing to a peace settlement "purple with revenge." Many liberals regarded the Covenant as a cloak for Anglo-French imperialism. Simultaneously, influential ethnic blocs, led by Irish-Americans, attacked the treaty because it either neglected national ambitions or punished their fatherlands too severely.

Sen. Henry Cabot Lodge, chairman of the Foreign Relations Committee, made full use of this growing opposition. An ardent nationalist, an intense partisan, and a master of parliamentary skill, Lodge stalled the treaty in the senatorial pipeline until sentiment could be rallied against it. He cleverly manipulated the votes of the dozen irreconcilables who held the balance of power between the moderates and the Wilsonian loyalists. Thus the anti-League diehards voted with the reservationists to attach Lodge's conditions to the treaty and then cast a "nay" ballot on the ultimate tally. It is not certain whether Lodge wanted, as he claimed, to make the treaty "safe" for America or whether his true aim was to keep his country out of the League.

Lodge, however, could not have succeeded without unwitting help from a president characteristically unable to compromise with a detested foe. Wilson was indeed willing to make certain changes in order to save the treaty; these changes, viewed in perspective, were not too far removed from Lodge's barbed demands. Wilson remained adamant on the main issues, however, and the treaty with reservations could not pass the Senate because a hard core of his docile followers voted against it on White House orders.

## Presidents and the Court

There have been, throughout the Court's history, recurrent clashes between the Court and executive authority—notably during Pres. Franklin D. Roosevelt's first two terms when a major political crisis arose over the court's invalidation of the main planks of the New Deal legislative program. While Congress was enacting new reform measures in 1935, the Supreme Court was invalidating some of the earlier New Deal laws. In January, by an 8–1 decision, it invalidated the National Industrial Recovery Act (NRA) code regulating the petroleum industry; in May it held by a 5–4 decision that the Railroad Retirement Act was unconstitutional. In addition, it held unanimously that the Frazier-Lemke Farm Bankruptcy Act of 1934 was invalid and that the NRA codes involved an unconstitutional delegation of legislative power to the president and overstretched the commerce clause of the Constitution. The NRA decision (*Schechter Poultry Corp.* v. *U.S.*) created a national sensation. President Roosevelt charged that the justices were taking a "horse-and-buggy age view" of federal regulatory power. In January 1936, in another decision of prime importance, the Court in the case of *U.S.* v. *Butler* invalidated the processing tax included in the Agricultural Adjustment Act.

President Roosevelt interpreted his landslide reelection in 1936 as an electoral mandate for continued reform. The Supreme Court, by its narrow interpretation of the commerce clause and the tax clause of the Constitution, sought to prohibit the federal government from engaging in various areas of economic regulation. By its broad interpretation of the due process clause in the Fourteenth Amendment, it was also prohibiting state regulation. Consequently, Roosevelt set out to change the membership of the Court. Without informing congressional leaders in advance, the President in February 1937 sent Congress a message proposing a reorganization of the court system that would give him the power to appoint one new justice for each justice who was seventy years of age or older, not exceeding six new justices in all. Some New Dealers and a few liberal Republicans in Congress supported the President's proposal, but a strong coalition of Republicans and conservative Democrats fought against the "court-packing plan," as it was called. They had behind them strong public support. To many Roosevelt supporters the court plan smacked of the methods of European dictators; they feared it would upset the system of checks and balances.

Meanwhile, the Court itself in a new series of decisions began upholding as constitutional certain measures involving both state and federal economic regulation. In March 1937 it upheld a state minimum wage law for women (*West Coast Hotel Co.* v. *Parrish*); in April it approved the Wagner Labor Relations Act (*Jones and Laughlin Steel Corp.* v. *NLRB*); and in May it held the Social Security Act to be constitutional (*Steward Machine Co.* v. *Davis*). Some employers had been openly violating these laws in the expectation that the Supreme Court would invalidate them. In each of these decisions the five men comprising the liberal and moderate wing of the Court voted in the affirmative, and the four more conservative justices dissented. These decisions, paving the way for extensive revision of constitutional law and governmental regulation of the economy, made the reorganization plan unnecessary. The Senate defeated it in July 1937 by a vote of 70–22. President Roosevelt had suffered a stinging political defeat, even though he no longer had to fear that the Court would block his program. Beginning in the summer of 1937 there were rapid changes in the Court as older members resigned or died; by 1942 every member of the Court except Harlan Fiske Stone and Owen J. Roberts was a Roosevelt appointee. The changing majorities on the Supreme Court after 1937 in fact extended a general presumption of constitutionality to New Deal legislation; only a handful of measures initiated by the national administration, generally of minor significance, were thereafter invalidated by the court.

No consistently strong president came in Roosevelt's wake until Lyndon B. Johnson, a canny Texan, consummate politician, and veteran majority leader in the Senate. Johnson, seizing every emotional and political advantage from John F. Kennedy's assassination (1963), effected an authentic revolution in government's role in American life. His legislative accomplishments made commonplace certain moves not previously dared by Congress, including federal aid to every aspect of public education and even to many aspects of private and parochial education. His administration revolutionized health care as well and realized progress in civil rights and race relations only dreamed of by earlier Abolitionists.

Then Johnson ran afoul of a current in public opinion that he had missed: the depth and intensity of American popular hatred of the escalation of the Vietnam War, which he had inherited. Prudently he decided not to seek reelection in 1968. His decision to step back from the test that would have toppled him forestalled a conflict with Congress, and possibly the Court, that might well have been historic.

# 12.
# Governing the States

In 1776 the thirteen British colonies in America proclaimed themselves to be independent states, and in 1781, under the Articles of Confederation, they formed a "perpetual Union." The perpetuity of the Union was not assured, however, for the Articles that established that "firm league of friendship" provided also that each state should retain its "sovereignty, freedom and independence"; in the years following, the states showed a strong disposition to exercise the sovereignty retained. The federal Constitution, drafted in 1787 and put into effect two years later, established a stronger national government—the "more perfect" Union that was needed. The Constitution made no reference to the troublesome question of sovereignty, leaving that issue to be disposed of in time—as it turned out, to be denied to the states by the Civil War.

## The Two Systems

The federal Constitution divides the powers of government between the national (commonly called federal) government and the states. The federal government has those powers that are delegated to it by the Constitution; in addition, it has the authority to make all laws that may be "necessary and proper" to implement the powers so delegated. The delegated powers are not numerous, but they are fundamental, including those to make war, to conduct foreign relations, to regulate interstate and foreign commerce, and, of course, to levy taxes. The last-named power may be exercised to pay and provide not only for the common defense but also for the general welfare. Federal power has been extended by constitutional amendments, but it has been expanded much more significantly by the liberal use that Congress has made of the "necessary and proper" clause of the Constitution and by the judicial sanction of such use.

In many areas of government responsibility, federal power and influence have been extended through a system of grants-in-aid to the states and through them to the local governments. The basic features of the system are that Congress, acting under its authority to appropriate money for the general welfare or under some other specific authorization such as education, highway, or public welfare laws, makes funds available to the states for a particular purpose, on condition that the states make matching appropriations for the same purpose and meet a standard set by Congress for the manner in which the federal-state funds shall be spent. Use of grants-in-aid expanded rapidly after the middle of the twentieth century, both in the number of projects supported and in funds appropriated for them. After the 1960s categorical grants to the states were largely abandoned in favor of a "revenue sharing" plan, returning to state and local governments a small, lump-sum share of the national revenue, leaving those governments independent to choose the purposes for which the money might be used.

The states retain all the powers not conferred upon the federal government by the Constitution and not prohibited by it to the states. The powers of the states are thus residual. They must be determined in large part by a process of subtraction. Naturally no precise result can be obtained when the powers to be subtracted are based on broad implications and are not definitely determined. The important national powers with respect to interstate commerce, taxation, treaties, post offices and post roads, and maritime jurisdiction have been construed broadly, almost without exception.

The U.S. Supreme Court has long been engaged in determining the line between national and state power. This is a continuing judicial duty in a federal system, for it is almost impossible to draw any definite or permanent line between national and state jurisdiction. The steamboat and the railroad, the telegraph and the telephone, the radio and television, and the airplane—all have been potent factors in the development of national authority. Railroads originally came under state regulation but later fell almost completely under national control. The so-called antitrust movement began in the states, but after the Sherman Anti-Trust Act of 1890 and the creation of the Federal Trade Commission in 1914, restrictive commercial practices came largely under national supervision. The broad and flexible powers of the federal authority are capable under the Constitution of further expansion and adaptation as new needs develop in the wake of economic, social, and technological change.

Historian James Bryce (later Lord Bryce) wrote in the 11th edition of *Encyclopædia Britannica* (1910–11) that "An American may through a long life never be reminded of the Federal government, except when he votes in Federal elections (once in every two years), lodges a complaint against the post office, or is required to pay duties of customs or excise." Obviously, the federal impact on the citizen's daily life has increased vastly since that time. Still, examples of state power exist on every hand. The United States has a limited criminal code, but the great body of criminal law is incorporated within state legal codes. The laws of contracts, torts, negotiable instruments, sales, and many others closely related to business are all state laws. Property laws are within the special province of the states, and so are those respecting wills and inheritance. Marriage, divorce, and domestic relations fall within the jurisdiction of the states. The states determine who may vote, subject to the limitations set forth in the Constitution of the United States or in the various amendments to that document. Practically all of the laws relating to political parties and elections are acts of state legislatures. Local governments are established and controlled by the states. Public education is a leading state function. As Bryce observed in the late nineteenth century:

> *The State, or local authority constituted by the State statutes, registers his birth, appoints his guardian, pays for his schooling, gives him a share in the estate of his father deceased, licenses him when he enters a trade (if it be one needing a license), marries him, divorces him, entertains civil actions against him, declares him bankrupt, hangs him for murder. The police that guard his house, the local boards which look after the poor, control highways, impose water rates, manage schools—all these derive their legal powers from his State alone.*

But attention should be called to the fact that developments after 1933 have greatly increased the importance of the national government, not only in the functions that it performs, but also in its influence over state governments. Unemployment compensation is theoretically under state control, for example, but in fact federal control over state action is maintained through a tax offset system by which a state is allowed to recapture ninety percent of a federal tax if the state complies with national law. A broad construction of federal power to regulate "commerce . . . among the several states" has brought about federal control over labor disputes and over wages and hours of labor in cases where a substantial part of the commodities in question are involved in interstate traffic in one way or another. Through the same power the national government has come to determine the planting acreage of crops and the conditions and prices in the marketing of milk. Through the enormous funds spent on public welfare programs, the government has also established a substantial role for itself in the area of social services.

Maintaining state power depends upon more efficient conduct of those governments and more effective cooperation among the states concerning mutual problems. The field of insurance regulation was held in 1944 to be subject to control by Congress as interstate commerce; Congress, however, elected to leave control to the states, and the continuation of such control will most probably depend upon the efficiency and uniformity of state regulation.

Throughout the territory of each state two governments operate—the nation and the state—each with its administrative and judicial organizations for the enforcement of its own laws. Federal revenues are collected through officers controlled from Washington; state revenues are collected by independent state and local officers. Taxes levied by the two are in some cases similar in character. The country and almost all states impose income taxes, but their administration is independent. Violations of state law are tried and punished in state courts, violations of national law in separate federal courts. A decision by the U.S. Supreme Court in 1945, however, made violation of a state law by a state officer punishable in federal courts in cases where the offense is violative of due process of law under the Fourteenth Amendment. In some cases the laws of both governments are directed to the same purpose and are substantially identical. The constitutions of both systems forbid that a person be twice put in jeopardy for the same offense, but in legal theory the two governments are so distinct that one act, forbidden by substantially identical laws of each, may in fact be punished by each as a separate offense.

The reasons for this sharp distinction between the two governments are historical. Articles of Confederation sought to act through the governments of the several states and not directly upon the citizens of those states. Government under these Articles failed because each state finally determined for itself whether it would enforce the policies of Congress. In the Constitution, the founding fathers might have sought to use the states as agencies for the enforcement of national law, as is largely done under the federal system of Switzerland; but under the historical circumstances it was natural to build up an independent federal administrative and judicial system. This system has steadily grown with the expansion of national activities.

For many years it was the established principle in the United States that the exercise of independent powers by the nation and the state forbade either government to tax the employees or securities of the other. This principle, which was based on the theory that "the power to tax is the power to destroy," was later largely replaced by the principle that each government may without discrimination tax the income of employees of the other. Moreover, the Supreme Court expressed the view that the national government may enter upon an enterprise personal in nature and forbid state taxation thereon, but that a similar state enterprise may be taxed by the national government.

State governments in the United States have a number of common characteristics. Each state is legally the equal of every other state in the federal system. Each controls the organization of its own state and local governments. Each has a written constitution providing for three branches of government, with a legislature of two houses (with one exception) elected by popular vote and a popularly elected governor as head of its executive branch. Each state has a judicial system not essentially dissimilar in external organization from that of the other states. Each state has created local governing areas for the performance of certain functions.

Superficially, all the state governments appear to be more or less alike and appear to be doing the same things. The constant shifts of population have prevented the development of sharp differences in governmental organization. Furthermore, from one state to another there has been considerable copying of political and legal institutions. Each state is distinguished from other states, however, not only in size and population but also in location, climatic conditions, and resources; these differences are indeed reflected in the political and governmental organization of the individual states.

## State Constitutions

The state constitutions in force vary a great deal in length and in content. Some were drawn up in an earlier period, and some bear recent dates. The constitution of Vermont, adopted in 1793, required fewer than 5,000 words; the Louisiana constitution of 1921, more than 200,000. The constitutions of Oklahoma, California, and a number of other states are highly detailed. Massachusetts boasts that it is governed by the constitution of 1780, but this constitution has been altered in form by so many amendments that it would hardly be recognized by its original framers. By amendment or by adoption of new documents, the states have attempted to readjust their institutions to meet changing needs. The national Constitution has proved a model for much of the development of state constitutional history, particularly with reference to the establishment of three coordinate branches of government.

In most of the states the constitutions establish the organizational plan for the three departments of government in some detail. They contain elaborate declarations or bills of rights, and most of then contain provisions regarding the organization of local government. Limitations on the power of state legislatures have multiplied through the years. Unfortunately, the authors of constitutions are inclined to include in these documents provisions regarding such matters as the salaries of state officials and the location of state institutions. Such elaboration of detail makes frequent amendment necessary, a process that is in almost continuous operation in a number of states.

State constitutions provide for four methods of change: constitutional convention; legislative proposal of amendments; proposal by popular initiative petition; and constitutional commission. All but twelve of the state constitutions expressly provide for constitutional conventions; in these twelve it is recognized as proper to employ such conventions for constitutional change. Ordinarily conventions assemble as a result of popular vote and submit their recommendations for popular approval.

Proposals of constitutional amendment may be made by the legislatures in all states. Methods of amendment through legislative proposal differ, but in all states except Delaware a legislative proposal of amendment must be submitted to and approved by popular vote before it becomes effective. Details of the amending process vary. In some states, as California, Louisiana, and New York, the adoption of amendments through legislative proposal is relatively easy; in others, such as Minnesota, the constitution is difficult or substantially impossible to amend.

The proposal of constitutional amendments through popular initiative petition, followed by popular vote, is a fairly late development, but this plan has been adopted by fourteen states. Among these states there is varying ease or difficulty in employing the initiative plan of amendment. In Oregon and four other states it is as easy to amend the constitution through initiative petition and popular vote as it is to enact a statute through the same devices. Where the plan of popular initiative has been adopted, it has merely been added to the two already existing devices of constitutional convention and proposal by legisltative action.

Except in Florida, constitutional commissions are created by statute, legislative resolution, or executive order, and their recommendations for constitutional revision are submitted to the legislatures for further action. The Florida constitution expressly provides for the creation of a constitutional revision commission, and its recommendations are not subject to legislative approval.

## Legislatures

In all the states except Nebraska, legislative power is exercised by a body composed of two houses. A plan for a unicameral legislature was first adopted by Nebraska in 1934, and it went into effect in 1937. The Nebraska legislature is composed of a single chamber of forty-nine members elected on a nonpartisan basis. In all the states with a bicameral legislature, the smaller of the two houses is called the senate. All but eight of the states call their larger house a house of representatives, and the eight have such varying titles as assembly, general assembly, and house of delegates. More than half of the states use the name *legislature* to designate the two houses together; nineteen use *general assembly*, and three use *legislative assembly*. Massachusetts and New Hampshire use the term *general court*, which was first employed in the colonial charter. In view of the fact that the legislative bodies have somewhat varying names in several states, it has been customary to refer to the larger of the two as the lower house and to the smaller as the upper house.

To a large extent the exact number of members of the two houses, or of one of the two houses, is left to legislative determination, subject to constitutional restrictions. The size of the two houses varies a good deal from one state to another. The Minnesota senate is the largest, with sixty-seven members, while Alaska and Nevada each have only twenty.

The size of the lower house ranges from forty in Alaska and Nevada to four hundred in New Hampshire. Membership of the lower houses is especially large in several New England states because of the system of town representation.

In a majority of states, senators are elected for four years and representatives for two. In some states, one-half the members of the senate are elected every two years so that the senate has continuous membership, as contrasted with the house, whose membership is chosen as a whole at each election. In Alabama, Louisiana, Maryland, and Mississippi, however, four-year terms have been provided for members of both houses, and a number of states have a two-year term for members of both houses.

In some states financial measures must originate in the lower house, and in most states the senate has certain powers with respect to confirmation of executive appointments. The provisions for impeachment of public officers also ordinarily prescribe that charges be brought by the lower house and that the officer be tried by the senate. On the whole, however, it may be said that from the standpoint of legislation the two houses of state legislatures have equal powers and do not represent basically different points of view.

Distinctions that once existed in many states have largely dissolved, although in a number of states differences in territorial representation have emerged. In the earlier state governments the substantially equal representation of local areas was not grossly unfair, because of the absence of great inequalities in their population. With the growing urbanization of the country and the concentration of population in cities, however, rural areas soon came to be grossly overrepresented in the state legislatures. The cities and, increasingly after World War II, the suburbs had far less representation than their share of the population entitled them to.

This inequity stimulated agitation for the reapportionment of state legislatures so as to equalize representation upon the principle of "one man, one vote." In 1962 the U.S. Supreme Court in a landmark decision, *Baker* v. *Carr*, ruled that urban residents in Tennessee were being denied "equal protection of the laws" by the failure of the state legislature to reapportion itself. This decision quickly led to suits and challenges in other states designed to eliminate rural overrepresentation in legislative bodies. As a result *Baker* v. *Carr* led to the reapportionment of both houses of many state legislatures, for the courts did not accept the argument that representation in one legislative body of a state must be based on area rather than population.

Members of state legislatures are chosen from local districts by popular vote. Proportional representation has been proposed but not adopted although in municipal elections it is sometimes used. All states follow the plan under which a candidate is elected who receives a plurality of the votes in his district. Under the first state constitutions provision was generally made for the annual election of members of legislative bodies and for annual legislative sessions. Frequent and regular sessions of the legislature were deemed essential safeguards of popular rights and were at that time thought sufficient. By the second half of the twentieth century, however, most state legislative bodies met in January of odd-numbered years. In the early 1970s this trend was reversed and the majority of the legislatures met in annual sessions. Constitutions ordinarily prescribe the number of days for which the session may continue. Biennial sessions are held in even years in Kentucky. Alabama and Mississippi experimented for a time with quadrennial sessions.

As is the case with the national Congress, the work of state legislatures is largely done through committees. A number of states have sought to devise a more orderly and reliable legislative pattern through the creation of legislative councils composed of representatives of the two houses, such councils to remain continuously in existence and to consider important matters of legislation with the aid of a permanent body of experts. An efficient and influential governor can exercise a distinct leadership in important matters of constructive legislation, but over a great many legislative enactments his influence is more likely to be negative than affirmative.

The governor has a veto power over legislation in all states except North Carolina; in most states, however, the veto can be overcome by a two-thirds vote of the legislature, although only a three-fifths vote is required in some states and a bare majority in others. There has also been a definite increase in the governor's control over appropriations, through the vesting in him of a power to veto separate items in appropriation bills. Such a power now exists in most states. A tendency has appeared in some states to extend the governor's veto power still further. The Washington and South Carolina constitutions confer upon the governor the power to veto any item or section of any bill presented to him, and a similar power exists in Alabama.

The veto power is not an idle weapon in the governor's hands. Its use and effectiveness depend upon several factors —the extent of the governor's constitutional power, the personality of the governor, and the political agreement or disagreement at the time between the governor and the two houses. Even where it is not exercised, the governor can exert influence over legislation by the threat of its use.

## Executives

In the first state constitutions the executive department was subordinate to the legislature. In most states the governor and certain other state officers were chosen by the legislature; an executive council, however, also chosen by the legislature, was placed on guard to prevent executive usurpation. Such an attitude toward the governor was natural in 1776 when unpleasant memories of royal governors was strong; but the governor's power almost immediately began to grow. New York in 1777 made its governor popularly elective, though at the time it created two councils—the council of revision and the council of appointments—to share with the governor the powers of veto and of appointment to office. Massachusetts (1780) and New Hampshire (1784) followed with the plan of popular election. Executive councils remain in Massachusetts, Maine, and New Hampshire.

In all states the governor became a popularly elected officer and hence independent of legislative dominance. Other state officers also became popularly elective, though some are still chosen by state legislatures. Until late in the nineteenth century the functions of state government were few and were chiefly conducted by a small group of popularly elected officers. As new needs developed, it has become increasingly common for major state administrators to be appointed rather than elected. In the late 1970s more than half of all state executives were appointed by the governor, slightly less than a third were elected, and the rest were picked by boards or the state legislature.

The statutory creation of new offices to be filled by the governor has increased his power, but without reference to any efficient supervision by the governor. Some states have as many as two hundred independent officers, most if not all of whom are appointed by the governor, but over whom it is physically impossible for the governor to exercise effective control. A later movement has sought to organize executive functions into a small group of departments, each under a director appointed by and responsible to the governor. Several states have established cabinets. One of the chief difficulties in building up an effective state executive system is that the governors of a few states are elected for terms of only two years. In most states, however, the term is four.

There has, indeed, been an increase in state executive power and leadership, but such leadership is often greatly handicapped by the fact that the majorities of one or both houses of the state legislature may be politically opposed to the governor. This lack of political harmony is more common in the states than in the national government.

## Courts

In the judicial field, states generally have courts of three main types:

1. Justices of the peace have a limited and inferior jurisdiction in both civil and criminal cases. Justices of the peace are ordinarily elected from towns or townships or from districts created for the purpose within the county. The jurisdiction of justices of the peace is strictly limited by statute, and their courts are not courts of record. Appeals are allowed from their actions to a court of general trial jurisdiction, and ordinarily the trial in the higher court is a trial *de novo* (from the beginning). The system of justices of the peace paid on a fee basis has not proved satisfactory and has been replaced in larger communities. In 1961 Connecticut abandoned its local courts altogether and substituted a system of district courts with legally trained, full-time judges.

2. In all states there are courts of general trial jurisdiction, known as superior courts, district courts, circuit courts, and in some states by a still different name. The court of general trial jurisdiction ordinarily has general authority to try all cases in law and equity. Five states still retain the old English plan of separate courts for the trial of cases at law and in equity, but most of the states have abolished this distinction. In some states—as in Arizona, California, and Ohio—the court of general trial jurisdiction is organized upon a county basis, and there is a separate court for each county. The more common plan, however, is to have the court of general trial jurisdiction go on circuit from one county to another, at least in the smaller counties of the state.

3. Each state has a court of review, the function of which is chiefly that of hearing appeals from the courts of general trial jurisdiction. This court is ordinarily termed the supreme

court; in Kentucky, Maryland, and New York it is called the court of appeals, and slightly different names are used in several other states. The highest court is usually given some original jurisdiction, but ordinarily this jurisdiction is small and its use is strictly limited by the court itself in order that time may be available to hear appeals from other courts.

Once these three branches of the judiciary are established, state judicial organization becomes to a large extent a mass of diversity. In many larger communities a municipal court has been organized that not only replaces justices of the peace but is granted a more extended jurisdiction. In a number of states there is also a so-called county court, with limited civil and criminal jurisdiction and usually also a fairly large authority over rather distinctly administrative matters, such as county affairs, elections, and charities. Where county courts exist independently of the court of general trial jurisdiction, they are often vested with authority in probate matters.

There are in addition other types of trial courts with special jurisdiction. Every large community has a juvenile court, and separate probate courts are not uncommon. Other specialized courts, such as domestic relations courts, morals courts, boys' courts, speeders' courts, and small-claims courts, have been established in many larger communities, often as branches of a municipal court. In some cases there are separately organized criminal courts, although ordinarily criminal jurisdiction is exercised by the courts of general trial jurisdiction. In all states the prosecution of criminal offenses is by and in the name of the state and is conducted by prosecuting attorneys, who are usually elected by the voters of the county. Under a decision by the Supreme Court in 1963, *Gideon* v. *Wainwright,* the state is required to furnish counsel for indigent defendants in all serious criminal trials.

The state judicial organization has placed great emphasis upon appeals from lower to higher courts. No case of any importance is regarded as finally settled until it has been taken to the highest court. Increased complexity of appellate court organization has resulted from the growing number of appeals to be heard. The increased mass of appellate work is handled in three ways: (1) by increasing the number of judges of state supreme courts; (2) by authorizing such courts to sit in sections; and (3) by creating intermediate appellate courts, standing midway between the trial courts of general jurisdiction and the highest court.

There are four methods of selecting judges throughout the United States: (1) in a majority of states judges are elected by the people; (2) in four states judges are elected by the legislature, and in one they are appointed by the legislature upon the nomination of the governor; (3) in six states the highest judges are appointed by the governor, subject to confirmation by the governor's council in Maine, Massachusetts, and New Hampshire, and to confirmation by the senate in Delaware, New Jersey, and Hawaii; (4) in eleven states the governor initially appoints the highest judges, who run on their records for retention in office. Certain inferior judges in other states are also appointed by the governor.

A 1934 California plan allows justices of the supreme court and of courts of appeal to become candidates for succession to office at the ends of their terms. If not, the governor nominates a suitable alternate, subject to confirmation by a special commission. In either case, under this plan a candidate is not opposed, but an election determines whether he shall become or remain a judge. By popular vote in any county the same plan may be adopted for the superior court.

In 1940 Missouri adopted a plan similar to that of California with respect to judges of the supreme court, the courts of appeal, and the circuit and probate courts in the city of St. Louis and Jackson County. Modifications of the Missouri plan were adopted by several other states. The Alaska constitution provides for the appointment of supreme, superior, and district court judges by the governor from nominations made by a judicial council. The judges are approved or rejected on a nonpartisan ballot at the first general election held three years after an appointment.

A major problem in judicial administration is the existence of crowded dockets (lists of legal cases to be tried). In some area this has assumed near astronomical proportions. In New York alone, more than one million civil and criminal disputes are brought before the state's judicial benches each year. This congestion has introduced great pressure for more efficient procedures in the state court systems.

## Interstate Relations

The national government was created by a small number of states that served, in effect, as creators of the country. States as units in a federal system were naturally more important when their number was only thirteen. The influence of increased numbers comes into perspective when it is realized that twenty-four of the additional states were created wholly out of territory acquired later by the United States and never were a part of the original thirteen states. These new states, forming more than half of the area of the country, are in a very real sense creatures rather than creators of the national government. With the increased importance of interstate relations, state boundaries largely became artificial lines, and national consciousness—strengthened by the Civil War— became politically dominant, especially since general state elections are usually held the same day as national ones.

Yet, though the states have come to be less important as political units in a federal system and have lost all status in international affairs, the increasing complexity of social and economic needs has brought them a heavier burden of governmental responsibility than ever before.

Within two decades after 1950, the cost of state government increased about fivefold and, despite the numerous and often generous federal-aid programs, a number of states had difficulties in financing the cost of new services. In considerable measure, however, such difficulties stemmed from the extreme reluctance of many legislators, particularly rural ones, to increase tax rates or to produce additional revenues through such means as abolishing property tax exemptions for certain interest groups or adopting a state income tax.

Many states proved slow to tackle the responsibilities imposed by modern developments, and hardly any states dealt effectively with the great metropolitan issues and crises. Active federal participation became necessary on fronts that were formerly almost entirely reserved to the states. But the pervasive activities of the national government did not retard state efforts. On the contrary, federal participation, often in the form of financial grants that states had to match in part, stimulated the states to greater exertion. In any case, after World War II the states greatly expanded their functions and increased their budgets, particularly for highways, education, health, and welfare; acting alone or in cooperation with the national government, they significantly strengthened their performance as vital units of government.

Authority for the states to cooperate with each other in regional compacts is contained in Article I, Section 10, of the U.S. Constitution, which provides that "No State shall, without the Consent of the Congress, . . . enter into any Agreement or Compact with another State, or with a foreign Power, . . ." The history of such compacts, in fact, predates the

Constitution by well over a hundred years. Several agreements of this kind were concluded during the colonial period and under the Articles of Confederation, from which the present compact clause was derived.

The compact is a formal contractual agreement between or among states that takes precedence over ordinary statute, usually receives congressional consent, and is enforceable before the U.S. Supreme Court. While the exact wording of the compact clause in the Constitution would indicate that congressional consent must always be obtained, judicial construction has modified this provision to some extent in *Virginia* v. *Tennessee*, 1893. Since that time the Court has held that consent may be implied where subsequent acts of Congress indicate recognition of action taken under provisions of the compact. In the same decision the Court added that only those agreements that affect the political balance of power within the federal system must have congressional consent.

Prior to the twentieth century the interstate compact was used infrequently, for such limited purposes as the determination of boundary lines and criminal jurisdiction over boundary waters. In 1921 creation of the Port of New York Authority established by compact the first joint administrative agency of a continuing nature. One year later the Colorado River compact, providing for allocation of waters among the upper and lower basin states, marked the first use of a compact to meet common problems on a regional basis. It also marked the beginning of a series of water allocation compacts in western states. With the formation in the mid-1930s of the Interstate Compact to Conserve Oil and Gas, providing for membership of all oil-producing states, the use of the compact transcended the regional level. The Interstate Compact for the Supervision of Parolees and Probationers, also drafted in the 1930s, sought and eventually achieved the cooperation of all the states in a joint administrative operation. Since that time the compact device has been used increasingly on a regional and national basis to provide interstate cooperation in a variety of fields including conservation, control and use of natural resources, environmental protection and antipollution efforts, provision of welfare and correctional facilities, education, law enforcement, mental health, and civil defense.

Influenced by the same reform pressures that brought about the Budget and Accounting Act, state and municipal governments also adopted budget systems. In the early 1970s all fifty states had budget systems, forty-six of them with an executive budget prepared by the governor and four with budget preparation committed to a board. In most states the legislative body had unlimited power to change the budget, except for possible constitutional restraints on the taxing or borrowing power; in four states the legislature's flexibility was more limited. Since many state legislatures met only once in each two-year period, twenty-four states had biennial budgets. In the twenty-six states where there were annual sessions of the legislature, the budgets were annual.

## Regulatory Powers

Although it is more conspicuous on the federal level, the states still retain and exercise considerable regulatory power in many areas. In the landmark case of *Gibbons* v. *Ogden,* 1824, Chief Justice John Marshall raised, but did not decide, the question whether the grant to Congress of power to regulate commerce among the states did not necessarily exclude the states from exercising like power. The later case of *Cooley* v. *Board of Wardens,* 1851, decided the issue in a manner that was thereafter uniformly followed. Some subjects are national in nature and thus demand a single uniform system of regulation. Concerning these, the power of Congress is exclusive. With other subjects, conditions differ from state to state, and in these cases diversity rather than uniformity is desirable; here the states, in the absence of pertinent federal legislation, have the power of regulation. On this ground the Court sustained a Pennsylvania law requiring foreign ships to engage a local pilot while in the port of Philadelphia. The test permits no easy or automatic application, since in essence it calls for striking a balance between national and state interests.

Participation in interstate commerce, however, is a federal and not a local right, and statutes requiring state licenses to engage therein are invalid. In general a state may prohibit a corporation not incorporated or licensed by it from doing business within its borders. But this prohibition cannot apply when the corporation is engaged in interstate commerce, and a state may not insulate any portion of its own intrastate commerce from interstate competition. For example, a state statute was held invalid that forbade natural gas producers in that state to pipe their product into other states until the needs of local consumers had been satisfied.

The regulation of rates for transportation from, to, and

through several states is obviously a matter requiring exclusive national control. There has been considerable litigation on the question whether the particular fixed rates involve interstate or intrastate transactions. State regulations of interstate commerce designed to protect the personal safety of citizens, or to secure adequate service, have been sustained. The courts have also upheld the state laws requiring railroads at highway crossing to check the speed of their trains, maintain watchmen, or eliminate grade crossings. In all these respects, however, if the regulation in question is found to hamper or burden the interstate commerce function of the railroad unreasonably, it becomes invalid.

About forty states have some requirement for registering each individual issuance of securities (stocks and bonds). Most states permit nonexempt securities—usually those of well-established companies traded on a national exchange or already registered under federal law—to be registered by mere notification to the state agency. Otherwise, securities must be the subject of a detailed registration statement disclosing the history and business of the issuer; names, addresses, and compensation of officers, directors, and large shareholders; underwriting and promotional arrangements; and other information by which the security may be evaluated. Financial statements and the principal corporate documents governing legal organization and structure must be furnished to the state along with the registration statement.

Many states also regulate the character and content of any prospectus or other advertising material used to solicit sales. Among the practices at which these provisions have been aimed has been the transfer of property—such as mining claims, patents, and other undeveloped assets—of speculative, unproved, or fictitious value, for securities having a face or market value equal to the inflated value of the assets. Such securities, sometimes called watered stocks because not backed by solid asset value, have then been sold to the public without adequate disclosure of the background.

Many states undertake no more than a full disclosure, on the theory that the government interest is limited to protecting investors against purchasing securities that they have no opportunity to evaluate. A few states, notably California, give the securities commissioner or other agencies power to prohibit the sale of securities deemed by the commission to be unfair or inequitable. These states usually issue rules indicating what promotional arrangements, in the form of compensation, share options, or bonuses, will be considered so unduly favorable to the promoters and unfair to the public as to preclude sales within the state or require protective orders, such as holding promoters' shares in escrow (safe keeping by a third person) until the company is established.

In 1956 a Uniform Securities Act containing all three types of state securities regulation was proposed by the National Conference of Commissioners on Uniform State Laws. It is a disclosure-type proposal and includes provisions whereby state regulations may be more closely coordinated with federal registration procedures. Thirty-two states had adopted statutes modeled substantially after the Uniform Act by 1978. State regulation is important in covering foods and drugs that fall outside the scope of the Federal Food, Drug, and Cosmetic Act because of the act's limitation to interstate commerce. The enactment of safety legislation has been contemporaneous with the passage of workmen's compensation acts and public health laws. States at an early date required inspections of steam-power boilers. Mine safety has been a subject for legislation in coal, ore, and mineral-producing states.

Before workmen's compensation acts were securely established as constitutional (around 1920), most state safety acts relied chiefly upon inspection, with indirect enforcement through civil litigation in damage suits brought by injured workmen. After 1920, when damage suits all but ceased because most workmen were limited to compensation claims, the chief mode of enforcement shifted to administrative boards with power to seek injunctions and to make rules, investigations, and reports. In a few states, such as Washington, educational standards of safety, as well as rules dealing with safe working conditions, were in the early 1960s issued by the supervisor of safety. Statutes that provide for apprenticeship systems, limit the hours of work, or require rest periods may be classified as safety laws because of their bearing on accident prevention. The constitutionality of safety laws in the second half of the twentieth century has usually been upheld unless there has been a showing of arbitrary action in a particular situation, and such regulations typically are enforced by inspection plus criminal or administrative sanctions. In additional to laws pertaining to industrial safety are statutes concerning regulation of traffic; inspection of theaters, schools, and other public places, plus highways and sidewalks, public carriers, and bathing beaches; and fire prevention. It should also be noted that collective bargaining agreements frequently contain provisions that have a bearing on industrial safety and that joint committees of management and employees often cooperate in formulating such policies and rules.

As early as 1877 the U.S. Supreme Court, in *Munn* v. *Illinois,* upheld the validity of an 1871 Illinois statute fixing maximum rates for storing grain in elevators. Chief Justice Morrison Waite, upholding the statute, noted the importance of the grain trade and the strategic position of grain elevators, which stand "in the very 'gateway of commerce,' and take toll from all who pass." The first regulatory commissions, generally those created prior to 1870, were largely advisory bodies and their chief concern was with the railroads. They made recommendations to state legislatures and railroad managements, appraised property taken by the railroads under the right of eminent domain, enforced safety standards, and generally served as fact-finding bodies. However, they had no control over rates. From 1870 to 1907, the first "mandatory" commissions developed as a result of the Granger movement. In 1871 Illinois passed a statute establishing the initial commission; similar statutes were enacted by Minnesota (1871), Iowa and Wisconsin (1874), and Georgia (1879). Finally in 1887 Congress established the first such federal agency, the Interstate Commerce Commission, to regulate the railroads. Most of the state regulatory laws had been designed to place a ceiling on railroad rates, either prescribing the maximum to be administered by the commissions or leaving their determination to the commissions.

Modern commission regulation began in 1907 with the creation of two powerful bodies by New York (under the leadership of Gov. Charles Evans Hughes) and Wisconsin (at the urging of Sen. Robert M. La Follette). In both states the legislatures extended the regulatory powers of the commissions to other utilities: railroad, gas, light, power, telephone, and telegraph companies. Both commissions, moreover, were delegated broad powers, including security regulation, examination of accounts and property, the fixing of rates, the requirement of detailed reports in prescribed form, and the right to prescribe uniform systems of accounts. These two powerful state commissions became models and by 1920 more than two-thirds of the states had similar regulatory commissions. After the stock market crash of 1929, state commissions were strengthened, their jurisdictions extended, and their powers further increased. Several additional federal commissions were also established to regulate interstate commerce. Today, all fifty states plus the District of Columbia have public utility or public service commissions, railroad commissions, and corporation or commerce commissions, which regulate the electric, gas, transportation, communications, and other industries.

Under the commerce clause of the Constitution, the expansion of federal jurisdiction has greatly increased the importance of federal preemption over the control of labor relations law. Indeed, this trend led to a uniform labor law policy throughout all industry engaged in or affecting interstate commerce. Under it the Supreme Court declared invalid any local state legislation in conflict with prevailing federal labor law. But the Court recognized the validity of state laws covering matters that did not affect interstate commerce, or where Congress expressly permitted the states to apply conflicting rules within their territorial limits. In various states, of course, there are many kinds of labor statutes. A few states have labor relations acts more or less resembling the National Labor Relations Act (NLRA); and many of them have anti-injunction acts modeled after the federal law. Many state acts aimed at the suppression or control of union recourse to strikes, boycotting, and picketing have been declared invalid by the Supreme Court and are thus no longer significant. Several of the states are experimenting with statutes intended to deal with special situations, such as public-utility disputes, in the hope that these statutes will stand up when their constitutionality is tested.

In addition to regulatory powers that are fundamentally the province of the states, the national government has thus left to the states much control over interstate commerce matters that are primarily of local concern. And the states have been allowed almost complete authority to police interstate highways within their borders.

The U.S. Constitution, however, also imposes certain specific prohibitions. By far the most significant ones are those derived from the Fourteenth Amendment, which stipulates that no state shall "deprive any person of life, liberty, or property without due process of law, nor deny to any person within its jurisdiction the equal protection of the laws." Since about 1930, a liberal judicial interpretation of those prohibitions has greatly enlarged civil liberties in general and the rights of racial minorities in particular.

# 13.
# Government at the Grass Roots

Some degree of local government characterizes every state in the world: the degree is all-significant. Local government means authority to determine and execute measures within a restricted area inside and smaller than the entire state. The variant—local self-government—is important because of its emphasis upon the freedom of the locality to decide and act in certain matters. There is more than a technical importance in the difference between the two concepts—local government and local self-government—since they are related to the distinction sometimes drawn between deconcentration and decentralization.

Modern local government has a twofold aspect—it is a mixture of both deconcentration and decentralization, of central convenience and acknowledgment that not all authority ought to be exerted by the central authority. The mixture is revealed by the extent to which some powers exercised by local governmental units are exercised under compulsion and fairly strict control of a central authority with financial assistance, while others are not. This mixture produces the high complexity of modern local government.

The history of local government in the United States exhibits growing awareness of its significance. This awareness is a product of a development of parochial and town life which began long before the modern state emerged between the fifteenth and seventeenth centuries. In New England, the local units, parishes, towns, cities emerged from their origins as spontaneous self-governing units.

In the U.S. the local constitutional status stresses two main features: (1) the variety of arrangements in the various states, and (2) the large degree of freedom of the local units, derived from early English township forms reinforced by migration into new lands. Nevertheless, that freedom is subordinate and defined by state statutes and charters giving corporate status. The special charter, referring to the individual city; the general charter, which is a statewide municipal code; the charter that confers status by classifying the local unit for privileges—these are various means of trying to give local units a status which relieves them of the need for repeated application to the legislature, while yet subjecting them to a firm pattern of permissions and limits.

In twenty-six states home rule charters, granted by the legislature, allow the city to draft its own charter by a local convention, sometimes requiring legislative ratification, sometimes not. Another system allows the local units to choose from among several forms of charter provided in a state general law. There is much independence and vigor, no hierarchy, little central administrative authority, but much judicial control to hold the units within their charter and statutory position. Direct relations between federal government and local units are increasing.

Unlike the federal government, which establishes its central organization for substantially all national activities, the state conducts a large part of its governmental business through locally elected officers. There is no one system of local government for the states or even for any one of them. The geography of local government in each state is a patchwork, with the same territory often occupied by from ten to twelve separate governing bodies, each with slightly varying boundaries and with independent powers. In the fifty states, there are more than 81,000 local governing units, of which slightly more than 3,000 are counties (parishes in Louisiana); approximately 17,000 are towns or townships; about 18,000 are cities or villages; and more than 21,000 are school districts. In addition, there are more than 21,000 special units, such as park and fire districts.

## Forms of Government

Certain types of organization are usual in local government. There are the county (parish in Louisiana); towns or townships (subdivisions or units of the county in most of the states where they exist, although the New England town was the original area for local government and is more important than the county); and city. In addition to the city, which is theoretically the chief unit of local government for urban areas, most state laws provide for the incorporation of small communities as towns or villages, with a simpler form of government. Besides these usual types of local government, other forms are common to all the states. Park and sanitary districts in more settled areas, drainage and irrigation districts in rural communities, road districts, school districts, and numerous others can be found, often occupying the whole or a part of the same territory as that covered by the county, town, or city.

Counties exist as geographic areas in most states except Alaska. These counties are organized as governmental units except in Rhode Island and Connecticut. Certain local areas, principally in Virginia but including also St. Louis, Mo., and Baltimore, Md., are independent of surrounding or neighboring counties, and perform within their boundaries both city and county functions. In the 1970s approximately 3,000 organized county governments existed in the United States, the number in individual states ranging from 3 in Delaware to 254 in Texas.

The principal organ of county government is usually an elective board of commissioners or supervisors, whose members may be chosen from districts or from the county at large. Three-member and five-member boards are most common; where provision is made for representation of townships, board membership ranges upward to fifty or more. The term in office varies from a single year to eight years with a four-year term most common; terms are frequently staggered. The county governing board is vested with both legislative and administrative powers. Foremost among its legislative powers are those of taxing, appropriating, and borrowing money on behalf of the county, although bond issues frequently require voter approval. In addition to these fiscal powers, boards commonly possess some legislative authority of a regulatory nature, such as power to license and regulate retail liquor establishments and various forms of commercial amusement in unincorporated areas of the county. In some states county boards have zoning authority. Administrative powers usually include control and supervision of county institutions and property, letting of contracts, settlement of claims against the county, and appointment of various county officers and employees.

Elective county offices, in addition to membership on the governing board, most commonly include those of sheriff, treasurer, clerk, coroner, assessor, superintendent of schools, surveyor or engineer, and recorder or register of deeds. The local prosecutor, though legally a state officer, is often elected from the county. Certain other county officers, such as highway commissioner, health director, and welfare superintendent, are more commonly appointed by the county board than elected. Also frequently included in the governmental organization are various special-function boards and commissions operating in such fields as agriculture, assessment, elections, hospitals, libraries, and planning.

A few U.S. counties in the second half of the twentieth century had managers patterned after the city managers found in many municipalities; a somewhat larger number had appointed executives with administrative authority less extensive than that of orthodox managers; and a few had elective executives similar to city mayors. The great majority of counties, however, were entirely lacking in any single executive officer charged with general oversight of county administration, such supervision as existed being provided by the multimember board of commissioners or supervisors.

Major county functions are law enforcement, judicial administration, construction and maintenance of roads, provision of public assistance to the needy, and the recording of legal documents. In some states, principally in the South, the county plays an important role in school administration. Other services and institutions provided by some counties include health protection, hospitals, libraries, parks, weed control, predatory animal control, fire protection, and agricultural aid.

County government is financed for the most part from local property taxes and state-aid funds, although fees and fines constitute minor revenue sources; occasionally counties levy sales taxes or other nonproperty taxes, or operate public enterprises of a revenue-producing nature.

In New England the town meeting has historically been the chief organ of government. The areas of these towns consist of from 20 to 30 square miles and usually include both rural territory and more compact village settlements. About three-fourths of them have fewer than 2,500 inhabitants each and hence may properly be classed as rural communities. When a community becomes larger, it is usually incorporated as a city, generally terminating the existence of town government within the new city limits.

The so-called town or township system of government is found in the great northern group of states extending from New York to Nebraska. These governments may be classified as follows: those, as in New York, which have the town meeting and township representation on the county board; those, as in Minnesota, which have the town meeting but no township representation on the county board; and those, as in Pennsylvania, which have merely a local township organization but no representation on the county board and no town meeting.

Efforts have been made to introduce the township system

into the states of the South and the West, but there the counties are ordinarily divided into subordinate districts, largely for administrative purposes; such districts, though sometimes called townships, usually have little if any independent authority in the field of local government.

In the United States, a city is an urban area incorporated by special or general act of a state legislature. Its charter of incorporation prescribes the extent of municipal powers and the frame of local government, subject to constitutional limitation and amendment. In common usage, however, the name *city* is applied to almost every urban center, whether legally a city or not, and without much regard to actual size.

As a type of community, the city may be regarded as a relatively permanent concentration of population, together with its diverse living places, social arrangements, and supporting activities, occupying a more or less fixed site, and having a cultural uniqueness that differentiates it from other types of human settlement and association. In their elementary functions and rudimentary characteristics, however, many cities are not clearly distinguishable from a town or even a large village. Mere size of population, surface area, or density of settlement are not in themselves sufficient criteria of distinction, while many of their social components (division of labor, nonagricultural activity, central-place functions, and creativity) characterize in varying degree all communities from the village to the metropolis.

While many cities have been deliberately founded by potentates or colonizers, others have "just grown." During their 7,000-year history, cities have been populated by clans, families, and individuals; they have been patterned in rectangular, oval, and irregular shapes. Cities have variously functioned as temples, fortresses, capitals, markets, and factory sites and have provided a place for agricultural, commercial, manufacturing, and a host of other specialized service activities. As a consequence, city life has given rise to a variety of social structures and personality types. The changing institutional order of the city has embraced any or all of these phenomena and has assimilated something from each. The city and its hinterland have traditionally been interdependent: the countryside focuses its social life and activity upon that of a central city, which, in turn encompasses the diversity of the hinterland.

The growth of urban population has naturally led to the development of the cities as the chief agency for meeting new local needs. As the walled medieval town often left its traditions at the heart of the modern European metropolis, so too did obsolete governmental patterns linger to complicate the administration of modern municipal services.

## Forms Of Management

In the United States, both national and state governments were slow to face the emerging urban problems of the nineteenth century. The cities, reflecting a traditional American suspicion of government, were governed through an ineffectual system of two-chamber city councils, mayors without power, and a multitude of elected officials. The legal status of the city as a corporation, operating within the strict bounds of specified powers delegated from the state governments, was another major handicap. Cities often lacked statutory power to exercise necessary control over individual actions. Rurally dominated state legislatures were either indifferent to urban problems or were tempted to meddle directly in local affairs to gain special privileges. When new municipal functions were authorized, state laws usually required that they be administered by semi-independent commissions detached from the administration of the mayor. As a result, local officials shielded by dispersed responsibilty often took advantage of the opportunities for corruption in such ways as awarding franchises for public utilities, enforcing building codes, or constructing public works.

By the end of the nineteenth century, municipal corruption had become a national scandal in the United States, and several reform movements gathered momentum. Among them were drives for greater home rule for cities, a shorter ballot, stricter enforcement of tenement-control laws, reform of police systems, city planning, and stronger executive control over city government. The National Municipal League, organized in 1894, became the educational center for changes in the structure of local government. It advocated and provided legal guidance for strengthening the position of the mayor, reducing the size of city councils, dispensing with superfluous elected officials, and abolishing many independent boards and commissions. Supported by growing public sentiment for reform, many states adopted municipal home-rule laws. These permitted a range of experimentation and local initiative that raised city government from disrepute to advanced professionalization within a generation.

*Home rule* refers to the concept of enabling U.S. cities to govern themselves without interference from state legislatures. The desirability of encouraging local authorities to assume responsibility for local governmental services has been recognized in most countries that follow Anglo-Saxon governmental traditions and in a number of others, such as Germany and Switzerland. This was the prevailing view in the United States immediately after the Revolutionary War.

During the nineteenth century, however, the legislatures, under one pretext or another, gradually extended their control over local affairs. The means used were usually either special acts granting or changing the charters for individual cities or general incorporation acts for classes of cities. Laws were even passed to change the names of municipalities, grant public utility franchises, and fix the pay of local employees. This excessive legislative control of cities was bad for both cities and legislatures alike. It tended to sap the initiative and responsibility of local officials, to promote governmental extravagance, and to decrease public interest in local government. Furthermore, the volume of local legislation was sometimes so great that it required too much of the legislators' time, thus preventing adequate consideration of major state issues.

As urban centers grew in importance, they became increasingly restive at state legislative interference. Municipalities were generally underrepresented in the legislatures because of failure to redistrict after each census or because of unwillingness to take account of the faster growth of cities. In 1962 the U.S. Supreme Court ruled in *Baker* v. *Carr* that federal courts had jurisdiction to hear suits brought to correct this imbalance, which had resulted in urban centers having a decreasing voice in the state legislatures that controlled them.

Beginning with Missouri in 1875, more than half the states had, by the second half of the twentieth century, adopted constitutional provisions conferring home rule on their cities. These clauses vary greatly. Some give cities broad powers "to determine their local affairs and government" (Wisconsin, 1924). Others enumerate the powers that cities may enjoy (Colorado, 1901). Some merely withdraw constitutional objections to a grant of home rule by the legislature (Utah, 1932), while others are so specific that they can be put into effect without further legislation (Oklahoma, 1907). Oregon in 1906 extended home rule to "every city or town," but many states limit it to cities of a certain size or even to a single city.

A few states extended home rule to counties and townships, but usually not to special-purpose governmental units such as school or park districts.

The heart of any home-rule article is the power it gives to the cities. These grants of power do not interpret themselves. In practice the state supreme court must decide if any specific matter is one of local concern or if the state's interest is paramount. Because the supreme courts are state organs, they often tip the scales against local autonomy. To prevent this, some states specify in detail the exclusive powers given to localities, thus creating a government within a government, or local sovereignty. If the state constitution can be amended easily (for example, by an initiative petition followed by a popular vote, as in California), a narrow judicial construction of local powers can be reversed by constitutional amendment. The campaign to detail statements of local powers more precisely also sometimes modifies judicial resistance to local self-rule.

After 1945 there was a tendency to veer away from tight constitutional formulas. It was proposed, for example that cities be authorized to exercise any powers within their boundaries that were not denied to them by the state constitution or by statutes that applied throughout the state. These proposals also commonly included prohibitions against the passing of special laws for a limited group of cities and against the imposition of financial burdens on cities such as legislative salary-fixing for city employees. Reliance was placed on political and financial responsibility for both cities and states rather than on constitutional fences erected around each level of government. This method of obtaining local autonomy was patterned on the federal-state relationships provided in the U.S. Constitution, in which the residual powers rest by definition with the states.

Three patterns of city government attracted national attention during the first half of the twentieth century. One—the commission form—is now only a matter of historical interest. It was launched in Galveston, Tex., in 1901, and later widely imitated. The members (usually five) of a small council served as administrative heads of a group of services. The mayor was simply the presiding member of the council and had no special powers. With time, the dispersal of responsibilty in the scheme revealed serious weaknesses, and the commission form gradually dwindled away. The two forms of government that were gaining in importance by mid-century were the strong-mayor type and the council-manager (city manager) type. Under the strong-mayor form, a popularly elected chief executive is given substantial authority to make appointments, initiate the budget, supervise government departments, propose public policy, and veto council actions. This became the dominant pattern in many larger cities. Most cities of more than 500,000 population operate under some form of mayor-council government, with general managerial assistance for the mayor provided by a chief administrative officer. The powers of the mayors vary widely, however, and the trend toward centralized administrative authority has been restricted by the continuing tendency for state legislatures to place new functions under semi-independent boards. Smaller cities have moved more slowly toward a strong executive than have the larger ones. Many continued at mid-century, however, to operate under strong-council, weak-mayor forms, with the council and its committees still the dominant element.

The council-manager form of government spread widely in the United States after World War II. Under it the city manager is the principal executive and administrative officer of a municipality. It was introduced in Sumter, S.C., in 1912. The next year Dayton, Ohio, became the first large city to adopt it. About one-third of U.S. towns and cities over 5,000 in population operate with some form of the council-manager plan (and about half with a council-mayor plan, one-eighth under the commission form, and the remainder under a town meeting form).

Under the council-manager plan, the voters elect only the city council, which appoints a city manager to administer municipal affairs under its supervision. The members of the council, usually five to nine in number, may be elected either at large or by wards. The mayor is a member of the council and serves as its presiding officer. He may be either designated to this position by the council or elected to it by the voters. The council acts only collectively, and its individual members, including the mayor, have no administrative functions. The city manager serves at the pleasure of the city council. Subject to its general supervision, he is in full charge of the administration of municipal affairs. He prepares the budget, appoints and dismisses personnel, and directs the work of the municipal departments. He attends all council meetings, presents recommendations on municipal business, and usually takes an active part in discussions.

Advantages of the council-manager plan are that it provides for a short ballot with only members of the city council elected by the people; that it unifies authority and political responsibility in the council; and that it centralizes administrative responsibility in an administrator appointed by the council. It is argued by some, however, that a disadvantage of the plan is that the manager generally comes from outside the city and is not familiar with its local problems. Another disadvantage is that too much power is placed in the hands of one man. But a manager has, in fact, no power of his own because the elected council makes all policy decisions and can remove him at any time.

## Services and Functions

In the United States the growth in governmental services accelerated after 1930. Much of the burden of administering and financing these services fell on local governments. Population shifts during and after World War II meant increased pressure for additional utilities, schools, improved streets, and related local services. Inadequate local tax sources, however, brought appeals for state assistance. Meanwhile state and federal governments were looking to local units to help administer new social programs. Financial aid to local governments, therefore, expanded and principally took the form of grants subject to state or federal standards of performance and related supervision. The problem of federal-state-local relations, including the allocation of tax resources, was consequently the subject of many studies by federal and state commissions.

A primary problem of local government is the existence of a large number of political units that are neither economically nor politically self-sustaining. Whereas other nations combine most local government functions within a single comprehensive administration, the United States has assigned many of these functions—especially education, health, and parks—to special authorities. The structure of local government varies with regional history. In the South and South Central region the chief unit is the county (or parish in Louisiana); in the North Central, the combined county and township; in New England, the town. The constitution of Alaska vests powers of local government in boroughs and cities. In some states, the people of each county may vote to divide the county into townships. In the late 1970s there were approximately 3,000 counties and parishes. The smallest had about 100 inhabitants, the largest (Los Angeles County, Calif.) about 7 million.

Recognition of the inadequacy of school districts inspired a consolidation movement that eliminated many units no longer capable of supporting an effective educational system. The total number was reduced from more than 125,000 in the 1930s to little more than 20,000 by the 1970s. Elsewhere proposals have been made to abolish certain units of township and county government that can no longer perform significant governmental tasks, but this has proved very difficult. After World War II, in fact, the number of municipalities and special districts steadily increased. The growth of special districts was particularly pronounced. There were around 8,000 in 1942; within 25 years there were more than 21,000. This expansion reflects a variety of pressures, especially the need for new forms of government in metropolitan areas to deal with problems that overlap the geographic jurisdictions of existing governmental units.

## Urban Growth

The surge of industry during the nineteenth century had a profound cultural impact on the cities of America; it was accompanied by rapid population growth, unfettered individual enterprise, great speculative profits, and remarkable lapses of community responsibility. Sprawling giant metropolitan cities emerged, offering wealth and adventure, variety and change. Their slums, congestion, disorder, and ugliness provoked the beginnings of the modern housing and city-planning movements. American cities were unbelievably congested, overbuilt, unsanitary, and unpleasant. Early regulatory laws enacted to ease these conditions set standards that improved slums of the time but seemed a century later to be impossibly low. The objective of improving urban housing recurred continually. Early significant progress in public health conditions resulted from engineering improvements in water supply and sewerage treatment.

Toward the end of the nineteenth century, another effort to improve the urban environment emerged with the recognition of the need for recreation. Parks were developed to provide visual relief and places for healthful play or relaxation. Later, playgrounds were carved out in congested areas, and facilities for games and sports were established not only for children but also for adults whose shortened workweek allowed more time for leisure activities.

Concern for the appearance of the city had long been manifest in Europe, in the imperial tradition of court and palace, the central plaza and great buildings of church and state. The resurgence of this tradition in the United States was evident in the "city beautiful" movement following the Chicago World's Fair of 1893. It was widely expressed in the growth of civic centers and boulevards, contrasting with surrounding disorder and ugliness.

During the sprawling growth of industrial cities in the early twentieth century, factories invaded residential areas, tenements crowded in upon residential neighborhoods, and the first skyscrapers overshadowed nearby buildings. To preserve property values and to achieve economy and efficiency in the structure and arrangement of the city, the need was felt to separate incompatible activities, to set some limits upon height and density, and to protect established areas from despoliation. City zoning laws were the result.

As transportation evolved from foot and horse to street railway, underground railway or subway, elevated railroad, and automobile, the new vehicles made possible tremendous urban territorial expansion. Workers were able to live far from their jobs, and extremely complex traffic systems developed. The new vehicles also rapidly congested the streets in older parts of cities. As traffic was threatened with strangulation, the need to establish new kinds of orderly systems was dramatized. Metropolitan growth so intensified these and other difficulties that people living in cities—who for the first time outnumbered the rural population—began to demand a concerted attack upon their problems. In response, city planning by mid-century came to focus not on any single reform but on upgrading all aspects of the urban physical environment. Planning was broadened to include those measures needed to foster a realization by business and civic leaders of their stake in city development, and of their opportunities to capitalize on it.

A still further complication arose, which had not yet been resolved by the late 1970s, with the introduction of social problem-solving to municipal government. Old-line city planning commissions and departments were not equipped for this function. Many cities set up human relations commissions, primarily to deal with racial problems. Other *ad hoc* agencies were introduced, sometimes outside of city government, to administer poverty programs. Health services planning, where it occurred, was also likely to be separate and often nongovernmental. Innovations and experiments were tried, and a few conclusions began to emerge. One was that the complexity of urban problems would require broad city planning (as the term was being redefined) in the same metropolitan area, to include simultaneously several levels of government—municipal, county, even state and federal—and also several functional agencies—transportation, health services, education, economic development, housing, recreation, and others. Another conclusion was that it was not practical to expect political processes to produce a single hierarchical planning structure, with some central comprehensive agency in a position of overall authority and responsibility. Instead there would have to develop relationships of collaboration, cooperation, and conflict-resolution, along the lines of what has been called "creative federalism."

## Metropolitan Government

Urgent problems arise from the governmental chaos that characterizes many metropolitan areas. As these areas develop, they overreach and include neighboring cities, villages, and other minor civil divisions; they often embrace two or more counties and not infrequently sprawl across state boundaries. They typically contain a multiplicity of units of local government ranging from as few as 15 in the smallest to 400 or more in the largest areas. In the area served by the Northeastern Illinois (Chicago) Metropolitan Area Planning Commission, for example, there are 900 semi-autonomous governmental units, without even including those in the contiguous Calumet (Gary-Hammond-Whiting-East Chicago) metropolitan area across the state line in Indiana.

Since local government units derive their respective and unequal powers from an external authority (the state), they bear no obligation to their neighbors and particularly none to the metropolitan area—a unit that has no legal status. Lacking a unified administrative organization, the parts (which comprise in fact an economic and social unit) are unable to act in concert in matters of deep common concern. Public health, water supply, sewage disposal, police and fire protection, traffic control, planning, and many other critical urban needs are left to the option of each unit that has appropriate authority—and are correspondingly neglected by units that lack sufficient power. Some units, notably the central city, provide a variety of services for the entire area, paying the capitalization and operating costs of those services, or at least of the public facilities they require, while receiving no financial assistance from other civil divisions in the area.

Numerous attempts to achieve governmental unification have been made to avoid the confusion created by the emergence of metropolitan areas. Examples of such attempts include metropolitan Toronto, Tokyo-to, and Greater Miami.

Miami adopted a commission-manager plan of government in 1921, but since 1957 a number of municipal functions have been taken over by a countywide government with broad powers over municipal affairs. Although this metropolitan government can absorb the municipalities, Miami is completely surrounded by incorporated areas that show no interest in annexation, and therefore any integration with the central city is difficult. The county board of commissioners, known as the Metro commission, is made up of nine members elected by the county as a whole; one member runs as mayor and serves as permanent chairman. The commission directs policy and appoints the county manager and sheriff. Judges for the Metropolitan court are selected by a modified "Missouri plan." The Metro commission also functions as a port authority, making policy and appointing a director for the Miami International Airport and the port of Miami. Public schools of the county, consolidated in 1945, are administered by an elected board of public instruction.

Unlike Miami's Metro, most such attempts at area consolidation have met with failure. Hence various kinds of partial solutions to the problem have been devised. One class of these is the special service district. Two or more civil divisions, or parts thereof, join together, sometimes creating a legal entity, for the mutual provision of a particular service such as water distribution, sewage disposal, or public health protection. Special service districts have proliferated in metropolitan areas. While they have no doubt met urgent needs in their localities, they have further complicated the administrative compositions of the areas. A second class of *ad hoc* arrangements for dealing with common problems is the metropolitan authority—a special administrative unit established on the basis of enabling legislation to deal with a single metropolitan-wide need, such as water supply, development of recreational resources, or transportation planning and development. The Port of New York Authority, established in 1921 by interstate compact between New York and New Jersey, is one example. It is managed by gubernatorial appointees and is thus independent of local politics and insulated against local influence. The effectiveness of this type of authority is indicated by its rapid spread among the larger metropolitan areas. Efficient as it has proven to be, however, the authority is no more than a partial solution to the problems of metropolitan government. Other proposals have been suggested and tried, but have not found wide acceptance.

One single-function Metro entity, the Municipality of Metropolitan Seattle, was established by popular vote in 1958, after the passage of an enabling act by the Washington state legislature. Of the six functions authorized by the legislature (water supply, planning, rapid transit, parks and recreation, garbage disposal, and sewage disposal), only the most pressing task of sewage disposal was permitted in the implementing act. The Metro area, as initially established, covered 230 square miles in northern King county, embracing ten incorporated cities and towns, including Seattle, plus unincorporated areas. Governed by a council consisting of representatives of the governmental units concerned, Metro quickly embarked upon the building of a sewage disposal system.

Throughout the nation in general, however, the central city, its satellite towns, and a variety of special districts remain a chaos of overlapping and competing jurisdictions. There usually is no metropolitan-wide authority competent to coordinate the functions of planning, land-use control, transit, recreation, prevention of water and air pollution, and other activities that demand attention on an area-wide basis. Because local jealousies and rivalries block the consolidation of metropolitan government, it seems probable that only new kinds of multipurpose districts, able to carry on area-wide functions while leaving local matters to community determination, are likely to relieve the situation.

In any case, variety and development are marks of contemporary local government. New functions are impending. Recognition that the small locality nourishes continuing human values may help counter tendencies toward increasingly centralized authority in state and nation. Associations of municipalities and professional officials already contribute considerably to the efficiency of localities, and their services are destined to become even more valuable in moderating the trend toward centralization. Meanwhile, the ever-increasing size and complexity of government on national and international levels in the final quarter of the twentieth century has served to revive a balancing interest in the local community and its government—government "at the grass roots."

# 14.
# The Impact of Sectional Conflicts

The role of intersectional conflict in the development of American political and governmental institutions has been profound. These conflicts have fallen into two categories, geographical and urban-rural, although considerable overlapping has been obvious, with East or North representing urban interests against a rural West or South.

## North-South Differences

Two issues have predominated among causes of sectional antagonism. The greater of these, which predates the Constitution, revolved around the drive to moderate or abolish the institution of slavery. A lesser issue centered much later on the drive to moderate or abolish the sale and consumption of alcoholic beverages. Interstate battling over water in the arid West has also been a minor issue. Even before the slavery question arose at the Constitutional Convention of 1787, interstate wrangling had occurred over the basis for representation in a new government. The issue polarized the small states against the large ones. It is interesting to note that James Madison correctly predicted that voting would reflect sectional, economic, and social beliefs rather than the size of state. Soon after the Connecticut Compromise resolved the representation problem with a bicameral Congress—one chamber with geographical representation, the other by population—Madison's forecast was borne out.

Difficulties became immediately apparent based on conflicting sectional interests, chiefly those between South and North. Northern delegates desired representation in the House of Representatives in proportion to wealth or free population. Those from Maryland southward insisted that slaves be taken into account either as persons or as property. On the other hand, Northern spokesmen wished to count the slaves in the apportionment of direct taxes, while Southerners said no. Ultimately it was agreed that representation should be in accordance with numbers, and that five slaves should be counted as three freemen for both representation and direct taxation.

Other delicate problems between North and South arose from divergent opinions regarding export duties, regulation of the oceanic slave trade, and navigation acts. The Southern delegates desired prohibition of export duties and laws that might give Northern merchants a monopoly over Southern maritime trade. Men from the deep South also desired a bar against action by Congress that would destroy the slave trade. New Englanders sought to secure as much of the Southern seaborne traffic as could be gotten for Yankee merchants; and, along with delegates from the upper South, they desired to abolish the oceanic commerce in slaves. After sharp disputes a compromise was finally reached in August. By its terms, export taxes were forbidden; the slave trade was exempted from federal interference for twenty years; and passage of navigation acts by simple majority was permitted. The delegation that had been instrumental in arranging the Connecticut Compromise also helped materially in arranging this sectional bargain.

The staple-crop economy featuring tobacco, rice, indigo, (declining sharply after the Revolution), sugarcane, and cotton shaped the character of the South. Because production on a big scale was most profitable, large agricultural units known as plantations grew up; although vast numbers of small, owner-cultivated farms remained, the plantation became a dominant factor in the society. Since crops were used for commercial purposes rather than for subsistence (such as prevailed in the backwoods), it paid the proprietor to expand his number of workers and thus increase production. The slow-maturing crops needed attention most of the year and thus required a permanent labor force.

Because the agricultural tasks were simple enough to be performed by unskilled labor working in gangs, owners resorted to the use of slaves. Thus the one-crop system, the predominance of the plantation, and the presence of a biracial population, with the blacks in a subordinate position, were all developed in the South early in the eighteenth century; their grip became ever tighter as "King Cotton" rose to become the predominant crop. By 1850 there were 3,204,000 slaves in the area, and it has been estimated that 1,815,000 of these were connected with the cultivation of cotton.

Ultimately, the complex of staple crops, plantations, and black bondsmen gave to the South qualities that made it a distinctive region and set it on an adverse sectional relationship with other parts of the United States. But until the nineteenth century, the sectional alignment was far from clear-cut. Historians now reject a once-prevalent interpretation which explained the differences between North and South in terms of the dissimilarities between Puritans in colonial New England and cavaliers (aristocratic gentlemen) in colonial Virginia. The British colonists who settled the two regions were not so sharply differentiated as the tradition has claimed. Moreover, in the colonial South, the plantation economy and slavery were rather narrowly confined to limited areas around Chesapeake Bay and in the coastal district of the Carolinas and Georgia. The Democratic, Presbyterian, Scots-Irish who populated the vast back country of the piedmont did not share in this regime. They practiced a subsistence economy, cultivated grain crops, had no use for slaves, and were frequently at odds with the aristocratic, Anglican planters. These subsistence farmers of the interior seemed to have more in common with the similarly circumstanced settlers in the interior of Massachusetts and the backwoods of Pennsylvania than with either group had with the grandees of the coastal districts—whether merchants princes in Boston, Mass., or planter-aristocrats in Charleston, S.C., or along the James River. Correspondingly, the latter groups showed a greater affinity for one another than for their neighbors to the west. The antagonism between the coastal and the interior districts was chronic and was repeatedly manifested in incidents of friction such as Shays's Rebellion in Massachusetts and the uprising of the Regulators in the Carolinas. At the time of the American Revolution this east-west division seemed likely to remain the primary line of sectional cleavage.

At that time, the divisions between North and South still remained somewhat tenuous. The leaders of both sections agreed in regarding slavery as an evil. At the same time, both sections practiced it, and it was sanctioned by law in every state. The actual concentration of slaves was overwhelmingly in the South—94 percent of all slaves in 1790 were held south of Pennsylvania. But many districts in the South had almost no slaves, and slavery was widely regarded as a localized and declining institution.

*Economic Divergence.* Between 1775 and 1830, however, both North and South experienced transformations that heightened their dissimilarities and generated deep antagonisms between them. The Northern transformation came as the region slowly began to industrialize. This process committed it politically to the idea of economic self-sufficiency within a national market protected by tariff walls, where agricultural areas and manufacturing areas would complement one another by producing to meet each other's needs and serving as markets for each other's products. Industrialization generated rapid economic change in the North, and this gave sanction to the idea of progress and to the idea of a free society in which the individual can alter his occupation and status to meet changing conditions. Moreover, the use of machines freed the worker from many brute tasks and, by increasing productivity, raised the standard of living.

Meanwhile, in the South the advent of the dominant cotton economy made it possible to convert the whole region to staple-crop agriculture, as had never been possible with tobacco, rice, and sugar. Cotton would grow almost everywhere in the South, and it was more flexible than other staple crops in lending itself to production on any scale, large or small. The cotton economy moved quickly into the up-country, thus obliterating most of the former divisions between the coastal and the piedmont areas. By carrying the plantation and slavery with it, it increased the value of slaves and reinvigorated the declining slave system.

Economically, the South looked to the British textile industry for its market, and it therefore opposed the growing economic nationalism of the North and West. Socially, the plantation system discounted the commercial values of thrift, prudence, enterprise, and progress; it exalted qualities of magnanimity, command, manly prowess, and physical courage; and it adopted a cult of chivalry, with a code duello (rules governing duelling), to enshrine these virtues. The Southern social philosophy, holding to a country-gentry ideal, presented a sharp contrast with that of the North, for it stressed the conservative values of status in a fixed social order rather than of freedom; of stability rather than of progress; and of a way of life rather than accumulation of wealth. Such an emphasis was almost inevitable in a region where one-third of the population occupied a position of fixed legal subordination.

*The Slavery Question.* The growing economic divergence between North and South, highlighted in the dissimilarity of their values, found a focus in the question of slavery. In the North, the antislavery sentiment of the Revolutionary era continued to grow. Between 1777 and 1804, every state north of Maryland either abolished slavery outright or provided for gradual abolition. The early antislavery movement was moderate in tone and sought to bring about emancipation gradually by persuading slaveowners to free their slaves voluntarily. But about 1830 it entered a new and more militant phase in which immediate abolition was demanded and slaveowners were denounced in most abusive terms. The militant abolitionists were always a minority, and historians disagree as to the extent to which the North became "abolitionized," but it is clear that antislavery sentiment was becoming more and more widespread. Two indexes to the strength of this feeling can be found in the immense popularity of Harriet Beecher Stowe's *Uncle Tom's Cabin* (1852), and the election to the presidency (1860) of Abraham Lincoln, who had said that "if slavery is not wrong, then nothing is wrong."

While the North passed from mild opposition to strong condemnation of slavery, the South passed from mild opposition to an unqalified defense of its "peculiar institution." Various Southern spokesmen defended slavery on the grounds that it was sanctioned by the Bible; that the Northern economic exploitation of wage earners was worse; that the Negro was biologically inferior; and that in a well-ordered society it was better for one class to be set apart for the menial duties. Belief that slavery was a "positive good" became a test of Southern orthodoxy.

With all the cultural dissimilarities and economic conflicts between North and South converted into a dispute on the slavery question, sectional antagonisms became both chronic and acute between 1830 and 1860. The South perceived that it was not growing as rapidly as the industrial North in wealth, power, or population. The region developed the psychology of an abused minority, and a number of political leaders, of whom John C. Calhoun was foremost, evolved elaborate constitutional arguments that proclaimed the ultimate sovereignty of the states and their right to secede from the Union.

The full explosive effect of the slavery question was to some extent kept out of politics by the fact that no one contested the right of individual states to permit or prohibit slavery within their own borders. The trouble came with expansion: whenever new lands were acquired, either by such means as the Louisiana Purchase (1803) or by the Mexican War (1846–47), contests erupted over the status of slavery as each territory advanced toward statehood.

A series of crises followed one after another. By the Missouri Compromise of 1820, slavery was banned in the Louisiana Purchase north of latitude 36° 30′ except for Missouri, which was subsequently admitted to the Union as a slave state. A bitter controversy unrelated to expansion occurred in 1832–33 with South Carolina's vigorous efforts to nullify the Tariff Act. In 1848–50 the confrontation over slavery focused on the territory acquired from Mexico. California consequently became a free state by its own choice and in accordance with the Compromise of 1850. In each of these crises a clash was averted by the adoption of certain measures of compromise between North and South—measures that have been compared to treaties between two nations. But despite these efforts to save the Union, relations between the sections became increasingly strained and escalated almost to the breaking point by a series of violent episodes in the 1850s —the repeal of the Missouri Compromise by the Kansas-Nebraska Act in 1854, open combat between antislavery and proslavery factions in "Bleeding Kansas," the 1857 decision of the Supreme Court in the Dred Scott Case that Congress could not prohibit slavery in the territories, and John Brown's daring raid at Harpers Ferry, Va., in 1859.

As early as 1796, in his Farewell Address George Washington used the expressions "the North" and "the South" (as well as "the East" and "the West"). He warned that the federal union would be in danger if a time ever came when political differences were based upon geographical lines. By 1860 that time was at hand. Americans then commonly talked as if there were but two sections, the North and the South, and took for granted that there was an irreconcilable conflict between them.

**The Civil War.** When Abraham Lincoln was elected president by a purely sectional majority on a platform pledging opposition to slavery in the territories, the states of the lower South took his election as a signal to act. Seven of them (South Carolina, Georgia, Florida, Alabama, Mississippi, Louisiana, Texas) adopted ordinances of secession and proceeded (1861) to form a new union, the Confederate States of America.

Lincoln denied the legality of their act and sought to maintain the authority of the Union. As a result, fighting broke out at Fort Sumter, in Charleston Harbor, S.C. (April 1861). Soon thereafter, four other states (Virginia, North Carolina, Tennessee, Arkansas) also seceded and joined the Confederacy. For four years, the United States and the Confederate states fought each other fiercely in the U.S. Civil War.

Southerners in the heat of secession and war believed that the "Southland" or "Dixie," as they now called it, had achieved a full and separate nationality, not only in the political but also in the cultural sense. Historians since then, with an eye to features of cultural distinctiveness, have also recognized an important degree of "Southern nationalism." It is a serious question, however, whether Southern separatism resulted primarily from deep cultural differentiation, or whether it was the reaction of a group who were still an integral part of the American people, but who had been psychologically (rather than culturally) alienated from their fellow Americans by a long period of minority status, conflicting interests, and defensive guardianship of the institution of slavery. The readiness with which the South returned to the Union after the war suggests the latter.

**Reconstruction.** In any event, the South lost the war, and this loss settled two questions. First, it killed the idea of state sovereignty and the right of secession. Second, it ended the institution of slavery. But there were other problems that the war did not solve, and that continued to make for Southern distinctiveness for another century. For one thing, the South maintained its reliance on a one-crop economy, and it continued to cultivate this crop with the toil of black folks, who discovered that as long as a person went on making his living by hoeing cotton, the transition from slavery to freedom did not altogether revolutionize his life. For another, the South continued to insist upon the inferiority and the subordination of the black. Slavery had been partly an economic system providing for the ownership of the labor force, and partly a social system of racial control, and though emancipation ended the one, it did not end the other.

During the so-called Reconstruction period (1865–77), the victorious Republican Party made more or less earnest efforts to assure racial equality, but those who wanted the party to help the blacks were probably never as numerous as those who wanted the freedmen to help the party. After the latter perceived that the party might fare better without black help, the crusade for equality was generally abandoned, and the South was left to work out its own arrangements. As a consequence, the institution of slavery was replaced by three others: the economic system of sharecropping, the political system of one-party politics, and the social system of segregation, supported both by law and by custom.

The system of sharecropping or tenancy resulted from

need for a new link between the soil and the cultivator: former slaves lacked funds to buy land; landowners lacked funds to pay wages. The one-party system was arranged to neutralize the political power of freedmen, who had been legally enfranchised by the Fifteenth Amendment (1870). The practice of legalized segregation, or separation of the races, it may be noted, was much older than the postwar segregation laws and extended far beyond the South.

The North attained its highest self-consciousness as a section during the Civil War. At that time "the North" was synonymous with "the Union." It included not only the free states but also the border slave states of Delaware, Maryland, Kentucky, and Missouri (though there was considerable pro-Southern sentiment in the border area, and Kentucky and Missouri were represented in the congress of the Confederate States as well as in that of the United States). The North gained two states with the admission of West Virginia in 1863 and Nevada in 1864. Except for a period at the beginning of the war, the North maintained control of all of the western territories except the Indian Territory (Oklahoma).

The twenty-three states of the Union (not counting West Virginia or Nevada) had a population of approximately 22 million, as compared with approximately 9 million (including more than 3.5 million slaves) for the eleven states of the Confederacy. The twenty-three states contained a disproportionate share of the economic resources of the entire country. The North possessed, for example, 81 percent of the factories and produced 75 percent of the nation's wealth.

But regional differences within the North reappeared even during the Civil War, when sectional unity was at its greatest. These wartime differences could be seen in such political controversies as that between Illinoisans demanding internal improvements (roads and canals) at federal expense and Pennsylvanians opposing them. The differences could be seen also in the agitation of the midwestern Peace Democrats, the so-called "Copperheads," who were motivated more by antagonism to the northeast and especially to New England than by attraction to the South.

During the postwar Reconstruction (1865–77) sectional self-consciousness persisted in the North, and even after that time it was kept alive by those Republican politicians who resorted to "waving the bloody shirt" (recalling wartime hatreds) for electioneering purposes. But in the last two decades of the nineteenth century the East-West division in national politics often predominated over the North-South division. In the reform movements culminating in the Populist revolt, western and southern farmers aligned themselves against "the interests" of the East. Thus "the North" gradually lost some of its validity as a sectional concept.

The Reconstruction era left an indelible imprint on the history of the United States. It fixed firmly on the national scene the economic revolution that had been begun during the war and was destined to make possible the remarkably rapid transformation of an essentially agrarian society into what was to become modern industrial America. It introduced a number of worthwhile reforms into the South. Courts were reorganized, judicial procedures improved, new and improved techniques of school administration were instituted, and more feasible methods of taxation devised. Many of the state constitutions adopted during the postwar years are still in existence. It is also true that the Reconstruction experience led to an increase in sectional bitterness, to an intensification of the racial issue, and to the development of one-party politics in the South.

***Mid-Twentieth Century.*** It became less feasible than ever to treat the North as a single, clear-cut entity, yet "the North" continued to be mentioned frequently in ordinary discourse, chiefly to indicate what was opposite from the South. Sectional self-consciousness in both the North and the South increased with the rise of civil rights for blacks as a major issue in national politics, especially after the Supreme Court's decision against school segregation in 1954. With respect to formal equality for blacks, Northern folkways were being resisted in the South, but the Northern pattern of life in many other respects was being readily accepted. Industrialization and urbanization, now proceeding even more rapidly in the South than in the North, tended to make the former more and more like the latter.

Part of the heritage of the Civil War were the Reconstruction amendments, notably the Fourteenth Amendment guaranteeing equal protection under state law. Numerous and significant have been the Supreme Court cases stemming from this amendment, cases alleging violation by states of the rights of free speech and assembly, religious freedom, and alleging denial of equal educational opportunity on racial grounds alone. Protection of such individual rights as guaranteed by the Constitution became the object of an increasing number of injunction (a legal order requiring or prohibiting a specific act) proceedings. The leading precedent confirming the rights of black students to education in a nonsegregated school was established by an injunction proceeding in 1954: *Brown* v. *Board of Education of Topeka.* The basis of granting relief in such cases is the actual or threatened violation by local or state authorities of rights guaranteed under the Fourteenth Amendment. By way of implementing the elective franchise and of preventing denial of the right to vote on grounds of race, color, or other restrictions, Congress has authorized the attorney general to institute injunction proceedings in the name of the United States.

Peculiar to the United States federal system is the problem of a federal court's enjoining (prohibiting) a proceeding in a state court and vice versa. The general principle is that no such injunctions shall be issued; but being courts of concurrent jurisdiction, the court that first obtains jurisdiction of the subject matter regards its authority as exclusive and employs the injunction to support its interpretation. The friction that might result from a liberal use of the injunction in this way was foreseen at an early date, and in 1793 Congress prohibited such use by the federal courts except in bankruptcy cases. The federal courts have, however, by a series of judicial decisions, established numerous exceptions to this broad statutory provision, as in the field of constitutional rights.

A second ground of state-nation irritation has concerned the use of the injunction by federal courts to restrain the enforcement of state statutes on the ground that they are unconstitutional. An appeal from such action lies to the U.S. Supreme Court, but during the interim a single federal judge has been able to nullify the entire administrative authority of a state. A related problem is the use of the injunction against administrative acts of public officials, as in the regulation of business, the collection of taxes, and the fixing of rates by public utility commissions. While the injunction here has the advantage of raising questions of the validity of the administrative action at an early date, the effect of such injunctions, which federal judges readily granted, has been to impede seriously the activities of one branch of government. These problems led Congress, by a series of statutes beginning in 1910, to prohibit the issuance of such injunctions except by a court consisting of three judges, one of whom should be a judge of a court of appeal, and to provide for expediting an appeal therefrom to the Supreme Court.

## East-West Differences

What is now the Middle West was at first *the* West. Although the frontier character of the Midwest slowly gave way in the nineteenth century, some sense of rivalry with the established northeast remained. From its beginnings the Middle West was tied more closely to the South and tended to support the Democratic party. As that party came to be the voice of the southern slaveholders in the 1840s, Middle Westerners, unhappy with both Whigs and Democrats, helped create the new Republican Party and contributed heavily to the Republican presidential victory in 1860. The region supported the Union with men and materials during the Civil War and for decades thereafter held the Democratic Party responsible for the war. The Republican Party reigned supreme in most of the Middle Western states much of the time from 1865 until the Great Depression of the 1930s.

As the frontier moved West, out of the newly settled territory which it left behind it came a goodly share of the nation's problems and not a few of its most bitter conflicts. The steady advance of population produced a recurring Indian problem. Wars and treaties and ultimate removal of the Indians to reservations were a logical outcome of the frontiersman's determination to possess the whole continent.

The same steady advance kept the land problem alive. The Preemption act of 1841 enabled the squatter to buy 160 acres; the graduation law of 1854 lowered the price to 12½ cents per acre; the Homestead law of 1862 gave the settler the land if he would cultivate it; heavy grants to the railroads paid for westward construction. At every step, Congress gave the settler his way against those who would have used the public domain to raise revenue. His insistent demands forced every public official to offer some land policy favorable to the people he represented.

The availability of cheap agricultural land generated a demand for internal improvements and aid to markets. The part which government should play in the building of roads, canals, and railroads, and government's right to pass protective tariffs (in part to create markets), occupied almost as much of Congress's time for two generations as did the land policies themselves. All were related to the matter of finance. To migrate to the frontier and to establish a farm in the West was not something that every American could afford to do. It has been estimated that in the mid-nineteenth century it took something like $1,500 to clear and stock an 80-acre farm in the new West. Most settlers had to borrow money, and thus a hostility to banks that restricted credit and a general debtor attitude that favored inflation characterized most frontiers. From Andrew Jackson to William Jennings Bryan such western attitudes played an important part in U.S. politics.

Westward expansion ultimately carried the settler across the border into Texas, and the idea of Manifest Destiny (inevitable U.S. expansion to the Pacific) led through the Mexican War to the acquisition of New Mexico and California. The moves to organize this vast, new territory then became entangled with the slavery issue. Where before the struggle had revolved about the merits of the institution itself, the struggle now broadened into one over the expansion of slavery into the territories. The character of western settlement and the kind of institutions that were to be developed had become part of the power struggle between North and South. The effort to shape the future of a frontier in Kansas, for instance, brought rivalry to open bloodshed.

In no way did the advancing frontier affect American life to a greater degree than in the creation of sectional conflicts. Each forward movement into another area meant the formation of a new society that might be under the political domination of some older state or into territories just beginning their roles in national life. In either case, the new group's needs and attitudes did not always agree with those of the more mature groups in the state or the nation. The result was conflict, and much of American history, local and national, is made up of the struggles and adjustments that resulted. State capitals have been moved, constitutions rewritten, and legislative programs reshaped to satisfy contending interests, old and new, east and west. One American state was divided. New western states were created out of land once claimed by older parent states. In one case frontiersmen, who had formed their state of Franklin, had to give way to the demands of North Carolina. One need only recall the part played by the young West in the American Revolution and in the War of 1812 to understand the frontier's part in early national affairs. The dominant role that it played in the economic struggles and in the slavery controversy in the years from 1815 to 1860 has already been noted. Even more significant as expressions of western as against eastern attitudes were the Granger, Populist, and Nonpartisan League drives of the late nineteenth century. Each revealed a marked democratic equality; each showed bitterness against eastern neglect; each bore a debtor flavor; and each tried to say that America stood for something that was being lost.

***Populist Movements.*** A political disaster befell the Republicans in the trans-Mississippi West in the elections of 1890, when their strength in the House of Representatives was reduced by almost half. A western boom had begun in this area in the late seventies when the tide of migration into the unoccupied farmlands beyond the Mississippi quickly led to the settlement of hitherto unoccupied parts of Iowa and Minnesota; this was followed by the pushing of the frontier westward across the Plains almost literally to the shadow of the Rocky Mountains. Discontent was already rife in the agricultural regions of West and South, and the McKinley Tariff Act added to agrarian resentment. A prolonged period of optimism and rising prices collapsed in 1887, to be followed by an economic and psychological depression.

Westward expansion was deliberately encouraged by the railroads that served the region. It was supported by satisfactory prices and encouraging foreign markets for wheat, the money crop of the Great Plains. For ten years, from 1877 through 1886, the farmers on the Plains had the benefit of an abnormally generous rainfall, leading many to assume that climatic conditions had changed and that the rain belt had moved westward to provide adequate rainfall for that area. Confidence was followed by unrestrained optimism that engendered wild speculation and a rise in land prices. Lured on by these illusions, many settlers went into debt to make improvements on their farms while small towns dreamed of becoming great cities and authorized bond issues to construct public improvements they felt would be needed.

The collapse of these dreams came in 1887. The year opened ominously. In January the Plains were swept by a catastrophic blizzard that killed thousands of head of cattle and virtually destroyed the cattle industry of the open range. The following summer was dry and hot, crops were poor, and, to compound the woes of the farmers, the price of wheat began to slide. The dry summer of 1887 was the beginning of a ten-year cycle of little rainfall and searingly hot summers. By the autumn of 1887 the exodus from the Plains had begun; five years later areas of western Kansas and Nebraska that had once been thriving agricultural centers were almost depopulated. The agricultural regions east of the Plains were less directly affected, though farm prices declined.

Although the disaster on the Plains bred a sense of doom and frustration, the lure of good land was still strong. When the eastern half of the present state of Oklahoma was opened to settlement on April 22, 1889, an army of eager settlers, estimated to have numbered 100,000, rushed into the district.

The collapse of the boom and falling agricultural prices caused many farmers to seek relief through political action. In 1888 and again in 1890 this discontent was expressed through local political groups, commonly known as Farmers' Alliances, which quickly spread from the West to the South where they attempted to seize control of local Democratic organizations. These alliances won some local victories and contributed to the discomfiture of the Republicans in 1890. They were not an effective vehicle for concerted political action, so in 1891 alliance leaders organized the People's, or Populist, Party. The Populists aspired to become a national party and hoped to attract support from labor and reform groups generally. In practice, they continued through their brief career to be almost wholly a party of farmers, with a platform tailored to meet the wishes of Western agrarians in particular. By the end of the century, Populist causes were mainly absorbed by the Democratic Party.

In similar fashion, political organization throughout the West followed economic developments. Territorial governments were quickly established; by 1890 all but four of these had become states, and the last had reached statehood by 1912. The constitutions which these states adopted were notable for their democratic provisions. Such advanced ideas as the initiative, referendum, and recall were introduced. Women were accorded a larger political place. Even as a territory, Wyoming granted women the vote, and both Wyoming and Utah did so as states. Montana elected the first woman to the U.S. Congress, and Wyoming the first woman governor. These states took the lead in passing eight-hour workday legislation, in limiting the hours of labor for women and children, in providing for the arbitration of labor disputes, and in increasing employer liability. Arizona included a provision for the recall of judges in its constitution, removed the provision under pressure, but reinstated it after statehood.

California, early a state (1850), never quite became a typical part of the American West. It had already progressed beyond early frontier stages before it became a part of the nation. It was always uniquely California, especially influenced by its Spanish origins and long coastline. The discovery of gold in 1848 did not greatly alter the situation. It made California part of the mining frontier and of a great trans-Mississippi West that became America's last frontier.

*Temperance Movement.* Out of the West and Middle West came the effective support for prohibition of alcoholic beverages, a movement which reached its climax with the adoption (1920) and thirteen-year life of the Eighteenth Amendment to the Constitution. Organized efforts to limit the use of intoxicating beverages did not begin on a large scale in the United States until the 1820s, under the leadership of Congregationalist and Presbyterian ministers. Early support came largely from eastern states, but nationwide organizations soon developed. The intensive religious revivalism of the 1820s and 1830s stimulated various movements toward perfectionism in human beings, including humanitarian doctrines, abolition of slavery, and temperance. Out of this wave of temperance concern, movements for state and local Prohibition began. The expression "teetotaling" came into being in this period because temperance supporters indicated their total belief in temperance by a "t" opposite their names on temperance rosters.

During the 1840s and 1850s temperance advocates were linked to a number of other movements of a religious and humanitarian nature. Sabbatarianism (strict observance of the Sabbath), home missionary movements, abolitionism, nativistic hostility to foreigners, and temperance were frequently blended in various combinations, many persons adhering to all of them. It was in this period that the temperance movement appeared as an important political link to other reform movements. The relation between temperance and abolition discredited the former below the Mason-Dixon Line, however; although it had begun well in the South, therefore, after 1840 the temperance movement met with slight appeal in Southern states.

In the decade after the Civil War two major temperance organizations emerged. Founded in 1869, the National Prohibition Party pledged in the 1872 presidential election to work for nationwide Prohibition. This political platform, and many others afterward, contained a reformist program expressing many of the same goals as the Grange (a widespread farmers' organization) and, in later years, the Populist Party. In 1874 the Woman's Christian Temperance Union (WCTU) was founded. Under the leadership of Frances Willard, it was the leading temperance organization of the 1880s and 1890s in the United States. It was also active in a number of other social reforms, including women's rights, the labor movement, and the Americanization of immigrants.

Both these organizations reflected two major concerns. One, manifested to a larger degree in the WCTU, was a concern for the problems brought about by the industrialization of American cities and accompanying waves of immigration. Large non-Protestant populations needed to be assimilated, and temperance advocates preached to them what they hoped would be a unifying set of middle-class values and habits. The second concern, felt strongly by the Prohibition Party, was a largely rural and small-town apprehension over the growing political power of the burgeoning cities. These developments culminated in the second wave of statewide Prohibition activity between 1880 and 1890.

The drive for Prohibition on a nationwide basis emerged out of a renewed attack on the sale of liquor in many states after 1906. The dry (nonalcoholic) fight had the support of churches, small towns, Progressivists, and rural political power. A major force throughout the campaign was antipathy to the growth of cities. As the United States became more urbanized, the impact of immigration made the rural-urban conflict increasingly important in American politics. That conflict had strong overtones of cultural differences. It was largely in the small towns and agricultural areas that temperance sentiment had its strongest support. Urban and eastern industrial areas were the centers of greatest opposition.

Especially in its rural segments the Midwest represented another major source of temperance support. Here again the complex of agriculture, Protestantism, and nativism worked together to develop the drive for Prohibition as an attack on the new industrial and alien cultures that had developed in the big cities. Although urban areas did contain many residents whose cultural roots in American middle-class values gave rise to an antipathy to drinking, the main political support for Prohibition was nevertheless heavily rural.

The political power of these outlying areas dominated state legislatures. Without it, the enactment of state Prohibition laws and the adoption of the Eighteenth Amendment would have been impossible. In a number of cases, statewide Prohibition came about through state legislative action rather than through statewide referenda. The political power of the rural areas was in fact even stronger in its legislative representation than its numerical majorities within the population.

The Progressive movement of the early twentieth century, although mainly an urban one, saw in the saloon and in the drinking that it fostered sources of the municipal corruption and industrial chaos that the Progressives sought to eliminate. In fighting for Prohibition they saw themselves resisting the organized underworld, the foundation of corrupt politics, and a prime source of the workers' low standard of living. Populist political sentiments, represented to some degree by William Jennings Bryan in the 1896 presidential election, were expressed in the antiurban quality of the Prohibition movement and in the attack on big business. Populists labeled the liquor industry an enemy that, like the railroads and the banks, put profits above human values.

In the twentieth-century movement for Prohibition, both the Progressive and Populist strands in American politics merged in the common thrust toward human perfectibility. Similar nativist sentiments contained also the efforts toward the reform of the immigrant, for whose improvement they felt a missionary zeal. By skillful management of political pressure and public opinion, the Anti-Saloon League harnessed the diverse elements of support for Prohibition beginning about 1906, leading to state dry laws covering more than fifty percent of the U.S. population by 1919. The following year saw adoption of the Eighteenth Amendment.

The early phases of the battle to repeal the Volstead Act (1920), which enforced Prohibition, featured polarization of industrial city against rural and small-town America. The power of Democrats in many industrial areas led to identification of that party with pro-repeal forces. It is important to recognize, however, the enormous effect the 1930s Depression had on Prohibition. First, it strengthened the economic argument favoring the restoration of the liquor and beer industries. While labor unions had been cool to the Eighteenth Amendment, after 1930 they became vociferous in demanding repeal as a way of producing jobs in related fields. Many businessmen saw in the abolition of the Eighteenth Amendment an opportunity to revive a source of tax revenue that might ease their own tax burdens. Second, it shifted America's attention to the problem of unemployment. These tended to make income levels and class differences far more important as political elements than those social and sectional antagonisms from which the Prohibition movement had drawn its fundamental strength. In 1933 Prohibition passed into history.

*Water Resources.* It is perhaps ironic that the principal remaining cause of intersectional rivalry in the United States after the liquor question has had to do with water. As irrigation enabled the development of farming in the arid and semi-arid regions of the West, federal control was increasingly exercised over the management of water resources. Irrigation had been practiced before A.D. 1000 by the Pueblo Indians in New Mexico and Central Arizona. The Spanish added a few *acequias* (ditches) of their own, often as part of the huge land grants belatedly made by the Mexican government in the hope of establishing agricultural communities as buffers against the encroaching Americans. In their turn these Americans, individually and through cooperatives, struggled to increase the paltry stream diversions. Adequate measures were not possible, however, until the Reclamation Act of 1902.

The Reclamation Service's first successful large-scale project in the nation was the Theodore Roosevelt Dam near Phoenix, Ariz., completed in 1911. The largest project in the Southwest was Hoover Dam on the Colorado River, completed in 1936 (though Glen Canyon Dam, upriver from Hoover and completed in 1964, closely approached it in size). But the water proved expensive and led to intensive cultivation of high-income crops: alfalfa, citrus, and long-staple cotton. It also led, in the case of streams crossing state boundaries, to complex legal disputes, the bitterest of which concerned the diversion of the Colorado River water far from its natural channels. Various state compacts were entered into by the claimants, but sectional jealousies militated against a solution. After World War II the water shortage was even more critical when developments associated with aviation and nuclear energy brought an influx of industry and population into urban areas of the Southwest.

Similar conflicts will arise from time to time as other resources abundant in one state or region are demanded by farms and industries in another. Coal, oil, gas, and lumber are examples. Interstate compacts offer the possibility of harmonious and cooperative development of such resources. Adjudication in federal courts, up to and including the Supreme Court, offer the prospect of resolving disputes that cannot be amicably settled by contesting states themselves. To precisely this purpose did the Constitutional Convention of 1787 speak in Article III, Section 2: "The judicial power shall extend . . . to controversies between two or more states. . . ."

# IV. Electing a Government

*"A President needs political understanding to run the government, but he may be elected without it."*

—Harry S. Truman

# 15.
# The American Electoral Process

An election is one means by which a society may organize itself and make certain formal decisions. Where voting is free, it is a system for determining political power relations in a society—a method of seeking consensus with a minimum of sacrifice of the individual's freedom. The essence of a democratic election is freedom of choice. In Soviet bloc countries and in certain developing countries the individual may be asked to go through some of the formalities of casting a ballot, but this often represents a mock election, not a valid one. The voter merely ratifies choices already made by the dictator or the ruling clique, rather than making any true selections himself.

Electoral systems had their beginnings in ancient times. In classic Greece most public officers were selected by lot, but a few posts requiring special qualifications were filled by election. For the most part voting was by show of hands in a public meeting, but in cases of ostracism and legal decisions, voting was made secret by means of white and black balls of stone or metal, or marked and unmarked shells. A Roman law of 139 B.C. allowed each voter to use a carved wooden ballot to indicate his choices for candidates for public office.

In medieval times elections were used for various purposes, principally religious, but the size of the electorate was extremely small. Indirect elections by means of electoral colleges (a body of electors) were used to select chief executives in Germany and in some Italian cities. In 1562 a papal bull required the College of Cardinals to select the pope by a secret ballot.

In modern times elections have been associated with the system of representative government, including the selection of both administrative officials and legislative representatives in some countries. The part that the electoral system plays in the machinery of government varies from country to country. The role of the electorate may be limited in varying degrees by the power of a hereditary second chamber (as in England), by royal power (in countries with a constitutional monarchy), or by the power of the courts (as in the United States). Ignorance, apathy, and lack of training may keep some voters from making their opinions count. In a free society voters must learn to make wise choices in spite of pressures—economic, social, and political—brought to bear upon them.

The real significance of an electoral system, then, depends upon its ultimate governmental effectiveness, its relationship to other political institutions, and the social system within which it operates. In considering the subject, therefore, the examination cannot be confined to the written text of the franchise acts alone but must consider the electoral system broadly, including all those means whereby a person becomes elected to a legislative assembly or some other government position.

## Constitutional Provisions

The American founding fathers treated the electoral process briefly in the U.S. Constitution. Three of that document's four references to the election of officials wisely left details to Congress or the states. The fourth reference prescribed the role of the electoral college in choosing the president and was amended twice to remedy technical defects. Five other amendments ratified in the last 175 years broadened citizen participation in the electoral system.

Article I, establishing the Congress, merely provides (Section 2) that representatives are to be "chosen every second year by the people of the several states" and that voting qualifications are to be the same for Congress as for the "most numerous branch of the State Legislature." It also stipulates (Section 3) that senators are to be chosen by the state legislatures, but this was changed to popular election by the Seventeenth Amendment (1913). Section 4 leaves to the states the prescription of the "times, places and manner of holding elections for Senators and Representatives," but gives Congress the power "at any time by law [to] make or alter such regulations, except as to the place of choosing Senators."

Five constitutional amendments gradually broadened the franchise. The first of these was the Fifteenth, ratified in 1870, which declared simply that "The right of citizens of the United States to vote shall not be denied or abridged by the United States or by any State on account of race, color, or previous condition of servitude." In addition to the popular election of senators (Seventeenth), the Nineteenth Amendment (1920) gave women the vote; the Twenty-fourth (1964) abolished the poll tax as a requirement for voting in federal elections; and the Twenty-sixth (1971) extended the franchise to citizens aged eighteen or older. In addition, the right to vote for president was given to citizen residents of Washington, D.C., by the Twenty-third Amendment, adopted in 1961.

Constitutional responsibility for the conduct of elections rests with the state governments (except in the case of Washington, D.C.).State laws set up election machinery and determine the qualifications for voting, subject to federal restrictions against discrimination because of race, color, previous condition of servitude, age (eighteen or over), or sex. Educational qualifications for voting have been imposed in some states. The application by some Southern states of educational or other qualifications to discourage or prevent voting by blacks was prohibited, however, by the Civil Rights Act of 1965.

Nonvoting, even by those legally entitled to the suffrage, is common. Countries vary considerably in how easy or difficult it is to vote. The United States—which has a lower level of voting participation than Australasia, Great Britain, Canada, and the northern European countries—ranks high in voting difficulty. In the United States a voter must first register, often months before political interest is stimulated by the campaign, and only then is he allowed to vote. In many other countries, voters are "registered" by government officials and do not have to do anything to get on the voter roll. In the United States, by the late 1970s advance registration requirements were coming under attack and four states (Maine, Minnesota, North Dakota, and Wisconsin) allowed "instant registration" on Election Day.

At the national level only members of the two houses of Congress and presidential electors are chosen by popular vote. A much more numerous group of state officers and an even larger number of county, city, and other local officers are elected directly by the people. When all these types of officers appear on one ballot or in one election, the voter is sometimes faced with the confusing task of choosing a hundred or more officials from among several times that number of candidates. The voter may also be asked to vote on issues as well as candidates through the initiative, the referendum, or the constitutional amending process. Under many state laws, moreover, proposals of municipal bond issues and other local questions must be submitted for popular approval at the same time. The short-ballot movement (electing only the most important officials) has made some headway in cutting down the number of elective offices, but the U.S. voter continued to be faced with the difficult challenge of making choices for a large number of candidates for both primary (a party preference poll) and general elections.

At the national level, U.S. political history has been characterized by a two-party system. Occasionally a third party has risen to importance as was the case with the Progressive Party under the leadership of Theodore Roosevelt in 1912. In the early years of the country, the Federalist Party represented the interests of strong nationalism; the Republican Party under Thomas Jefferson stressed the interests of the states. By the 1830s the Jeffersonian Republicans had become dominant and had changed their name to Democratic Party. The Federalists had disappeared by this time, and the Whigs became the opposing major party. The Whigs were eventually replaced by the Republicans, who elected Abraham Lincoln to the presidency in 1860. Since that time, the Republicans and Democrats have been the only parties with enough political power to win a national election. Third parties have, however, influenced the programs of the major parties, and, on occasion, their choice of candidates.

## Suffrage

The history of voting rights in America has been one of step-by-step extension of the franchise. Religion, ownership of property, and race disappeared one by one as legal bars to the right to vote. But women—even those qualified by every test but sex—were almost universally denied the vote, even after the attainment of "universal manhood suffrage." The movement for women's suffrage in the United States started in the early nineteenth century during the antislavery agitation.

Such women as Lucretia Mott showed keen interest in the antislavery movement and proved themselves effective public speakers. When Elizabeth Cady Stanton joined the antislavery forces, she and Mrs. Mott decided that the rights of women, as well as those of the black slave, needed redressing. In July 1848 they issued a call for a women's rights convention at Seneca Falls, N.Y., adjourning to Rochester after a two-day session. It was followed in 1850 by a convention in Worcester, Mass., under the auspices of Lucy Stone and a distinguished group of Eastern suffragists. The movement, however, still lacked the dynamic force it needed. This was soon supplied by Susan B. Anthony.

At first no method of extending the suffrage was considered except amendments to state constitutions. The first attempt along this line was made in Kansas in 1867, immediately after the close of the Civil War. An amendment was submitted at the same time to enfranchise freedmen. Both were defeated, and even though the Territory of Wyoming granted women the right to vote in 1869, it became apparent that an amendment to the federal Constitution would be a preferable plan for the nation as a whole. Miss Anthony and some of the women's suffrage leaders demanded that such an amendment enfranchise not only blacks but women as well. Most men who had been the strongest advocates of women's suffrage opposed this demand, and they were supported by some of the women who feared that it would imperil the success of the Fourteenth Amendment. Women were not included in this amendment, and therefore, when a Fifteenth was later found necessary to strengthen it, they were also excluded.

The next step in the campaign was the formation (1869) of the National Woman Suffrage Association, with the declared object of securing the ballot for women by a Sixteenth Amendment to the Constitution. Mrs. Stanton was elected president and Miss Anthony chairman of the executive committee. This organization held a national convention every year thereafter for fifty years and appeared before committees of every Congress to plead for the amendment. Its leaders soon learned that pressure from the states on congressional representatives would be necessary, and they therefore began to organize women in each state. In the autumn of 1869 another group, headed by Lucy Stone, organized a national association called the American Women Suffrage Association solely for this purpose. In 1890 the two organizations united under the name of the National American Woman Suffrage Association and worked together for almost thirty years. After the deaths of the founders of the movement, their work was continued by Anna Howard Shaw and Mrs. Carrie Chapman Catt, who headed an organization that eventually included many thousands. Individual states yielded and began to enfranchise their women; each such state increased the members of Congress elected partly by women. These members were thus obliged to vote for an amendment to the federal Constitution.

It was found, meanwhile, that state legislatures could give women the right to vote for presidential electors and, in some states, the right to vote in municipal and local elections. Arkansas and Texas permitted women to vote in primary elections, which were more important in those states than general elections. Campaigns were vigorously conducted to persuade the legislatures to submit to the voters amendments to the state constitutions conferring full suffrage in state affairs. This was accomplished in New York in 1917 and proved the greatest victory yet achieved. By 1918 women had acquired equal suffrage with men in fifteen states, offering the only instance in the world where the voters themselves gave the franchise to women. Most of the forty-eight legislatures had already adjourned, and yet thirty-six of them had to ratify the Nineteenth Amendment before November 1920 in order for women to vote in the next presidential election. Many special sessions were called for this purpose, and fourteen months later, on August 26, 1920, ratification was complete.

The extensive urbanization of blacks during this time had a profound effect upon their status and especially on the way they viewed themselves. Crowded together in the large cities, the descendants of slaves were no longer afraid to speak out against the injustices that a white society continued to inflict upon them. Some began to talk of the "New Negro," not only in literature but also in politics. The National Association for the Advancement of Colored People (NAACP) was campaigning against lynching, while individual blacks were battling the exclusively white Southern Democratic primary election. In a series of cases beginning in 1927, they sought to have the U.S. Supreme Court outlaw the exclusion of blacks from these primaries. In 1927 and 1932, victories were won when the Court ruled that state legislation empowering the Democratic Party to exclude nonwhite citizens was unconstitutional. A case was lost in 1935, however, when the Court observed that if the Democratic Party excluded blacks without state authorization, the Fifteenth Amendment had not been violated. Final victory came in 1944, when the Court asserted that since the Democratic primary was an integral part of the elective process, blacks could not be excluded from participation.

In the North, meanwhile, blacks were beginning to make themselves felt politically. In 1915 Oscar DePriest was elected Chicago city council alderman from the densely populated

South Side. Two years later the blacks of New York sent E. A. Johnson to the state assembly. In 1928 some black voters turned from their traditional choice of the Republican Party to the Democrats, in the belief that they would do more for them. The same year they sent DePriest to Congress, the first black to serve there since 1901. In 1930 they used their political influence to block the confirmation of John J. Parker for the U.S. Supreme Court because they regarded him as an enemy of their race. By the time that Franklin D. Roosevelt ran for president in 1932 on the Democratic ticket, the black minority was in a position to use its growing political strength to force greater consideration from the major parties. Black influence in politics grew steadily thereafter, particularly in the Democratic Party, although the first black U.S. senator elected (1966) since the Reconstruction era was a Republican, Edward W. Brooke of Massachusetts.

## Nominations

The Constitution does not specify the process by which candidates are nominated for political office. Conventions for nominating candidates originated during the presidency of Andrew Jackson (1829–37), after years of growing dissatisfaction over nominating procedures. The first president, George Washington, had been so clearly the outstanding national leader of his time that no formal action was necessary to identify him as a candidate before the election. But when it became necessary to choose a successor from among several possibilities, it grew apparent that as a preliminary step the field must be narrowed if the electoral arrangements of the Constitution were to operate effectively. By the election of 1796, the beginnings of party organization in Congress were able to solve the problem; presidential nominations were made in this period mainly in informal congressional party caucuses.

The term *caucus* originated in Boston, Mass., in the early part of the eighteenth century, when it was used as the name of a political club, the Caucus or Caucas Club. There public matters were discussed and arrangements made for local elections and the choosing of candidates for office. A contemporary reference to the club occurs in the diary of John Adams in 1763, but other sources suggest that it was in operation as early as the 1720s.

In 1816 James Monroe was nominated by the caucus of what was then the Democratic Republican Party, in transition from the Republican Party of Jefferson to the Democratic Party of Andrew Jackson. Monroe was elected, and his administration—known as the Era of Good Feeling—was marked by a virtual disappearance of such organized political parties as had existed previously in Congress. In 1820 Monroe required no nomination for a reelection that was almost unanimous. In 1824, however, the popular vote was divided among four candidates who had come to public notice in one way or another. None of the candidates had a majority of the electoral vote, and the election was therefore thrown into the House of Representatives for settlement. John Quincy Adams was chosen president, although Jackson had been the leading candidate and had received the highest number of both popular and electoral votes.

Jackson was called upon by the legislature of Tennessee to run again in 1828, and he agreed to do so. By that year the Jackson men were so strongly organized that no formal action was needed to identify their candidate, although there had been talk of calling a national convention. Jackson won the presidency in 1828 without difficulty. A clarification of party lines followed in Congress, but the congressional party caucus, which had been under increasing attack, was too discredited for restoration as a nominating agency.

The opposition parties of the time held the first recognized national party conventions in preparation for the elections of 1832. The Anti-Masonic Party met at Baltimore, Md., in September 1831, with 116 delegates representing thirteen states, and chose William Wirt as its presidential nominee. The National Republican Party, which is generally identified as a predecessor of the Whig Party and the present Republican Party, held a convention at Baltimore in December 1831, at which it nominated Henry Clay. The Jacksonians met at Baltimore in May 1832 as the "Democratic-Republican Convention," hailed Jackson as their chief, and nominated Martin Van Buren for vice-president. This was the first national convention of the present Democratic Party, which has held similar meetings regularly ever since.

The National Republicans held no convention in 1836 and were replaced in 1840 by the Whigs, who held national conventions through 1852. After that year the Whig Party disintegrated over the issue of slavery. It was succeeded mainly by the Republican Party, which originated in 1854 and has held national conventions in preparation for every presidential election since 1856. Third parties and minor parties have also occasionally held national assemblies. As generally used, however, the phrase *national political convention* refers to the quadrennial meetings of the two major parties that have alternated in winning presidential elections since 1832—the Democrats on the one hand, and the Republican Party and its predecessors on the other.

The national nominating conventions have been among the most criticized of political institutions throughout their history, and criticism increased as the conventions became more visible in the modern television era. Similar types of party conventions formerly were used to select party candidates for elective positions in state government and in Congress, but most states shifted to the use of primary elections for such offices early in the twentieth century. A similar change, to create a national presidential primary to nominate the candidates for president and vice-president, has been proposed intermittently for many years.

The national conventions of 1968 inspired an unusual amount of public dissatisfaction both by their procedures and by their outcomes, with the result that various reform proposals were revived. Congressional committees undertook study of proposed constitutional amendments that would provide or permit some form of national presidential primary. Most of these proposals would involve procedures similar to those used in state primaries; such procedures, however, become cumbersome, time consuming, and expensive on a nationwide basis. Petitions to get on the ballot of a national primary, for example, could require as many as 700,-000 signatures, with a quota from every state, all to be obtained within a limited period and to be placed on file in Washington not less than sixty days before the election. Few candidates could meet the financial and organizational campaign requirements that would result. Reluctant candidates, such as Adlai Stevenson and Dwight Eisenhower in 1952, might not even make the attempt.

More promising lines of congressional action might include either (1) a simple form of constitutional amendment granting general authority to Congress to legislate on presidential nominating procedures or (2) the exercise by Congress of its undoubted existing authority to make recommendations to the states and to the political parties, coupled with some provision for financial inducements to persuade compliance. The first alternative was favored by Senator Estes Kefauver but opposed both by those who wanted no action at all and by those who preferred the incorporation into the Constitution of a mandatory plan, spelled out in detail. The second alternative was favored by some members of Congress as a way to achieve a gradual improvement both in convention procedures and in delegate selection, without making any overall change so drastic that the results would be unpredictable.

State governments could do much to improve delegate selection and preconvention campaigning within their borders. In 1955 Florida adopted a statute, recommended by a group of political scientists, under which organized slates go on the ballot under the name of the presidential candidate they favor; these slates can also run on a "no-preference" basis when the preconvention situation is especially uncertain. Other states, led by Oregon, moved to widen the choice in their presidential preference polls by authorizing a specified state official to put all nationally recognized candidates on the ballot—a system somewhat remote from delegate selection and one that could result in so many candidates being listed on the ballot that no one would achieve a majority in the preferential vote.

Both national party organizations organized study groups to recommend improved procedures. Some changes were made in 1968, and others followed. The Republican convention of 1968 was a much more orderly convention than that of the Democrats, in which every aspect of procedure was questioned. The Democrats, however, managed to make some genuine reforms, especially the abolition of the party's long-standing "unit rule," under which the majority of a state delegation could determine its entire vote if so authorized by state party authorities. Historically, this rule had always been rejected at Republican national conventions. Later, it had been used only by a minority of states, mainly Southern, in Democratic conventions. More important, probably, was the Democratic action giving notice that future state delegations should be selected through processes assuring voter participation in the presidential-election year and under rules that called for more representation of women, blacks, and other groups who had been traditionally underrepresented at the convention and in other national political institutions.

Opinion among political scientists remained generally favorable to the continuation of national party conventions, coupled with the view that many detailed reforms were needed to clarify procedures, strengthen popular control, and assure fair representation of all interests in the ultimate choice of candidates. The continued evolution of the conventions in response to reformist pressure seemed much more feasible than any sudden or drastic change or outright abolition.

## Primaries

Another effort at reform led to the primary election, an institution peculiar to the United States. Nominating conventions for offices below the presidential level eventually became subject to abuses that led first to their regulation and ultimately to their elimination for most offices except president and vice-president. Observance of early laws relating to selection of delegates was optional, parties being permitted but not required to conform to their provisions, and the laws were limited to certain areas.

After the year 1800 mandatory regulations transformed the primary into an election conducted by public officials at public expense. Even before these laws were tested a demand arose for direct voter nomination. The direct primary was used by the Democratic Party in Crawford County. Pa., as early as 1842, but it was not until the twentieth century, when the Progressive movement tended to divide both parties, that the system came into general use. In 1903 Wisconsin, under the leadership of Gov. Robert M. La Follette, passed the first mandatory, statewide direct primary law. The movement spread so rapidly that by 1917 all but four states had adopted the direct primary for some or all statewide nominations. After the passage of laws in Utah (1937), New Mexico (1938), Rhode Island (1947), and Connecticut (1955), some form of direct primary was used in every state. Primaries in most states are mandatory and cover nominations to all state and county offices, but optional primaries survive in several Southern states. Michigan, New York, and Indiana are among the states that use conventions for nominations to certain state offices. In most states provisions apply only to parties polling a fixed minimum of votes at the last election.

Direct primaries in the states vary widely in detail, and dates of primary elections vary from spring to fall. Various methods are used to place names on the ballot. The simplest is a declaration of candidacy, with or without a filing fee. The more popular method is by petition signed by a certain number of political supporters of the aspirant. In an increasing number of states the primary is preceded by official or unofficial conventions and candidates so designated are listed first on the ballot. Preprimary endorsing conventions are provided by law in Colorado, Connecticut, Idaho, Massachusetts, New Mexico, and Utah. In Rhode Island party committees may endorse candidates and their names appear in first place on the primary election ballot. On the other hand, California in 1963 prohibited party organizations from officially endorsing candidates and required nominees of unofficial clubs to be labeled "unofficial" on the ballot. In most states an aspirant for nomination may compete only in the primary of the party in which he claims membership, but in a few states it is possible for the candidate to seek the nomination of both parties simultaneously.

Particularly interesting and important are the variations in qualifications for voting in the primary. Some primaries are "open" in the sense that no declaration of party affiliation is required; the voter may participate in the primary of either party and move from one party to another in successive contests. Sometimes, as in Wisconsin, the participant receives the ballots of all parties and may decide which to use in the privacy of the voting booth, whereas in those states following the Minnesota plan a "blanket" ballot is provided on which the names of all candidates are arranged in party columns.

In 1935 Washington adopted a blanket ballot that permitted the voter to cross back and forth between the parties at the same primary; for example, he might vote for a Republican aspirant for the gubernatorial nomination and at the same time choose a Democrat for Senator. The "closed" primary, used in all but eight states in 1970, limits participation to party members. Voters may be required to enroll as members of a party at the time of registration, to state their party choice at the polling place, or to swear that they meet a specified test of party membership if their right to participate in the primary is challenged. The usual tests are support of the party's candidates at the last general election or the intention to support the candidates of that party at the next general election.

The merits of open and closed primaries have been widely debated. It is argued that the open primary permits participation by independents who are unwilling to declare a party affiliation and that it prevents intimidation of voters. Its opponents say that it destroys party responsibility by permitting those who have no continuing allegiance to the party to control its nominees, and that it permits members of one party to "raid" the primaries of the other party.

In most states the candidate polling the highest number of votes becomes the nominee, but by the early 1960s most Southern states, in which Democratic nomination was equivalent to election, required a second or "runoff" primary if no candidate received a majority of the votes in the first contest. Preferential voting (indication of a first, second, and third choice), tried by several states, had been abandoned by all of them.

Studies made in the 1950s and 1960s tended to support the hypothesis that the primaries had altered the character of political competition, at least in the case of nominations for state legislative posts. Even in two-party areas the effective choice had tended to be transferred to the primaries of the majority party, and the vitality of the minority party was weakened.

Attempts have been made to extend the idea of direct nominations to the office of president of the United States. By election of delegates to the nominating conventions, and by preference voting for president, or both, some states have attempted to bring the national conventions within the control of the party membership. The first mandatory presidential primary law was adopted by Wisconsin in 1905, and by 1916 laws varying widely in type and effectiveness were in operation in twenty-four states. After that the movement lost ground. Studies published in the 1960s suggested that primary contests did indeed affect the actions of national nominating conventions, and there was a revival of interest in presidential primaries. In 1972 there were twenty-three of them, and George McGovern's deft accumulation of convention delegates through this means helped assure in advance his nomination by the Democratic convention. Four years later there were seven more state presidential primaries, and Jimmy Carter used a similar approach to ensure his nomination even before the Democratic convention met.

Primary elections have offered state legislatures an opportunity to demonstrate originality. A number have undertaken nonpartisan primaries for judicial and local office, and by the late 1970s two states, Louisiana and Mississippi, had established primaries in which all candidates (for nonfederal office) ran on a single ballot regardless of party affiliation or the lack of it. Any candidate polling a majority larger than fifty percent was elected at once.

# 16.
# The Two-Party System: An Improvisation

A political party is a group of people attempting to bring about the election of their candidates for public office and, by this means, to control or influence the actions of government. A political party is only one of several types of groups that seek to control the personnel and policies of government. As defined here, political parties are instruments of democratic or republican regimes in which the chief governmental officials are chosen by popular election. A clique of military officers that gains control of a government by its command of the nation's armed forces is hardly a political party, although it may masquerade as such. Under dictatorships, one-party systems have often been established to bolster the power of the dictator. Such parties may be effective props for the regime but are in reality extensions of the governmental control apparatus rather than genuine political parties. The essential condition for the existence of political parties is freedom to form organizations that strive for power by electoral methods. Under other circumstances groups of citizens may influence government or form part of a coalition supporting it, but without freedom of competition for power, political parties cannot exist in the strict sense of the phrase. Hence, the Communist Party of the Soviet Union, the Nazi Party of Hitler's Germany, and the Fascist Party of Italy could not have been considered political parties as that usage is generally understood. In some countries—such as France, Italy, and India—the Communist Party gained acceptance as a bona fide political organization and wielded immense influence.

Pressure groups differ from political parties in that they seek to influence government primarily by such means as propaganda and persuasion. These pressure groups consist of individuals or federations of associations held together by some common interest; exertion of influence on government policy is generally only one means of advancing the association's purposes. Professional societies, for example, make themselves heard by public authorities when matters of concern to them are under consideration, but influencing public policy is not the sole objective of such societies. The line between political parties and pressure groups is sometimes blurred, but an important distinction may be drawn from the fact that pressure groups, unlike political parties, neither nominate candidates for public office nor desire to accept the responsibility for management of government.

In the eighteenth century, on both sides of the Atlantic, the word *party*, like *faction*, suggested something politically unwholesome if not actually subversive. In his Farewell Address (1796) George Washington warned against "the baneful effects of the party spirit generally." Thomas Jefferson, who would later found a great political party himself, once angrily dismissed a partisan controversy: "If I could not get to heaven but with a party, I would not go there at all." Contemporary voters also often disdain parties, contending that they themselves are "independent" and "above party." In most countries, nevertheless, particularly in those with long traditions of successful party government, political parties are regarded as essential to popular government.

Party competition for power is in a sense a sublimation of civil warfare, and a party can be considered a kind of political army consisting of segments of the population with certain compatible aspirations. People bind themselves together in parties for much the same reasons that they join together in warring factions. A common economic interest, for instance, may be susceptible of promotion or defense by political methods. Labor and peasant parties are examples that are paralleled by parties dominated by industrial interests.

Whatever the factors may be that draw people together in parties, these organizations perform functions indispensable to popular government. They select candidates for public office and present them to the entire electorate, which may then choose from among the contenders. The process of nomination of candidates is in most countries highly informal; caucuses or inner cliques of the leaders of a party determine its candidates. In the United States, however, because of abuses within party organizations in making nominations. the process is regulated by law. Most candidates are selected at a direct primary election, but candidates for president and vice-president are chosen at national party conventions.

In addition to nominating candidates, parties define the issues before the electorate in campaigns and elections. They present not only a choice among candidates but a choice among governmental programs. At times, particularly in countries with a dual party system, the differences between party programs are by no means sharp. In the United States the issues between the Republican and Democratic parties are often more notable for their similarities than for their differences. Nevertheless, the general direction and emphasis of a particular party program may be closer to the beliefs of a voter than those of the opposite party. In multiparty countries such as France, numerous separate parties pursue programs tailored to fit the views of comparatively small segments of the population. Parties also carry a large part of the burden of education and debate incidental to the voters' choice of governments. Especially since the development of universal suffrage, the conduct of campaigns and other work related to the electoral process has become extremely burdensome and costly.

## Party Organization

As with all but the most rudimentary associations, a political party possesses organizational machinery through which it acts. Such organization is, in effect, the government of the party. It is the apparatus through which party decisions are made and inner factional disputes are settled. It tends, in fact, to be the essence of the party. Parties pose as mass organizations and adopt all the paraphernalia of representative government for control of their affairs, but everywhere their management tends to be controlled by a few. In theory only, political parties are associations with vast memberships. In practice, membership is an affiliation with no real obligation for participation in party management, usually representing nothing more than a voter's current association. Members leave the operation of the party machinery to the inner core of professional and semiprofessional party workers. This arrangement works only because party leadership must continually respond to membership interest in order to maintain its following.

The supreme authority within the party is a national convention meeting every four years, directly or indirectly representing the entire membership. These vast Democratic and Republican assemblies consist of more than a thousand delegates each, selected by state party conventions or direct primaries. Their business is to nominate presidential candidates, adopt platforms, and designate party officials. Both parties maintain national headquarters and staffs, whose activities and importance increase as an election approaches.

Local party organization conforms to the structure of local government. City and county party organs are tied into state party organizations, which in turn occupy a place in the national party structure. Although provision is often made for committees and conventions based on congressional districts, the city or county party machinery is more generally the center of power locally.

The nature of a nation's politics is profoundly influenced by how much power is exerted nationally over local party actions. The central offices of British parties, for example, are able to exercise great influence over the choice of candidates by local party associations. This relationship within the party organization is reflected in the fairly high degree of discipline prevailing within the party groups in Parliament. Unity within the majority party lays the basis for, but does not assure, a stable and firm governmental policy. In the United States, however, arrangements prevail between national and local party organizations.

The national bodies are only loose federations of state and local party machines. Relatively slight control of local party actions is exercised by the national leadership of each party. In the past, local party organizations have rebuffed attempts even by such strong party leaders as Woodrow Wilson and Franklin D. Roosevelt to influence the selection of candidates for the House and Senate. Local party autonomy is accompanied by weak cohesion within party groups in Congress and by consequent difficulty in enacting party programs into legislation. In practice, most legislation is passed by combinations of votes that cut across party lines.

Soon after political parties sprang up in the United States, they came to exert considerable influence over elections at all levels. Few candidates but those of the two leading parties have had much chance to be elected. Various voting methods of the parties thus became indispensable to the very process of government itself, and they are now controlled in great detail by state legislation.

One of the first examples of such official control was the printing of the ballot. Before 1888 parties printed their own ballots and consequently determined the conditions under which the names of their candidates should appear. Serious abuses arose under this arrangement, particularly with respect to the secrecy of the ballot. Beginning in 1888 the states officially adopted the so-called Australian (secret) ballot, with ballots printed at governmental expense. State laws regulate the entire process, whether ballots are cast by hand or voting machine.

Under the Australian ballot system, the parties take great concern over the manner in which candidates are listed. Massachusetts and a number of other states adopted a plan whereby the names of the candidates (with party designation) are grouped under the titles of the offices. This arrangement makes it necessary for the voter to mark separately the name of each candidate of his choice. Most states, however, adopted the so-called party-column ballot, which varies in different places, but whose fundamental purpose is to facilitate straight-ticket voting. Usually all the candidates for one party appear in a single column so that a voter may vote for all of them at once. If the voter does not wish to follow the straight party ticket, he must vote for each candidate separately.

Control by law over the official ballot was followed by detailed regulation of the methods of party nomination and of the machinery of political organization. Through primary elections, voters in most states choose their party committeemen. State laws determine the power of such committeemen, the manner in which they shall form the various party-governing bodies, and how party organizations shall frame platforms. This kind of governmental regulation was largely occasioned by a feeling that party organizations themselves control the government and that they should, therefore, be subject to legal control themselves. As the costs of political campaigning have risen, the necessity of regulating the financial affairs of parties has drawn increased attention.

## Party Functions

When a party is first created, it may stand for political principles that set it apart from others. For the main part, however, parties serve as convenient devices for the operation of government and for presenting the public with political issues as they arise. Such issues are not created merely by the existence of two opposing parties; during much of the time, in fact, few issues exist to arouse controversy at all. At such times parties may proclaim principles but actually have no sharp differences. When issues are altogether absent, parties still perform the functions of narrowing the choice for the voter at the polls and of binding together the machinery of government after an election.

A movement for nonpartisan elections sprang from the

belief that national parties should not control the election of local and judicial officers. In a number of states judicial officers are therefore nominated and elected through ballots bearing no party designations. But usually a candidate must be actually sponsored by an effective organization if he is to win. The nonpartisan movement has accomplished more in municipal than in state elections.

The climactic function of the party in U.S. politics is the nomination and, if possible, the election of a president. It is, in fact, the goal of winning the presidential office that primarily serves to hold parties together as national coalitions. Otherwise, state and local party organizations might have little reason for joining in a nationwide alliance. Although effective power resides at the state and local levels rather than the national party headquarters, an incumbent president is able to exert a good deal of central control over his own party, through patronage (political appointments), and because party fortunes are inevitably linked with the success of his administration.

The quadrennial conventions at which presidential candidates are nominated are the chief instrument through which the national parties function. Voting power at both the Republican and Democratic conventions is parceled out among the states in terms of population and the extent to which the state has supported the party at a previous election. Two-thirds of the states select their delegates by party conventions or committees; one-third by primary elections.

The tactics used in winning elections have undergone considerable change in the post-World War II years. At one time an effective party organization was a basic prerequisite for a successful campaign. The activity of party workers served to "sell" a candidate to the voters, and the organization enjoyed corresponding influence in state and local politics, especially.

With the arrival of new media of communication, particularly radio and television, however, a candidate is able to reach the voter directly. The party organization, therefore, has lost some importance as a channel of communication between candidate and voter, though organizational support remains a valuable political asset. A related development that party organizations have sometimes viewed with misgiving has been the emergence of the volunteer, nonpartisan group for the purpose of supporting particular candidates, especially for president. While these volunteer groups have drawn many individuals into political activity who would not work through the machinery of regular party politics, they are to some extent competitors with party organizations for patronage and the other rewards of power.

## Party Beginnings

Political tactics used in winning U.S. elections underwent significant change at two points roughly a century apart—in the 1840s and again after World War II. The origin of American political parties may be said to have been in Washington's own Cabinet, despite his antipathy to partisanship. It started with the fiscal system that Secretary of the Treasury Alexander Hamilton devised around his Bank of the United States to solve the critical debt and credit problems facing the young nation at the end of the Revolutionary War. The Bank (chartered in 1791) had authority to issue notes, backed with gold and government bonds, that would be used to redeem the public debt and could provide the nation with a universally acceptable currency. The entire debt would thus be funded by the Bank of the United States at a uniform rate of interest and gradually retired by tax receipts. In one brilliant stroke the public credit was restored and worthless securities turned into fluid capital.

Hamilton's fiscal system was more, however, than an economic program. It also emerged as a political platform designed to ensure the permanence of the Constitution. The wealthy and the powerful in the nation were bound to the federal government by the strongest of all ties—economic self-interest—for it was they who had speculated in the debt and benefited from the funding system. To James Madison in Congress, this was unfair to the many small investors who had helped finance the Revolution and had been forced to sell out to speculators. Madison also had misgivings about the constitutionality of the Bank, for nowhere did the Constitution specifically empower Congress to grant such a charter. Washington was uncertain about the matter and consulted his Cabinet. Hamilton argued that the authority to create a bank was "implied" in the authority to levy taxes, coin money, and pay the debt. Jefferson, on the other hand, felt that Congress should not exceed its expressly delegated powers.

The result of this division of opinion over Hamilton's fiscal system was the gradual evolution of political parties. The opposition, led by Jefferson and Madison, objected to the centralizing tendencies of the Federalist system and its alliance with business. They also criticized Washington's habit of holding weekly levees (receptions) in fancy dress and felt that his practice of addressing Congress in person was reminiscent of royal speeches from the throne in England. By 1792 the followers of Jefferson and Madison were calling themselves "Republicans," implying that their opponents were "monarchists." Though neither Washington nor Hamilton favored a monarchy, the accusation had a great deal of propaganda value for the opposition, particularly among the small farmers of the West and South who did not understand the intricacies of Hamilton's fiscal system. Even so, Washington was reelected by unanimous vote of the electoral college in 1792, the Republicans concentrating on an unsuccessful attempt to replace Vice-Pres. John Adams with the New York Anti-Federalist George Clinton. Until 1793 the "Republican interest" was nothing more than a small circle of followers grouped around Madison in Congress.

What crystallized the Federalists and Republicans into actual parties was the impact of the French Revolution and the outbreak of war in Europe. The French Revolution in 1789 excited the general sympathy of Americans, but genuine diplomatic problems for the United States resulted when war broke out four years later as European monarchies aligned themselves against republican France. Horrified by the Reign of Terror in France, Federalists also recognized that the nation was dependent upon Britain for commerce, credit, and manufactured goods. Jefferson, on the other hand, supported the French Revolution and felt that "the liberty of the whole earth was depending on the issue of the contest."

Like Washington, Hamilton had been one of the foremost among the founding fathers who had deplored the idea of political parties, equating them with disorder and instability. He had hoped to establish a government of superior persons who would be above party. Yet he became the leader of the Federalist Party—a political organization in large part dedicated to the support of his policies. Hamilton placed himself at its head because he needed organized political support and strong leadership in the executive branch to get his program through Congress. Washington usually supported Hamilton's policies and in effect became a Federalist. In attempting to carry out his program, Hamilton frequently interfered in Jefferson's domain of foreign affairs. Detesting the French Revolution and the egalitarian doctrines it spawned, he tried to thwart Jefferson's policies that might aid France or injure England and to induce Washington to follow his own ideas in foreign policy. Hamilton went so far as to warn British officials of Jefferson's attachment to France and to suggest that they bypass the secretary of state and instead work through Hamilton and the president in matters of foreign policy. This and other aspects of Hamilton's program led to a feud with Jefferson from 1791 to 1793, in which the two men attempted to drive each other from the Cabinet. They used party newspapers to attack each other and the policies each espoused, and each tried to turn Washington against the other. It was Hamilton's domestic and foreign policies that gave the Federalist Party its program and created the bitter hostility that made it so short-lived.

In 1796, after Washington refused to run for a third term, his vice-president, John Adams, was chosen president, defeating Jefferson. Hamilton and other Federalists had urged electors to cast an equal vote for Adams and Thomas Pinckney (the other Federalist in the contest), partly in hopes that Jefferson, who was elected vice-president, might be excluded altogether. Another part of their motivation, it seems, was the possibility that Pinckney might receive more votes than Adams and thus be elected president, though he was intended for second place on the Federalist ticket. The electoral college cast 71 votes for Adams, 68 for Jefferson, 59 for Pinckney, and 78 scattered among other candidates.

Adams's four years as president (1797–1801) were marked by a succession of intrigues that embittered him throughout his later life. They were also marked by events such as the passage of the Alien and Sedition acts, which brought discredit on the Federalist Party. Factional strife broke out within the party itself; Adams and Hamilton became alienated, and some members of Adams's own Cabinet looked to Hamilton rather than to the president as their political chief. The United States was at this time drawn into the vortex of European complications, and Adams. instead of taking advantage of the militant spirit which was aroused, patriotically devoted himself to securing peace with France, much against the wishes of Hamilton and his adherents.

While the Federalists controlled the government until 1801, their inability or unwillingness to organize politically, their neglect of the arts of consultation, persuasion, and discipline, and their failure to devise a program of broad national appeal doomed them. The name of their party had become synonymous with favoritism, influence, and monopoly.

The accomplishments of the Federalists were great, nevertheless. They organized the new federal government in all its branches, giving it an administrative machinery that in the main endured; they established the doctrine of neutrality toward European conflicts that stood the United States in good stead as a poor, defenseless country preoccupied with its own continental expansion; they laid the basis for lasting friendship with Britain; and they fixed the practice of a liberal construction of the Constitution—not only by Congress but above all by the U.S. Supreme Court, which, under the leadership of John Marshall (who had been appointed chief justice by Pres. John Adams), stamped large portions of Federalist doctrine on the national system. Their economic accomplishments of fiscal integrity, credit worthiness, and protection of property and the investing process also were impressive achievements.

## Nineteenth Century Developments

Federalist party morale was impaired by internal dissension and intrigues. The party took up the Republican weapon of states' rights and in New England carried sectionalism dangerously near secession in 1808 and also in 1812–14 during the movement opposing the War of 1812. By 1817 it was practically dead as a national party. It is sometimes said that Federalism died because the Republicans took over its principles of nationality and accepted its economic ideas. This is true in part. But it fell principally because its great leaders, John Adams and Alexander Hamilton, became bitter enemies; because neither proved even remotely comparable to Jefferson as a party organizer and leader; because the party could not hold the support of its original commercial, manufacturing, and general business elements; because it opposed sectionalism and espoused a growing nationalism toward the issues that ended in the War of 1812; and because, after 1801, it failed to adjust itself to the emerging democratic spirit of the country. In New England, where the Federalist Party persisted longest, it represented a "cordial union between the clergy, the magistracy, the bench and bar and respectable society"; this coalition had to fail in an expanding United States.

*The Democrats and Slavery.* Jefferson's Republican Party continued under various designations with such leaders as James Madison and James Monroe until, during the presidency of Andrew Jackson, it came to be known as the Democratic Party. Although from the outset this party had formed a strong opposition in Congress, it did not win control of the administration until Jefferson became president in 1801. Throughout the next forty years, except during the administration of John Quincy Adams (1825–29), the party was in control of the government. Madison and Monroe, both close friends and disciples of Jefferson, served in the presidency a total of sixteen years.

Although Jefferson had established the Republican Party on the principle of popular government, as opposed to the Hamiltonian concept of direction by national economic groups, all the members of the so-called Virginia school of presidents were aristocrats in birth, breeding, education, and environment. It was not until the election in 1828 of Andrew Jackson, a frontiersman from Tennessee, that a "man of the people" entered the White House to become the second great figure in the party's annals. The Jeffersonians in effect had held the party in trust for the people, whereas Jackson would turn it over to them.

Jackson emphasized Jefferson's original principle of strict interpretation of the Constitution. His great political battle, which he won, was to deny a renewal of charter to the United States Bank, inasmuch as he feared the weight of its influence in national affairs. He also asserted the authority of the national government in strong terms. When South Carolina threatened to nullify federal tariff legislation and if necessary to secede from the nation, Jackson issued a proclamation declaring that no state had a constitutional right to withdraw from the federal union.

Between 1837, when Jackson retired, and 1860, four Democratic presidents were elected—Martin Van Buren, James K. Polk, Franklin Pierce, and James Buchanan. Although the Democrats lost to the Whigs in 1840, the death of Pres. William Henry Harrison in 1841 brought to the presidency John Tyler, who had been and remained more of a Democrat than a Whig. The real party history of this period is involved with the futile struggle of politicians and statesmen to ignore or compromise the slavery issue. The Democratic Party during the Van Buren administration came increasingly under the dominance of the South, which was firmly convinced that its economic, social, and political interests were bound up in the preservation and extension of slavery. The South demanded the right to extend slavery into new territories and states as the only way to prevent the great industrial states of the North from becoming too strong in the federal government. The South also wished to ensure the perpetuation of its peculiar institution.

By 1850 the slavery issue had assumed such aggravated form that working out an accommodation (such as the Missouri Compromise of 1820) had become extremely difficult. A final effort, however, was made in the Compromise of 1850, proposed by Henry Clay and accepted by majorities in both the Whig and the Democratic Parties. On the basis of this arrangement, the national Democratic conventions of 1852 and 1856 assumed that the issue had been settled.

Subsequent events proved this assumption completely erroneous. No matter how politicians sidestepped the question in their speeches and platforms, the overwhelming issue was still slavery. The final crack-up came in 1860, when the delegates assembled for the Democratic convention in Charleston, S.C. The majority of the platform committee of this convention proposed a plank stating that each new state or territory must have the right to enter the federal union on its own terms, as expressed in a constitution adopted by vote of its residents, whether prohibiting or recognizing slavery. Pending adoption of a local constitution, the platform declared for free settlement in new states and territories, which meant that Southerners could establish themselves there with their "property," including slaves.

When the convention rejected this resolution and adopted a minority report ignoring any specific slavery declaration, the Southern delegates withdrew. The Northern Democrats adjourned to Baltimore, Md., and nominated Stephen A. Douglas of Illinois as presidential candidate. The Southern faction, reconvening in Richmond, Va., adopted the rejected majority report on slavery and then met in Baltimore, where it nominated John C. Breckinridge of Kentucky as its candidate.

Inevitably, this North-South split was disastrous to the Democrats. Not until 1884 did the party again elect its candidate. From 1860 to 1932, the Democratic Party was in administrative power for only sixteen years.

*The Anti-Masonic Party.* During the late 1820s an Anti-Masonic Movement (opposing secret fraternal organizations) had grown up in the Middle Atlantic states and evolved into a political party for a brief period. The Anti-Masonic national nominating convention of 1831 in Baltimore was the first of its kind in U.S. political history. Thirteen states were represented by 116 Anti-Masons. The convention required a special three-fourths (rather than a simple) majority to nominate, establishing the precedent for the two-thirds rule used by the Democrats in subsequent national conventions for more than a century. William Wirt of Maryland, attorney general under Monroe and Adams, was nominated for president, although substantial elements in the convention favored endorsing Clay, who became the National Republican nominee. The Anti-Masonry issue had by this time, however, became secondary to the issues of internal improvement and the protective tariff; Wirt himself was a Freemason.

The Anti-Masonic Party's achievements in national elections were few. In the presidential contest of 1832 it carried only Vermont. At the same time the party won a large number of seats in the Twenty-third Congress (1833–35), but few thereafter. Its influence, nonetheless, lingered in other ways. Its national convention system was followed in 1831 and 1832 by the National Republicans and the Jacksonian Democrats, and subsequently by the major U.S. parties. And several of the party's leaders became founders of the Whig Party and others became prominent in the Democratic Party.

***The Whigs.*** From about 1834 to 1854 the Whigs constituted a major U.S. political party. Its lineage may be traced back through the National Republicans to the Federalists. During the administration of John Quincy Adams differences developed between his and Clay's supporters and those of Jackson. The Adams-Clay faction became known as National Republicans and was influential for a few years.

The Whig Party was formed following the overwhelming victory of the Democrats in electing Pres. Andrew Jackson to a second term in 1832, chiefly on his issue of "killing" the second Bank of the United States by refusing to renew its charter. Drawing strength and support from three main groups—Eastern capitalists, Western farmers, and Southern plantation owners—the Whigs generally espoused the cause of propertied and professional people (without, however, being antilabor) and, above all, the principle of national unity. In the beginning they were united by the bonds of opposing "executive usurpation" under President Jackson and of winning to their ranks the great bulk of the Anti-Masonic Party membership. A twofold strategy lay behind the choice of the term *Whig:* to avoid the handicap of functioning any longer under a name identified with the disastrous defeat of 1832, especially since the loser in that campaign, Clay, was one of their main leaders; and, by implication, to fasten on the Jacksonian Democrats the odious label of Tories.

Senators Clay of Kentucky and Daniel Webster of Massachusetts gave the Whigs their best and most sustained leadership; yet Gen. William Henry Harrison (1840) and Gen. Zachary Taylor (1848), neither of whom represented any well-known political views, were their only successful presidential candidates—and both men died in office, with serious consequences for the party. Sen. John C. Calhoun of South Carolina, spokesman of the great slaveowners of the South, supported the Whigs until the close of the 1830s, primarily because of Jackson's ruthless opposition to nullification; Calhoun, however, later returned to the Democratic fold.

Not yet fully organized by 1836, the Whigs supported three candidates in that election (Webster in the East, Harrison in the West, and Hugh L. White in the South), but in 1840 they nominated the old Indian fighter Harrison and John Tyler, a leading Virginia planter. This was the famous "Log Cabin and Hard Cider" campaign of "Tippecanoe and Tyler Too." The Whigs won, but Harrison died within a month after his inauguration as president; Tyler, a southern Whig, proved to be so much more concerned about states' rights and slavery than about the program of either Clay or Webster that these factions secured Tyler's formal ejection from the party. In 1844 the Whigs nominated Clay as their standard-bearer and drafted their only real platform, one stressing the need for a well-regulated currency, a tariff for revenue, distribution to the states of the proceeds from the sale of public lands, limitation of the presidential office to a single term, and reform of executive usurpation—all in line with Clay's American System of tariff protection and internal improvements proposed in the 1820s. Perhaps, however, because of his indecisive position on the "reannexation of Texas," the key issue of the Democrats, Clay lost, and James K. Polk won.

In 1848 the Whigs again offered a military hero, General Taylor of Mexican War fame, as their candidate and succeeded a second time in gaining the White House, only to have their leader die (July 1850). On the accession of Millard Fillmore to the presidency, the greatest question before the country was that of the extension or prohibition of slavery in the newly acquired territories. Faithful to the key Whig principle of preserving national unity, Fillmore sided with Clay in the effort of the "great compromise" to forge a final solution to this irrepressible issue. When the Clay-sponsored

Compromise of 1850 became law, the Whigs hailed it as a lasting settlement and looked forward to the next campaign.

The drift of Southern Whigs into the Democratic organizations of the South imposed on the Democratic Party an increasing conservatism on matters of slavery. Eventually this development would impair the strength of the Democratic Party in the North, but the danger did not become obvious until after the campaign of 1852. After the Compromise of 1850 old-line Whigs staked their party's future on the continuing national acceptance of the extension of the Missouri Compromise line westward to California. This refusal to face the moral implications of the slavery question alienated the antislavery Whigs of the North without stopping the drift of Southern Whigs into the Democratic Party. By 1852 it was clear that the Whig Party was doomed as an effective political organization. The Whigs nominated Gen. Winfield Scott, an inept politician; the Democrats, Franklin Pierce, who carried all but four of the thirty-one states.

*Origins of the Republican Party.* What provided the antislavery politicians with their opportunity to produce a major shift in American politics was the introduction of the Kansas-Nebraska Bill into Congress in January 1854. In introducing the bill, Sen. Stephen Douglas of Illinois was concerned with organizing these territories to facilitate the building of a transcontinental railroad into the city of Chicago. But Douglas's vigorous response to Western pressures quickly collided with pressures from Southern extremists who demanded, in exchange for needed Southern votes, that Douglas's bill specifically repeal the Missouri Compromise line and establish two territories instead of one. By substituting the principle of popular sovereignty for the Missouri Compromise line, Douglas's bill removed a great mass of territory from the settlement and offered it as a prize for which the sections would have to struggle. It transferred the conflict, moreover, from the remote deserts and mountains of the Southwest to the almost contiguous and reputedly rich lands of Kansas. Never before had the slavocracy appeared so insatiable.

In failing to anticipate the violent sectional reaction to his Kansas-Nebraska Act, Douglas committed one of the grossest political blunders in American history. By reopening the one issue that could reforge the Free-Soil coalition (opposing extension of slavery to the territories) of 1848, his action immediately threw the existing parties into chaos. The

American or Know-Nothing Party, a secret, oath-bound organization that was pledged to oppose the influence and power of foreign-born citizens, had been formed earlier and had begun to assume the place of the Whig Party. It proved quite successful in state elections and now aspired to become a broad national party. The Know-Nothings intended to ignore slavery, but by 1854 many of its leaders were forced to take a position against the Kansas-Nebraska Act.

With no party name other than "Anti-Nebraska Men," thousands of advocates from Maine to Illinois began joining together in opposition to Douglas's measure. In 1854 small group meetings were held in a half-dozen states—the earliest in Ripon, Wis. A mass meeting on July 6, at Jackson, Mich., attended by former Whigs, Democrats, and Free-Soilers, adopted the name *Republican*. This was an appealing title not only for those who recalled Jeffersonian "republicanism" but also for those who placed the national interest above sectional interests and were opposed to states' rights. No American party ever rose so swiftly; it carried the congressional elections that fall in the North, forced many of the Whig and Know-Nothing leaders into a union with it, and succeeded in controlling the House of Representatives of the Congress that met in 1855.

The Democrats, who had comprised practically the only cohesive party in 1852, now faced the latest and strongest of their broad-constructionist opponents. The Republicans were from the beginning strongly nationalistic. Although the party did not propose to abolish slavery where it already existed, it did aim to exclude slavery from those territories where it did not yet exist. It was the only party that ever assumed an outright antislavery position, labeling slavery as a moral, social, and political evil, and denouncing both the Kansas-Nebraska and the Fugitive Slave Acts.

An informal meeting in Pittsburgh, Pa., on February 22, 1856, planned the first Republican national convention, which assembled in Philadelphia, Pa., on June 17. Its platform advocated denial to Congress of the right to recognize slavery in a territory; it held instead that Congress not only had the right to abolish slavery in the territories but ought, indeed, to do so. This view, no longer that of the extremists, was representative of widespread sentiment throughout the North. John C. Frémont, who was widely known for his Western exploration and who had been elected senator from California in 1849, was the party's nominee for president. He won 114 electoral votes, but was defeated in a three-way contest against Millard Fillmore, candidate of the Know-Nothing and Whig Parties, and the conservative Democrat, James Buchanan, who was elected.

During the next four years the nation drifted toward war between the sections. On May 16, 1860, the Republican National Convention met in Chicago, Ill., and nominated a former Whig congressman from that state, Abraham Lincoln. In a four-party contest, Lincoln led the Republicans to victory. The new party had displaced the Whigs in the North as the main opposition to the Democrats.

Lincoln's primary focus was the preservation of the Union. The outbreak of rebellion in the South (1861) and the quick secession of eleven states led to the Civil War and consequently played havoc with existing party lines. For four years the armed conflict came to no positive conclusion. In the autumn of 1864 the president faced the necessity of going to the people at the stated election time but did so with slight hope of a vote of endorsement. His supporters confessed their weakness. In calls for a convention and in the convention, these Republicans called themselves the "Union" Party. This party, with Lincoln as its nominee and a war Democrat, Andrew Johnson, as vice-presidential nominee, managed to defeat the Democrats, who declared the war a failure. The struggle was pressed to a successful conclusion (1865), but the assassination of Lincoln, who died on April 15, brought about a complete realignment of political forces.

**Republican Dominance.** Within a year of the end of hostilities, the Republican Party had reappeared and was clearly determined to retain control of the government. In so doing, it was taking a form that was to prove the most powerful yet seen in the history of U.S. political parties. Throughout the following thirty years, the Republicans and the Democrats—who by the autumn of 1866 appeared as the one vehicle of strong opposition—fought for supremacy in the government—the Republicans usually winning. Except for the terms of Democratic Pres. Grover Cleveland (1877–81, 1893–97), the remainder of the nineteenth century (and the dawn of the twentieth) belonged to the Republicans.

In the years of chaotic Reconstruction, the government had kept troops in the South and attempted to confer political power upon the unprepared freedmen—an attempt that was abandoned as a failure by 1877. The Republican Party organization was revealed in this period to be of narrow interest and often selfish purpose, ruled by a small and usually self-perpetuating group of politicians who made party regularity a fetish. To the support of modest and unimaginative electoral tickets rallied voters from villages and county districts in the old East and the new West—mostly men of small means attached to the traditions of their pioneering forefathers. The main Republican appeal was frankly to businessmen as the nineteenth century ended.

The tariff was included in the Republican platform as an issue in the campaign of 1896, but as election day approached much greater prominence was given the question of the free and unlimited coinage of silver, which the Democrats supported. William McKinley of Ohio was nominated by the Republicans on a gold standard platform and won the election. There followed a burst of U.S. expansionism in world affairs. The party in power vigorously pursued the Spanish-American War (1898). As a result, the nearby island of Cuba won independence, and Spain was forced to cede the Philippine Islands, Guam, and Puerto Rico to the United States, Hawaii was also annexed at this time.

## Twentieth Century Developments

A new era in Republican Party domination was dawning. Theodore Roosevelt was supported for the vice-presidency in the campaign of 1900 by Republican Party boss T. C. Platt, who was anxious to get him out of New York politics. Roosevelt had a large and enthusiastic following among the delegates from Western states and was nominated against the wishes of both McKinley and party boss Mark Hanna, who, however, bowed to the will of the convention. The problem of the party managers was one of first magnitude when, in the autumn of 1901, the assassination of President McKinley brought to the presidency the independent and imaginative Roosevelt. Since the Republican Party did not possess a definite party program, as it had in 1897, there was both opportunity and need for a leader who could reshape its appeal and its purpose. This the new president proceeded to do.

*Theodore Roosevelt.* Roosevelt's course was to attack the business trusts that had become extremely powerful, an attack not upon big business as such but upon industrial combinations that believed themselves superior to the government as well as to the public interest. His position on the trusts and his aggressive action in the coal strike of 1902 were extremely popular.

Roosevelt's widespread popular support won him reelection in 1904 and gave to his second administration a more personal character than had prevailed in the preceding three years, however, the overthrow in 1910 of the Republican majority in the House of Representatives ended fourteen years of complete control of the national government and revealed the strength of Western Republican insurgents.

In February 1912 Roosevelt announced that he was willing to accept the Republican nomination, thus attempting to obtain control of the party machinery to make the party organization responsive to the demands of its voters. State primary elections revealed Roosevelt's popularity, but William Howard Taft won the nomination and Roosevelt's supporters thereupon bolted the party and organized the Progressive Party (also called Bull Moose Party) with a platform calling for a change in political machinery and an aggressive program of social legislation. The Progressives nominated Roosevelt for president and Gov. Hiram W. Johnson of California for vice-president.

**_Woodrow Wilson._** The Democrats had again split disastrously in 1896, this time on the issue of free and unlimited coinage of silver as advocated by their candidate, William Jennings Bryan of Nebraska. Their adherence to economic radicalism under Bryan again made the Democrats a minority party, but in 1912 they were the beneficiaries of the Roosevelt-Taft split and were able to elect Woodrow Wilson, former governor of New Jersey. Under the slogan of the New Freedom, Wilson urged more complete federal regulation of banking and industry, strengthening the antitrust statutes, and a drastic revision of the tariff laws. Wilson was narrowly reelected in 1916. He mobilized the country's resources for the defeat of Germany in World War I and inspired the creation of the League of Nations.

At the end of World War I the Republicans returned to power, electing Sen. Warren G. Harding of Ohio as president. By the time Harding died in August 1923 and was succeeded by Vice-Pres. Calvin Coolidge, the Republican Party had become more than ever a coalition of sectional leaders and divergent economic interests. Its outstanding national figures were not regulars but insurgents such as Sen. Robert M. La Follette of Wisconsin, who led his followers out of the party in 1924. In the three-party election of that year Coolidge rode to victory on a wave of economic prosperity that held steady until after the election of Republican Herbert Hoover in

1928. The worldwide depression that overtook the U.S. economy in 1929, plus defections by Republicans in Congress, led to Hoover's defeat in 1932 by Gov. Franklin D. Roosevelt of New York, a triumph in which Roosevelt carried all but six states. In 1936 the party's victory was overwhelming, with only Maine and Vermont voting Republican. Roosevelt was reelected in 1940 and again in 1944.

**Franklin D. Roosevelt.** Roosevelt's domestic program, coupled with heavy relief expenditures during the Depression and the large federal expenditures for World War II, won votes for the Democrats and stimulated the economy at the same time.

Domestic reform was pushed aside when the United States entered the war in December 1941. Roosevelt had already transformed the United States into an "arsenal of democracy," and he now became a major leader of the Allies. He died on April 12, 1945, before the war ended, and was succeeded by Vice-Pres. Harry S. Truman.

Truman was often thwarted by a conservative coalition of Republicans and Southern Democrats. From 1947 on he was preoccupied with foreign problems, especially Soviet expansion, the Cold War, and finally the Korean War (1950–53). Truman was elected president in 1948, defeating Thomas E. Dewey in a remarkable upset victory, but he declined to run for reelection in 1952, and the Democrats nominated Gov. Adlai E. Stevenson of Illinois.

By choosing for their 1952 presidential candidate a popular World War II general, Dwight D. Eisenhower, the Republican Party returned to power under the dominance of its liberal-moderate wing, as opposed to its conservative wing led by Sen. Robert A. Taft of Ohio. Eisenhower's moderate course in domestic and foreign affairs attracted much non-Republican support, and in 1956 the Republicans renominated him and his vice-president, Richard M. Nixon, of California. Eisenhower defeated Democratic candidate Stevenson for the second time. The Democrats, however, won control of Congress and in 1958 increased their majority.

**John F. Kennedy.** In 1960 the Democratic Party nominated Sen. John F. Kennedy of Massachusetts for president and Sen. Lyndon B. Johnson of Texas for vice-president. In a vigorous campaign—highlighted by televised debates with the Republican candidate, Vice-Pres. Nixon—Kennedy attacked the Republican administration for lack of leadership and won the election, though by a very close popular vote. Yet the heavily Democratic Congress was reluctant to pass administration-sponsored legislation. After Kennedy's untimely assassination on Nov. 22, 1963, President Johnson was able to push through Congress much of the legislation proposed by Kennedy. In 1964 the Democratic National Convention nominated Johnson to run for president with Sen. Hubert H. Humphrey of Minnesota as his running mate. The Republicans nominated a leading conservative senator, Barry M. Goldwater of Arizona, and a New York congressman, William E. Miller.

The election on November 3 was an overwhelming Democratic victory. The Republican national ticket carried only Arizona and five states of the deep South. The Johnson landslide cut across all levels of government, bringing with it large Democratic majorities in Congress and in state legislatures throughout the country and led to a wave of legislation dealing with education, health care for the aged, air and water pollution, urban blight, unemployment, depressed areas, and the desire of blacks for full citizenship. More and more concern, however, arose over the war in Vietnam. The 1966 elections cut Democratic majorities in Congress and lost gubernatorial seats.

***Richard M. Nixon.*** In 1968 Nixon, Eisenhower's vice-president, who had been defeated by Kennedy in 1960, made a comeback and swept to a first-ballot nomination by the Republicans. His running mate was Gov. Spiro T. Agnew of Maryland. Their campaign capitalized on the electorate's dissatisfaction with the escalation of the Vietnam War, and a rapidly worsening urban crisis on many fronts—housing, crime, education, and civil rights. Despite a third-party campaign by George C. Wallace, candidate of the American Independent Party, the Republicans won. However, although Nixon and Agnew were easily reelected in 1972, the unprecedented events of 1972–74 brought the Republican Party to a low ebb. The 1974 elections gave the Democrats massive majorities in Congress. These majorities were not significantly reduced in 1976 when a Southern Democrat campaigning in an anti-federal-bureaucracy vein, Jimmy Carter, narrowly defeated Republican Gerald R. Ford, who had been appointed to succeed Agnew and then succeeded the ousted Nixon.

# 17.
# Minor Parties in America

Strong ideology or other special interest has usually motivated third parties, while consensus on a broad span of issues has characterized the major American parties. The issue of slavery galvanized a number of minor parties, among them one of the first in the United States—the Liberty Party, organized in 1839–40 to oppose and restrict the political power of the slave states. It contributed somewhat to Henry Clay's defeat in 1844; a few years later it was virtually absorbed by the Free-Soil Party.

The ideology uniting Free-Soilers was not the abolition of slavery but resistance to the presence of black labor—either free or slave—in the territories. "Let the soil of our extensive domains," as they stated in their 1848 platform, "be kept free for the hardy pioneers of our own and the oppressed and banished of other lands, seeking homes of comfort and fields of enterprise in the New World." The final plank contained their historic slogan: "Free soil, free speech, free labor, and free men." They nominated former president Martin Van Buren of New York for president and Charles F. Adams of Massachusetts for vice-president but polled only slightly more than ten percent of the popular vote for president. In 1852 they did only half as well, and in 1856 the remnants of the party were absorbed into the Republican Party.

## American Party

The American Party, which became known as the Know-Nothing Party, flourished in the decade before 1860 and stressed a strong nativist (pro-American, anti-foreign) viewpoint. Its roots lay in the Federalist-Republican struggles of the early years under the Constitution when the foreign ideas and influences of Jefferson's followers aroused strong opposition. As immigration increased and Roman Catholic immigrants grew in numbers, the geographical segregation and the clannishness of foreign city voters gave them a power that politicians strove to control. In labor disputes and political feuds such immigrants—especially the Irish and Germans—displayed great power and at times gave offense by their criticism of American institutions.

At immigration centers, such as Boston, Philadelphia, and

New York, the Roman Catholic Church was held by some to be perpetuating foreign power on American soil. Many regarded it as a transplanted foreign institution, un-American in both organization and ideas. Thus numerous nativists became involved in anti-Catholic and anti-Irish city riots, and in local elections they endorsed anti-foreign candidates for public office in order to uphold "Americanism."

First known by a variety of names, including the Order of the Star Spangled Banner, the (Native) American Party began its national career in 1845. With Whig support the nativists carried New York City and Boston but soon lost the support of the Whigs, and by 1847 the national organization was disappearing. In the early 1850s nativism was revived politically by a rising tide of immigrants. The phantomlike Know-Nothing movement had sprung from nativist secret societies and lodges whose main attraction was their ritualistic mysteriousness. The use of handclasps, signals, and passwords formed a part of the Know-Nothing lore. Emulating the Masons, the organization was secret; when interrogated about it, the members were supposed to answer that they knew nothing, hence the name.

The times were propitious for the success of such an aggressive third party. In 1854 the Know-Nothing gains were remarkable. Renaming itself the American Party, it reached its greatest strength during the height of the national struggle over slavery. It elected governors, legislatures, or both in four New England states and in Maryland, Kentucky, and California. Thereafter the organization spread like wildfire—especially in the South, where there were, paradoxically, few immigrants. The party straddled the slavery issue, but northern Know-Nothings were swept into the antislavery movement in 1854. The national platform of 1856 (adopted by a secret grand council) included anti-alien and anti-Catholic planks and offered political sops to both North and South on the slavery issue. The party's unsuccessful presidential nominee that year was Millard Fillmore. Eight months later a Republican Party wave swept the Know-Nothings out of the North, and by 1859 the party was confined to the border states. The equally unsuccessful antiwar Constitutional Union Party—the "Do-Nothing" Bell-Everett Party of 1860—was mainly composed of Know-Nothing remnants. The year 1860 practically marked the disappearance of the Know-Nothings as a political power.

Two other groups that took the name American Party appeared in the 1870s and 1880s. An antiliquor, Bible-quoting party organized itself as the National Christian Association in 1872. It proved ineffectual and was reduced by the 1880s to backing Prohibitionist candidates for office. In 1886 another American Party appeared in California. This group elected various state and local officials, participated in pro-vigilante activities, and took part in the anti-Chinese agitation that rocked San Francisco. With unemployment rampant, the party's demands for Oriental exclusion and delayed naturalization for other aliens proved temporarily popular.

During the hard times following the panic of 1873, another minor party flourished briefly under the designation of Greenback (paper money) Party. It was essentially a protest against deflation and against a return to the gold standard. The Greenbackers, mainly consisting of Western farmers, demanded that the amount of paper currency issued during the Civil War be maintained or expanded as a means of keeping money in circulation and helping to keep prices up. The movement gained enough strength to halt the retirement of greenbacks for a while but was not able to prevent the return to the gold standard in 1879. The Greenback Party eventually merged with the Free Silver movement of the 1880s and 1890s, which had similar objectives but advocated the use of silver instead of paper currency.

The People's Party of the United States of America (Populist Party) was founded at Cincinnati, Ohio, May 21, 1891, at a mass convention of delegates representing discontented farmers of the Northwest and the South. In 1892 the Populists nominated James B. Weaver of Iowa for president and James G. Field of Virginia for vice-president. In the presidential election of that year they polled twenty-two electoral votes and more than one million popular votes. By fusing with the Democrats in certain states, the Populists were also able to elect several members of Congress, three governors, and hundreds of minor officials and legislators, nearly all in the Northwest. In the South most of the farmers refused to endanger white supremacy by voting against the Democratic Party.

Populist gains in the midterm elections of 1894 were considerable, but when the Democrats nominated William Jennings Bryan in 1896 on a free silver platform the Populists endorsed him, although nominating their own vice-presidential candidate, Thomas E. Watson of Georgia. After Bryan's defeat, most Populists became Democrats.

## Progressive Parties

Three times in the first half of the twentieth century a political party using the name "progressive" became active in U.S. presidential campaigns—1912, 1924, and 1948. The Progressive Party of 1912 began as an insurgent outbreak among Republican members of Congress in 1910 against the Speaker of the House of Representatives, Joseph G. Cannon. Opposition to the administration of President Taft crystallized in 1911 when the National Progressive Republican League was organized by Sen. Robert M. La Follette of Wisconsin. Theodore Roosevelt soon placed himself at the head of that movement. Alleging unfair tactics on the part of the "Old Guard," his followers left the Republican National Convention in Chicago, Ill. (June 1912), and Roosevelt was nominated for the presidency by a Progressive (Bull Moose) National Convention, also held in Chicago.

During World War I partisanship was in abeyance, but upon the end of the war the old Republican rift soon reappeared. The administrations of Harding and Coolidge encountered dissatisfaction among farmers, and in 1924 Wisconsin and other farm states held a conference for progressive political action. The result was a new Progressive Party that nominated Senator La Follette for president and Sen. Burton K. Wheeler of Montana, a Democrat, for vice-president. The party platform promised a "housecleaning" of executive departments, public control of natural resources, public ownership of railways, and tax reduction. The Republicans denounced the alleged radicalism of the La Follette platform, ignored Democratic attacks, and won the election. La Follette claimed nearly 5 million votes but carried only Wisconsin; after his death in 1925 the party dissolved.

Unlike its predecessors, the Progressive Party founded by Henry A. Wallace in 1947–48 stressed foreign issues in its platform—principally abandonment of the Marshall Plan and the Truman Doctrine (to help economic recovery of European countries). Formally organized in Philadelphia, the party named Wallace as its 1948 candidate for president and Sen. Glen H. Taylor of Idaho for vice-presidential candidate. That year the national convention of the Communist Party of the U.S. announced its support of the Wallace-Taylor ticket. In the election the party polled only 1,156,103 popular votes and won no electoral votes.

Another politician of the same name, Alabama Gov. George C. Wallace, figured in a third-party effort twenty years later when he headed the American Independent Party's national slate. Rallying white resistance to federal racial-desegregation efforts, and conservative opposition to excesses of "liberal" bureaucrats, he won forty-six electoral votes in 1968. While seeking the regular Democratic nomination in 1972, Wallace was partially paralyzed by a would-be assassin.

Although no major U.S. political party has ever used the name *Conservative,* from the first years of the republic conservative ideas have been continually at work in American politics. Both the Federalist Party of New England and the Republican Party of Virginia exhibited different aspects of conservative thought and practice—the first with its emphasis on fiscal order and national security, the latter with its attachment to the rural interest. During the Civil War, spokesmen for both North and South declared that theirs alone was the truly conservative stand.

The word *liberal* was seldom employed in the United States until the coming of World War I and did not become truly popular until the first administration of Pres. Franklin D. Roosevelt. During the Roosevelt years and World War II, conservatism came to carry connotations of regression and wealthied self-interest. But about 1948 the spirits of conservatives began to revive. Several books by reflective conservatives gained wide attention, and certain political leaders began once more to use the word with more approval. Among them was Republican Sen. Robert A. Taft, who described himself as a "liberal conservative."

The failure of a truly radical party to win the votes of any considerable number of Americans probably accounts for the lack of need for a formal organization of American conservatives: no challenge was ever strong enough to break down the barriers between the established Republican and Democratic parties and blend their respective conservative elements. In the past the absence of a distinct aristocracy and the existence of numerous opportunities for personal advancement tended to discourage the formation of theoretical or class parties, whether conservative, liberal, or radical. As the United States entered the mainstream of world affairs, during and after World War II, however, and stood opposed to the threat of Soviet Communism, there became evident in America a growing desire for a distinct political philosophy to oppose Marxism. As in Europe, the result was the renewed popularity of conservative doctrines. In practical politics, the ascendancy of Sen. Barry Goldwater of Arizona—the most vigorous figure among conservative politicians of the early 1960s—was an indication of this changed climate of opinion, though he was defeated in the 1964 presidential race.

## Communist Party

Communism emerged in the United States only after Russian Communists encouraged left-wing elements to separate from the Socialist Party in 1919 and to imitate Moscow by creating a Communist Party. After subsequent dissension had splintered the party, and deportation from the United States had removed some of its noncitizen leaders, Moscow ordered creation in 1921 of an open party that could operate legally. Thus emerged the Workers' Party of America, but the Communist Party was continued as a secret group until 1923, when Moscow ordered its complete elimination. Characteristic factional conflict continued within the legal party, requiring Moscow's intervention in 1929 to restore party discipline. A Communist Party of the United States was then recreated as an avowed section of the Communist International.

Dissolution of the Communist International by Moscow in 1943 to curry favor with Western democracies in the joint war against Hitler's Germany required reorganization of its U.S. affiliate. The Communist Party's constitution, in its revised form that had been adopted in 1938, contained no statement of relationship to Moscow. The party sought to associate itself in the public mind with American democratic traditions. This trend toward masking the party's revolutionary role and its Moscow orientation was accentuated with passage by the U.S. Congress in 1940 of the Voorhis Act requiring registration of organizations subject to foreign control. The party adopted a new constitution and went so far as to re-form in 1944 into what was called a "political association," having as its stated aim collaboration within the historic U.S. two-party system aiming at victory in the war.

Defeat of Germany and Japan in 1945 brought an immediate change to the U.S. Communist Party on orders from Moscow. The mask of political association, which had proved effective in recruitment of politically uninformed Americans during the period of wartime collaboration with the U.S.S.R., was put aside. The Communist Party of the United States was re-created, but its constitution sought to avoid anticipated distrust on the part of U.S. patriots by retaining the earlier espousal of democratic traditions. Following Stalin's death in

1953, revelation of his excesses as personal dictator over the Communist Party of the Soviet Union caused many resignations from the party, as did mounting exposure of party aims by U.S. scholars and public associations, and enactment of restrictive legislation. Membership fell to 8,000, according to a 1958 estimate of a congressional committee.

Following revelation of Communist infiltration of the federal bureaucracy and in the heat of hostility against Communist China during the Korean War, the McCarran Act was enacted in 1950. It made criminal "knowingly to combine or conspire with others to perform any act which would substantially contribute to the establishment within the United States of totalitarian dictatorship, the direction and control of which was to be vested in any foreign government, foreign organization, or foreign individual." Laws of similar intent were enacted in some states. Communists were excluded thereby from the school system as teachers, from foreign travel, and from labor union leadership — without disqualifying their unions from the protection of the Taft-Hartley Act. Some state laws denied them the right to run for any elective office. An act of Aug. 24, 1954, further hampered the Communist Party, and it claimed that it had been "outlawed."

Communist Party senior officials were convicted in 1949 under the Smith Act of 1940, and the U.S. Supreme Court upheld the convictions. The 1940 act made it a criminal offense to advocate overthrow of any government in the United States by force or violence. Subsequent convictions elicited a clarification from the Supreme Court in 1957 that teaching and advocating forcible overthrow of the government were not punishable under the Smith Act so long as such teaching and advocating were divorced from the effort to instigate action.

Enforcement of state antisedition laws was nullified by a Supreme Court decision in 1956 declaring a Pennsylvania statute an unlawful assumption of authority in a field preempted by the federal government. The effect of the 1954 "outlawry" remained unclear when no judicial review of the statute occurred immediately and the Communist Party ceased to run candidates, although it continued to hold congresses.

The party's long legal battle against the registration requirements of the Subversive Activities Control Act of 1950 ended in 1961 when the U.S. Supreme Court upheld the act as regulation and not prohibition, but the party continued to resist. In 1964 the Supreme Court declared unconstitutional prohibition of foreign passports to all Communists without consideration of degree of engagement in party affairs. In 1965 the Supreme Court rejected the 1950 act's requirement that individual Communists register as violating the Fifth Amendment. Emboldened by these legal victories, the Communist Party held a congress in 1966 and announced resumption of open activities.

## Socialist Party

In 1900 two small American Socialist groups joined forces to nominate a presidential slate headed by Eugene V. Debs, who polled nearly 100,000 votes. Following the campaign, the older groups dissolved and formed the Socialist Party to serve as "the party of the working class and those in sympathy with it," dedicated to bringing about "a system of collective ownership by the entire people of the means of production and distribution." The immediate demands in the party's platform included women's suffrage, old-age pensions, unemployment insurance, health and accident insurance, increased wages, reduced working hours, direct legislation, and public ownership of utilities.

During the next eleven years, from 1901 to 1912, the party grew steadily in numbers and influence. Its membership increased to 118,000; its presidential vote, with Debs as candidate, from 97,000 to nearly 900,000; its representation in public office from zero to more than 1,000, including 56 mayors, more than 300 aldermen, numerous state legislators, and one congressman, Victor L. Berger from Milwaukee.

In 1912 the party was engaged in a vigorous internal struggle with the followers of William D. Haywood, leader of the Industrial Workers of the World (IWW), who emphasized direct industrial action, including sabotage and the general strike, as a means to a cooperative social order. The majority of the party adhered to their belief in parliamentary action and amended their constitution to exclude from membership those who advocated sabotage and violence. In 1913 Haywood was expelled from the party's executive committee. The controversy led to the withdrawal of numerous "direct actionists" from the party. In 1916 the party nominated an antimilitarist for president and rolled up a vote of more than half a million.

When the United States entered the war in April 1917, the Socialist Party at its St. Louis convention declared "its unalterable opposition to the war just declared." During the next year many of the party's journals and meetings were suppressed by the government; Debs was arrested for delivering an antiwar speech at Canton, Ohio, and was sentenced to a federal penitentiary for ten years. While Socialist activity came to a standstill in many parts of the country, it took on renewed vigor in other sections. In New York City, Morris Hillquit, Socialist candidate for mayor on a platform that called for an early and democratic peace, received 146,000 votes, helping elect ten assemblymen and seven aldermen.

On Nov. 7, 1917, the Russian Bolsheviks staged their successful revolution. Many members of the Socialist Party were of the opinion that the United States was ripe for a similar revolution and urged the adoption of Bolshevik tactics and the joining of the Communist International. To aid their cause, they swelled party membership rolls with recent immigrants from countries of Eastern Europe who were better acquainted with the institutions of their homelands than with those of the United States.

The struggle over socialist versus communist tactics culminated in the Chicago convention of the Socialist Party in late August 1919. The left-wing elements in the party were defeated and withdrew to form the Communist and Communist Labor parties. Though the Socialist Party's membership during the struggle was greatly reduced (numbering 26,766 after the convention), the party's vote in 1920 with Debs—still in prison—again as its nominee, exceeded 900,000. In 1924 the Socialists endorsed the La Follette Progressive Party ticket in hopes that a continuing Progressive or Farmer-Labor party might evolve from it, but when no new party materialized, the Socialists returned to their traditional policy of supporting their own candidates.

Debs, five times Socialist presidential candidate, died in 1926, and the party turned to Norman Thomas, writer, lecturer, former Presbyterian minister, and co-executive director of the League for Industrial Democracy, as its new standard-bearer. In 1928, when many were predicting that the "new capitalism" was guaranteeing permanent prosperity to the country, Thomas received but 267,200 votes. Four years later, however, in the midst of the Depression, his vote total increased to 884,781.

Various factions developed within the party over "the road to power" and the possibility of limited cooperation with the Communists in the fight against world fascism and reaction.

This controversy led in 1936 to the withdrawal of several hundred party members and their organization of a Social Democratic federation. The 1936 convention decisively repudiated any political united front with the Communist Party. During the next few years antagonism to the Communist Party was progressively sharpened by the American Communists' support of Stalin's policies. In its drive to surmount the economic depression in the following four-year period (1933 –36), the Roosevelt administration embodied in its New Deal legislation many immediate demands of the Socialist Party platform in the fields of social security, housing, public power, and labor-management relations.

During the 1940s and 1950s the Socialists continued to nominate presidential candidates in campaigns emphasizing that their economic goal was not the public ownership of all industry but an economy aimed at equality of opportunity in which public, cooperative, and private ownership could exist side by side. In the 1960s the party gave up nominating its own presidential candidate but campaigned for the Socialist platform, stressing the necessity for an honest, meaningful political realignment.

While the Socialist Party's electoral successes have been less than its founders had hoped, since the beginning of the century and especially since the 1930s, the party has seen a great many of its demands met by government action initiated by the major parties, especially the Democrats. Such demands have included the expansion of public educational, health, recreational, housing, and social security services; the conservation of natural resources; the strengthening of labor legislation; the end of racial discrimination; economic and cultural aid to underdeveloped countries, and international agreements for disarmament with strict inspection and controls.

Explicit Socialist objectives have been reflected in the platforms and legislative agendas of both major parties from time to time—a fact helping to demonstrate that contrasts between two-party and multiparty systems are often exaggerated. Both Democratic and Republican parties have been influenced importantly and repeatedly by the goals and agitations of minor parties. Indeed the coalescent nature of the major parties—their ability to absorb members and digest programs of special-interest groups—may account for the continued vitality of both Democrats and Republicans.

# 18.
# The Election Campaign

The election campaign is an American institution that first emerged in recognizable form at the close of the Jackson era. It was a direct result of the evolution of democracy in America—a gradual process, indeed, with few great landmarks.

The word *democracy* itself is relative and must be redefined in each age. Black persons were generally excluded from political participation until after the Civil War, and women were not given the vote until 1920. Among free, white, adult males, who never numbered more than about fifteen percent of the total population, there was a considerable amount of democracy even in the colonial period.

Property qualifications for voting, common in the colonies, did not exclude many in a society of landowners. The Revolutionary period marked a small step toward greater democracy, for the early state constitutions generally reduced property qualifications for voting. Pennsylvania opened the vote to all taxpayers, and most states abolished religious tests. The Jeffersonians talked much about the "common man" but did little to give him the vote. After the War of 1812 a surge of constitutional revision on the state level gradually expanded the suffrage. Constitutions drawn during the Revolutionary era were revised by Maryland (1810), South Carolina (1810), Connecticut (1818), New York (1821), Massachusetts (1821), Virginia (1830), and North Carolina (1836). In addition, the new states of the West, though generally imitative in their political institutions, tended to adopt the more democratic features of eastern constitutions.

## Election of 1840

The Jacksonians, not noticeably involved in this leveling process, did not directly benefit from it. Not until 1840 was there any significant increase in voter participation in a presidential election. In the Eastern cities, moreover, workingmen were almost evenly divided in their political allegiance. Elsewhere, there were many voters who supported Jackson, not as a great democrat, but because he represented the virtues of energy and forcefulness that they admired. It is nevertheless true that the Jacksonians developed a rhetoric that appealed to the hopes and frustrations of the common man.

The rhetoric itself, even if only veneer, represented a new direction in American politics. The successful propaganda techniques of the *Washington Globe*, edited by Jackson's intimate adviser Francis Preston Blair, evidenced a new concern for public opinion. The same was true of the Jacksonian concept of rotation in office, which rested on the assumption that any honest and reasonably intelligent man was capable of managing the government. Supporters of Adams were dismissed and replaced with loyal Jacksonians. Though Jackson replaced less than a fifth of the federal officeholders, the concept of using the federal patronage as a reward for victory marked an important aspect in the development of party organizations. If the flowering of the spoils system in the post-Civil War period ultimately produced governmental corruption and mismanagement, it nevertheless represented to Jackson a vital step in the evolution of democracy. The success of the techniques of the Jacksonians in appealing to the common man was evident to their opponents. In 1840 when the Whigs captured the presidency for William Henry Harrison, they succeeded only by assimilating the methods of popular appeal pioneered by the Jacksonians.

One landmark in the process of broadening popular participation in politics was the emergence of the national nominating convention. When the Democrats adopted the idea in 1836, Martin Van Buren, Jackson's handpicked successor, was the presidential candidate of the first Democratic National Convention.

The Whig Party was just getting off the ground, albeit slowly. Its name implied opposition to Jackson, whose antagonists styled him "King Andrew" to decry what they saw as his dictatorial style. The Whigs were more coalition than party, slow to achieve formal organization and hard put to agree on anything. They put forward candidates in 1836 but did not hold a nominating convention until 1840. Only once in their twenty-year history were they able to agree on a platform. In 1836 they opposed Van Buren with several regional candidates. Hugh Lawson White carried Tennessee and Georgia, and Daniel Webster collected some electoral votes in New England; William Henry Harrison did even better in the Northwest.

Harrison, a Virginian by birth, a Westerner by adoption, was a hero of the Indian campaigns in the War of 1812. He was a typical Whig candidate—a military hero possessing the valuable assets of vague ideology and broad popular appeal.

When the Whigs held their first nominating convention in 1840, they chose him to seek the presidency. For his running mate the Whigs sought Southern support by nominating an old Jeffersonian, John Tyler of Virginia. As a candidate Harrison was inarticulate and content to let the politicians run the show. The result was a campaign that introduced hoopla to the search for votes. It instituted the use of campaign songs, political slogans, and party insignia. The Democrats referred to Harrison as the "log cabin and hard cider" candidate to deride his identification with the wild Ohio frontier where he had settled. The Whigs immediately adopted miniature log cabins and cider jugs as their major identifying symbols. Harrison, victor over the Indians at the Battle of Tippecanoe, was known as "Old Tip," and under the euphonious slogan "Tippecanoe and Tyler Too," the Whigs ignored political issues and concentrated on parades and picnics.

The Democrats also had used songs, ballyhoo, and slogans to solicit votes during this "first modern election campaign." The popular expression "OK" is said to have originated during the campaign, representing "Old Kinderhook," referring to Van Buren's New York birthplace. The voters turned out in larger numbers than ever before. They chose the Whig, William Henry Harrison, seeming to accept the evaluation of one of the anti-Van Buren slogans of the campaign: "Van, Van, the used-up man!" The inauguration ceremonies, March 4, 1841, were conducted in a cold drizzle. Harrison, the old campaigner, insisted on delivering his lengthy inaugural address without hat or overcoat. He caught a cold, developed pneumonia, and died a month later. John Tyler became president—the first vice-president to succeed to that office.

## Election of 1844

Two explosive issues dominated the campaign of 1844. John C. Calhoun, President Tyler's secretary of state, that spring had signed a treaty of annexation with Texas. Calhoun candidly admitted that his purpose was to add to slave territory, and that was enough to ensure the treaty's rejection by the Senate. The Whigs controlled the Senate but the president, though elected as a Whig, had no control over the party machinery. Henry Clay was the real leader of the Whigs, and he greatly feared the impact of the expansion issue. The Democratic leader Van Buren had similar fears and the two tried to remove the issue from the approaching campaign by putting out simultaneous letters opposing the annexation of Texas on the grounds that it would cause a war with Mexico.

The other popular issue addressed demands by American settlers in the Oregon territory (which by treaty was occupied jointly by the United States and Britain) for admission to the Union. Clay was nominated by the Whigs on an antiexpansionist platform. At the Democratic convention Van Buren was abandoned by the expansionist Southern delegates, who engineered the nomination of the first "dark horse" candidate, James K. Polk of Tennessee. The sectional issue was avoided by linking Texas with Oregon, so free territory as well as slave would be added to the Union.

Campaigner Polk surprised the country by taking a positive stand on the two burning issues. While other candidates hedged on Texas, he demanded annexation. While other candidates evaded the Oregon problem, he openly advocated a drastic change in policy in the boundary dispute with Great Britain, using the slogan "54° 40′ or fight." His election was close but decisive—a popular plurality of about 38,000, and 170 electoral votes against 105 for Henry Clay. Many in the North suspected that the Democrats' drive for expansion was a Southern conspiracy to add to slave territory. In fact, an anonymous letter was published during the campaign falsely depicting Polk as a slaveholder.

## Slavery Issues

Inevitably the hastening controversy over slavery shaped the national campaigns from 1848 through 1860. In 1848 the Democratic nominee Lewis Cass, who—like Webster and James Buchanan—had lost out to Polk at the 1844 convention, campaigned on the doctrine of "popular sovereignty," which would allow the people of the West to decide for themselves whether their territory should be slave or free. Former President Van Buren, again denied renomination by his Democratic Party, ran under the banner of the new Free-Soil Party. The Whigs, too divided as usual on the slavery issue to agree on a platform, named another military hero whose political views were unknown—Gen. Zachary Taylor, a slaveowning Virginian, who won narrowly.

By 1852 the Whigs were well advanced in the process of dissolution. They simply avoided the slavery issue. That year's Whig military hero, Gen. Winfield Scott, carried only four states. In 1856 success for the new Republican Party hinged on the widespread conviction that only a North united on the principle of free soil could prevent the spread and ultimate triumph of slavery. To dramatize this warning Republican orators even accused the Democratic Party of attempting to establish slavery in Kansas under the subterfuge of popular sovereignty. The Republican convention, meeting in Philadelphia, nominated for president John C. Frémont, an Army officer and explorer of the West. The party platform demanded the immediate admission of Kansas as a free state and the construction of a railroad to the Pacific, supported by federal aid. The Democrats, meeting in Cincinnati, nominated James Buchanan. As they had done in their three previous conventions, the Democrats supported strict limitations on federal power, especially on the matter of slavery in the states. At Cincinnati they reaffirmed their devotion to the principle of popular sovereignty as embodied in the Kansas-Nebraska Act. The remnant of the Whig Party, including the Know-Nothings of the North and those Southern conservatives who had no interest in any further debate on slavery, nominated Millard Fillmore.

In November only Maryland gave Fillmore a majority, although he gained more votes in the South than did the Whig Party in 1852. The Democrats succeeded in electing Buchanan, but the party throughout the North was clearly in retreat. All the free states but five favored Frémont. For the first time in the history of the country a distinctly antislavery candidate actually came near to capturing the presidency. Buchanan won by sweeping the South and holding Pennsylvania, Indiana, and Illinois in the North.

A major element in a relatively minor election campaign in 1858 came to have significance well beyond the question of who would represent Illinois in the U.S. Senate. A former one-term Whig congressman named Abraham Lincoln entered the senatorial election of 1858 as a Republican, determined to drive home the wedges already splitting the Democratic Party. Stephen A. Douglas was the perfect opponent for this purpose, since he was the leading candidate for the Democratic presidential nomination in 1860. During the early weeks of the campaign Lincoln pursued the "Little Giant" around Illinois to take advantage of Douglas's larger crowds. Finally in July, Lincoln and his friends challenged Douglas to a debate. Douglas, knowing that he had everything to lose, accepted reluctantly. The two agreed to meet in the seven congressional districts where they had not campaigned.

Slavery in the territories was the main question at issue in the debates. Douglas promised free territories without needless civil strife through the normal functioning of popular sovereignty. But Lincoln knew that Douglas, if forced to defend his views of popular sovereignty, must alienate either the voters of Illinois or the leaders of the South. For years Douglas had struggled to avoid this dilemma. He had escaped a quarrel with the South over the Kansas-Nebraska Bill by terming it merely "a question of self-government." He had refused to question either the Cincinnati platform of 1856 or the Dred Scott decision. But a current issue over a constitution proposed for Kansas that would protect slave property already there gave him no choice but to offend Southern extremists. He had to make a decision between Illinois and the South. Lincoln predicted what it would be. "He cares nothing for the South—he knows he is already dead there," Lincoln wrote late in July. "He only leans Southward now to keep the Buchanan party from growing in Illinois."

In Freeport, Ill., on Aug. 27, 1858, Lincoln posed the question that plagued Douglas and the Democratic Party: "Can the people of a United States territory . . . exclude Slavery from its limits prior to the formation of a state constitution?" Douglas responded with a tone of impatience: "I answer emphatically, as Mr. Lincoln has heard me answer a hundred times at every stump in Illinois, that in my opinion the people of a Territory can, by lawful means, exclude slavery from their limits prior to the formation of a State Constitution. . . It matters not what way the Supreme Court may hereafter decide as to the abstract question . . . slavery cannot exist a day or an hour anywhere, unless it is supported by local police regulations." Thus the people of a territory had the lawful means to introduce or exclude slavery. Constitutionalism, he regretted, had simply confused the issue.

Nonintervention was the key to Douglas's philosophy. At Jonesboro, Lincoln put it to the test again. He asked Douglas if, as a member of Congress, he would vote to give slaveowners protection for slave property in the territories. This was a crucial question—one which the South would soon force remorselessly on the national Democratic leadership. But Douglas again answered emphatically. For Congress to give such guarantees, he said, would defy the principles of popular sovereignty. Douglas's realism and devotion to the democratic process forced him into strong positions that were offensive to Southerners, and he knew it. Lincoln's questioning, in forcing Douglas to repeat what he had stated earlier, merely dramatized the hopelessness of continued Democratic unity. Douglas won the senatorial race in the Illinois legislature later in 1858, but Lincoln saw the lasting significance of the debates. "Douglas had the ingenuity to be supported in the late contest both as the best means to break down, and to uphold the Slave interest," he wrote in November 1858. "No ingenuity can keep those antagonistic elements in harmony long. Another explosion will soon come."

By 1860 the population of the United States had reached 31 million, an increase of more than 8 million in ten years. As the decennial increases of population became larger, so did the divergence of the sections in population, and still more in wealth and resources. Two more free states came into the Union during the late fifties—Minnesota (1858) and Oregon (1859). Kansas continued to clamor for the same privileges. The free and slave states, which had been almost equal in population in 1790, stood now 19 million to 12 million. Of the population of the slave states, the 4 million slaves and the 250,000 free blacks were not so much a factor of strength as a possible source of weakness and danger. No serious slave uprising had taken place in the South for a generation, but John Brown's attack in 1859 on Harpers Ferry and the alarm that it carried throughout the South were tokens of a danger that added an alarming prospect to the threat of civil war.

## Election of 1860

When the Democratic convention of 1860 met at Charleston, S.C., the final strand of the last national political organization parted: the Democratic Party itself divided on the issue of slavery. Before the convention reached the nominating process, it broke up over the platform. No amount of accommodation could close the gap between the Southern platform, demanding full federal intervention in behalf of almost nonexistent slave property in the territories, and the Douglas interpretation of popular sovereignty. Northern delegates were determined that the national party should cease to be the agency of the slave interests, as it had been under Buchanan. As debates on the platform gripped the convention, the exchanges became hotter and delegates began to grapple on the floor, cheered on by the galleries. The assembly moved noisily toward disruption.

When the first show of strength in the voting convinced Southern leaders that they could not control the convention, they refrained from contesting the will of the Douglas supporters. When the platform was adopted by Northern votes, William L. Yancey led his Alabama delegation out of the hall amid the howling of the spectators, followed closely by the delegations from Mississippi, Louisiana, South Carolina, Florida, and Texas. The dominant leadership of the Southern democracy now stood in open defiance of the North. Eventually the Douglas Democrats reassembled at Baltimore and, after provoking a second secession of Southern delegates, nominated Douglas for the presidency. Southern Democrats, meeting at Richmond and then at Baltimore, selected John C. Breckinridge of Kentucky as their nominee.

The remnants of the old Whig and Know-Nothing parties, assuming the name Constitutional Union Party, met at Baltimore and nominated John Bell of Tennessee. This group hoped to attract the support of all Americans who were tired of the perennial debate over slavery.

For the Republican Party, meeting at Chicago, the challenge was clear. The returns of 1856 revealed that, with the votes of Pennsylvania and Illinois or Indiana, the party would have been successful. The former Democrats in the party were now ready to accept a platform that would secure the votes of these states. As a result the Republican platform of 1860 had a much broader appeal than that of four years earlier. The need to capture the Northern conservative vote explains in large measure the rejection of Seward and the nomination of Abraham Lincoln of Illinois.

In the November election Lincoln carried the entire North, yet he was a minority president, polling scarcely forty percent of the total votes cast. Both the Republican and Democratic parties increased their voting percentages over 1856, largely at the expense of the Know-Nothings. Lincoln increased the Republican vote in Pennsylvania, New Jersey, Indiana, and Illinois; his gains were made largely in the rural districts. Douglas ran a strong second to Lincoln in the popular vote, 1,383,000–1,866,000, but carried only one state— Missouri—and three of New Jersey's electoral votes. The Constitutional Union Party, having adopted no platform on slavery, had a wide appeal in the Unionist border states, carrying Virginia, Kentucky, and Tennessee. Breckinridge carried the remaining slave states. Lincoln's victory, however, did not result from the Democratic schism. Had all his opponents agreed on one candidate, he would still have carried all his states except California and Oregon, leaving him a majority of twenty-one electoral votes. Lincoln's victory resulted from the fact that he carried, often by narrow margins, those heavily populated regions of the United States where political and economic power had been accumulating for a decade. Lincoln's election demonstrated beyond any doubt what the politics of the fifties had often denied—that the South had been reduced to minority status.

Lincoln's conduct of the war enjoyed little support in Congress, in the press, or among party leaders. The Radical Republicans abused the president unmercifully, and even most moderate party members refused to defend him. But Lincoln was never overwhelmed, for he was a consummate politician. If congressional leaders would not conform to his program, there were powerful weapons in the presidential arsenal that he could employ. Through the astute use of federal patronage, he could bend politicians to his purposes.

Lincoln wanted the renomination in 1864 and used the distribution of spoils to gain this end. Congressmen might condemn his policies, but he demanded and won their support of his candidacy. Through patronage Lincoln held the advantage over his Radical opponents, many of whom favored another Fremont nomination. The Radicals could hardly replace him without condemning the Republican administration of the war. Lincoln's agents maneuvered behind the scenes; by convention time they had lined up enough votes to secure his nomination without opposition.

The ensuing campaign was a veritable mud bath. Vilification and vituperation were heaped upon the president and his opponent. When the presidential ballots were counted in November, it was obvious that neither Lincoln nor the Republican Party had captured the overwhelming support of Northern voters. With the entire South out of the Union, the returns of 1864 gave Lincoln but fifty-two percent of the popular vote. Almost half the ballots were marked for McClellan, the Democratic nominee representing a party whose platform demanded peace (with some reservations) and charged Lincoln with administrative failure. McClellan, however, disagreed with the antiwar position of many Democrats and actually repudiated his party's platform. Apparently the main pillar that upheld Lincoln and his party was the predominating Union sentiment of the North.

After the end of the war, the murder of Lincoln, and the accession of Vice-Pres. Andrew Johnson to the White House, another significant "off-year" congressional election campaign took place in 1866. Johnson, a war Democrat from Tennessee, had been nominated in 1864 with Republican Lincoln on a pro-Union ticket. But by 1866 the President, who had broken with the Republican leadership, was forced increasingly to rely on Democratic support. The so-called National Union Convention, which met in Philadelphia in midsummer 1866 in an effort to abate sectionalism and endorse the president's policies, included a large number of war Democrats, moderate Southerners, some Republicans, and a few Whigs, especially from the border states. The convention declared that the Southern states had a right to representation in Congress. The Radical Republicans, meeting in convention, declared for the tough policy of the Radical-dominated Congress. Johnson began campaigning, journeying all the way to Chicago and denouncing his congressional opponents at every stop. He lost no opportunity to abuse his antagonists in intemperate language. The strategy backfired on the president. His enemies won two-to-one control of the House of Representatives.

## Election of 1868

At its national convention in Chicago in May 1868, the Republican Party nominated Gen. Ulysses S. Grant for president, with Schuyler Colfax as his running mate, and adopted a platform that endorsed congressional Reconstruction measures. On the vital question of universal suffrage for freedmen, the platform declared that the guarantee by Congress of equal suffrage to all loyal men of the South was "demanded by every consideration of public safety, of gratitude and justice, and must be maintained; while the question of suffrage in all the loyal states properly belongs to the people of those states." Nowhere in the North was the black an important element in the population, but the North nevertheless revealed an unwillingness to apply to itself the doctrines of civil rights it imposed on the South. Between 1865 and 1868 Connecticut, Wisconsin, Minnesota, Kansas, Ohio, and Michigan refused to grant blacks the right to vote. The plank in the Republican platform revealed the unwillingness of the party to make a direct issue of universal male suffrage. The platform also contained a plank calling for payment of the public debt, which would have caused currency contraction.

For the Democrats who met in convention in New York during July 1868, the currency question dominated all others. Many Democrats accused the Republican leadership of producing the agricultural depression of 1866 through the policy of retiring greenbacks. The Democratic platform favored using greenbacks as legal tender and endorsed Congressman George H. Pendleton's "Ohio Idea" for paying the national debt in greenbacks. Other Democrats added to the platform the charge that the Reconstruction measures of the Republican Congress were unconstitutional and void; they demanded that the Southern states be restored to their former rights and given control over their own elective franchise. The party nominated Horatio Seymour, war governor of New York, for the presidency and Francis P. Blair, Jr., of Missouri for the vice-presidency.

Grant's popularity in the North, together with Republican strength in those Southern states reconstructed under Negro suffrage, gave the Republicans an easy victory. Seymour carried only Delaware, New Jersey, New York, and Oregon in the North; Maryland, Kentucky, Georgia, and Louisiana in the South. The knowledge that the Republican victory had been gained through the freedmen's vote in the reconstructed states led Republican leaders to ignore their platform pledge to leave to the states the question of black suffrage in the North. Under Republican leadership, Congress submitted to the states for ratification the Fifteenth Amendment. It declared that "the right of citizens of the United States to vote shall not be denied or abridged by the United States or by any state on account of race, color, or previous condition of servitude." By March 1870 it had been ratified.

As Grant's administration progressed, Republican reaction began to appear against the excesses of the Radicals in their midst. The party's idealists, led by Sen. Charles Summner, Carl Schurz, and several leading editors, started to challenge the central core of party command. By 1872 these insurgents had created the Liberal Republican movement within the party. Summner launched an attack on the Republican leadership in the Senate in May 1872, charging it with deserting the principles of the party. In the interest of party harmony, he said, he would have let the matter ride except for the fact that many Republicans were attempting to bring about Grant's renomination. There was, he added, no standard of competence that Grant could meet. Summner wondered why fellow Republicans would seek the renomination of a man who had so thoroughly corrupted the presidential office and the basic institutions of the nation.

Grant's renomination by the Republican convention sent

the Liberal Republicans into open revolt. Yet the Liberals' convention at Cincinnati was so completely ruled by the machinations of petty politicians that the will of the leaders was subverted. The convention proceeded to nominate New York editor Horace Greeley for president and adopted a platform drafted with a view to capturing Democratic support. The maneuver succeeded, for the Democratic convention endorsed the Liberal Republican candidate. Greeley's personal idiosyncrasies, plus the fact that he had signed the bail bond of Jefferson Davis, made him extraordinarily vulnerable to Republican jibes. Greeley's earlier radicalism, lifelong opposition to the Democratic Party, high tariff views, and well-known eccentricity were endlessly rehearsed in the campaign and compelled many who would have liked to see Grant defeated. The president won reelection easily with a popular majority that more than doubled his previous vote. Greeley died a few weeks after the election, and his electoral votes were scattered among various rivals.

During the campaign the scandals of the Crédit Mobilier affair began to come to light. Its revelations finally exasperated voters so long content to ignore the lesser scandals of the Grant era, and the 1874 congressional campaign turned on corruption in office. At last Grant's critics could command an audience of eager listeners. The election gave the Democrats control of the House of Representatives for the first time in fourteen years.

## Election of 1876

The presidential election of 1876 is remembered not for its campaign, which was unexciting, but for the electoral crisis precipitated by the counting of the vote. In brief, the Democrats won the vote and the Republicans, after four months of tension and doubt, won the count.

The dominant forces in American life in the last quarter of the nineteenth century were economic, not political. This fact was reflected in the ineffectiveness of political leadership and in the absence of deeply divisive issues in politics, except perhaps the continuing agrarian agitation for a greater money supply. There were colorful political personalities who had gained their following on a personal basis rather than as spokesmen for a program of political action. No president of the period was truly the leader of his party, and none apparently aspired to that status except Grover Cleveland during his second term (1893–97). Such shrewd observers of American politics as Woodrow Wilson and James Bryce agreed that great men did not become presidents; and it was evident that the nominating conventions of both major parties commonly selected presidential candidates who were "available" in the sense that they had few enemies.

In the absence of leadership from the White House, public policy was largely formulated in Congress. As a result public policy commonly represented a compromise among the views of many congressional leaders—a situation made the more essential because of the fact that in only four of the twenty years from 1877 to 1897 did the same party control the White House, the Senate, and the House.

The Republican Party appeared to be dominant in national politics. Their success was achieved in the face of bitter intraparty schisms that plagued Republican leaders from 1870 until after 1890, and despite the fact that in every election campaign after 1876 they were forced to concede the entire South to the opposition. The Republicans had the advantage of having been the party that had defended the Union against secession and had freed the slaves. When all other appeals failed, Republican leaders could salvage votes in the North and West by reviving memories of the war. A less tangible but equally valuable advantage was the widespread belief that the continued industrial development of the nation would be more secure under a Republican than Democratic administration. Except in years of economic adversity, the memory of the war and confidence in the economic program of the Republican Party were normally enough to insure Republican success in most of the Northern and Western states.

## Election of 1880

There were three prominent candidates for the Republican nomination in 1880: Grant, James G. Blaine, and Secretary of the Treasury John Sherman. Grant had a substantial and loyal bloc of delegates in the convention, but their number was short of a majority. Neither of the other candidates could command a majority; on the thirty-sixth ballot the weary delegates nominated a compromise candidate, Congressman James A. Garfield of Ohio. To placate the "Stalwart" or pro-Grant faction, the convention nominated Chester A. Arthur of New York for vice-president.

The Democrats probably would have been willing to renominate their 1876 candidate, Samuel J. Tilden, in 1880, hoping thereby to gain votes from those who believed he had lost previously only through fraud. But Tilden declined to become a candidate again, and the Democratic convention nominated Gen. Winfield S. Hancock as its candidate for president. Hancock had been a Union general during the Civil War, but he had no political record and little familiarity with questions of public policy.

The campaign failed to generate any unusual excitement and produced no novel issues. As was true in every national election of the period, the Republicans attempted to win support by stressing their role as the party of the protective tariff and by asserting that Democratic opposition to the tariff would impede the growth of domestic industry. Actually, the Democrats were badly divided on the tariff issue and during the campaign General Hancock dismayed political leaders of both parties by declaring that the tariff was an issue of only local interest. Garfield won the election with an electoral margin of 214–155. His plurality in the popular vote was, however, a slim 9,000. He carried all but three of the Northern states, while Hancock carried all the former slave states.

Upon Garfield's assassination his vice-president, Chester A. Arthur, entered the White House. President Arthur hoped for nomination to a full term by the Republicans in 1884. His administration had won the respect of many who had viewed his accession to office with misgivings. It had not, however, gained him any powerful following among the leaders of his party. The strongest candidate for the Republican nomination was James G. Blaine, who had been an unsuccessful aspirant for the nomination in 1876 and 1880. His candidacy still aroused opposition from those who believed he was too partisan in spirit or that he was vulnerable to charges of corrupt actions while Speaker of the House many years before. Despite opposition, he was nominated on the fourth ballot.

The Democratic candidate, Gov. Grover Cleveland of New York, was in many respects the opposite of Blaine. He was a relative newcomer to politics. He had been elected mayor of Buffalo in 1881 and governor of New York in 1882. In both positions he had earned a reputation for political independence, inflexible honesty, and an industrious and conservative administration. Though he was stolid in appearance, his record made him an attractive candidate for many who accepted the dictum that "a public office is a public trust." This was, in 1884, a valuable asset, and it won for Cleveland the support of a few outstanding Republicans and some journals of national circulation that usually favored Republican nominees for office.

As in 1880, the campaign was almost devoid of issues of public policy—only the perennial question of the tariff appeared to separate the two parties. Cleveland had not served in the army during the Civil War, and Republicans made an effort to use this fact, together with the power of the South in the Democratic Party, to arouse sectional prejudices against him. During the campaign it was revealed that Cleveland, a bachelor, was the father of an illegitimate son, an indiscretion that gave the Republicans a moral issue with which to counteract charges of corruption against their own candidate. Another shabby element of the campaign was the use of the phrase "Rum, Romanism and Rebellion," by Rev. Samuel D. Burchard as a slur on the Democratic Party in a campaign speech made in Blaine's presence in New York City on October 29. Blaine did not disclaim the phrase; whether he heard the statement at all is open to question, but it was immediately publicized by Democrats to rally New York's Irish-Americans against Blaine.

The election was close. On the evening of the voting it was apparent that the result depended upon the vote in New York State, but not until the end of the week was it certain that Cleveland had carried New York by the narrow margin of 1,149 votes and had thereby been elected president. In the electoral college Cleveland got 219 votes to Blaine's 182.

In 1888 the Democrats renominated Cleveland, although it was thought he had endangered his chances of reelection by his outspoken advocacy of tariff reduction. The Republicans had their usual difficulty in selecting a candidate. Blaine, who had told friends he regretted having been a candidate in 1884, refused to enter the race. No other person in the party commanded substantial support. From among the many who were willing to accept the nomination, the Republicans selected Benjamin Harrison of Indiana, a Union general and the grandson of Pres. William Henry Harrison.

Cleveland had won respect as a man of integrity and courage, but neither he nor Harrison aroused any great enthusiasm among the voters. One feature of the campaign noted by observers was the broad expenditure of money to influence the outcome. This was not a new phenomenon, but the free spending of money to carry doubtful states and the apparent alliance between business and political bosses had never before been so open. The results were again close. In the popular vote, Cleveland had a plurality of almost 100,000 votes. In the electoral college, however, Harrison had a margin of 233–168 and was elected. The only states that voted differently from four years earlier were New York and Indiana, both of which were carried by the Republicans in 1888. The Republicans also gained control of both houses of the Fifty-first Congress.

In 1892 the Democrats, despite the bitter protests of Tammany Hall (the New York political organization), nominated Cleveland for president a third time. The Republicans renominated Harrison. The campaign was a quiet one despite the underlying tension in the nation. The Populists, essentially agrarian in nature, had emerged after 1890 to offer a liberal challenge to the two conservative parties. Under the leadership of James B. Weaver of Iowa, they boldly championed the free coinage of silver as well as other reforms, while Cleveland and Harrison emphasized the tariffs in their appeals for votes. Cleveland won the election with a popular vote of 5,556,918 to Harrison's 5,176,108 and Weaver's 1,027,000. Although Cleveland gained less than a majority of the total popular vote, he received 277 electoral votes to Harrison's 145 and Weaver's 22.

## Election of 1896

In the midterm elections of 1894 the Republicans recaptured control of both houses of Congress. This result indicated the discontent produced by the continuing depression. It also guaranteed that, with a Democratic president and Republican Congress, there would be little action in domestic legislation while both parties looked forward to 1896.

At their convention in St. Louis the Republicans selected Gov. William McKinley of Ohio as their presidential nominee. He had served in the Union Army during the Civil War, and his record as governor of Ohio tended to offset his association with the unpopular tariff of 1890. His most effective support, however, was provided by Mark Hanna, a wealthy Cleveland businessman who was McKinley's closest friend.

The Democratic convention in Chicago was unusually exciting. From the beginning it was apparent that it was controlled by groups hostile to Cleveland's financial policies, and it took the unprecedented step of rejecting a resolution commending the administration of a president of its own party. The debate on this resolution culminated in a famous speech by William Jennings Bryan, whose eloquent forthrightness in support of silver and in defense of agrarian interests won him not only the applause of the convention but also its nomination for the presidency. A former congressman from Nebraska, Bryan was only thirty-six years old—the youngest man ever to be a major party's candidate for president. By experience and conviction, he shared the outlook of the agrarian groups that dominated the convention.

Bryan conducted a vigorous campaign. It was the first time a presidential candidate had carried his case to the people in all parts of the country, and for a time it appeared that he might win. The worried conservatives charged that Bryan was a dangerous demagogue, and they interpreted the campaign as a conflict between defenders of a sound economic system that would produce prosperity, and dishonest radicals who championed reckless innovations that would undermine the financial security of the nation. On this interpretation they succeeded in raising large campaign funds from industrialists who feared their interests were threatened. With this money, the Republicans were able to turn the tide and win a decisive victory. Outside the South, Bryan carried only the Western silver states and Kansas and Nebraska.

## Election of 1912

Ensuing election campaigns generated little light or heat until 1908. Although Roosevelt recommended Taft to the electorate as the best man to carry out his policies, the election that year was much closer than the previous one had been. In cutting down the Republican majority in Congress from the 1904 figure and particularly in winning important governorship contests in the Middle West and Far West, the Democratic Party, with Bryan as its candidate for the third time, started to reverse the Republican trend, a reversal which was to be much more noticeable in the congressional elections of 1910. A good part of the reason for this political turn lay in the rifts within the Republican Party.

The split between Roosevelt and Taft and the former's ill-fated Progressive (Bull Moose) adventure of 1912 coincided with the emergence in New Jersey of a reformist governor, former head of Princeton University, Woodrow Wilson. His initiative with the legislature in his own state amounted to a triumph on the eve of the campaign for the presidential nomination. Wilson's rapid and resounding success in New Jersey brought him clearly into the arena of national politics.

He was not slow to develop an active campaign. But when the Democratic National Convention met in Baltimore in June 1912 to select a candidate for president, Wilson's chances were not highly favored as compared with those of the leading candidate, Champ Clark. The contest was prolonged, but on the forty-sixth ballot he received the necessary two-thirds vote and was nominated.

In the presidential campaign that followed, the clarity and positive quality of Wilson's domestic program soon won for him the leadership of the Democratic Party and of the entire progressive movement throughout the nation. He called for expanded exercise of federal authority not so much for the regulation of industrial enterprise as for its emancipation from the control of privileged groups. He rejected Roosevelt's New Nationalism, which implied active government intervention on behalf of social justice and the economic welfare of the underprivileged. The purpose of his program (the New Freedom, as he called it) was to restore unrestrained opportunity for individual action. By its emphasis upon the idea of liberation, the New Freedom appeared as a revival of traditional Democratic principles; it redefined those principles, however, to meet twentieth-century social and economic conditions.

In the election Wilson received 435 electoral votes as against 88 for Roosevelt and 8 for Taft. His popular vote was one million less than that of his two chief opponents combined, and in only fourteen states (all of them in the South) did he receive a clear majority. Because of the division of Republican votes, the election put both houses of Congress under Democratic control, and in the country at large Wilson could reasonably expect support from the Progressives for his legislative program of reform.

## War Years

After World War I broke out (1914), Wilson was determined to avoid involvement. In 1915 the British liner *Lusitania* was sunk, however, by a German submarine without warning; more than 1,000 persons were drowned, among them 128 Americans. Wilson displayed long-suffering patience in the negotiations of the ensuing weeks. "There is such a thing as a nation being too proud to fight," he declared in a public address shortly after the sinking of the *Lusitania*. He spoke bravely, and his will to compel Germany to abide by the established rules of cruiser warfare was unshakable. His protest to Germany was, in fact, so strongly worded that Secretary of State Bryan resigned rather than sign it. In the spring of 1916, when a rupture with Germany again became imminent because of the torpedoing of the channel steamer *Sussex*, Wilson protested in terms that amounted to an ultimatum, finally drawing from Berlin a more comprehensive pledge to abandon the ruthless submarine campaign altogether. For the next seven months, relations with Germany were less disturbed.

This diplomatic victory not only postponed American intervention in the war, but proved of political value to Wilson in the presidential campaign of 1916, in which he was the Democratic candidate. It gave strength to the argument that he had vindicated the rights of the United States successfully and at the same time had "kept us out of war." The slogan made a strong popular appeal, especially west of the Mississippi. The Republicans, who nominated Charles Evans Hughes, denounced the president as hesitating and cowardly, both in his dealing with Germany and in his handling of the Mexican problem, involving civil war and a new government there. A Republican newspaper cartooned a human backbone with the legend, "Lost in Washington." Wilson's opponents criticized his legislative reforms as demagogic and cited a legislative act (urged by the president to avert a railroad strike) as a surrender to labor. On the eastern seaboard and in most of the industrial centers of the Middle West, the reunited Republican Party could count on success, but in the farming districts west of the Mississippi and on the Pacific coast, Wilson showed great strength; he drew largely from the Progressives, who refused to follow Theodore Roosevelt back into the Republican fold. The result of the November 7 election was so close that for twelve hours a Republican victory was generally conceded. Only as returns from the West came in was it determined that Wilson had been reelected by 277 electoral votes to 254 for Hughes, and that he had a popular plurality of 9,129,606–8,538,221.

After the war, part of the explanation for the rejection of U.S. participation in Wilson's masterpiece, the League of Nations, was his stubborn determination not to compromise; another part was the willingness of Republican senatorial leader Henry Cabot Lodge to gain political advantage for his party from the issue. The president was by this time a very ill man, having had a stroke in the midst of a national speaking tour in defense of the League. He hoped to the last that the election of 1920 would prove a "solemn referendum" on the League issue, one in which the people would overrule the Senate.

The atmosphere of 1920 was hardly one in which a great foreign policy issue like the League could be rationally debated. Demobilization after the war's end had come without a plan and with stunning rapidity. Within a few weeks after the armistice, the government canceled thousands of contracts for supplies and rapidly dismantled the war agencies. The unplanned reconversion produced shortages of goods, unemployment, and price inflation. Returning war veterans, unable to find work, were in real distress; labor, confronted with rising prices, resorted to strikes when manufacturers refused its demands. The movement of black labor to the North during the war set the stage for postwar race riots; the formation of two Communist parties in the United States, plus some incredibly foolish acts of alien radicals, brought to a head the anti-Red (Communist) campaign led by Wilson's attorney general, A. Mitchell Palmer. Mass immigration of impoverished Europeans into the country was linked to a growing radicalism, and demands for absolute immigration restrictions and for a cutting of all foreign ties bred a wave of superpatriotism. In such an atmosphere the elections of 1920 were held.

The Republican convention in Chicago was largely controlled by a group of conservative senators. Jealous of the wartime increase in the power of the president at the expense of Congress, they determined to pass over the leading candidates for the convention and finally gave the nomination to a fellow senator, Warren G. Harding, whose main qualifications appeared to be his affability, his rock-ribbed conservatism, and his disinclination to lead. Then they chose Calvin Coolidge of Massachusetts as their vice-presidential nominee. The Democrats at San Francisco did little better. Passing over well-known party members, they settled on Gov. James Cox of Ohio for president and Franklin D. Roosevelt for vice-president. During the election campaign the League issue was thoroughly obscured; Harding's cloudy and at times almost incoherent exhortation for a return to "normalcy" probably won a great many more voters than it alienated. The elections proved to be a complete triumph for the Republicans, who not only won both houses of Congress with solid majorities but also elected Harding with the greatest popular majority since pre-Civil War days.

## Election of 1924

With Harding's death in San Francisco on Aug. 2, 1923, little changed in the total political complexion of the White House. If anything, Coolidge was more conservative and more responsive to business interests than Harding was. He openly admired business leaders and men of great wealth and disliked liberals, radicals, and change. The already booming prosperity made him a hero of business circles as well as of a good many other people. The Republican Convention of 1924 nominated him on the first ballot with only thirty-four votes going to Sen. Robert La Follette and ten to Hiram Johnson by way of protest. The Democrats, expecting to take advantage of the Harding scandals and the continuing agricultural distress, threw away their chances in the notorious struggle between their two leading candidates for the nomination, Alfred E. Smith and William G. McAdoo. After 103 ballots the Democratic convention nominated John W. Davis as a compromise, but by that time the party was so split between the Eastern, anti-Prohibition, Catholic faction and a Southern, Prohibitionist, Protestant group that even Davis considered the nomination "worthless." Dismayed by the conservative cast of both candidates of the two major parties, many liberals, Republican progressives, Socialists, and labor representatives quickly united and formed the Progressive Party, which nominated Robert La Follette at its meeting in Cleveland, Ohio. In the following election Coolidge easily won a far greater popular vote than the combined totals of Davis and La Follette. The new Congress, moreover, was so overwhelmingly Republican that the dissident Western progressives no longer held a balance between the major parties.

Four years later Calvin Coolidge may have been surprised at the reception of his cryptic public statement, "I do not choose to run." Taking his words at their face value, the Republicans, except for the delegates from the farm states, nominated Herbert Hoover. His Democratic opponent was Alfred E. Smith, who by 1928 was obviously the best known and most successful Democratic politician. For four terms Smith had been an able and liberal governor of New York; he was a favorite of the Eastern urban group in the party, and his platform was designed to appeal to the farmers in the Middle West as well. But the outcome of the election was influenced by the country's booming prosperity, Smith's stand against Prohibition, his thoroughly urban lower-class background, and his Roman Catholic religion. Hoover won an easy victory, carrying a majority of the old Confederate states and polling more than 21 million popular votes to about 15 million for Smith. Even so, Smith had carried Massachusetts and Rhode Island and had sharply reduced the usual Republican majorities in the great Northern cities and in the agrarian states of the Middle West. The tide that had elected three Republican presidents in the decade had begun to recede, and the election of 1928 foreshadowed what was to happen in 1932.

The Republican National Convention, which met in Chicago on June 14, 1932, endorsed the Hoover administration and on the first ballot renominated the President and Charles Curtis. The Democrats met in the same city on June 27 and after some maneuvering nominated Franklin D. Roosevelt of New York, who in primaries had won a substantial majority of the delegates, though fewer than the two-thirds necessary to win the nomination. When John Nance Garner, Speaker of the House of Representatives, broke a threatened deadlock by releasing his own delegates to Roosevelt, he was then chosen to run for vice-president. Roosevelt, though crippled since 1921 by infantile paralysis, immediately flew from Albany to Chicago and broke precedent by delivering his acceptance speech to the assembled delegates in person. In it he pledged himself to "a new deal for the American people." Editorial writers and cartoonists picked up the phrase, and Roosevelt's program soon became known as the New Deal.

## Roosevelt Years

In the campaign that followed, Roosevelt had little difficulty in persuading voters that the only hope of recovery from the Depression lay in a change of administration. He toured the country, promising aid for farmers, businessmen, and the unemployed, together with governmental economy and a balanced budget. He appealed strongly to Republican progressives as well as to Democrats and was especially popular in the South and the West. President Hoover campaigned vigorously in the final weeks, warning that under Roosevelt conditions could get much worse. It was of little avail. Roosevelt carried every state except six, with fifty-seven percent of the popular vote and 472 electoral votes to 59 for Hoover. The Democrats secured an overwhelming majority in both the House and Senate. The 1936 election simply reconfirmed Roosevelt's mandate and enlarged his congressional majorities. World War II overshadowed the campaigns of 1940 and 1944, in which he easily won unprecedented third and fourth terms.

Upon the sudden death of the President on April 12, 1945, Harry S. Truman became president of the United States. The problems he faced were known to him only in a general way, for he had not had close association with the administration. Eightieth Congress, dominated by conservative Republicans, ignored Truman's program, and in the 1948 campaign the Republicans seemed almost certain of victory. They renominated Gov. Thomas E. Dewey of New York, who had lost to Roosevelt in 1944, and for vice-president chose Gov. Earl Warren of California.

The Democrats nominated Truman, and for vice-president, Sen. Alben Barkley of Kentucky. A third party, the Progressive Party, calling for a more conciliatory policy toward the Soviet Union, nominated Henry A. Wallace; a fourth party, the States' Rights Democrats (Dixiecrats), protesting civil rights provisions in the Democratic platform, nominated Gov. J. Strom Thurmond of South Carolina. President Truman's chances seemed hopeless, but he embarked upon a vigorous whistle-stop campaign directed against the conservative congressional Republicans. Mustering the support of labor, discontented farmers, and northern blacks, Truman surprised nearly everyone by defeating Dewey. The popular vote was 24,106,000–21,970,000 and the electoral vote 303–189. Thurmond received 1,169,000 votes and 39 electoral votes; Wallace received 1,157,000 votes. The Democrats recaptured the House (263–171) and the Senate (54–42).

## Election of 1952

While he was serving as commander of Supreme Headquarters of Allied Powers in Europe (SHAPE), Gen. Dwight D. Eisenhower's name was entered in the 1952 Republican state presidential primaries, a number of which he won. After he retired from his military post, the general's supporters campaigned actively for his nomination. When the Republican convention met in Chicago, sentiment was about evenly divided between him and Sen. Robert A. Taft of Ohio, but Eisenhower was nominated on the first ballot. Sen. Richard M. Nixon of California was named Republican vice-presidential candiate.

The Democratic National Convention, also held in Chicago, nominated Gov. Adlai E. Stevenson of Illinois as its presidential candidate and Sen. John Sparkman of Alabama for vice-president. Like Eisenhower, Stevenson had been a reluctant candidate in the early stages of the preconvention campaign.

Eisenhower vigorously attacked the administration, charging it with responsibility for events leading to the Korean War and promising that, if elected, he would visit Korea before his inauguration. Republican campaigners denounced scandals among the Democratic administrators and continued to make accusations of Communist infiltration in government offices. President Truman vigorously defended his administration and supported Stevenson, who conducted an energetic and impressive campaign.

In November the popular vote of more than 61 million was the largest in the nation's history. Eisenhower carried thirty-nine states (442 electoral votes); Stevenson carried nine (89 electoral votes). Eisenhower carried the Southern states of Florida, Virginia, Tennessee, and Texas. Republicans gained control of the House and won a narrow 48–47 margin in the Senate, not including one independent Republican. Gubernatorial contests in thirty states resulted in twenty Republican victories.

The new president had run far ahead of his party ticket, attracting portions of the labor vote that had been consistently Democratic for twenty years, as well as a substantial black vote in the cities and a widespread Midwestern farm vote. His noncommittal policy in domestic affairs weakened the influence of labor elements in the Democratic Party and strengthened liberal elements within the Republican Party.

In 1955 and again in 1956 the president suffered a heart attack and surgery for ileitis, and although he was renominated enthusiastically, his health and problems of succession and the caliber of the vice-president became matters of debate. Vice-President Nixon was unanimously renominated with Eisenhower. Adlai E. Stevenson was again nominated by the Democrats at their convention in Chicago, with Sen. Estes Kefauver of Tennessee as his running mate.

The outcome of the election was determined in large measure by external events. Late in October an apathetic electorate was aroused when Eastern Europe and the Middle East burst into flames. The final days of the campaign were dominated by events outside the United States—the outbreak of an anti-Communist revolt in Poland; a violent anti-Communist revolution throughout Hungary; invasion of Egyptian territory by Israel, which claimed self-defense against border depredations; and the swift attack of Great Britain and France upon Egypt for the purpose of regaining control of the Suez Canal, which Egypt had seized in July. Stevenson, meanwhile, had proposed an end to nuclear tests by international agreement because of dangers from radioactive fallout. He also urged a cut in the Selective Service draft. The electorate voted overwhelmingly for Eisenhower, who carried all but seven states. It was more a personal than a party victory, however, for the Democrats won control of both houses of Congress.

## Election of 1960

As President Eisenhower's second term neared its end in 1960, the two major U.S. political parties nominated comparatively young presidential candidates—both Navy veterans of World War II—at their national conventions. The Republican nominee, Vice-President Richard M. Nixon of California, was forty-seven; the Democrat, Sen. John F. Kennedy of Massachusetts, was forty-three. Nixon's campaign was devoted largely to defending the record of the Eisenhower administration in which he had served for eight years as vice-president. Kennedy's main contention was that the Eisenhower administration had been lacking in vigor and imagination. He urged that steps be taken to stimulate the nation's economic growth and "get the country moving again." The most dramatic feature of the campaign was a series of television appearances (publicized as "debates") during which the two candidates stated their positions and answered questions from newsmen. On November 8 Kennedy defeated Nixon in the most closely contested election of the century. Kennedy won 303 electoral votes to Nixon's 219, but in the popular vote of more than 68 million, Kennedy's margin was only 118,000. The Democrats retained control of both houses of the Eighty-seventh Congress but with a somewhat smaller majority than they had held in the previous one.

When Vice-Pres. Lyndon Johnson became president after Kennedy's assassination (November 1963), Johnson skillfully capitalized on the national shock and grief, winning massive advances in civil rights and anti-poverty legislation. He was nominated by acclamation in 1964 and decimated the conservative slate named by the Republicans and headed by Sen. Barry M. Goldwater of Arizona.

In the winter of 1967–68 a rising tide of opposition to the Vietnam War arose as casualties mounted and victory seemed impossible for either side; thus the war became the major issue in the 1968 campaign. Antiwar forces had gained a champion in 1967 when Democratic Sen. Eugene J. McCarthy announced that he would oppose President Johnson for his party's presidential nomination. He ran well against Johnson in the New Hampshire primary (March 1968), winning forty-two percent of the vote to Johnson's forty-eight percent.

Shortly thereafter Sen. Robert F. Kennedy (Dem., N.Y.) announced his candidacy and challenged McCarthy's leadership of the antiwar Democrats. Then, on March 31, Johnson announced his decision not to seek or accept the Democratic nomination for another term. Hubert H. Humphrey announced his candidacy in late April. On June 5, while Kennedy was in Los Angeles celebrating his California primary victory over McCarthy, the New York senator was fatally shot. Sen. George S. McGovern, a Kennedy supporter, entered the race in early August.

In late August Humphrey was nominated at the Democratic National Convention in Chicago, with Sen. Edmund S. Muskie of Maine as his running mate. The convention was marred by violent disorders in the streets of Chicago arising from opposition not only to the Vietnam War but also to party positions and procedures. Earlier in August, the Republicans had met in Miami Beach, Fla., and nominated Richard M. Nixon for president and Gov. Spiro T. Agnew of Maryland for vice-president. George C. Wallace, former governor of Alabama, headed the American Independent Party, with Gen. Curtis E. LeMay as his running mate.

The election in November was close in the popular vote between Humphrey and Nixon, but Nixon won a decisive electoral vote majority, 301 votes to 191 for Humphrey and 46 for Wallace. The Democrats, however, held a majority of 243–192 in the House and 58–42 in the Senate.

## Election of 1972

The inroads into regular Democratic strength and solidarity made by antiwar activists in 1968 helped set the stage for the 1972 preconvention campaigns. Senator McGovern, following the tactics of John Kennedy and Barry Goldwater, organized a superbly efficient campaign to secure convention delegates, and a month before the 1972 Democratic convention he was virtually assured of the nomination—which in fact he won. His first choice for running mate, Sen. Thomas Eagleton, became the first vice-presidential nominee to withdraw from a national ticket when his earlier psychiatric treatment was publicized; he was succeeded by a Kennedy brother-in-law, Sargent Shriver.

The Democrats in 1972 had in McGovern, however, a candidate well to the left (more radical) of the nation at large, making in reverse the same mistake the Republicans had made with the conservative Goldwater eight years before. McGovern was decisively repudiated by the voters after a shrill and bitter campaign. Nixon, twice vice-president, rejected by the voters of the country in 1960 and by those of California in 1962, and barely elected over Humphrey in 1968, had his landslide election at last.

The mandate, of course, was vitiated and eventually ruined by the Watergate scandals (1972–74). Two elements of the 1972 election campaign, however, were to have repercussions on future elections. One of these was the McGovern refinement of the Kennedy and Goldwater methods of securing delegates many months before the national party convention assembled. In his successful quest for the Democratic nomination in 1976, a virtual unknown on the national stage, Jimmy Carter, briefly a Georgia legislator and a one-term governor, won the nomination beyond dispute many weeks before Democratic convention time. The technique, which involves pre-nomination financing adequate to do the necessary public-opinion sampling, as well as vigorous primary campaigning, was certain to be emulated.

The second significant outgrowth of the 1972 campaign was increased federal control over the regulation and financing of election campaigns resulting from the Election Campaign Act of 1974. This response to the Watergate scandal created federal subsidy (on a matching-funds basis) for presidential campaigns and strict spending limits on all candidates who availed themselves of the subsidy. It also established more stringent reporting requirements on the sources of contributions than had been imposed previously. Numerous aspects of the law were immediately attacked in court, and late in 1975 the Supreme Court forced certain modifications in the "watchdog" Federal Elections Commission; it upheld the main thrust of the bill, however, thus imposing federal regulation for the first time in any substantial way upon the electoral process itself.

# 19.
# The Mechanics of Election: Voting and Counting

"Who votes is not as important as who counts." This cynical observation is not without validity. The mandates of many officeholders in American history, from president to alderman, have been clouded by uncertainties—or certainty—about irregularities in the counting process.

With the increasing size of an electorate, the counting and other administrative problems of conducting elections have become more and more complicated. The aim of election administration is to safeguard the rights of the voters, to serve the convenience of the voters, to keep the expense of holding elections to a minimum, to provide the best method for translating the votes into seats, and to prevent fraud. The devices to achieve these ends have been registration laws, ballot laws, laws governing the casting and counting of the votes, laws regarding the assignment of seats, and corrupt practices acts.

## Registration and Poll Tax

When an election is to be held, registration machinery must be set up to determine who is entitled to vote under the law, and to establish safeguards against voting by persons who are not. Registration procedures should impose the least possible burden upon the voters that is consistent with the achievement of these objectives. They should also provide means for keeping the voter lists up to date. Proper identification of the voter is the key to a sound registration system. In some states the signature of the voter is used as an adequate means. The voter signs his name at the time he registers and again when he applies to vote. The polling official compares the two signatures and establishes the identification. (In India and parts of Africa, where there are many illiterates, a fingerprint is used for this purpose.) Demands for registration by mail are heard from time to time, and occasionally for no advance registration at all. The latter proposal depends upon the voter's being able to present positive evidence of his identity, residence within the jurisdiction, and absence of any disqualification based on age, citizenship, or felony conviction.

Poll taxes (a fee charged before a person can vote) former-ly were a prerequisite to voting in several states. Ten South-ern states enacted the requirement between 1889 and 1902. In its origins the tax is associated with the agrarian unrest of the 1880s and 1890s, which culminated in the rise of the Populist Party in the West and the South. The Populists, a low-income farmers' party, gave the Democrats in these areas the only serious competition they had experienced since the end of Reconstruction. The intensity of competition led both parties to bring blacks back into politics and to compete for their votes. Once the Populists were defeated, the Democrats amended their state constitutions or drafted new ones to include various disfranchising devices. The poll tax was one of these. Its purpose was to disfranchise blacks and possibly also to weaken politically the poor whites who had made up the backbone of the Populist Party.

Beginning in 1920 the poll tax was abolished by state ac-tion in North Carolina, Louisiana, Florida, Georgia, South Carolina, and Tennessee. In 1937 the Supreme Court unani-mously upheld the constitutionality of a Georgia poll tax. Constitutional amendments to abolish the tax were submit-ted to the voters in Arkansas, Virginia, and Texas, but failed to pass. The tax still prevailed in these states as well as in Alabama and Mississippi at mid-century, with rates ranging from one dollar to two dollars per year. In Texas and Arkan-sas, failure to pay merely disfranchised a person for that year only and did not create an obligation that had to be paid in subsequent years if the person wished to vote. In Alabama, Virginia, and Mississippi the tax was in some degree cumula-tive. As a requirement for voting for federal offices, however, the poll tax was prohibited in 1964 by the Twenty-fourth Amendment to the U.S. Constitution. A poll tax that was not a requirement for voting, as in New Hampshire, was not affected by the amendment. Later the Supreme Court went beyond the Twenty-fourth Amendment by ruling that under the "equal protection" clause of the Fourteenth Amendment states could not levy a poll tax as a prerequisite for voting in state and local elections, thus rendering the tax ineffective.

## Major Concerns

Throughout the Western world in the nineteenth century great parliamentary fights were waged around the process of polling (receiving and recording the vote). The issue was to secure the freedom of the voter from outside influence, protection against ballot-altering, and honest counting of the votes. The first was secured by the proper organization of the whole electoral procedure; the second by the institution of the secret ballot; and the third by associating the representatives of the contending parties with the supervising officer of the proceedings, usually a public official.

Before 1884 the general practice in the United States was either open voting by voice or hand, or, where this rudimentary and clumsy process had been superseded, voting by ballot. At first each party printed its own ballot (or party "ticket"), and party workers hawked them aggressively at or near the polling place. After the presidential elections of 1884 the Australian ballot system was extensively adopted. Now ballots are printed at public expense, handed to the voter in the polling place, marked and folded (if paper) in secret, and deposited by the voter or, unopened and unread, by a poll worker in the presence of the voter. Ballots in some states are officially numbered and identifiable by reference to a counterfoil retained by the officials. Increasing use is made of voting machines and punched-card ballots to assure greater speed and honesty in counting.

## Absentee Voting

Absentee voting in the United States was first provided for during the Civil War, when eleven states permitted men serving in the Union Army to vote in the presidential election by absentee ballot or by proxy. There was relatively little interest in the soldier vote during the Spanish-American War or World War I. During the latter, the War Department cooperated with those states that provided machinery for absentee voting within the U.S., but not overseas.

The first use of the absentee ballot by civilians was authorized by a Vermont law passed in 1896; five years later a similar measure was adopted in Kansas. Between 1917 and 1942 the number of states that extended this privilege to their citizens increased from twenty-eight to forty-five. By the 1960s all states had established a system of absentee voting. In the 1950s and 1960s the absentee voting laws of the states began to assume a rather uniform pattern, with the result that by the 1970s most states provided absentee voting procedures for all eligible voters who did not expect to be able to vote in person on election day. Although all states allow absentee voting by those in military service, a few states still restrict civilian use of the absentee ballot to those in certain occupations, such as government employees and students. Most states now permit shut-ins, the sick, and the physically disabled to use this procedure.

The usual method of absentee voting is by mail. Several states, however, have made provision for voting in person in advance of election day. The trend has been toward extension and liberalization of the privilege of absentee voting as well as toward great uniformity of methods among the states. These trends have been stimulated in part by a campaign conducted by the Department of Defense to encourage states to liberalize and simplify their voting requirements for the benefit of absent servicemen.

## Voting Systems

Voting machines were first used in the United States in Lockport, N.Y., in 1892. Because of the high costs of purchase, trucking, and storage, not to mention problems of repair and maintenance, use of these machines grew slowly. They are available in several sizes, some operating mechanically, others electrically, and have been found to be most economical when about 450 voters use one machine.

Each voting machine is a complete polling booth and is surrounded by curtains to insure privacy. The entire list of candidates and referendum questions appears on the face of the machine in much the same way as on a paper ballot. Near the name of each candidate and each question, there is a pointer that voters must move into position, or a handle to turn, to indicate their preference. Some machines also make provision for write-in votes. Within the machine are counters that record and count the votes for each candidate or question. Each candidate's total vote accumulates throughout the election period so that the final count on each machine is ready the moment the polls close and can be dispatched to central headquarters immediately. Each voting machine is inspected by election officials before the voting begins and is sealed after the total vote has been recorded.

In the 1960s the computer revolution began to bring improvements to election administration. Electronic voting systems began to appear. There are two basic types, one in which votes are punched on a tabulating card and computers are used to count them, and the other in which votes are cast on paper ballots and then are counted by ballot-reading devices triggered by variations in light density. The first punch-card voting system was marketed in some Ohio localities as early as 1960. Meanwhile Los Angeles County in California supported development of a paper ballot-counting mechanism that could handle up to 600 paper ballots per minute. Another counter, privately developed, could accommodate ballots with as many as 299 positions. The leading punch-card voting system can handle 240 ballot positions and sells for about one-tenth the cost of a voting machine.

## Electoral College

At the national level, the Constitution has interposed another counting system between the precinct and the presidency—the electoral college. Actually, the "college" is plural: there are fifty state colleges (bodies) of electors who are elected and actually do meet in the state capitals to cast their vote for president and vice-president. Each state chooses a number of presidential electors equal to the number of its members in the national House of Representatives, plus its two senators.

The plan of the Constitution was that these electors should actually exercise a choice as to who should be president. However, almost since the beginning of the present government, candidates for the presidency and vice-presidency have been nominated by the great political parties of the country in advance of the choice of electors. These political parties also nominate within each state their candidates for presidential electors. These candidates for electors are usually pledged in advance to vote for the candidates nominated for national office. For this reason, everybody knows who will be president immediately after the November election, when the electors themselves are chosen. In this respect, as in others, unwritten law, developed by usage, has altered the operation of the written text of the Constitution. In recognition of the fact that presidential electors are merely a device for casting a certain number of votes allotted to the state, at least one-third of the states now provide for a direct vote for candidates for president and vice-president and omit from their ballots the names of candidates for presidential electors. Although each state has power to appoint its presidential electors in such a manner as its legislature may direct, every state legislature has surrendered its right to choose electors and has provided that its electors shall be chosen by popular election on a general ticket nominated by each party.

Political strategy is to win the big blocks of electoral votes from the more popular states such as New York, Illinois, or California in order to accumulate a majority of electoral votes. As a result, presidential candidates are often nominated from such states. Following the national nominating conventions, presidential candidates often concentrate their campaigning on these populous states, especially those that have a habit of swinging from one party to the other. Half the candidates for president in the century following the American Civil War were or had been governors of such states.

There have been several proposals for altering the method by which presidents are elected. The simplest of these new plans provides for the abolition of the electoral college and the election of a president by direct popular vote. Another proposal is that the electoral vote in each state be divided among all candidates in proportion to the popular vote they received in that state. It has also been suggested that each state be divided into a number of election districts for the purpose of electing a president, and that single electors be chosen from each district rather than voting for all electors on a statewide basis as is presently done. The ostensible purpose of these proposals is to prevent the election of a president who has a majority in the electoral college but not in the popular vote. Both Rutherford B. Hayes in 1876 and Benjamin Harrison in 1888 were elected president under the electoral college system although receiving a smaller popular vote than their principal opponent.

The election of 1876 led to one of the gravest domestic political crises ever to confront the nation. The Democratic Party faced that year with confidence that, for the first time in twenty years, it could elect a president. Democratic victories in the midterm elections of 1874 and the success of Southern Democrats in recapturing most of the former Confederate states were evidence of a resurgence of party strength. The Democrats further improved their chances by nominating Samuel J. Tilden, the reform governor of New York, as their candidate for president.

The Republicans were in a less enviable position. The party was divided and tarnished by revelations of corruption. Their most popular personality was Sen. James G. Blaine of Maine, but he was disliked by the "stalwart" (nonreformist) wing of the party, with which former Pres. Ulysses S. Grant was associated, and it was widely believed that he had improperly used his influence in Congress in the interests of certain railroads. These disabilities cost him the nomination; instead of Blaine, Governor Hayes of Ohio was nominated.

The campaign itself was unexciting, but confusion concerning the outcome set the stage for four months of tension and political maneuvering without parallel in the history of the country. On the night of the election it appeared that Tilden had won, and most Republican leaders were prepared to concede. One Republican, William E. Chandler of New Hampshire, noted that if Hayes had carried three Southern states—South Carolina, Florida, and Louisiana—he would have 185 electoral votes to 184 for Tilden. On the face of the popular returns, Tilden had carried all three states and no one disputed that he had a national plurality of more than 250,000. Chandler, however, boldly asserted that Hayes had won the three Southern states, and other Republicans joined him in this assertion. The situation was complicated by the fact that in all three states the election boards were controlled by Republicans. (There was also some doubt about the electoral vote from Oregon, but the votes of the Southern states were the crux of the controversy.)

Although Hayes had polled a majority of the popular vote in Oregon, and in spite of wrongdoing by both parties in Louisiana and South Carolina was probably entitled to their electoral votes as well, he almost certainly had been defeated by Tilden in Florida. Tilden, therefore, had won the election beyond much doubt by an electoral vote of 188-181.

Each party quickly sent observers into the disputed states to observe and, if possible, to influence the official canvass of the votes. The result was almost inevitable. The election boards in all three states rejected returns from districts apparently carried by the Democrats and revised the official tallies so that the vote as certified showed that Hayes had carried all three. If these returns went unchallenged, Hayes would be elected president.

The Constitution leaves the manner of selecting electors to state law; the electoral ballots are sent to the president of the Senate, who "shall, in the presence of the Senate and House of Representatives, open all certificates, and the votes shall then be counted." This provision left unanswered several questions of vital importance. Might Congress or an officer of the Senate review or challenge the acts of a state's certifying officials? Might it even examine the choice of electors? And if it had these powers, might it delegate them to a commission? The fact, moreover, that in 1876 the Republicans controlled the Senate and the Democrats controlled the House, made it much more difficult to reach any harmonious settlement of these issues.

On Jan. 29, 1877, after weeks of acrimonious discussion in and out of Congress, including threats of civil war, Congress created an electoral commission to pass upon the contested returns. Many more Democrats than Republicans voted for this measure. The decisions of the commission, which was given "the same powers, if any" possessed by Congress were to be final unless rejected by the two houses acting separately. Five Democratic and five Republican members of Congress, plus five Supreme Court justices (including two of each party and a fifth chosen by these four), composed the commission. This fifteenth member, so crucial to the outcome of the electoral vote-counting, was expected to be Associate Justice David Davis, who was not clearly associated with either party. However, a few days before President Grant signed the Electoral Commission Law, the legislature of Illinois, whose twenty-one electoral votes had been cast for Hayes, the Republican, had elected Justice Davis to the U.S. Senate. When word reached the Justice, he declined to serve on the electoral commission, and the four justices already on the commission picked Justice Joseph P. Bradley, a Republican whose record on the Court made him acceptable to the Democrats.

The official process of opening and counting the electoral votes occupied all of Febraury and was interrupted frequently by the reference of disputed votes to the commission. In each instance, the commission decided the issue in favor of the Republicans by a strictly party vote of 8–7.

Convinced that the Republican certification boards had fraudulently rejected many valid votes for Tilden, the Democratic leaders abandoned their customary adherence to states' rights and insisted that the electoral commission go behind the official returns to correct the injustice. With as much inconsistency, in view of their usual support of national power at the expense of states' rights, the Republicans argued that the sovereignty of a state made unconstitutional any probing into its official returns.

Accepting this latter contention virtually as argued, the eight Republicans on the commission overrode their seven Democratic colleagues and accorded the electoral votes of Florida and Louisiana to Hayes. On February 23, by unanimously assigning South Carolina and Oregon also to his column, it awarded him the presidency by a margin of one electoral vote (185–184 for Tilden).

The Democrats could still block the completion of the electoral process if the Democratic House refused to attend the joint session at which the completion of the count was to be held and the result formally announced. There was a division among Democrats in the House as to what course they should pursue, but after a week of ominous bluster enough Democrats joined the Republicans to permit the final joint session to be held. In the early morning hours of March 2, 1877, the last votes were counted and it was announced that Hayes had been elected—only forty-eight hours before Inauguration Day. He became president of the United States, first taking the oath of office privately on Saturday, March 3, to avoid being sworn in on the Sabbath, and was publicly inaugurated on Monday the 5th.

The Resolution of the crisis had been accomplished through the cooperation of Southern Democrats. They came from a section that had been devastated by war and represented constituents who had no desire to repeat that experience. More subtle forces, however, also influenced their decision. In the confused weeks after the election, friends of Hayes recognized that he could be elected only if Southern moderates were persuaded that it was to their interest to acquiesce in such an outcome. The absolute minimum that would satisfy the South was a promise that the remaining federal troops would be withdrawn from that section and that the national administration would do nothing to prevent popularly elected Democratic governors from taking office in the three states still controlled by Republicans. This minimum, however, was not enough to win the cooperation of many Southern congressmen. As further evidence of good faith, it was proposed that Hayes would include in his Cabinet at least one Southern Democrat and that he would support efforts of Southern capitalists to obtain subsidies for railroad construction in the South. Negotiations were carried on through intermediaries, and an understanding was reached that Hayes would accept these proposals. Many Southerners shared the generally conservative views of Hayes on economic questions, and they had confidence in his integrity. Though they believed that Tilden had been elected president, they were willing to accept Hayes on the basis of the compromise worked out by his colleagues.

Both Hayes and Tilden had approved the idea of the commission before it was broached in Congress. Hayes believed that intimidation of black voters by Southern whites had reduced the Republican vote in the three Southern states and given Democrats an unfair advantage—certainly true in two of the states. Tilden only reluctantly approved the commission, but failed—or refused—to provide vigorous or direct leadership in the crisis.

One Republican activist was Sen. James A. Garfield, a future president. During the Grant administration he had defended the use of federal troops in the South, a measure which he frankly regarded as essential to the maintenence of the Republican Party in those states. In the election of 1876 he was one of the "visiting statesmen" whose presence in New Orleans strengthened the hand of the returning board of Louisiana in recounting the vote of the state for the Republican ticket. Named to the electoral commission, he voted to resolve every doubtful electoral vote in favor of Rutherford B. Hayes.

The Democrats retained their control of the House of Representatives in this unusual election, and through the investigation of the Potter committee in 1878-79 attempted to show Republican corruption and irregularities in connection with the disputed presidential contest. Findings of the committee reflected on persons close to Hayes, notably John Sherman. They did not involve the president himself beyond showing that, in keeping the bargain struck for him during negotiations, he had rewarded certain carpetbag politicians of dubious character with federal positions. The Republican *New York Tribune* in October 1878, meanwhile, published translations of a large number of telegrams sent in code by Democrat operatives while the election was still in dispute. The telegrams revealed that close associates of Tilden were involved in negotiations to bribe election officials, counteracted the exposures of the Potter committee, and spoiled Democratic plans to capitalize on the fraud issue in the 1880 campaign.

The electoral crisis and its resolution had a significance beyond the immediate questions of bribery and corruption, however. Critics of the settlement called it a bargain between Southerners and the Republicans, or, as some said, "the compromise of 1877." Others said Tilden had been sacrificed to make "a Southern holiday." But the acceptance without violence—which had been threatened early in the dispute—of the decisions of the electoral commission so soon after the Civil War gave a welcome reassurance to the American people that self-government and domestic peace were not incompatible.

# V. The System and Human Nature: Corruption, Exposure, Persuasion, and Reform

*"The office of government is not to confer happiness, but to give men opportunity to work out happiness for themselves."*

—William Ellery Channing

# 20.
# Corrupting the Body Politic

If one illustration were needed for the fact that human nature can impair the purity of the political system, the varied improprieties and illegalities of the electoral crisis of 1877 might suffice. Unfortunately, others abound, and in great variety. Before reviewing them, however, it may be well to note the encouraging aspect of the study of political corruption: it still makes news. In other words, American history has revealed that political corruption has been neither universal nor constant.

In the sense of *political* corruption, the primary dictionary-definition of corruption serves perfectly well: impairment of integrity, virtue, or moral principle. Political corruption may be divided into three categories according to the objectives of both corrupter and corrupted: power, material gain, and benefits for friends. Obviously, there is a great degree of overlapping among these categories, and there is also considerable semantic confusion over the precise meanings of words often used in discussing political corruption.

*Corrupt practices* as a general term originally embraced bribery and the use of other undue influence to gain political "favors" or other ends. Beginning in the nineteenth century, however, the phrase came to be limited in common usage to practices threatening the integrity of elections.

*Spoils system*—a term usually used with negative overtones—describes the patronage system of rewarding the party faithful with appointment to public office. It involves political activity by public employees in support of their party and removal from office if their party loses the election. A change in party control of government necessarily brings new officials to high positions carrying political responsibility, but the spoils system extends personnel turnover down to routine or subordinate governmental positions whenever civil service does not apply. In the most extreme form of the spoils system the primary test for appointment is faithfulness of party service, with almost complete disregard of competence to perform the duties of the public office concerned. The term apparently originated with a speech made in 1832 by Sen. W. L. Marcy in which he asserted that "to the victor belong the spoils of the enemy."

"Spoils system" is sometimes applied loosely to the great variety of means by which money may be transferred more or less indirectly from the public treasury to the party coffers; it is also applied to other abuses of governmental power for partisan advantage. So used, the term includes abuses in the management of public expenditures, irregularities in the granting of franchises and other privileges, partisan favoritism in the administration of criminal law, discrimination in the levy of taxes, and other corrupt uses of public power. For this discussion, however, the term will be limited to its narrower usage related to political appointments to public office.

Although patronage existed in colonial times, the spoils system came to full bloom in the period 1800–29. When Thomas Jefferson became president in 1801, he found the public offices filled with persons generally hostile to him and to his party. Without espousing the principle of rotation in office, he replaced enough Federalists with Jeffersonian Republicans to assure a more even distribution between the two parties in the civil service. Yet in both appointments and removals partisan considerations were not the sole criterion; it remained for Andrew Jackson (elected 1828) to introduce the principle of the spoils system into the national government—yet even Jackson did not make wholesale removals on political grounds. Spoils practices had been instituted earlier in the governments of both states and cities. The system first rooted in New York; it was established almost as soon in Pennsylvania. By 1828 in all the states of the North and West, the system existed or strong groups desired to introduce it.

In his annual message in 1829 Jackson presented a reasoned philosophy of the spoils system. "There are," he said, "perhaps few men who can for any great length of time enjoy office without being more or less under the influence of feelings unfavorable to the faithful discharge of their public duties. Their integrity may be proof against improper considerations immediately addressed to themselves, but they are apt to acquire a habit of looking with indifference upon the public interests and of tolerating conduct from which an unpracticed man would revolt." Rotation in office, then, was not an evil but a positive good. "The duties of all public offices are," he declared, "or at least admit of being made, so plain and simple that men of intelligence may readily qualify themselves for their performance; and I cannot but believe that more is lost by the long continuance of men in office than is generally to be gained by their experience."

The same attitude underlies the provision in many state constitutions, especially in the South, limiting a governor (and certain other officials) to a single term in office. Variations permit a governor to hold the same office more than once but not to succeed himself, or to serve not more than two terms. The mistrust of officialdom implicit in this kind of restriction is part of the populist character, which was an element of Jackson's approach to politics. More precisely, perhaps, the mistrust is less of officialdom than of the human weakness to succumb to temptation. Demonstrations of the wisdom of such concern have been abundant. Popular suspicion that a political figure is involved in corrupt activities, however, is not necessarily always accurate.

Henry Clay was a candidate for the presidency in 1824 but ran fourth and last in the election. This excluded him from consideration when the contest was decided in the House of Representatives. There the leading contestants were Andrew Jackson and John Quincy Adams. The Kentucky legislature instructed Clay to vote for Jackson, but he refused to do so. He threw his support to Adams, who was elected. Adams then made Clay his secretary of state. Jackson was furious, and he and his followers raised the cry of "bargain and sale." Clay marshaled impressive evidence to show that he had decided to vote for Adams before coming to Washington. The charges of corruption would not disappear, however, and were periodically resurrected with damaging effect on Clay through the rest of his life.

## Tammany and Tweed

Tammany Hall, the popular name of the executive committee of the Democratic Party of New York County, has been popularly identified with political corruption intermittently since early in the nineteenth century. The Society of St. Tammany, as it was named when it was created in 1789, was under the control of Aaron Burr until his political downfall after killing Alexander Hamilton in a duel in 1804. The society was influential in bringing about victories of the Republican (later called Democratic) Party and was richly rewarded, particularly by Jefferson after he became president in 1801.

Politically, the Democratic Party was organized as an apparently distinct body; in reality, however, the Tammany society controlled the political mechanism in New York and the real power passed into the hands of ward leaders, later organized as the executive committee of the party. As early as 1806–07, revelations of widespread corruption of Tammany city officials resulted in the removal of the controller, the superintendent of the almshouse, the inspector of bread, and others. Despite such proved charges, many of the removed officials, including the society's founder, remained powerful Tammany sachems (an Indian word for leader). The election of its grand sachem, Martin Van Buren, as president of the United States in 1836 enhanced Tammany's prestige. Within a few years, however, the astute, unscrupulous, and engaging Fernando Wood, several times mayor of New York, organized the political power of immigrant groups into gangs to break with and later control Tammany Hall.

Another shrewd and corrupt leader acquired control of Tammany after the Civil War. William Marcy Tweed had held a variety of municipal offices when he became chairman of the Tammany General Committee and grand sachem of Tammany Hall. Tweed gained absolute power in the New York City Democratic organization, controlling both nominations and patronage. While serving as a state senator, he extended his influence to state politics and in 1870 forced a new city charter through the legislature. This charter created a board of audit by means of which Tweed and his associates seized control of the city treasury. By such devices as faked leases, padded bills, false vouchers, and unnecessary repairs, the "Tweed ring" systematically plundered the city of sums estimated at from 30 million to 200 million dollars. As a result of a joint exposé by the *New York Times*, the cartoons of Thomas Nast in *Harper's Weekly*, and the efforts of the noted lawyer and reformer Samuel J. Tilden, the notorious Tweed Ring was overthrown, a number of corrupt municipal judges were removed, and Tweed himself was jailed.

During the same period Republican organizations came under intermittent attack for corrupt activities. Governor Tilden broke up New York's Canal Ring, a conspiracy of politicians and contractors that defrauded the state in connection with the construction of the Erie Canal. To this day construction contracts are a major factor in political corruption. Republican quarrels arose over the lavish patronage potential of the New York Custom House, which had been long noted for the most flagrant abuses of the spoils system. Chester A. Arthur, an important figure in Sen. Roscoe Conkling's New York Republican machine, was appointed collector of customs for the Port of New York by Pres. Ulysses S. Grant. Although he combined experimental civil service examinations with patronage considerations in making appointments and made few removals for political reasons, his management did not satisfy the reform convictions of President Hayes; a nonpartisan commission was therefore appointed by Secretary of the Treasury John Sherman recommending sweeping changes. The president asked for the resignation of Arthur, but he refused to retire under fire and was removed from his position in July 1878. Arthur's business conduct of the office was not impugned, but he was regarded as too involved in machine politics to carry out a reform program.

Circumstances led to Arthur's nomination for vice-president with James A. Garfield in 1880. His nomination was coldly received by the public; when, after his election and accession, he became actively engaged on behalf of Conkling in a major conflict with President Garfield over New York patronage, the impression was widespread that he was unworthy of his position. Upon the death of Garfield (Sept. 19, 1881) Arthur took the oath as his successor. Coming at a period of intense factional controversy and following the assassination of Garfield, which had profoundly shocked the public mind, the accession of Arthur to the presidency created serious apprehensions. The widespread expressions of dismay in the press at the probable outcome of an administration in the hands of such an alleged factionist and spoilsman are said to have deeply wounded Arthur. But his performance in office, scrupulously administered in a spirit devoid of factional animosity, established the confidence of the nation and won for him the approval of many of his severest critics. Contrary to the general expectation, his appointments as a rule were unexceptionable, and he earnestly supported the Pendleton Act, passed in 1883, for the reform of the civil service. Vindicated by his performance in the presidency, Arthur fared better than many of his contemporaries in cleansing his name of stains of corruption that some of his associations had brought on it.

## The Grant Administration

The two decades following the Civil War saw a remarkable succession of political scandals. The period was a veritable golden age of boodle. The Republican Party was firmly in control of national affairs. Congress, almost monolithically Republican, had been riding high since seizing control of Reconstruction from Pres. Andrew Johnson, and Grant's election in 1868 placed the White House in friendly hands. Grant's innocence in political matters, his ineptness, and his general indifference to governmental policies rendered him an easy victim for the Republican bosses of the Northern state machines. These party chiefs, free of disciplinary threats from the executive, reduced the Congress to a state of total irresponsibility.

The most serious national scandal of Grant's first administration resulted from the rapid expansion of railroads with federal assistance. Between 1862 and 1872 grants were made to the Union Pacific and Central Pacific companies, and to other connecting corporations, to build railways from the Missouri River to the Pacific Ocean. By 1869 these roads had spanned the continent. Various grants were also made to other roads, both transcontinental and Middle Western. The new railways, tempted by such opportunities, often extended their lines into regions that were totally undeveloped.

Extravagances in construction and operation were aggravated by "construction rings" of railway officials and by rolling stock companies who received extravagant prices as the result of favoritism. These conditions rendered the roads no longer able to meet the demands of stockholders without imposing rates that the Western farmers deemed excessive. Due largely to support from Northern businessmen and the complacency of Northern voters enjoying the postwar boom, Grant was reelected in 1872, despite a Republican split and a Democratic campaign centering on Grant's incompetence.

During the campaign it was learned that Vice-Pres. Schuyler Colfax, Grant's new vice-presidential nominee Henry Wilson, and a number of other prominent Republican politicians were involved in the Credit Mobilier of America (a construction and finance company). Experience had already taught veteran railroad organizers that more money could be made from construction contracts than from the operation of a completed road. This promised to be doubly true in the case of the Union Pacific, which was supported by federal loans and land grants although it proposed to span a vast unpopulated region between the Missouri River and Great Salt Lake. Crédit Mobilier was part of a complex arrangement whereby Thomas Durant, Oakes Ames, and other men in control of the Union Pacific Railroad contracted with themselves for construction of the railroad. Chartered in 1859 as the Pennsylvania Fiscal Agency and taken over by Union Pacific men in 1864, Crédit Mobilier was itself a contractor for only the first 247 miles of road. Thereafter it functioned as the guarantor of extravagant contracts awarded to Ames and J. W. Davis and assigned by them to seven trustees chosen from the inner circle of Crédit Mobilier and the Union Pacific. The trustees received payments from the Union Pacific (more often in its stock and bonds than in cash), paid the actual costs of construction, and distributed the profits among holders of Crédit Mobilier stock. These arrangements, while facilitating the disposal of Union Pacific securities and speeding completion of the railroad, enabled the men in control to enrich themselves by converting Union Pacific assets and credit into construction profits. In the process, the railroad was overcapitalized and impoverished.

Crédit Mobilier became a public scandal when it was revealed that in 1867–68, Oakes Ames, whose financial responsibilities did not prevent his serving as congressman from Massachusetts, had tried to win friends for the company by selling shares of its stock to a number of his colleagues at prices far below their market value. The initial revelations were sensationalized in the press, and congressional investigations in 1872–73 developed the affair into a scandal of major proportions. At last the magic spell that seemed to have given the Republican Party a protective immunity even under the leadership of Grant broke with the Panic of 1873.

Despite the widespread questioning of Republican leadership, the scandals continued. The revelations that certain congressmen had been effectively bribed with gifts of stock in the Crédit Mobilier damaged the reputations of numerous prominent Republicans. Enormous frauds in the collection of internal revenue by the Whisky Ring, with the connivance of federal officials, were revealed in 1875; at the same time Secretary of War William W. Belknap resigned to avoid impeachment for corruption in the conduct of Indian affairs. The administration was further discredited by the forced resignation in 1876 of Secretary of the Treasury Benjamin H. Bristow after he had successfully exposed the Whisky Ring, and of Postmaster Gen. Marshall Jewell, who had resisted the spoils system in his department. By 1876 the collapse of the Grant administration was truly astonishing. Then, on the eve of the 1876 Republican National Convention, came new and shocking revelations about James G. Blaine, who had been Speaker of the House of Representatives during the sordid improprieties of the Grant administration. Blaine was charged with using his office to profit from a financial transaction involving the Little Rock and Fort Smith Railroad. Though he made a brilliant speech in Congress attempting to exonerate himself, the incident's publicity, plus a heatstroke suffered on the eve of the convention, adversely affected Blaine's chances in the close nominating race, which was won by Rutherford B. Hayes.

## Garfield and Prohibition

Still another casualty of this remarkable age of corruption was James A. Garfield. Charges were made against Garfield that involved a problem of political ethics, which a later generation was to call a conflict of interest. With one or two of these charges Garfield dealt frankly and successfully, but the Crédit Mobilier affair proved quite embarrassing. Garfield, among others, had received in January 1868 an offer of a gift of stock in this company, which was then seeking legislative favors. Without recognizing until later the impropriety of the whole proceeding, he had kept the matter in abeyance for more than two years before refusing to have any more to do with it. His denials could thus be only partial and not as convincing as he might have wished.

From that bitter experience in 1874 Garfield learned a lesson. He had been admitted to the bar and in his early years in Congress had accepted an occasional case; now he had found that clients who desired legal services were not easy to distinguish from those who needed political influence. From that time on, in spite of a meager salary that barely covered expenses, Garfield refused all legal assignments. Not all the beneficiaries of Crédit Mobilier and the other devious dealings of the era were so circumspect. Garfield, at least, was able to go on to the presidency, however briefly.

Concern expressed in recent years over the influence of organized crime in politics and its major thrust in the gangster era during national Prohibition (1920–33) should not obscure the fact that the foundations of such power had been laid earlier, nor the fact that after Prohibition was repealed, this type of criminal activity became more highly organized and no less ruthless. At least as early as the 1850s in New York and the 1870s in Chicago, systematic cooperation between criminals and politicians had become habitual. In return for campaign contributions and the intimidation of voters, the politician protected the criminal in the courts and winked at the existence of gambling and prostitution. The extortion of money (called "protection") from a business by threats of bombing or other disruption was solidly established on the docks of New Orleans and in the gambling houses of Chicago before the turn of the century.

## Harding and Teapot Dome

Warren G. Harding was a prosperous Marion, Ohio, newspaper publisher and a regular, high-tariff, nationalist, conservative Republican. In 1920 his party's national convention became deadlocked in choosing among three outstanding presidential prospects. Overnight conferences of conservative leaders decided somewhat tentatively on Harding, who had served one term in the U.S. Senate, as an alternate who, if elected president, would "go along" with them.

In conscious imitation of Pres. William McKinley, Harding did not make a speaking tour but conducted a "front porch" campaign. Although his intellectual limitations could not be entirely concealed, he was the beneficiary of the country's war weariness and reaction against the idealism of Pres. Woodrow Wilson. The electorate welcomed the "return to normalcy" Harding proposed, and he was the easy victor.

Harding's cabinet, like most cabinets, was a melange of men of native ability and political or industrial experience and party leaders who claimed office as a reward for services rendered the new president. The outstanding names were those of Charles Evans Hughes and Herbert C. Hoover, who became secretary of state and of commerce, respectively. Andrew W. Mellon was secretary of the treasury. Political and personal debts were paid by the choice of Albert B. Fall as secretary of the interior, Harry M. Daugherty as attorney general, and Will H. Hays as postmaster general. Fall was Harding's Senate colleague from New Mexico, Daugherty his political mentor and campaign manager, and Hays the chairman of the Republican National Committee. The conduct of administrative and political affairs by the latter group and others less prominent in the new administration soon brought intense criticism upon the President and the Republican Party. Some key men appointed to the regulatory agencies publicly confessed that they were against government regulation. Some appointees to the cabinet or lesser posts were so biased in favor of business, and so antilabor and antifarmer in their outlook, that they quickly lost the confidence of these latter groups. Attorney General Daugherty, instead of negotiating with the unions during the coal and railroad strikes of the early twenties, preferred to obtain sweeping injunctions against labor from friendly courts and then use federal troops to support his antilabor convictions. After his appointment as Chief Justice of the Supreme Court by Harding, former Pres. William Howard Taft wrote that he had been elevated to the Court in order to reverse some past decisions.

A 1910 act of Congress had stipulated that certain oil-bearing federal lands be set aside and designated by the U.S. government as naval oil reserves. Reserve no. 1 embraced 38,000 acres of public and private lands in Elk Hills, Calif; reserve no. 2 contained 30,000 acres of public and private lands in the Buena Vista Hills, Calif; and reserve no. 3, Teapot Dome, Wyo., contained 9,321 acres of public lands. In an act of June 4, 1920, Congress directed the secretary of the navy to conserve the properties and lease them if necessary for protection against drainage by adjoining private lands. The policy reflected by the acts was to "maintain a great naval petroleum reserve in the ground."

Harding's secretary of the navy was Edwin N. Denby, and before he had been in office three months he innocently consented to a proposal by Interior Secretary Fall that the oil reserves be transferred from Navy to Interior jurisdiction. On May 31, 1921, at the instigation of Fall, Harding signed an executive order effecting the transfer.

Secretary Fall thereupon entered secret negotiations with Harry F. Sinclair of the Mammoth Oil Company. In less than a year, on April 7, 1922, Fall issued, without competitive bidding, a lease covering all of the lands in reserve no. 3 (Teapot Dome) to the company, granting it the exclusive right to take and dispose of oil and gas from the reserve. No imminent danger existed that the oil would be lost by drainage. In 1921 and 1922 Fall also secretly negotiated contracts and leases with Edward L. Doheny covering lands in reserves no. 1 and 2, executed in 1922 with the Pan American Petroleum and Transport Company and the Pan American Petroleum Company, both controlled by Doheny. All of these leases and contracts were also signed by Secretary of the Navy Denby, but the courts found that Denby was passive throughout and had signed under misapprehension and without full knowledge of their contents.

The leases and contracts came under investigation by committees of the U.S. Senate, where it was disclosed that shortly after the signing of the Teapot Dome lease, Fall and members of his family received from an unknown source more than $200,000 in Liberty bonds under circumstances indicating that the bonds came from a company organized by Sinclair and others receiving benefit from the lease. Also, it appeared that prior to the execution of the Pan American contracts and leases, Doheny, at Fall's request, sent $100,000 in currency to Fall as a "loan" which had not been repaid.

On February 8, 1924, a joint resolution passed by Congress stated that it appeared from the evidence that the leases and contracts negotiated by Fall with Sinclair and Doheny were executed under circumstances indicating fraud and corruption, without authority on the part of the officers purporting to act for the United States and in defiance of the settled policy to maintain in the ground a great reserve supply of oil adequate to the needs of the Navy. It declared the contracts and leases to be against the public interest and directed the president to institute suits to cancel them and to prosecute any civil or criminal actions that might be warranted.

Cancellation of the leases and contracts was later confirmed in separate cases by the U.S. Supreme Court. The Court ruled that the leases and agreements were made fraudulently and that the executive order of May 31, 1921, transferring the administration of the reserves to the secretary of the interior was illegal. In criminal actions Doheny and Sinclair were acquitted of charges of bribery and criminal conspiracy, but Fall was convicted in 1929 and became the first cabinet officer in the nation's history to be sent to jail.

At the time in 1923 when Montana's Senator Thomas J. Walsh was gathering evidence that would expose the oil lease scandal—not yet known to the public—Washington buzzed with rumors about wholesale looting by the alien property custodian and the director of the Veterans Bureau. Attorney General Daugherty, meanwhile, was charged with having received payments from violators of Prohibition laws. He was forced out of office by Pres. Calvin Coolidge, who succeeded to the presidency after Harding's death on a cross-country tour just as the scandals, wholly unknown to him, were beginning to be revealed. Daugherty was tried twice and each time refused to testify on the grounds that he might incriminate himself. Other lesser officials were imprisoned, and still another committed suicide. In some ways the decay of the Harding regime in a mass of corruption was reminiscent of the shabby denouement of the Grant administration. Both presidents were personally scrupulous men faithfully trusting associates and subordinates who proved untrustworthy.

## Watergate

A different kind of trust, and a different kind of corruption, characterized the other great political scandal of the United States' first two centuries. In 1972 Richard M. Nixon, like Harding fifty-two years earlier, won an epochal landslide. In his bid for a second term as president, he defeated liberal Democrat George McGovern by eighteen million votes, winning nearly two-thirds of the total ballots cast and carrying forty-nine states and 520 electoral votes to McGovern's seventeen votes from Massachusetts and the District of Columbia. A year and nine months later Nixon left office in disgrace, a scant step ahead of impeachment, leaving behind him the rubble of one of the gravest constitutional crises ever to confront the United States.

Unlike Harding, however, Nixon bore personal responsibility for some of the illegal and improper actions in the great Watergate crisis of 1972–74. Unlike Harding, Nixon was the principal intended beneficiary of the unlawful conspiracies in the case. And unlike the Harding case, the currency of corruption in the Watergate scandal was power, not money.

Lord Bryce wrote in 1921 that "not many American presidents have been brilliant and some have not risen to the full moral height of their position, but none has been base or unfaithful to his trust, none has tarnished the honor of the nation." Never before had corruption touched a president himself. The Watergate scandal came to symbolize not only administrative corruption but unconstitutionality.

The affair first came to light briefly in June of 1972 when a small band of men was arrested during and after a bungled burglary attempt of the Democratic headquarters in Washington's Watergate apartment complex. Links to the Nixon White House were discovered but quickly denied; the matter would have dropped out of sight except for the tenacious reports of a pair of nonpolitical journalists named Bob Woodward and Carl Bernstein of the *Washington Post*. That newspaper's insistent coverage of the Woodward-Bernstein discoveries, followed by revelations growing out of the trial of the Watergate burglars, led eventually to a Senate investigation that documented a wide variety of excesses by the Nixon reelection campaign effort in 1972. It was learned that Nixon agents had infiltrated Democratic offices and had undertaken sabotage of the nomination campaigns of strong Democratic presidential contenders to enhance the chance of the weakest, McGovern. Such efforts had been lavishly financed with

a fund of hundreds of thousands of anonymous one-hun-
dred-dollar bills, which turned out to have been unlawfully
contributed by various individuals and corporations, often
aggressively solicited by various presidential agents.

Then the Senate hearings virtually stumbled onto the fact
that the Nixon White House had been "bugged" earlier to
record historic conversations and that tape recordings of incriminating conversations had been made. The contents of
the tapes and other evidence led to a full-scale inquiry by the
House Judiciary Committee as to whether the president
should be impeached.

The various trials which ensued concluded with the conviction of a long list of Nixon's major and minor aides, including his attorney general and original campaign manager,
John N. Mitchell. Mitchell became the second Cabinet officer
in U.S. history to be jailed for criminal activity (after Harding's interior secretary, Albert B. Fall).

The nation was momentarily diverted from the Watergate
scandal when Vice-Pres. Spiro T. Agnew announced that he
had been informed that he was under investigation in connection with alleged kickbacks by contractors, architects, and
engineers to officials of Baltimore County, Maryland, where
Agnew had been county executive until 1967 and governor
until 1968. On August 8, 1973, he held a televised news
conference to deny any wrongdoing, but two months later he
resigned and pleaded no contest to a charge of evading income taxes on $29,500 of unreported income in 1967. In
return for this plea (tantamount to a felony conviction), the
Justice Department dropped all other pending charges.

Agnew became the first vice-president to resign under a
cloud. It is possible that he could have become the first vice-
president to be impeached, but the case was almost wholly
obscured by the Watergate affair, and the criminal investigation into his activities had not generated enough public attention to set the stage for impeachment by the time he resigned.
It is noteworthy that the two historic scandals of the Nixon
presidency involved totally different modes of corruption, the
Agnew case being typical of those in which material gain is
the objective, the Watergate affair being motivated by considerations of power and prestige.

The various Watergate trials and investigations revealed
testimony and other evidence making clear how the situation
developed and in large measure why. Nixon's most trusted
advisers were not politicians in the traditional sense of the

word but relative newcomers to electoral politics. His attorney general's outlook on government had been conditioned by his career as a leading expert in municipal bond financing arrangements, whereby public corporations are constructed to circumvent constitutional limitations on borrowing by state or local governments. His closest personal aide, H. R. Haldeman, had been an advertising executive who recruited many eager young converts from his field—converts who viewed political processes in the sterile terms of market analysis and marketing campaigns.

Something of a "bunker mentality" had developed in the Nixon inner circle after the riotous street demonstrations of the 1960s, and the White House tended to visualize subversion everywhere. After trying diligently, if covertly, to enhance McGovern's chance of being nominated by the Democrats, the Nixon group became convinced that Cuba's Communist dictator Fidel Castro was giving McGovern financial support; it was to the end of uncovering proof of this suspicion that the original Watergate burglary was directed.

It was extremely important to Nixon and his inner circle that he "win big" in 1972 after the barest of victories in 1968 over Hubert Humphrey. This determination, plus extravagant fears about the motivation of Democrats and protesters, the absence of a commitment to traditional political practices and values in many of his people, and the warping effect of having access to virtually unlimited money led to the debacle.

On Aug. 9, 1974, Richard M. Nixon resigned as president of the United States of America. He alone, among the thirty-six men to have held the presidency at the time, was driven from that high office by Article II, Section 4 of the U.S. Constitution. The fact that Nixon resigned before the full House of Representatives could act on the three articles of impeachment recommended by its Judiciary Committee in no way alters the fact that it was the process that forced him out. The House would have impeached him by an overwhelming margin, and he realized this even before new evidence revealed that he had deceived his own defense counsel and chief defenders about his involvement in Watergate. After those revelations, conviction by the necessary two-thirds majority of the Senate shifted from likelihood to virtual certainty. But before those last steps—formal impeachment by the whole House, the public spectacle of a trial before Senate and nation, and the degradation of conviction

—the president chose what in effect was a plea of no contest and resigned. In this step, too, he was the first.

## Impeachment

Impeachment found its way into law in England in the fourteenth century, where it was used intermittently until 1806. In 1787 it was built into the U.S. Constitution. Its purpose was to make possible the punishment of a guilty, highly ranked federal official, while lesser officers could be brought to justice in ordinary courts of law. At the same time, the process would allow for acquittal if the accused were adjudged guilty by less than the overwhelming margin of 2–1. Benjamin Franklin reminded the Constitutional Convention that prior to the adoption of impeachment, whenever a first magistrate was brought to justice, "recourse was had to assassination in which he was not only deprived of his life but of the opportunity of vindicating his character." James Madison saw the need to defend the community "against the incapacity, negligence or perfidy of the chief magistrate." The convention agreed by a vote of 8–2 that the executive be removable on impeachment, with only Massachusetts and South Carolina dissenting.

Article II, Section 4 states:" The President, Vice-President and all civil Officers of the United States, shall be removed from Office on Impeachment for, and Conviction of, Treason, Bribery, or other high Crimes and Misdemeanors." The meanings of treason and bribery are clear enough; what then are "high crimes and misdemeanors"? One constitutional lawyer has said that a collection of unanswered traffic tickets would amount to "high misdemeanors" if the U.S. Senate said it did. When Gerald Ford was serving in the House of Representatives, he led a pious and vain effort to impeach Supreme Court Justice William O. Douglas for allowing some of his writings to be published in a magazine Ford considered pornographic. At that time he declared, "An impeachable offense is whatever a majority of the House of Representatives considers it to be at a given moment in history."

"Strict constructionists"—notably the defenders of presidents fighting impeachment—argue that high crimes and misdemeanors must be indictable offenses, that is, explicit violations of law. This was the case with Nixon's defenders as it had been with those of Pres. Andrew Johnson 106 years before. The eleven articles of impeachment against Johnson attempted to identify specific acts as high crimes (two) and misdemeanors (nine), each article ending with some such stipulation as "did then and there commit and was guilty of a high misdemeanor in office." Although the argument about what constituted high crimes and misdemeanors raged across the country as well as in Congress, no consensus ever developed. Some of Nixon's last-ditch defenders have argued that the Congress with its top-heavy Democratic majority was nothing but a lynch mob, determined to drive him from office at all costs. A review of the history of the Fortieth Congress, which impeached Johnson and barely acquitted him, is instructive in this respect.

Most historians have romanticized the role of Andrew Johnson as victim, with the Radical Republicans in the House as villains. The fact is incontrovertible, however, that the Republicans enjoyed massive dominance in the Congress that impeached and tried Andrew Johnson. The seventeenth president was a Tennessee Democrat who was elected vice-president under a Republican, Abraham Lincoln, in 1864, and who served all but the first six weeks of Lincoln's second term. All seats in both houses of Congress apportioned to the eleven Confederate states were vacant during the Civil War, and when the Johnson impeachment came to issue before the Fortieth Congress in 1867 and 1868, only Tennessee had been readmitted to the Union. Thus in the House, 51 normally Democratic votes were vacant seats, as were 20 in the Senate. Thus the Republicans had a "veto-proof Congress," with 74 percent of the votes in the House and 78 percent in the Senate. By contrast, in the Ninety-third Congress, which forced Richard Nixon to resign, Democrats controlled the House with only 57 percent and the Senate with 58 percent margins that are trifling by comparison.

There are a few parallels between the two cases, separated by slightly more than a century in time. Although Lincoln and Johnson had won the 1864 election with 55 percent of the popular vote, the Tennessee Democrat did not inherit even the modest popularity that the murdered Lincoln had gained. From the start his relations with Congress had been difficult and his foot-dragging and outright interference in the Reconstruction course set by Congress made him enemies by the dozen.

Nixon, who had gained reelection with a historic landslide, was nevertheless personally unpopular, the beneficiary in 1972 of a massive resistance to his opponent more than a personal or political endorsement for himself. The arrogance of his principal aides reduced his congressional defenders.

In the case of Johnson, his sympathetic support for Southern leaders so recently rebels became increasingly apparent. This, and his manifest distaste for the Radical Republicans' program of enfranchising and otherwise aiding Southern blacks, moved the press to step up editorial demands that he be impeached. The roster of newspapers thus assailing Johnson included many that had previously supported him.

In the Nixon impeachment, as the president's innocence of ordering or leading the cover-up of the Watergate scandal and related excesses became more and more problematical, public support dwindled fast. First, there was damaging testimony before the Senate Watergate committee, then incriminating tape transcripts, and finally the evidence presented to the House Judiciary Committee. The totality of all available information painted a dismaying picture of complicity and deceit. As this happened the moderate and conservative press that had held out hope for his exoneration deserted him and began demanding his impeachment—again including, as 106 years earlier, the *Chicago Tribune*.

Although the party alignment against Nixon was much less heavily weighted than the hostile imbalance that faced Johnson, the GOP ranks of the Fortieth Congress were split much more deeply than the split existing between Southern and Northern Democrats on which some of Nixon's supporters sought to rely. The Radical Republicans in the Congress of 1867–68 were counterbalanced almost evenly on key Reconstruction issues by their conservative Republican fellows. Then, as in 1974, economic and other problems impinged on the impeachment question: a severe post-Civil War recession and sharp controversy over monetary policy.

However, the actions for which Johnson was impeached had been not only public but flamboyant. The Congress had legislated its program for reconstructing Southern society, giving the blacks meaningful freedom, and uniting a country shattered by civil war; the president had impeded, delayed, and countermanded. Congress enfranchised blacks and sent Union troops to oversee their voting; the president named Southern politicians as governors and changed military orders; he fired Republican postmasters and named Democrats in their stead, and threatened more of the same in order to garner local support for his programs. The Congress legislated the Tenure of Office Act, requiring Senate approval for the dismissal of any presidential appointee who had to be confirmed by the Senate. It later became apparent that the act was unconstitutional, but Johnson both observed it and scorned it, striking no consistent pattern. Finally he fired his secretary of war, an act of defiance provoking the ultimate collision.

In the Nixon case all the transgressions had been secret. The president's men had engaged in a host of unlawful actions to ensure what was already certain: that he be elected not narrowly but by a landslide. They had, in effect, set aside the operation of the Constitution and laws as they related to adversaries of the president — whether political campaign opponents, detractors, or even suspected traitors against whom the law seemed to find no effective sanctions. The original actions on behalf of the president had been covert; then they had been disguised and covered up; finally it became apparent that the cover-up, clearly involving obstruction of justice and a variety of illegal actions, had been participated in, and even led, by the president of the United States.

Here was the difference: secret abuse of the law by Nixon and his men, flagrant rejection of the law by Johnson. Libertarians among the Republican conservatives of 1868 hesitated to join the vengeful radical throng, and although most senators voted "guilty" against Johnson, he was spared because one man, Edmund Ross of Kansas, voted with the Democrats.

The same kind of legislators—libertarians among 1974 Republicans—were first stunned, then outraged, by the abuse of civil liberties on behalf of a Republican President, who then urged on a conspiracy to cover its own tracks. Republicans gamely insisted on his innocence, and then, as they realized they had been deceived, decided to vote to impeach.

Defenders of Nixon who continued to see him as innocent, as conspired against and betrayed by the press, argued that the House Judiciary Committee had been weighted against the president, and that the whole excursion had really been a hanging party. But by comparison with the only other presidential impeachment, the 1974 Nixon affair was a very model of comportment, of discreet conduct, and determination to be fair. Only a few of the Democrats on the Judiciary panel revealed constant hostility and fiery speeches against the actions of the president. Most Democrats seemed subdued and uncheered by the prospects.

In the Johnson impeachment, bias was evident everywhere. In the House the Radical Republicans who had successfully pressed for impeachment were exultant in their declarations. One saw the Johnson administration as "an illustration of the depth to which political and official perfidy can descend." Such florid proclamations embarrassed conservative Republicans, one of whom wrote to his wife, "They are determined to ruin the Republican Party." Like others, he was much dismayed by Andrew Johnson, who, he wrote, "*does* continue to do the most provoking things. If he isn't impeached it won't be his fault."

When Johnson's trial actually took place in the Senate it was presided over, by constitutional mandate, by the Chief Justice of the United States, Salmon P. Chase—who had let it be known to one leading Democrat that if Andrew Johnson were denied the Democratic presidential nomination later in 1868, he would be willing to accept it. Under the succession laws then in force, an impeached Johnson would be succeeded, there being no vice-president, by the president pro tempore of the Senate, Benjamin F. Wade—who sat in the Senate during the trial and voted for impeachment. He came within one vote of becoming president himself. The prospect was not lost on conservative Republicans who mistrusted him; more than one observed that but for Wade's obnoxious character Johnson would have been convicted. Sen. David T. Patterson of Tennessee, Johnson's son-in-law, also took part in the trial—and voted for acquittal. Senator Ross—who has been immortalized as the courageous Kansan who cast the crucial vote against conviction—was a conservative Republican who shortly thereafter aligned with the Democrats.

If the Johnson impeachment left no precedents to be emulated in future exercises of that awesome responsibility, it did leave some very poor examples of conduct that the future might shun. And these were indeed shunned during the Nixon impeachment proceedings. In 1974 lamentations were heard among the more partisan Democrats and other antagonists of the former president, that he had been allowed to resign and had thus escaped the actual mill of impeachment. This line of reasoning argues that he was not suitably punished. The hue and cry escalated again when Gerald Ford subsequently granted Nixon a full and complete pardon for any crimes he may have committed during his tenure in office. "Suitable punishment," of course, is a subjective judgment. It is not difficult to imagine that the disgrace of being forced from the presidency of the United States was, of itself, harsh and sufficient punishment for a man who long looked wistfully toward the history books. Consideration must also be given the U.S. Constitution's concern for protecting the republic from the wrongdoer and his associates, a concern that the founders judged to be coequal with punishment. Again, that concern is met equally well by forced resignation.

As for justice, "Shall any man be above Justice?" George Mason of Virginia asked his fellows in the Constitutional Convention in 1787. "Shall the man who has practised corruption & by that means procured his appointment in the first instance be suffered to escape punishment, by repeating his guilt?" The impeachment process answers "No" convincingly. The Constitution has enabled the United States to survive external and internal storms and has become the Earth's oldest continuing instrument of government.

Certainly the generation that witnessed the series of tragedies known collectively as the Watergate affair has ample reason to comprehend the value and vitality of the Constitution and the wise division of powers that it delegates to the three departments of the national government. When the president violated his constitutional obligation to take care that the laws be faithfully executed, the Senate, the House, and the judiciary remained steadfast to their constitutional trust, and the president was driven from high office for obstructing justice without disruption of the constitutional processes of the national government.

In addition, the Watergate affair teaches anew a lesson that the Supreme Court had previously recorded in these simple words in *United States* v. *Lee* (106 U.S. 196, 220):

> *No man in this country is so high that he is above the law. No officer of the law may set that law at defiance with impunity. All of the officers of the law, from the highest to the lowest, are creatures of the law and are bound to obey it. It is the only supreme power in our system of government.*

# 21.
# The "Fourth Branch":
# The American Press

The governors of the American colonies in the seventeenth century viewed the press suspiciously (in somewhat the fashion of Richard M. Nixon three centuries later). Royal charters commonly contained provisions for licensing the press, but the governors regarded printing as dangerous. As a result, free speech and free printing had no standing.

## Colonial Beginnings

An early press was in operation at Cambridge in the Massachusetts Bay Colony in 1639 and another by 1663. Presses were set up at Boston in 1674 and at Philadelphia eleven years later, but nothing that could properly be called a newspaper was published in the American colonies until Benjamin Harris issued his *Publick Occurrences Both Forreign and Domestick* (Boston, 1690). Packets of newspapers were brought over from England, and at least two issues of the *London Gazette* were reprinted in the colonies. A few professional newsletter writers did some business, and private letters of news were passed from hand to hand. Ballads, proclamations, and pamphlets contained some news. In 1689 Massachusetts leaders compiled and published a news broadside entitled *The Present State of New-English Affairs* in order "to Prevent False Reports" and to tell of minister-educator Increase Mather's efforts in behalf of a new charter following the overthrow of Gov. Sir Edmund Andros.

Actually, early colonial books—made in America—played a definite role in fabricating a uniquely colonial mentality among settlers from various European backgrounds. Many colonial books expressed the dissidence existing in the colonies. The first book published, the *Bay Psalm Book*, was an expression of Puritan discontent with the ecclesiastical settlement in the mother country. Many other religious books were of a similar nature.

In 1690 Benjamin Harris, London bookseller and publisher who had fled England after imprisonment for printing a seditious pamphlet, issued in Boston the first of his *Publick Occurrences Both Forreign and Domestick*, to be "Furnished once a moneth (or if any Glut of Occurrences happen, oftener)," on September 25. Four days later the governor and council suppressed it. This first American newspaper, which was thus ended summarily with its first issue, was a newsy three-page paper (the fourth page being left blank for private correspondence).

Fourteen years passed before the next American venture in newspaper publishing. In 1704 John Campbell, newsletter writer, bookseller, and postmaster, established the *Boston News-Letter*, the first continuously published American newspaper, and issued it "By Authority" for fifteen years. Thereafter it was published until the time of the Revolution; then, as a Tory paper, it was suspended shortly before the British evacuation of Boston. In 1719 William Brooker was appointed postmaster at Boston, and since Campbell refused to turn over the *News-Letter* to him, he founded the *Boston Gazette*. This paper had a long and influential career; during the struggle for independence it was edited by Benjamin Edes and John Gill, who were called "trumpeters of sedition" by their Tory enemies. It survived the Revolution but perished in 1798.

First printer of the *Gazette* was James Franklin, who had as apprentice his thirteen-year-old brother Benjamin. When Brooker lost both post office and newspaper in 1721, and the new proprietor took the printing of the *Gazette* to another shop, Franklin started another paper called the *New-England Courant*. During its five and one-half lively years, the *Courant* was a spectacular sheet, first as an opposition organ critical of the Mather regime, and later, after the council had banned James Franklin as a publisher, as a repository of periodical essays. To evade the council's order, James put his brother Benjamin in as nominal publisher.

Newspapers were establishment voices, too. William Bradford founded the first New York newspaper in 1725 under the title *New-York Gazette*. It was definitely an organ of government in that colony, and when a bitter contest between Gov. William Cosby and political leaders among the colonists developed in 1733, John Peter Zenger was induced to start an opposition paper. His paper, the *New-York Weekly Journal*, was supported by the contributions of James Alexander and other popular political leaders, much as James Franklin's crusading paper in Boston had been aided by a group of dissident writers there. Zenger's paper quickly became a political organ, consistently opposing the policies of Cosby.

For a year the paper continued scathing attacks on the governor until, in November 1734, Cosby issued a proclamation condemning the "divers scandalous, virulent, false and seditious reflections" and offering a reward for the apprehension of their author. On November 17, 1734, Zenger was arrested for libel and until the following August remained in prison, continuing to edit the *Journal* from his cell. When his case finally came to trial on August 4, 1735, he was defended by a noted lawyer from Philadelphia, Andrew Hamilton. Hamilton offered to prove the truth of the statements in Zenger's paper but, in accordance with English law, the judge, a supporter of the administration, refused to allow that procedure; instead, he instructed the jury simply to decide whether the statements in question had actually been printed and to leave the decision as to whether they were libelous to the court. Hamilton, however, urged the jury to consider itself competent to make that decision and stated Zenger's cause so eloquently that it returned a verdict of not guilty. The aged but intrepid Hamilton won Zenger's release on the ground that a fundamental English liberty was at stake. This early recognition of the right of juries to decide whether statements said to be libelous actually were libelous was an important step toward the freedom of the press from censorship by a biased judiciary, although the principle was not established as a legal precedent for many years.

American newspapers in the colonial period were modeled on those of England. The common size was four pages, each about ten inches by fifteen inches. Extra pages were sometimes added if there was heavy advertising. News story headings were little more than datelines. The successful papers had good patronage of advertisements, which were set single-column with little display, so that a page of them resembled modern classified makeup. Paper was obtained chiefly from England until the tax on that staple stimulated American manufacture. The collection of rags, from which paper was then made, was regarded as a patriotic duty during the Revolution. Manufacture of ink, type, and presses was also built up in America when importation was interrupted.

Chief news sources were the English newspapers, since interest in events in the homeland was paramount among the colonists. The second important source was "exchanges"— papers published in other American towns. The rule was for an editor to cover any news of first-rate importance in his own neighborhood for his own publication, and for other papers to clip these items; thus all colonial papers were members of an informal cooperative news-gathering system. Local news coverage was not intended to be thorough, and small happenings were usually disregarded; there were no local reporters, and the editors were commonly imbued with the concept of news as historical record. Sources other than those mentioned were letters from other cities or from England brought in by friends of the editor; word-of-mouth reports by ship captains, postriders, and travelers; and official documents and communications. With the coming of the Revolutionary War English papers were cut off almost entirely, and military operations interfered with colonial communications; patriot committees were active, however, in sending news bulletins from one town to another.

There were no editorial pages, but comment was interspersed with the news. Political and economic dissertations, satirical essays on social customs, and poetry were common.

## Partisan Papers

Parliament's adoption of the Stamp Act in 1765 taxed colonial newspapers and aroused them to bitter opposition and noncompliance. One of the leading Patriot newspapers in this era, which continued to the end of the American Revolution, was the *Boston Gazette*, to which Samuel Adams and his group contributed.

John Adams described his cousin as a plain, modest, and virtuous man, but Samuel Adams was, in addition, a propagandist who was not overscrupulous in his attacks upon British officials and policies, and a passionate politician as well. In innumerable newspaper letters and essays over various signatures, he described British measures and the behavior of royal governors, judges, and customs men in the most adverse terms. The British troops who were sent to Boston in 1768 offered a fine target for his propaganda, and he saw to it that they were portrayed in the colonial newspapers as brutal soldiers oppressing innocent citizens and assailing their wives and daughters.

One of the most influential molders of public opinion in the colonies just prior to the Revolution was an English author and humanitarian named Thomas Paine. In 1774 he emigrated to America on the recommendation of Benjamin Franklin. In Philadelphia he successfully edited the *Pennsylvania Magazine* for eighteen months, coming to know such influential people as Pres. John Witherspoon of the College of New Jersey (later Princeton), scientist David Rittenhouse, and physician-patriot Benjamin Rush, who encouraged him to publish *Common Sense* (which he did on January 10, 1776). This pamphlet, voicing with emotional fervor most of the persuasive arguments for independence from England, is credited by Washington with having "worked a powerful change in the minds of many men." It proved extremely popular, combining appeals to both idealists and those interested in colonial economic advancement. While serving in the army as Gen. Nathanael Greene's volunteer aide-de-camp, Paine began his series of influential tracts called *The Crisis*, opening with the inspirational lines, "These are the times that try men's souls." As secretary of the congressional committee of foreign affairs, he became involved in the controversy regarding Silas Deane's agency in obtaining French aid (1779). Paine's indiscretion in publishing secret documents in the hands of the committee made it necessary for him to resign his secretaryship. His later position as clerk of the Pennsylvania Assembly acquainted him with many revolutionary leaders, and he accompanied John Laurens to France in 1781 to secure aid. Paine's *Public Good* (1780) included one of the first calls for a national convention (looking toward something like a federal constitution) to remedy the ineffectual Articles of Confederation; this work also illustrates his advocacy of a strong union to which states' rights were to be subordinated.

There were, of course, Royalist papers as the colonies were girding for war, and one of these was the *Pennsylvania Evening Post*, founded in 1775 by Benjamin Towne and appearing three times a week. In 1783 he made it the first American daily newspaper. Generally it consisted of only two pages and was a rather shabby sheet. Towne was indicted for treason a few months after he made his paper a daily, lasting seventeen months. John Dunlap and David C. Claypool's *Pennsylvania Packet and Daily Advertiser* began daily publication in 1784. It was very successful, as was the *New York Daily Advertiser*, founded in 1785 by Francis Childs; the latter was the first American paper to be founded as a daily.

Dailies came into the picture less for the purpose of giving timely news than because publishers wished to compete with the coffee-shop bulletins in giving reports to merchants of the offerings of importers just as soon as ships arrived in the harbors of Philadelphia and New York. The political papers of the cities also adopted daily publication rather generally by the end of the eighteenth century, leaving the weeklies to the smaller towns.

As national issues developed, newspapers took up the cudgels of partisan strife. In helping shape public opinion on political issues, they early emerged as an informal arm of the government—later to be called the "fourth branch." From the second administration of George Washington until after the Civil War, ardent partisanship in journalism was the rule. The mercantile papers, as well as those admittedly established as political organs, took sides; when the penny papers appeared in the 1830s, with their emphasis on local news and human-interest features, they, too, were soon involved in party controversy. At its height during the first two decades of the nineteenth century, this partisanship resulted not only in slanting and distorting news but in personal abuse and vilification of political figures, duels and assaults among editors, and much debasement of the newspaper's chief duty of disseminating the news accurately, fairly, and fully. The situation improved in the 1840s and 1850s, but it was not until the doctrine of partisan independence made its great gains in the 1870s that biased reporting of public affairs abated.

The first national political organ was John Fenno's *Gazette of the United States* (1789–1818), which advanced the Federalist position. It was established in New York City when the capital was situated there and later moved with the government offices to Philadelphia. There its great rival was Philip Freneau's *National Gazette* (1791–93), the voice of the Jeffersonian Republican (later Democratic) Party. Alexander Hamilton and Thomas Jefferson, rivals in Washington's Cabinet, were the respective sponsors of Fenno and Freneau in their editorial efforts. Supplanting the *National Gazette* as spokesman for the Republicans was the *Philadelphia Aurora*, founded in 1790 by Benjamin Franklin Bache, grandson of Benjamin Franklin. Another notable political paper in that city was *Porcupine's Gazette* (1797–99), edited in vitriolic fashion by William Cobbett, at the time a refugee from England. In Boston Benjamin Russell's *Columbian Centinel* became a nationally recognized Federalist organ; founded in 1784, it was in many respects an excellent newspaper. Noah Webster, later famous as a lexicographer, established the *American Minerva* in New York in 1793 as a Federalist organ; four years later this paper adopted the name *Commercial Advertiser*, which it kept for more than a century.

One cause of the Alien and Sedition Acts (1798–1801) was the prevalence of abusive attacks on public officers, though the immediate occasion was the threat of war with France and the administration's fear of disloyalty. There were about twenty-five arrests under the Sedition Act and eleven trials resulting in ten convictions. Actions under the common law brought total convictions to fifteen, of which eight related to newspapers. But the censorship involved was greater than these figures indicate. The acts expired with the John Adams administration (1797–1801). Two years later Alexander Hamilton, in an argument for a new trial in the case of Harry Croswell, editor of the *Hudson* (N.Y.) *Wasp*, advanced the "Hamiltonian doctrine," used by Andrew Hamilton to win Peter Zenger's freedom: that *truth is an effective defense in a libel suit*. This principle was later made part of most state constitutions.

The *National Intelligencer*, established in Washington in 1800 as the organ of the Jefferson administration by Samuel Harrison Smith, proved to be mild in partisanship and reliable in news. Conducted after 1810 by Joseph Gales, Jr., and W. W. Seaton, the *Intelligencer* was considered by other papers for many years as the authority on Washington news. It was displaced as the government organ, however, when Andrew Jackson became president. Duff Green's *United States Telegraph* (1825) was Jackson's first Washington paper; it was supplanted in 1830 by the *Washington Globe*, edited by Francis P. Blair. Also associated with the *Globe* were Amos Kendall, editorial writer, and John C. Rivers, business manager, who, with Blair, were members of Jackson's "kitchen cabinet" of political advisers.

In New York, meantime, James Cheetham's *American Citizen* was the vituperative organ of the George Clinton faction of the Democratic Party during the first decade of the nineteenth century. Established largely in order to combat Cheetham's sheet was the *New York Evening Post*, founded in 1801 by Alexander Hamilton and friends associated in a joint-stock company. William Coleman was its first editor; he was followed in 1829 by William Cullen Bryant, who edited the paper until his death in 1878.

## The Penny Press

The chief characteristics of the penny press of the 1830s were smaller size, a one-cent price in comparison with the six cents charged by the larger papers, and adaptation to lower economic and social levels of readership. The penny papers featured local and human-interest matter, preferred news above support of a party or mercantile class, exposed abuses of banks and churches, and tended to give a realistic picture of the news scene despite taboos. The first successful penny daily was the *New York Sun*, founded in 1833 by Benjamin H. Day. Most important of its rivals in this field was the *New York Herald*, begun two years later by James Gordon Bennett. Three New York printers, William M. Swain, A. S. Abell, and A. H. Simmons, founded the *Philadelphia Public Ledger* in 1836 and the *Baltimore Sun* in 1837; Swain was chiefly responsible for the former and Abell for the latter over many years. In 1841 Horace Greeley founded the *New York Tribune* as a penny paper, and ten years later the *New York Times* was started by Henry J. Raymond, George Jones, and Edward B. Wesley at the same price. All these New York papers except the *Sun* soon went to the two-cent price, enlarging their size and scope. The penny papers initiated what may be called modern journalism by their emphasis on local news and timeliness. They were leaders in the use of expresses and the telegraph for quick transmission of news, and their large circulation and advertising receipts enabled them to improve their news services and install fast cylinder presses.

Bennett and Greeley, rival editors through three decades (both died in 1872), were leading figures in a period of personal journalism. Bennett was one of the most original of editors, initiating financial and society departments and playing a part in many other innovations. In his initial issue he outlined his policy: "We shall support no party—be the agent of no faction or coterie, and care nothing for any election, or any candidate from president down to constable"; and to this he consistently adhered.

Greeley was the great idealist, a crusader against slavery and intemperance and in favor of westward expansion. Ardently patriotic, humanitarian in sentiment, but distrustful of radical solutions for the ills of society and disdainful of Jacksonian democracy, Greeley became a liberal Whig. His views, expressed in the *New Yorker*, caught the eye of New York State's Whig political boss, Thurlow Weed, who employed him to issue campaign weeklies in 1838 and 1840. These periodicals substantially aided the Whig cause in New York State and marked the beginning of Greeley's political partnership with Weed and William H. Seward, governor of

New York. In 1841 he founded the *New York Tribune*, a daily Whig paper dedicated to reform, economic progress, and the elevation of the masses. The *Tribune* set a high standard among the papers of its day in news gathering, intellectual stimulus, and moral fervor. It developed a good clientele in New York City and a tremendous circulation as a weekly in the hinterland. Its editorial columns became a potent political influence.

For several years Greeley worked closely with Weed and Seward in liberalizing the Whig Party in New York State and in influencing Whig politics nationally. He became increasingly bitter over the failure of his political partners to support him for high public office. In 1854 he determined to take an independent course in politics and dissolved the relationship.

The *Tribune* had taken an antislavery stand in the 1840s but became violently opposed to slavery in the next decade. Greeley was dubious about the Compromise of 1850, especially its Fugitive Slave provision, but he vacillated on the measure as a whole. The Kansas-Nebraska Act of 1854 provoked his bitterest moral condemnation. He took a prominent part in organizing the Republican Party in 1854–55 and supported its nominee, John C. Frémont, for president in 1856. He and his paper were now anathema among the slaveholders. He was publicly caned by Congressman Albert Rust of Arkansas in 1856 and threatened with violence if he ever entered the South. He constantly fed the rising antislavery crescendo in the North, bitterly attacking the Dred Scott decision of 1857, the slave trade, and Southern manners and morals.

Greeley helped defeat Seward for the Republican presidential nomination in 1860. This started a feud with Weed that went on for years. The *Tribune*'s editor preferred the conservative Edward Bates of Missouri as a presidential candidate and had no enthusiasm for Lincoln. He did, however, support the latter in the campaign of 1860.

As secession materialized after Lincoln's election, Greeley's position became obscure. He urged letting "the erring sisters depart in peace," apparently believing that absence of coercion would gain time and best guarantee the maintenance of the Union. His opposition to any compromise with slavery extension remained firm, but his dread of war was paramount.

Greeley pursued an erratic course during the Civil War.

He early became convinced that the abolition of slavery was essential and joined the Radicals in urging emancipation of the slaves. But he also wanted the war brought to a speedy end and was greatly distressed by Union defeats and the mounting cost of the struggle in lives and treasure.

Greeley's interest in politics remained keen after the war was over. Zealous for a large measure of equality for freedmen, he supported the Fourteenth and Fifteenth amendments and urged the impeachment of Pres. Andrew Johnson. Repeatedly he sought state and national office but was never elected. He supported Ulysses S. Grant's campaign for the presidency in 1868, though without enthusiasm. He finally became convinced that Grant's attempt to maintain Radical Reconstruction in the South was a failure. He was also irritated by the administration's refusal to cut military expenditures and to resume the redemption of paper money with gold or silver coin, and he felt that Grant was thwarting his ambitions in New York State. Greeley thus finally broke away from the Republican Party, joined the dissenters known as the Liberal Republicans, and accepted nomination for the presidency by them and by the Democrats in 1872.

In the dreary campaign of 1872 Greeley was so mercilessly attacked that, as he said, he scarcely knew whether he was running for the presidency or the penitentiary. Overwhelmed by the strain of the campaign, exhausted by his vigil at the bedside of his dying wife, harried by his debts and by the decline of his influence in the *Tribune* office, Greeley sank into a deep depression and died November 29, 1872.

## Civil Strife and the "Mugwumps"

The American Civil War was well covered by special correspondents, more than 150 of whom served Northern papers. Military restrictions, government control of telegraph lines, and mob violence—all sporadic—curbed press activity, but there was no regular and consistent censorship. A number of papers were forced to suspend publication by military commands or the post office department.

Among these were the *New York Daily News* and the *Chicago Times*. The *News*, founded in 1855, was a penny paper, organ of the Tammany Democratic organization; it had come into the hands of Benjamin Wood, brother of Fernando Wood, New York's mayor. The Woods were strongly proslavery, and a combined military and postal blockade forced the *News* to close down for eighteen months in 1861–

62. The *Chicago Times*, founded in 1854, had been bought by Wilbur F. Storey in 1861. Its editorial attacks on the Union cause led Gen. A. E. Burnside to seize and suspend the paper, but after three days President Lincoln requested that the order be rescinded. He let his generals suspend several newspapers, but only for short periods. In a letter to one of his generals he expressed his policy thus: "You will only arrest individuals and suppress assemblies or newspapers when they may be working palpable injury to the military in your charge, and in no other case will you interfere with the expression of opinion in any form or allow it to be interfered with violently by others. In this you have a discretion to exercise with great caution, calmness, and forbearance." Considering the dangers and provocations of the time, Lincoln was quite liberal in his treatment of the opposition press. He was by no means the dictator critics often accused him of being.

Before the Civil War partisanship seemed more important than truth to many papers. When the organization of Kansas as a territory left the matter of slavery to be decided by its settlers, the antislavery forces of the North and Northwest agreed to help populate the region with people who had antislavery views. They formed emigrant associations that shipped men and families to Kansas, arming them for their protection in the new country. Southern newspapers called for similar measures in the South, but with less success. They feared that Southern men without slaves, settling a new state, might agree to prohibit slavery. Only slaveholders were trustworthy proslavery men, and such men were not likely to take slaves to Kansas and risk their ownership. Except for the proximity of Missouri, Kansas would have favored free soil from the beginning. Encouraged by political extremists, Missourians crossed over into Kansas and voted heavily in the first territorial election. The struggle soon grew into a minor civil war, the two factions fighting battles, capturing towns, and paroling prisoners.

Unfortunately newspaper reports from Kansas bore little resemblance to the truth, and the region became a symbol of Southern aggression. Even the Abolitionist Theodore Parker once wrote, "I know of no transaction in human history which has been covered up with such abundant lying." Violence was as inevitable in Kansas as was the region's destiny to be free, but whether "bleeding Kansas" bled or not was unimportant. What mattered for Republican editors was the fact that the Republican Party was entering its first national campaign and it needed the Kansas issue desperately. For those who followed events in Kansas by reading the Republican press, terror was stalking the land.

By the 1870s, a growing number of newspapers declared their independence of political control. Dating from the secession of Republican papers from the Ulysses S. Grant forces in 1872, what was sometimes called the "mugwump" (politically independent) movement gained in strength and caused the defeat of James G. Blaine in 1884. By 1880 one-fourth of American newspapers were listed in the directories as independent; by 1890 the proportion had reached one-third. By the 1950s one-half the daily papers listed themselves as "independent" and another one-fourth as "independent Republican" or "independent Democratic."

## Pulitzer, Hearst, and Yellow Journalism

Joseph Pulitzer, Hungarian-born immigrant who had made a success of the *St. Louis Post-Dispatch*, which he had formed in 1878 from the unimportant *Dispatch* (founded in 1864) and John A. Dillon's *Post* (founded 1875), upset the New York newspaper situation in the 1880s and did more than anyone else to set the pattern of modern journalism. In 1883 he bought the *New York World* and soon made it the country's most successful newspaper.

The *World* had come into the hands of Democratic politicians and financiers. To the *World*, as to the *Post-Dispatch*, Pulitzer gave a tone of aggressive editorial independence. He supported Grover Cleveland for the presidency in 1884, 1888, and 1892. He was sympathetic to labor; in 1892 he took the side of the striking steel workers at Homestead, Pa. He opposed William Jennings Bryan for the presidency in 1896 and became an advocate of war with Spain.

The *World* was largely responsible for bringing on the New York State legislative investigation of insurance companies in 1905. In 1909 the U.S. government successfully sought an indictment against Pulitzer for criminally libeling Pres. Theodore Roosevelt, J. P. Morgan, Elihu Root, and others in connection with allegations about the disposition of the $40 million paid the French Panama Canal Company, but the case was never prosecuted.

Pulitzer's success was carefully examined by other publishers, among them California's William Randolph Hearst, who invaded New York journalism in September 1895 by buying the unsuccessful *Morning Journal*, which he made a one-cent newspaper of highly popular type. By the use of numerous illustrations, colored magazine sections, glaring headlines, sensational articles on crime and pseudoscientific topics, and jingoism (extremely nationalistic policy) in foreign affairs, the *Journal* shortly reached an unprecedented circulation. Under Hearst's control the *Journal* attacked England in the Venezuela affairs, supported William Jennings Bryan in 1896, and vied with Pulitzer's *World* in 1897–98 in demanding war with Spain through hysterical propaganda against that nation based on exposures of Spanish atrocities in Cuba. This jingoism was not limited to the *Journal* and *World*, though they were leaders in it. (Some techniques of the "yellow (sensational or lurid) journalism" period became more or less permanent and widespread, such as banner headlines, colored comics, and copious illustration.)

Hearst supported Bryan again in 1900, bitterly assailing William McKinley and Mark Hanna as tools of the trusts. An editorial statement in April 1901 that "if bad institutions and bad men can be got rid of only by killing, then the killing must be done," led Theodore Roosevelt in his first message after McKinley's assassination to denounce "exploiters of sensationalism," words he later (1906) declared were meant for Hearst.

The success of the *Journal* led Hearst to establish the *Chicago American* (1900), the *Chicago Examiner* (1902), and the *Boston American* (1904). He purchased other newspapers and by 1925 he owned newspapers in cities of every section of the United States. He opposed U.S. entrance into World War I; he waged unremitting warfare against the League of Nations and demanded payment of the war debts in full. Late in 1916 the British and French governments denied Hearst the use of their mails and cables.

While Hearst was expanding his realm, two grandsons of *Chicago Tribune* editor and proprietor Joseph Medill became copublishers and coeditors of the paper. When Joseph Medill Patterson went on to New York to buy the *Daily News*, which he built into an immensely successful tabloid, Robert R. McCormick stayed at the *Tribune* and led it to set records in the United States for standard-size newspaper circulation and in the world for advertising revenue. *Tribune* enterprises expanded to include major publishing, radio, and television facilities. *Tribune* editorial policies voiced outspoken opposition to Prohibition, the Roosevelt and Truman administrations, and U.S. political involvement in overseas conflicts. From 1925 until his death in 1955, McCormick was among the most powerful and controversial figures in journalism.

The era of "yellow journalism" may be said to have ended shortly after the turn of the century, with the *World*'s gradual retirement from the competition in sensationalism and the rise of the *New York Times*. Adolph S. Ochs, publisher of the *Chattanooga Times*, in 1896 acquired control of the financially faltering *New York Times* and steadily strengthened the paper's journalistic and financial position. The influence of Ochs upon newspaper publishing in the United States was marked and highly beneficial. Entering New York publishing when yellow journalism was at its height, in competition with the richest and most powerful newspapers in America, he boldly adopted the slogan "All the News That's Fit to Print" and devoted his paper, not to sensationalism, but to giving intelligent readers a daily news report that was trustworthy and complete. In a few years he made the *New York Times* an outstanding example of journalistic enterprise.

## Muckraking

For all the austere influence of Ochs and the *Times*, however, yellow journalism had thoroughly whetted the public appetite for sensationalism and the news arrestingly presented. This continuing demand was supplied by the "muckrakers," an unorganized group of writers whose approach would later be called investigative reporting. They were completely identified with pre-World War I reform and the "literature of exposure." The name was given to them disparagingly, deriving from Pres. Theodore Roosevelt's speech of April 14, 1906, which, borrowing a passage from John Bunyan's *Pilgrim's Progress*, denounced "the Man with the Muckrake . . . who could look no way but downward."

But "muckraker" also took on honorable connotations of social concern and courageous exposition. The emergence of the new genre was heralded in the January 1903 issue of *McClure's Magazine*, featuring articles on municipal government, labor, and trusts, written by Lincoln Steffens, Ray Stannard Baker, and Ida M. Tarbell.

The intense public interest aroused by articles critical of political and financial rings, unsavory aspects of housing, labor, insurance, and other subjects rallied writers, editors, and reformers. Leader of the reform writers was Charles Edward Russell, whose exposes ranged from *The Greatest*

*Trust in the World* to *The Uprising of the Many*, the latter seeking to report methods being tried elsewhere in the world to extend democracy. Brand Whitlock wrote *The Turn of the Balance* (1907), a novel opposing capital punishment, and was also reform mayor of Toledo, Ohio. Thomas W. Lawson, a Boston financier, in "Frenzied Finance" (*Everybody's*, 1904–05) provided the decade's major exposé of corporate irresponsibility. Edwin Markham's *Children in Bondage* was a notable attack on child labor. Upton Sinclair's *The Jungle* and Samuel Hopkins Adams's *The Great American Fraud*, combined with the work of Harvey W. Wiley and Sen. Albert J. Beveridge, brought about passage of the Beef Inspection Act and the Pure Food Act. David Graham Phillips's series "The Treason of the Senate" (*Cosmopolitan*, 1906), which inspired President Roosevelt's remarks about "the Man with the Muckrake," was influential in leading up to the passage of the Seventeenth Amendment to the Constitution (popular senatorial elections). Muckraking as a movement largely disappeared between 1910 and 1912, although the influence of the periodical press continued intermittently.

## Illustrating the News

Often the major impact of periodicals and daily press alike came from illustration. The United States did not have a publication oriented to pungent political cartoons, in the manner of France's *La Caricature* and England's *Punch*, until after the American Civil War. Single-sheet cartoons, usually lithographed, were common; the publishers, among whom were Currier & Ives, overshadowed the artists at first. Two circumstances may have combined to delay the appearance of a great American caricaturist: first, the fact that above all the middle third of the nineteenth century in the United States was an age of oratory; second, that the combination of the telegraph with the facilities of the daily paper made the news—especially during the war—even more desirable than opinion. The great fighting words of the time (*copperhead*, for example) came from editorial writers rather than artists. The earliest important personal caricaturists and political cartoonists were David Claypoole Johnston (1799–1865) and Thomas Nast (1840–1902). Nast first made his name with war cartoons in *Harper's Weekly*. In the boom days of the 1870s Nast became a master of personal satire; his style and scale gave full effect to his ruinous attacks on "Boss" Tweed and other grafters. He was an outstanding symbol-maker and is probably the creator of the Democratic donkey as well as of the New York tiger—the label for Tammany Hall.

The development of photoengraving paved the way for photojournalism and when Joseph Medill Patterson founded the New York *Illustrated Daily News* in 1919, he emulated the London *Daily Mirror*, first newspaper illustrated exclusively with photographs. Within five years the *Daily News* had the largest circulation in the country.

German editor Stefan Lorant's axiom that the camera should be used like the notebook of a trained reporter, to record events as they occur, was introduced in the United States when Henry R. Luce founded *Life* magazine in November 1936, with Alfred Eisenstaedt as staff photographer. Only a few weeks later *Look* magazine began publication. Numerous others appeared subsequently in the United States, but none matched the success or the influence of *Life* and *Look*. The rapid development of magazine and newspaper photography, and motion picture photography in the form of the newsreel, brought an unprecedented immediacy to journalistic coverage of World War II.

Graphic reporting in the First World War had brought the press into collision with censorship. (More than seventy-five U.S. newspapers had their mailing privileges withdrawn under the Espionage Act.) But the ubiquity of the camera in World War II enabled the American people to see as well as read about the realities at the front. News magazines—notably *Time* and *Newsweek*—had risen to considerable influence and mass circulation.

At the same time broadcast journalism was creating a corps of radio news correspondents, and after World War II, when television became a reality, its merger of sight and sound gave a new dimension to the political influence of "the press." The term *news media* was coined to embrace news magazines and newspapers as well as radio and television. Increasingly *the media* came to be understood as the electronic or broadcast media, and more and more as television.

## Propaganda

War coverage by the print media had brought delayed prose descriptions and black-and-white still photographs of action to readers at home, but the Korean War was the last to be so reported. Color television was perfected before U.S. involvement in the Vietnam War, and it made that conflict what has been called the first living-room war. Scenes of carnage and destruction that were the subject of protest demonstrations on American college campuses and at the Capitol became live action on the nation's nightly news programs on television—on which Americans were increasingly relying for news. This effect was reinforced in the print media as full color photographs of war action appeared constantly in the weekly news magazines. The result was to place the news media in the service of antiwar propaganda, and growing popular dissatisfaction with American involvement forced a series of changes in political direction in the United States, including the eventual abandonment of the Vietnam War.

Propaganda is the dissemination of information—facts, arguments, rumors, half-truths, or lies—to influence public opinion. As a systematic effort to persuade, it is an act of advocacy in mass communication, involving the making of deliberately one-sided statements to a mass audience. (The one-sidedness of U.S. television coverage in Vietnam was inevitable. Only U.S. forces permitted television cameramen to cover combat. North Vietnam refused to permit such coverage. Therefore the world saw only Americans killing Vietnamese on its TV news—never North Vietnamese killing South Vietnamese.)

The one-sidedness of propaganda is not necessarily deceptive, although it is well known that one-sided presentations often spread and nourish false images by emphasizing only the good points of one position and the bad points of another. Hence one aim of public policy in popular government is to maintain a public forum in which the competing propagandas of political parties and interest groups correct and balance one another's lies and exaggerations.

The audience of any established channel of communication has selected itself on the basis of predispositions that cannot be disregarded. During World War II U.S. broadcasters to Germany quickly learned that crisis audiences differ from other kinds. Clandestine listeners who had risked their lives to hear news from the outside world were furious when all they could tune in on was entertainment.

The history of propaganda in religion and revolution makes it clear that dangerous propagandas need to be in devoted hands. More and more frequently, in the United States at least, political parties have employed professional public relations advice or agencies to plan and direct the propaganda and other aspects of their campaigns. Neither

U.S. party, incidentally, was able to take effective propaganda advantage of the Vietnam War.

## Television vs. Print

Television journalism, including its coverage of special events, has had a profound impact on domestic policies, indeed has engendered wholesale changes in the ways in which political candidates are selected, money is raised and spent, and campaigns are conducted. It has made the politician's conduct in office open to public scrutiny. Publicity about the extravagant charges in 1950–54 of Wisconsin's demagogue, Sen. Joseph R. McCarthy, made him a national figure; television exposure in the "Army-McCarthy hearings" probing a dispute between Senator McCarthy and the secretary of the army finally brought him down.

The successful election campaign of Richard Nixon in 1968 was a classic example of the successful use of all the techniques of national persuasion via the mass media. The televised investigation into the Watergate scandal by a special Senate committee, followed by the televised deliberations of the House Judiciary Committee over impeachment, left resignation as Nixon's only alternative to impeachment.

The "print media" have not abdicated to television the responsibilities of the press as the "fourth branch" of government. Newspapers remain alive and well. The 1971 case of the "Pentagon Papers" is one in point. The *New York Times* obtained a covertly supplied copy of a secret government study of the history of U.S. involvement in Vietnam and began publication. The Department of Justice won an injunction temporarily banning further publication of the series by the *Times*. Meanwhile other papers began publishing articles based on the study. The U.S. Supreme Court ruled in favor of the *Times* and publication was resumed.

Other "leaks" have raised serious questions about the ability of government to function if it may keep no secrets whatever. The position of government has usually been that secrecy is often necessary in the interests of national security, equity among competing groups, and justice. The position of the news media usually has been that secrecy is widely abused to hide improper and unlawful activities by government officials.

It is a debate that has gone on since the founding of the republic. The continuation of the debate, and its outcome, is important to the survival of the nation.

## 22.
# Between Elections:
# Citizen Impact on Government

In its original meaning, *lobbying* referred to the efforts of individuals to influence the votes of legislators, generally in the lobby outside the legislative chamber. In its broadest modern sense it means any attempt by individuals or groups to influence the decisions of government. It is most commonly associated with the activities of private interests, often called pressure groups, although even public officials may be said to lobby when they attempt to influence the making of public policy by other officials.

Because politics involves a struggle for power, lobbying in some form is inevitable in any political system. Any group that makes claims upon other groups or upon society finds it nearly impossible to stay out of politics, for even in a simple society the power of government to say who gets what and how is too important to ignore. In a modern industrial society, where regulation extends in some degree to almost all human activities and relationships, the decisions of public officials may be of crucial importance; they are and must be subject to the close and continuous attention of the groups they affect. Conversely, the government must heed the pressures of group demands. Even the most authoritarian rulers must take into account the army, the priesthood, or some other politically influential elements. In a free society, the government's obligation to consult the governed is recognized and institutionalized through guarantees of freedom of speech, press, and assembly, and the right of people to petition the government for a redress of grievances. Lobbying occupies a dominant position in the constitutional system as it is necessary to the preservation of self-government.

If lobbying is necessary for self-government, why does it have such a bad reputation in the United States? In the nineteenth century its poor reputation was deserved and much of it has hung on. Lobbying then was largely a matter of personal influence in which many lobbyists plied legislators with wine, women, and money. Moreover, the moral climate of public life was low. U.S. Senators were not chosen by the people but by state legislators, and many of them virtually belonged to the interests that engineered their selection. Many state legislatures were notoriously corruptible. It was said that Standard Oil millionaire Harry Payne walked into the Ohio legislature with two satchels of money and walked out with a U.S. Senate seat. This situation has improved. Lobbying never will be wholly above suspicion, but several congressional investigations in the twentieth century have made it clear that modern efforts to influence legislation, an unceasing activity, generate headlines of corruption only relatively infrequently.

Several reasons for these trends may be suggested. Exposure of corruption by muckraking writers at the turn of the century undoubtedly had some effect. Direct election of senators and the opening of legislative hearings to the public diminished the influence of interest groups enjoying favored access to officials. Modern investigative reporters succeed in penetrating the most private recesses of government, and secret improprieties are almost impossible to keep secret. But most important, perhaps, has been the growth of giant economic and professional associations. The typical national association is a federation of state and local units, capable of operating at every level of government. Typical examples of this kind of association are the National Association of Manufacturers, the Chamber of Commerce of the United States, the American Medical Association, the AFL-CIO, the American Farm Bureau Federation, and the National Farmers Union. With their large memberships and resources, the associations have found it more effective to lobby through their members and to create a sympathetic public opinion than to court individual officials.

Two areas in which scandal does arise from time to time are exceptional rather than typical. These are lobbying by agents of foreign interests, which are by definition outside the American political tradition, and the lobbying implications of campaign finance, legal and illegal.

One of the reasons for the frequent criticism of lobbying in the United States is to be found in the fact that lobbies can easily be seen. The group struggle is brought out into the open by the structure of tripartite government and the character of political representation in a democracy. Because they were more concerned with protecting minority rights than with effectuating majority will, the makers of the federal Constitution deliberately set obstructions in the way of control by a temporary majority. They provided a separation of powers that institutionalized conflict between president and Congress, and not even the unifying influence of strong political party ties has been able to overcome it. They gave to each branch of government some power to check the action of the other branches, thus making obstruction easy and cooperation difficult. There are, moreover, not one but fifty-one governments in the United States, each exercising authority guaranteed to it by the Constitution. In this framework the national parties are merely federations of state and local parties, largely incapable of carrying out a promised program of action. Power is further dispersed in Congress among standing committees, and localism is strengthened by the individual member's dependence on his constituency. With power so fragmented, the group struggle is bound to be public. This makes it easy for participants to denounce the lobbying of the other side; as Sen. Jim Reed once said, "a lobbyist is anyone who opposes legislation I want."

Lobbying in the United States takes many forms. Group interests may be represented openly before legislative committees and administrative tribunals. Public officials may be "buttonholed" in legislative lobbies, offices, hotels, bars, restaurants, or private homes. Letters may be written or telephone calls made to public officials, and "grass-roots" campaigns may be organized for this purpose. Organizations seeking to influence public policy may provide favored candidates with money and service—including radio and television coverage for public speeches and friendly mention or outright endorsement in the publications of the organization. Research and writing services may be made available to public officials when legislation is being developed. Much substantive information may be supplied to congressmen and their legislative assistants by lobbyists representing various and often conflicting points of view on pending legislation. For example, on one fairly complex piece of legislation a trade association may put forward an industrial position, several corporations the views of their own management, union representatives the interests of labor, a chamber of commerce the position of local businesses in the area affected, a civic organization such as the League of Women Voters the results of its own study of the issue, or a "public interest" lobby an antibusiness argument. Religious, environmental, professional, recreational, and other groups may add their views. A few days of hearings and conversations can amass a great volume of carefully researched and documented information and reasoned arguments supporting all the diverse views that Congress must consider before enacting a far-reaching piece of legislation.

In some lobbying activities massive public relations campaigns employing all the techniques of modern communication may be launched to influence legislators by mobilizing public opinion. The persons who lobby in these ways may be full-time officials of a powerful association, individual lobbyists with many clients who pay for their services, or ordinary citizens who take the time to state their hopes or grievances. Some of the most effective lobbyists are former congressmen, key staff aides, or administrative officials whose principal asset is that they "know their way around."

### Regulating Lobbying

The regulation of lobbying poses difficult problems. It is necessary somehow to curb the excesses of pressure groups without restricting their right to represent their members or the members' constitutional right (First Amendment) "to petition the Government for a redress of grievances." The national government and more than half the states regulate lobbying. Most laws relating to lobbying, (such as the Federal Regulation of Lobbying Act of 1946, which requires that lobbyists register and report contributions and expenditures and that groups they represent must make similar reports) are based on the assumption that lobbyists can't do much harm if their activities are publicized. The efficacy of these laws is doubtful; the 1946 federal law, for instance, is poorly written, has no provision for proper administration or enforcement or even for effective publicity, and requires only summary and superficial information. Tax-exempt status may be revoked when a nonprofit organization devotes a substantial part of its resources to influencing legislation.

Indirect lobbying—group activity designed to influence government by shaping public opinion—has proved almost impossible to regulate. Campaigns addressed to the public through newspapers, magazines, television, radio, books, pamphlets, and public speeches are protected by constitutional safeguards. The Supreme Court of the United States has made clear its intention not to permit laws for the regulation of lobbies to infringe upon freedom of speech or of the press. Although the Federal Regulation of Lobbying Act covers efforts made "directly or indirectly" to influence the passage or defeat of any legislation by Congress, the Supreme

Court in 1953 (*United States* v. *Rumely*, 345 U.S. 41) said that "lobbying" should be construed in its commonly accepted sense as "representations made directly to the Congress, its members or its committees." The next year, in upholding the constitutionality of the lobbying law (*United States* v. *Harriss*, 347 U.S. 612), the court reinforced its interpretation of the narrow scope of the law.

An area of ambiguity in the regulation of lobbying has been the provision of campaign financing by interests having a legislative ax to grind. The escalating cost of conducting an election campaign since the advent of computerized opinion-polling, television, and jet air travel has made campaign gifts an effective way to a politician's heart.

Federal law has long prohibited political contributions by business firms and labor unions. Organized labor, however, found an effective device to sidestep this prohibition in the creation of political action committees supported by voluntary contributions of members and not by union dues. Thus labor has been able to reward its friends in Congress and the legislatures with campaign contributions and also with competent research and other assistance.

Some corporations have explored similar arrangements, but in rather gingerly fashion, for legal prohibitions against corporate contributions to election campaigns were stringent. It has long been supposed—and occasionally proved in court—that some corporations compensate executives covertly or indirectly for campaign gifts ostensibly made from their personal funds. Revelations of the Watergate scandal demonstrated beyond dispute that some corporate executives have been willing (sometimes voluntarily, sometimes under pressure or solicitation from presidential emissaries) to give corporate funds for campaign purposes in flat violation of law. The Federal Election Campaign Act of 1974 finally made explicit the right of business organizations, like labor unions, to maintain separate political funds supported by voluntary contributions.

From time to time improper lobbying activities by representatives of foreign interests come to light. This kind of concern has been widely voiced about Germany before World Wars I and II, the Soviet Union at various times, the Republic of China ("the China Lobby") in the 1940s, and the Republic of Korea in the 1970s, among others. Where the currency is entertainment, such activity may be either proper or a borderline case, but where it is money it is explicitly unlawful.

## Referendum and Initiative

Apart from lobbying—and writing or visiting one's representatives in government—citizens have few opportunities to affect the course of government between elections. Two such opportunities are offered by the referendum and initiative, methods by which the wishes of the electorate may be expressed with regard to proposed legislation. These means exist in a variety of forms. The referendum may be obligatory or optional. In most states amendments to constitutions proposed by legislatures are subject to an obligatory referendum. If optional, a specified number of voters may demand by petition a popular vote on a law passed by a legislature. By this means actions of a legislature may be overruled.

The referendum may be constitutional or legislative, depending on the nature of the matter that is referred. In the United States questions subject to the obligatory referendum are mostly constitutional, while those subject to the optional referendum are invariably legislative. In addition to the obligatory and optional forms, legislative bodies may choose to submit certain questions to a referendeum, either to decide the issue or merely to advise the legislature.

By the initiative a specified number of voters may invoke a popular vote on a proposed state or local law or a proposal to amend the state constitution. In its direct form a proposal supported by the requisite number of voters is submitted directly to a popular vote for decision. Under the indirect form the legislature has an opportunity to enact such a proposal. If rejected, the proposition is submitted to a popular vote, in some instances accompanied by an alternative proposal or by a statement of its reasons for rejection.

The obligatory referendum on state constitutional amendments proposed by state legislatures, first adopted by Connecticut in 1818, was the prevailing method for such amendment in the second half of the twentieth century. In some states a referendum is obligatory on bond issues, and it is also widely used in local government for bond issues, tax questions, and related matters. Because of the detailed nature of most state constitutions and the necessity for their frequent amendment, issues many voters find dull are nevertheless often referred to them for decision.

Initiative and referendum were imported to the United States from Switzerland, where this form of "direct legislation" came into use in the liberal reaction after the Paris revolution of 1830. The movement to adopt these devices in the United States was led by populists and various reform groups that were hostile to machine rule, distrustful of legislatures, and had deep faith in democracy. They believed that by granting the people a means to overrule legislative action and to initiate popular votes on legislation, abuses then characteristic of state legislatures might be prevented. Conservative groups were hostile to the adoption of the institution of direct legislation. The chief resort to direct legislation was in the Western states, principally California and Oregon. It did not however, fulfill either the hopes of its advocates or the fears of its opponents. In practice the referendum is used by groups that feel aggrieved by an action of the legislature and hope to persuade a majority of the electorate to support their demand that the law not go into effect. The initiative tends to be used by groups that have failed to induce the legislature to enact a desired law. The initiative and optional referendum have proved much less important than the obligatory referendum in bringing issues to the voters. In the legislative process as a whole, the initiative and referendum are relatively unimportant in relation to the volume of legislation affected. Woodrow Wilson called them a "gun behind the door," ready to be used when abuses arise.

## The Concept of Recall

Another populist import from Switzerland is the device of recall, by which voters may remove a public official from office before the expiration of his regular term. Now used principally in this country, the recall is based upon the principle that officials are mere agents of the popular will and as such should be constantly subject to its control. Under the plan, if a specified percentage of the electorate is dissatisfied with an official's conduct and signs a petition for his removal, the officer must face a general election.

Though the general principle of the recall is simple, there are many variations in its practical application. Under some plans the choice of a successor is determined in a subsequent election, but for economy's sake the two are often combined in one election. The vote required to remove an official is usually a simple majority of those voting. The percentage of signatures required to force an election ranges widely, the average being about twenty-five percent of those who participated in the last general election in that electoral district. An officer elected at a recall election serves out the unexpired portion of the vacated term.

The recall is, in fact, resorted to infrequently and then almost entirely for local officers. It once found statewide application in North Dakota in 1921, when the governor, attorney general, and commissioner of agriculture were removed. It has rarely been applied to judges.

In Switzerland recall was made applicable not only to individuals but to the entire legislature. It was suggested in the U.S. Articles of Confederation and discussed in the Constitutional Convention of 1787, but its first practical application in the United States was in 1903 in the city charter of Los Angeles, Calif. It was soon adopted by many cities with the commission form of government as the most effective way to control the commissioners, in whose hands great power was placed. It was subsequently adopted in Oregon (1908), California (1911), Arizona, Idaho, Washington, Colorado, and Nevada (1912), Michigan (1913), Louisiana and Kansas (1914), North Dakota (1920), and Wisconsin (1926). Most of these states had many elective officers—not subject to removal by the governor—who were, in effect, beyond administrative control during their terms of office.

The concept of recall was also applied in the early twentieth century to various proposed restraints on the judiciary. In 1912 the Progressive Party advocated "recall of judicial decisions." Under the leadership of former Pres. Theodore Roosevelt the Progressives proposed that "when an act, passed under the police power of the State, is held unconstitutional under the State Constitution, by the courts, the people . . . shall have an opportunity to vote on the question whether they desire the act to become law, notwithstanding such decision." The 1912 proposal was not adopted, and in some states the recall was made inapplicable to judges on the ground that the judiciary should be independent of popular passions and political pressures.

A general increase in the size of electorates, plus a greater demonstration of responsibility on the part of executives and legislative bodies alike, tended to diminish use of the recall in the second half of the twentieth century. Its effectiveness may be better measured by the restraining influence of the threat of its use than by the incidence of its actual application. Petition, often in the guise of lobbying, remains the most effective means of citizen impact on the conduct of government between elections. And the next election always offers the most effective restraint on excess by an elected government official: defeat.

# 23.
# Patterns of Reform

The impulse to reform is strong in the United States, and Americans' indulgence of that impulse has had far-reaching effects on their political system. The political history of this country could be conveniently divided into chapters marking significant waves of reform, from the drive to perfect the Articles of Confederation to the move to prevent future "Watergates." Tides of reform have waxed and waned.

The administration of Andrew Jackson had the good fortune to coincide in the 1830s with a broad impulse toward social reform. Although the Jacksonians seldom indulged in crusades for human betterment, they benefited from the prevailing atmosphere of social progress. American individualism, born of the need to fashion a civilization out of the wilderness and enhanced by the virtual absence of governmental control, was responsible for a wide variety of ideas for curing the ills of mankind. An equally important factor in shaping the reform impulse was evangelical Protestantism. Lacking any great intellectual creed or body of doctrine, evangelical religion laid stress on a personal religious experience. A personal conversion, demonstrated by good works, made the individual responsible for social progress and bred a generation of reformers.

Every aspect of American society was subjected to intense scrutiny by active minds. Though many proposals bordered on the absurd, others resulted in genuine progress. In the field of education Horace Mann in Massachusetts and Henry Barnard in Connecticut instigated reforms that led to improved methods of teacher training, consistent allocations of state funds, and modern curricula. In the area of prison reform the Auburn Penitentiary in New York experimented with individual cells, separation of hardened criminals from lesser offenders, and productive rehabilitation. Dorothea Dix personally led a nationwide crusade for care of the insane, promulgating the idea that insanity was a curable disease and advocating the establishment of asylums. The Temperance crusade won an initial victory when Maine adopted statewide prohibition in 1846, and by the Civil War nearly every Northern state had adopted restrictions on the manufacture and sale of alcoholic beverages.

## Slavery

It was inevitable that the attention of reformers would be attracted to the most prominent ill of American society—slavery. Gradually the various reform movements became merged in the overriding crusade against bondage. Prior to 1830 opposition to slavery was most prevalent in the South, where it took the form of movements for gradual emancipation or efforts to recolonize black people in Africa. On Jan. 1, 1831, William Lloyd Garrison published in Boston the first issue of *The Liberator*. Founded on the principle that slavery was a moral wrong, *The Liberator* stood for immediate, uncompensated emancipation. Two years later Garrison founded the American Antislavery Society, and as the association spread through the North it forced politicians to take a stand on the moral issue of slavery, contributed to the growing sectionalism throughout the country, and made political compromise increasingly more difficult. Garrison's actual following was small, and it is quite possible that as great an influence was exercised by the evangelist Theodore Dwight Weld, who with his "Seventy Apostles" carried the gospel of antislavery throughout the North. Also, the writing and oratory of free blacks, of whom Frederick Douglass (an escaped slave) was the most important, is not to be underestimated.

The abolitionist movement in the United States labored under the handicap that it threatened the harmony of North and South in the Union, and that it ran counter to the Constitution, which left the question of slavery to the individual states. Therefore the Northern public remained generally unwilling to adopt Abolitionist policy and was distrustful of such Abolitionist extremism as John Brown's raid at Harpers Ferry (1859). Even when convinced of the evil of slavery (as they were by Harriet Beecher Stowe's *Uncle Tom's Cabin* [1852]), most Northerners rejected abolitionism. They were prepared, however, to resist the spread of slavery into new territories. The election of Abraham Lincoln as president on the basis of this issue in 1860 led to the secession of the Southern states and hence to the Civil War (1861–65). The war, in turn, led Lincoln, who had never been an Abolitionist, to emancipate the slaves in areas in rebellion (1863) and led further to the freeing of all other slaves by the Thirteenth Amendment to the Constitution (1865).

## Periods of Excess

Although a popular mood to reform may occur spontaneously, as in the era of Jackson, the reformist urge is inevitably fueled by periods of excess. The high standards of integrity, nonpartisanship, and permanence of tenure established by George Washington prevailed, on the whole, in the federal government until 1829. The growth of political parties, however, and their struggle for supremacy, soon showed that it would be hard to keep public service outside the sphere of party politics. While there was a certain amount of hiring of political friends and firing of political enemies under the five presidents who succeeded Washington, the idea of the spoils system did not become the dominant philosophy until the inauguration of Andrew Jackson in 1829. Jackson advocated rotation in office as a means of keeping public service responsive to the will of the people. Political patronage, however, led to successive waves of removals and new appointments and caused a rapid decline in the efficiency of government.

Mounting agitation for elimination of the spoils system came to a climax with the assassination of Pres. James A. Garfield by a disappointed office seeker in 1881. Public indignation was demonstrated in the next year's fall elections, and most of the candidates who advocated civil service reform were successful. When Congress met, this matter received attention from the first day of the session until passage of the Civil Service Act on Jan. 16, 1883. That act, with minor changes, remains as the law still governing the federal civil service today. It created the Civil Service Commission and established the basis for selection of employees as the result of open competition in pertinent examinations. It guaranteed the right of citizens to compete for and, if eligible, to be appointed to a job in the federal service, without regard to politics, religion, race, national origin, or any factor other than merit and fitness. Every president after Chester A. Arthur, who signed it into law, extended its coverage. In 1883 the act covered only ten percent of the 130,000 federal positions; by the 1970s it covered eighty-six percent of the approximately 3 million positions, with at least eleven percent covered by other special merit systems.

The scandals of graft and general corruption in the executive and legislative branches of government that characterized the Grant era and lingered after it, contributed to the development of civil service legislation and to the formation of regulatory agencies such as the Interstate Commerce Commission, the Federal Trade Commission, and others.

National scandals were replicated in the states. New York,

perhaps, led the country in this connection as in most others. During the decade following the Civil War, "boss" rule and wrongdoing characterized government operations on the state, county, and city levels. Postwar demoralization, the antiquated government structure, the pressure of business interests for franchises and contracts, and the tightening grip of political machines such as that of "Boss" William Tweed were the major causes of corruption. The Democratic Party generally controlled the governorship between 1875 and 1895 under such important leaders as Samuel Tilden (1875–76), who broke up the "canal ring," Grover Cleveland (1883–84), and David B. Hill (1885–91). During these years the Republican Party was divided by factional strife, with the leader, Roscoe Conkling, quarreling with Republican presidents Rutherford Hayes, James Garfield, and Chester Arthur for control of patronage, especially in the New York Custom House.

The governorship passed to Republicans between 1895 and 1910 because the public by then charged the Democrats with corruption and responsibility for the depression of 1893, and because the Republicans were ably led by Theodore Roosevelt, "Boss" Tom Platt, and Charles Evans Hughes. N.Y. Governor Hughes (1907–10) brought about the regulation of insurance and utility companies, introduced many labor reforms, including the state's first workmen's compensation law, and took steps to conserve forest and water resources. The split between the Progressive followers of Theodore Roosevelt and the conservative Republicans gave the state to the Democrats in 1910 and 1912. An intraparty fight between Democratic Gov. William Sulzer and "Boss" Charles Murphy of Tammany Hall led to the impeachment of Sulzer in 1913. He was found technically guilty of perjury, misrepresentation of campaign expenditures, and concealment of evidence. More important than these quarrels were the labor laws passed after the disastrous Triangle Shirt Waist Company fire in New York City in 1911. Robert Wagner, with the aid of Alfred E. Smith and Frances Perkins, made a thorough examination of labor conditions and their recommendations were enacted into legislation.

Muckraking writers exposed shocking exploitation of child labor, which had been a subject of socialist agitation. In the 1870s and 1880s many states enacted child labor laws, and this kind of reform was extended gradually. The federal government became involved in the field at a 1909 White House conference on child welfare, which was repeated a decade later. A federal Children's Bureau was set up under Grace Abbott. Congress in 1916 and again in 1919 enacted child labor laws that were found unconstitutional by the Supreme Court. A child labor amendment to the Constitution was submitted in 1924 but was not ratified. Eventually, New Deal legislation in 1938 effectively asserted federal control in the child labor field.

Reform leaders did not confine their activities to a single cause, often transferring their energies to a new cause when an old one achieved acceptance. Many activists in the cause of child labor law reform emerged from the women's suffrage movement after the Nineteenth Amendment was ratified in 1920. The pioneer of the latter movement, Susan B. Anthony, herself came out of the abolition and temperance movements. She was a schoolteacher and organizer of temperance societies when she became an agent for the American Antislavery Society. In collaboration with Elizabeth Cady Stanton she published a New York liberal weekly, *The Revolution* (1868–70).

Demanding for women the same civil and political rights extended to black men by the Fourteenth and Fifteenth amendments, she claimed her right to vote as a person and citizen in 1872. She was arrested, tried, and convicted, but she refused to pay the fine. From then on she campaigned for a federal women's suffrage amendment through the National Woman Suffrage Association (1869–90), through the National American Woman Suffrage Association (1890–1906), and by lecturing throughout the United States. With her close associates she compiled and published a four-volume work, *The History of Woman Suffrage* (1881–1902). In 1888 she organized the International Woman Suffrage Alliance. She died in Rochester, N.Y., March 13, 1906, fourteen years before the eventual triumph of her last cause—which occurred on the centenary of her birth.

The temperance movement, which had attracted Susan B. Anthony, had many crosscurrents and conflicting elements. Its time eventually came, however, and the case of Prohibition proved an unusual one in the annals of reform.

The excesses of the reform drive became sufficiently burdensome to the public that it demanded reform of the reformation; thereupon the repeal of "the noble experiment" became inevitable.

## Civil Rights Revolution

No excess of reform has attended the plight of black Americans, given freedom and equal rights by proclamation and amendment, but denied them by systematic and near-universal discrimination. After World War II, pressures built up in many sectors of society to bring some meaning at last to equality of rights and opportunity for all citizens. Between 1946 and 1950 the Supreme Court took cognizance of civil rights violations in a variety of cases involving public transport, real estate, and education.

In the historic decision of May 17, 1954, *Brown* v. *Board of Education of Topeka, Kansas,* the Court declared that separate educational facilities are inherently unequal and therefore unconstitutional. The decisions in this and other school desegregation cases stimulated a mass movement on the part of blacks to end segregation and other inequalities.

The winds of change had begun to blow quite forcefully in the 1950s, and conditions were created that led to what has been commonly referred to as the Negro Revolution or the Second Reconstruction. In 1955 the blacks of Montgomery, Ala., began to boycott city bus lines to protest a white driver's abuse of Mrs. Rosa Parks, who had refused to move to the back of the bus with other black passengers. Led by the Rev. Dr. Martin Luther King, Jr., blacks succeeded in forcing the bus company to desegregate its facilities. Soon they were picketing and boycotting other businesses in Southern and Northern communities. In 1960 four students from a black college in North Carolina entered a variety store, made several purchases, sat down at the lunch counter and ordered coffee. When they were refused service they remained in their seats until the store closed. This was the beginning of the sit-in movement which spread rapidly through the South and to some places in the North. Young blacks and their white colleagues sat in white libraries, waded into white beaches, and slept in the lobbies of white hotels. Many of them were arrested for trespassing and disobeying officers who ordered them off the premises.

In May 1961 the Congress of Racial Equality (CORE) sent "Freedom Riders" through the South to test segregation laws and practices in interstate transportation. The jails of several Southern communities soon became crowded with Freedom Riders who had been arrested for alleged violation of the law. Then began a wave of demonstrations, marching, picketing, and boycotting that characterized the drive for equality in 1962 and 1963, culminating in the great march on Washington, D.C., to rally against racial discrimination.

In still another way the civil rights revolution reached a new stage in 1960, when both major parties wrote into their platforms a pledge to seek equality. President John F. Kennedy created a stronger President's Committee on Equal Employment Opportunity from a committee established by former Pres. Dwight D. Eisenhower, with Vice-Pres. Lyndon B. Johnson as chairman. Kennedy also sent federal troops to protect a black student, James Meredith, when he enrolled as a student at the University of Mississippi, as President Eisenhower had done earlier to protect black students at Central High School in Little Rock, Ark. Finally, Kennedy signed a long-awaited order prohibiting discrimination in federally assisted housing.

In 1963, the centennial of the Emancipation Proclamation, civil rights leaders organized a massive march on Washington to demonstrate the importance of continued progress, and leaders of the 250,000 black and white marchers were received at the White House. President Kennedy had already asked Congress to enact laws that would guarantee the civil rights of all citizens, and the presence of the marchers dramatized the need for such legislation.

After the assassination of President Kennedy (November 1963), the new president, Lyndon B. Johnson, pledged to carry on the fight for equality. Together with congressional leaders of both parties, he succeeded in July 1964 in getting Congress to enact the most far-reaching civil rights bill it had ever passed. It forbade discrimination in public accommodations, threatened to withhold federal funds from communities that persisted in maintaining segregated schools, and established a Community Relations Service to assist communities in desegregating their facilities. Most blacks praised the legislation as ushering in a new day in race relations. Meanwhile, a significant increase in black political power had become apparent—an inadvertent result of the concentration of blacks in urban ghettos in the North. By 1970 blacks were sitting in lawmaking bodies in every Northern state where black people were concentrated in the large cities. In 1967 Cleveland, Ohio, and Gary, Ind., elected black mayors Carl Stokes and Richard Hatcher, respectively. In succeeding years larger and smaller cities and towns, North and South, elected black chief executives. Blacks also served as state and municipal judges, city commissioners, corporate counsels, and in a variety of other important elective and appointive offices. They were elected to school boards in various parts of the country and also won statewide positions, as, for example, the election of Edward Brooke to be attorney general of Massachusetts and then to the U.S. Senate (1966).

## Political Contributions and Campaigns

"The purification of politics is an irridescent dream," snorted John J. Ingalls, the Kansas Senator of the 1870s, himself a rabid waver of the "bloody shirt" over reconstruction issues. Yet it has remained a goal as well as a dream for reformers.

Piecemeal action toward reform was taken during the nineteenth century, especially in penal statutes against bribery and related abuses. Somewhat later, certain states and the U.S. Congress moved to limit the assessment of political contributions from public officeholders. It was not until 1890, however, that New York adopted its publicity law, the first state enactment attempting to bring about disclosure of the sources and uses of campaign money. This effort became a cornerstone in other states and was followed by federal reporting requirements; the first was adopted in 1910.

Although corrupt-practices legislation in the United States attempted and accomplished more than in other countries, it was characterized in general by faulty conception, imperfect draftsmanship, and casual enforcement. Over the years, state legislatures and the Congress addressed themselves to various types and modifications of controls. Because of constitutional uncertainties arising out of earlier federal legislation, the Corrupt Practices Act of 1925 repealed previous laws and made no effort to control nominating primaries or conventions. It required the treasurer of every political committee with activities in two or more states to file periodic reports with the clerk of the U.S. House of Representatives. These were to identify sources of contributions of $100 or more, plus total receipts and expenses with name and address for each expenditure of $10 or more. Candidates for House and Senate were required to file similar statements. The law limited spending for Senate campaigns to $10,000 and for the House to $2,500, and it continued a 1907 prohibition against campaign-giving by national banks or corporations organized under authority of Congress.

The Hatch Act of 1939, amended in 1940, extended existing controls over federal civil-service employees by prohibiting all federal employees other than policymaking officers from taking an active part in political campaigns. No political committee with activities in two or more states could legally receive or spend in excess of $3 million during any one year, and no one could give more than $5,000 a year to any candidate, party, or special campaign committee. (State and local groups were not covered.) However, court interpretations permitted individuals to give to as many separate committees as their resources and the imagination of campaign fund raisers would permit, and political committees proliferated.

The Watergate scandals prompted further efforts at reform, and in 1974 a new campaign finance act with far-reaching implications was adopted. Earlier a partial federal subsidy of presidential campaigns had been enacted, allowing taxpayers to direct that one dollar of their federal income tax be put into a fund apportioned between the two major national political party organizations for their presidential campaigns. This public financing was augmented by the new law, which provided an automatic $20 million for each major party nominee, with minor party candidates qualifying for support based on performance at the polls. Candidates accepting public funding could not accept private contributions, thus effectively limiting allowable campaign spending.

The 1974 law specified that presidential primary candidates could qualify for up to $5 million in matching funds by raising private gifts of $250 or less in twenty states to a total of $100,000; the national nominating conventions were subsidized, too ($2 million each for Republicans and Democrats, less for minor parties). The act put stringent limits on spending, holding presidential candidates to $20 million plus two cents per eligible voter that could be raised by the national committees. Candidates not seeking federal support were allowed to spend an extra $4 million for fund raising. Congressional candidates also were sharply limited in spending. Senators were allowed to spend $100,000 or eight cents per voter, whichever was larger, in primaries and fifty percent more in general elections. House candidates were allowed to spend a flat $70,000. All limits were indexed to permit increases with inflation in future years.

As enacted in 1974 the law undertook to remove the advantage of a wealthy candidate by limiting the contribution of a person's own money to his campaign to $50,000 for presidential candidates, less for congressional candidates. At Supreme Court hearings, immediate challenges overturned the limitations on what a candidate could contribute to his own campaign. The Court also struck down limitations on spending in House and Senate races and removed spending limits on presidential candidates who do not accept federal subsidy.

The act limited what individuals could contribute to $1,000 for each candidate in an election and restricted independent national or state political committees to $5,000. It also placed stringent disclosure and reporting requirements on candidates and political committees. A weakness of prior reporting and disclosure laws had been that it was difficult for reporters or others to secure the cooperation of the clerk of the House or the secretary of the Senate in gaining access to the records. A bipartisan Federal Election Commission created by the new law effectively put this information into the public domain without delay.

The same commission was also given power to rule on questions of the legality of various contributions of cash, goods, or services, and to interpret federal election law. It could audit and investigate, subpoena witnesses, and go to court to enforce the law where necessary through civil suits. The commission was originally created with members chosen by both houses of Congress and the president, but the Supreme Court ruled that all members must be presidential appointees since its functions essentially belonged in the executive. These defects were corrected, and the commission was able to function beginning with the 1976 elections.

The post-Watergate attempts at improving conditions governing campaign finance and conduct offer an interesting commentary on the American approach to reform as a whole. Faced with abuses on a large scale, popular demand soon calls for reform. Legislative remedies often follow with impressive speed, but they often are drafted imperfectly and may violate constitutional safeguards in certain instances. Court tests—arising with surprising rapidity when the public interest demands—protect the Constitution and point out directions for congressional improvement.

It is true that the nation's founding fathers could not have foreseen such modern developments as television, jet propulsion, and computerized opinion polling. They did, however, design a system of government that has proved capable of coping with enormous, unpredictable challenge, such as the Watergate scandal. Recognizing these remarkable political roots in the eighteenth century is the touchstone to understanding American government.

# Bibliography

## The New Encyclopaedia Britannica (15th Edition)

**Propaedia**: This one-volume Outline of Knowledge is organized as a ten-part Circle of Learning, enabling the reader to carry out an orderly plan of study in any field. Its Table of Contents—consisting of 10 parts, 42 divisions, and 189 sections—is an easy topical guide to the *Macropaedia*.

**Micropaedia**: If interested in a particular subject, the reader can locate it in this ten-volume, alphabetically arranged Ready Reference of brief entries and Index to the *Macropaedia*, where subjects are treated at greater length or in broader contexts.

**Macropaedia**: These nineteen volumes of Knowledge in Depth contain extended treatments of all the fields of human learning. For information on *The U.S. Government: How and Why It Works,* for example, consult: Administrative Law; Arbitration; Armed Forces; British Empire and Commonwealth; Bureaucracy; Censorship; Church and State; City Government; Civil Law; Civil Service; Civil War, U.S.; Common Law; Conservatism; Constitutional Law; Constitution and Constitutional Government; Courts and the Judiciary; Criminal Law; Electoral Processes; Federalism; Foreign Aid Programs; Health and Safety Laws; Human Rights; Ideology; Intelligence and Counterintelligence; International Agreements; International Law; International Relations; Jury; Labour Law; Liberalism; Nationalism; Police; Political Parties; Political Power; Political Systems; Production and Consumption, Government's Role in; Public Administration; Public Opinion; Revolution, Political; Slavery, Serfdom, and Forced Labour; Sovereignty; Special-Interest Groups; State, The; Tax Law; United Nations; United States, History of the; United States Outlying Territories; War of Independence, U.S.; Welfare and Security Programs. For biographical and geographic entries, check individual names.

## Other Publications

Corwin, Edward Samuel. *The Constitution and What It Means Today.* 13th ed. Revised by Harold W. Chase and Craig R. Ducat. Princeton, N.J.: Princeton University Press, 1973. Supplement, 1975.

Danielson, Michael N.; Hershey, Alan M.; and Bayne, John M. *One Nation, So Many Governments.* Lexington, Mass.: Lexington Books, 1977.

Ferguson, John H., and McHenry, Dean E. *The American System of Government.* 13th ed. New York: McGraw-Hill, 1977.

Glendening, Parris N., and Reeves, Mavis Mann. *Pragmatic Federalism: An Intergovernmental View of American Government.* Pacific Palisades, Calif.: Palisades Publishers, 1977.

Irish, Marian D.; Prothro, James W.; and Richardson, Richard J. *The Politics of American Democracy.* 6th ed. Englewood Cliffs, N.J.: Prentice-Hall, 1977.

Kelly, Alfred Hinsey, and Harbison, Winfred A. *The American Constitution: Its Origins and Development.* 5th ed. New York: Norton, 1976.

Woll, Peter. *American Bureaucracy.* 2d ed. New York: Norton, 1977.

# Index

## a

# n

# The Inquisitive Mind

Bantam/Britannica Books were created for those with a desire to learn. Compacted from the vast Britannica files, each book gives an in-depth treatment of a particular facet of science, world events, or politics. These accessible, introductory volumes are ideal for the student and for the intellectually curious who want to know more about the world around them.

☐ 12486 **THE ARABS:**
   **People and Power**    $2.50

☐ 12487 **DISASTER:**
   **When Nature Strikes Back**
             $2.50

☐ 12488 **THE OCEAN:**
   **Mankind's Last Frontier** $2.50

☐ 12485 **THE U.S. GOVERNMENT:**
   **How and Why It Works**  $2.50

# Bantam Book Catalog

Here's your up-to-the-minute listing of over 1,400 titles by your favorite authors.

This illustrated, large format catalog gives a description of each title. For your convenience, it is divided into categories in fiction and non-fiction—gothics, science fiction, westerns, mysteries, cookbooks, mysticism and occult, biographies, history, family living, health, psychology, art.

So don't delay—take advantage of this special opportunity to increase your reading pleasure.

Just send us your name and address and 50¢ (to help defray postage and handling costs).

---

**BANTAM BOOKS, INC.**
**Dept. FC, 414 East Golf Road, Des Plaines, Ill. 60016**

Mr./Mrs./Miss_____
(please print)

Address_____

City_____ State_____ Zip_____

Do you know someone who enjoys books? Just give us their names and addresses and we'll send them a catalog too!

_____

Mr./Mrs./Miss_____

Address_____

City_____ State_____ Zip_____

_____

Mr./Mrs./Miss_____

Address_____

City_____ State_____ Zip_____

FC—9/78